SAMUEL ELIOT MORISON'S

HISTORICAL WORLD

Samuel Eliot Morison's

Historical World

IN QUEST OF A NEW PARKMAN

Gregory M. Pfitzer

Northeastern University Press

BOSTON

Northeastern University Press

Library of Congress Cataloging-in-Publication Data

Pfitzer, Gregory M.
Samuel Eliot Morison's historical world : in quest of a new
Parkman / by Gregory M. Pfitzer.
p.   cm.
Includes bibliographical references and index.
ISBN 1-55553-101-6 : $29.95
1. United States—Historiography.   2. Historiography—United
States.   3. Morison, Samuel Eliot, 1877–1976.   4. Historians—United
States.   I. Title
E175.P48   1991
973'.072—dc20   90-23592
CIP

Designed by Virginia Evans

This book was composed in Trump Medieval by Coghill Composition Company in
Richmond, Va. It was printed and bound by Arcata Graphics/Kingsport in Kingsport,
Tenn. The paper is Glatfelter offset, an acid-free sheet.

Manufactured in the United States of America
95 94 93 92 91   5 4 3 2 1

For Mia

CONTENTS

ILLUSTRATIONS

ACKNOWLEDGMENTS

I would like to thank Mrs. Emily Morison Beck for her generous permission to use her father's papers in the Samuel Eliot Morison Collection at the Harvard University Archives and for her kindness in agreeing to read the entire manuscript. Her keen editorial skills have greatly improved the quality and the substance of the writing. Mrs. Beck also granted me several interviews at her home in the early stages of work. These interviews yielded insights into the work of her father and saved me countless hours of misguided research. In addition, I am indebted to Michael Morison, the historian's grandson, who commented on the entire manuscript and provided me with numerous insights into the personal vision of Samuel Eliot Morison.

I would also like to thank the libraries and staffs of several institutions who opened up their collections to me, including: Harley Holden, Clark Eliott, and the excellent staff of the Harvard University Archives, for their permission to quote the Morison papers and for their prompt attention to my many requests for materials; the Houghton Library of Harvard University for permission to quote from their collections on Morison, Barrett Wendell, and Van Wyck Brooks; the Library of Congress, Manuscripts Division, for permission to cite the papers of Albert J. Beveridge; the Rare Book and Manuscript Division of the Butler Library of Columbia University, for use of the James Truslow Adams papers; the Sterling Library of Yale University, for permission to quote from the papers of Charles M. Andrews; the Connecticut State Library, for permission to cite the papers of William Goodwin; the Franklin Delano Roosevelt Library, for permission to cite its Hyde Park Library correspondence; the Archives of the Naval War College, for permission to quote from the papers of Admiral Richard Bates; and the Naval Operations Archives, for permission to quote materials relevant to Morison's *History of United States Naval Operations in World War II*.

A special thanks to Henry Steele Commager, who spent an afternoon at the Somerset Club in Boston setting me straight on Morison's career and to his wife Mary Powlesland Commager, who provided me with important information on the collaboration of her husband and Morison on *The Growth of the American Republic*. In addition, I wish to thank Thomas Synnott, Roger Pineau, and Philip Lundeberg for information related to Morison's work on the naval history, and I give a special note of thanks to Thomas Boylston Adams, who arranged for me to discuss my project with several of Morison's friends, including publisher Ted Weeks, at the Tavern Club near the Boston Common.

I received funding from several summer grants provided by an anonymous donor through the History of American Civilization Committee at Harvard

University and through travel grants provided by Knox College and administered through the generosity of Dean John Strassburger. In addition, I wish to thank Dean Eric Weller of Skidmore College for assistance with computer needs. Without this financial support the project would have taken years longer to complete.

I have several personal debts to pay as well. To my graduate advisors at Harvard, whose patience and expert advice saw this study through to completion when it was a dissertation, I owe an inestimable debt. Professor Alan Brinkley advised me at each step of the writing, and his unequalled knowledge of twentieth-century American history helped me to understand the events that shaped Morison's career. To Dr. David H. Donald I owe a still greater debt. This work could not have been completed without his expert advice on all aspects of historical writing. It is altogether proper that he advised in the preparation of this manuscript, since Morison greatly admired Donald's work ("that fellow can write," Morison told Alfred A. Knopf) and since Donald may be the greatest living adherent to Morison's conception of history as literary art. Whatever glimmers of style shine through the pages of this work are due to Dr. Donald's careful revisions of the manuscript. I also wish to thank Bill Frohlich of Northeastern University Press for his editorial suggestions and for his patience in waiting for the various drafts of this book, sometimes hopelessly delayed by unavoidable personal and professional commitments.

Several fellow graduate students and personal friends, Gordon Hylton, Neil Jumonville, and Tom Siegel, joined me in a study group that met biweekly for several years while this work was in progress. Their comments on drafts of this manuscript when it was a dissertation were invaluable in helping me think through the project. They also offered emotional support of a kind that only dissertation students can understand, and I hope they know that I am eternally grateful to them. In addition, I wish to thank several colleagues at various institutions of higher learning with which I have been affiliated. To Charles Bassett and Pete Moss of Colby College, I wish to express my sincere thanks for preparing the intellectual ground for this work. To George Steckley, Penny Gold, Rodney Davis, Mikiso Hane, and Stephen Bailey of the Knox College History department, I extend my thanks for friendship and advice given during the period in which this book was written. And to my new colleagues, Mary Lynn, Joanna Zangrando, Wilma Hall, Dave Marcell, and Mary Nell Morgan, I wish to express my appreciation for support during the trying final months of production.

I wish to acknowledge my general debt to several works in the field of American historiography on which I have leaned heavily in certain sections of this book. David Noble's *Historians Against History* first interested me in the history of historical thought; John Higham's *History: Professional Scholarship in America* introduced me to major transitions in the various schools of thought in the American historical profession; and Peter Novick's *That Noble Dream* clarified a good deal of the confusing recent history of the American Historical Association. I also wish to acknowledge my debt to three memorial tributes published shortly after Morison's death by Wilcomb Washburn, Bernard Bailyn, and William Bentinck-Smith.

Most of all, I would like to thank family members who encouraged me when my confidence sagged. A special debt of appreciation is owed to my in-laws, Charles and Mary McCrossan, and to my adopted in-laws, the Cullinanes, for untold sacrifices made during the writing of this book. Thank you also to my mother, Jeanne, sister Margaret, brother Gordon, and especially to my brother Gary, and my father, Dr. Emil A. Pfitzer, who proofread and edited parts of the manuscript, and to my children, Michael and Sally, who figured more prominently in the conceptualization of this work than they will ever know. Most of all, I would like to express my love and appreciation to my wife, Mia, who not only typed and proofread but also endured with patience and good humor the constant strains bookmaking places on a young family. This work is dedicated to her.

Gregory M. Pfitzer

Saratoga Springs, New York
1990

PREFACE: THE GREAT SPHINX

For all their talk about objectivity and detachment, historians can sometimes be superstitious people. It seemed mysteriously prophetic to me, for instance, that on the very day nearly a decade ago when I first considered writing on the historical world of Samuel Eliot Morison a statue of him was being unveiled in Boston. Equally mysterious was the force that compelled me to cancel my afternoon plans, fight the crowds on Boston's notorious subway system, and risk a drenching on an overcast day in order to attend an unveiling. I felt then, as I do now, that some spiritual energy directed me toward the statue, and, in the dozens of trips I have made to the monument since the unveiling, that energy has never failed to register its effect on me. While I am neither mystical nor arrogant enough to presume that such a force was intended for *me* alone, its intensity suggested that certain subjects cry out so loudly for historical treatment (even from beyond the grave) that they emit a kind of magnetism to which historians are irresistibly drawn. As a student of the past living in an age of rationalism, I had always assumed that historians chose research topics according to principles of free will; but the power of this force made me suspicious that subjects may pursue historians as actively as we pursue them and in ways that few of us fully understand.

Taking the subway from Harvard Square to the Charles Street stop on Boston's Red Line that curious day, I turned a single question over and over in my mind: Why would the city of Boston erect a statue to a historian? To be sure, Morison was one of the most prolific and well-respected twentieth-century American historians, having written and edited nearly sixty volumes of history, including two Pulitzer Prize–winning biographies and a monumental fifteen-volume history of the United States Naval operations in World War II. Through numerous articles and books, Morison had practically invented the field of maritime history so far as the professional study of it was concerned. He had revived scholarly interest in an entire century of American history, the seventeenth century, and had restored the reputation of a whole people, the Puritans, in several works on early New England culture. He produced several of the most popular textbooks ever written, and his works, which were frequently Book-of-the-Month Club selections, were translated into fourteen languages and have sold thousands of copies. These accomplishments notwithstanding, I could not explain why a city which, despite its rich intellectual history, had never memorialized her considerable historians in such a fashion would dedicate this statue to Morison. Where were the statues in Boston to William Prescott, Francis Parkman, or Henry Adams? I wondered.

The question grew as I walked the several blocks from Charles Street station to the Commonwealth Plaza Mall. The six other monuments erected on the Mall since the land was leased to the city more than one hundred years ago suggested that Morison would be in rare but odd company. No consistent principle of selection seemed at work as I passed by the statues of Alexander Hamilton, William Lloyd Garrison, Domingo Sarmiento (educator and president of Argentina), Leif Eriksson, John Glover (commander of the Navy during the Revolutionary War), and Mayor Patrick Collins. Nor could I find any commonalities among those gathered around the veiled Morison statue when I arrived at Boylston and Exeter streets minutes before the ceremony. Those seated on the makeshift platform next to the statue I took to be members of the Back Bay Federation and the George B. Henderson Foundation, which had commissioned the statue.[1] Press and television reporters were on hand, setting up equipment and speaking casually with Morison's daughter, Emily Morison Beck. People ranging from the old to the very young circled the draped statue in an orderly progression, each reading the inscriptions on the rocks at the base of the statue and glancing up in highly individualistic ways at the shrouded figure. A group of curious college students gathered on the outskirts of the crowd, drawn from their fraternity houses along Commonwealth Avenue by the mystery of the cloaked figure and the announcement that Mayor Kevin White was expected soon.

The ceremony itself only piqued my curiosity about the business of sculpting monuments to historians. After a series of brief dedications, the keynote address was given by Thomas Boylston Adams, a direct descendant of the Boston Adamses and a family friend of Morison's when the historian lived in Concord. In his speech, entitled "Samuel Eliot Morison: Passionate Historian," Adams testified to the power of Morison's work with a personal anecdote. "One afternoon Mr. Morison—it was always Mr. Morison to us—was standing in the path [outside his house] with his hand held up in a signal to stop," Adams recalled. "Here's a book for you," he said, handing the young Adams a copy of his recently published *Maritime History of Massachusetts*. "That night I forgot my homework," Adams confessed, and he read the volume cover to cover. "Mr. Morison had caught me in the net of his style," he noted, and "I shall never escape." On behalf of thousands of other Boston readers, Morison "took his famous free-flowing fountain pen in his hand," Adams concluded, and "with the alchemy of a genius, he told stories with such truth and passion as to illuminate the important past and project light into the shadows of the future."[2]

Truth and passion may be the keys to good historical writing, I thought, but they still did not explain why the city had chosen to erect a statue to a historian. Hawthorne, Emerson, and Thoreau had combined both elements in their writings, but no statues to them graced the Mall. Adams was silent on this point, explaining only that Morison's contribution was "a question of creation" best understood by "fellow artist" and sculptress of the Morison monument Penelope Jencks. "The sympathetic bronze of Penelope Jencks must speak for itself," Adams announced at the close of his speech, and with that, Emily Morison Beck unveiled the Jencks work, leaving the crowd to evaluate its worthiness and rationalize its presence.[3]

Unshrouded, the statue increased rather than decreased my curiosity about Morison and his reputation. Somewhere in the monument's massive shapes and lines I suppose I expected to find an answer to the riddle of Morison's importance; instead I discovered an enigmatic Great Sphinx that raised many questions but solved few. What was I to make, for instance, of the contrast between the decidedly unpretentious figure of Morison, clothed in simple weather gear and sailor's cap, and the pedantic almost oracular inscriptions carved along the base of the twenty-ton piece of granite on which he sat? What was I to assume about the ambiguous body language of the figure Jencks had sculpted? Morison bears the casual, informal, contemplative attitude of a New England fisherman, gazing without plan or purpose at the incessant sea. Yet he is positioned in the manner of Rodin's thinker, evoking ancient connections and vast thoughts. Several months after the unveiling I questioned Thomas Boylston Adams about these contrasts, and his comments were a preview of the ideas he expressed later that same month in an article for *Yankee* magazine entitled "Passion and Truth Are the Life of Memorials." Arguing that "Boston is simply loused up with heroic figures in attitudes fixed on posterity by imitators of late Hellenistic sculpture," Adams praised the contemporary quality of Jencks's work, citing its many contrasts as symbolic of the diversity and complexity of Morison's life.[4] But, still, what was I to make of the statue in the first place?

In the months and years ahead, the rugged form atop the granite rock inspired me to search for answers to the riddle of Samuel Eliot Morison's greatness. Often such explorations raised still more puzzling questions. Several weeks after the unveiling ceremony, I met with Mrs. Emily Morison Beck and expressed my desire to write about the career of her distinguished father. Giving her kind permission for me to consult the Morison papers in the Harvard University Archives, she called my attention to a restriction prohibiting their use for a biography. "I do not believe in having biographies written of historians during their lifetime or shortly after," Morison wrote his heirs, adding that he preferred "to live and be remembered" through his works.[5] Such restrictions increased the mystery of him for me. Why would a historian who had built his career on writing biographies and consulting the private papers of public figures place restrictions on his own? Was he trying to obscure history, and if so, could he be the same truthful and passionate historian Thomas Boylston Adams had celebrated in his address "Truth and Passion"? To write a work on Morison's historical craft, as I intended to do, it was not necessary to probe too deeply into the historian's private life—his family history, his love relationships, his social habits, his club affiliations, and his personal eccentricities. But I wondered, would readers feel cheated by the omission of details about his boyhood in Boston, his years as a Harvard undergraduate and graduate student, his private reflections on World War I, his personal attitudes toward the depression, his involvement in World War II, his individual impressions of the cold war, and his reaction to the 1960s?

I soon discovered, however, that in directing would-be biographers to his works, Morison was not excluding them from a consideration of his life. Writers of history, no matter how detached they claim to be, create a persona in their works, and rarely has there been a historian as publicly forthcoming about his private life as Morison. His many books, articles, and lectures are highly autobiographical in character and comprise a vast storehouse of information about his habits and preferences. In Morison's published works as much as in his private papers, I discovered the fascinating and complex man Jencks had captured in her sculpture. Rumored to be shy and sensitive in his private life, Morison was outspoken and controversial in his writings. At times he could be humorous and witty, as in his reminiscences of nineteenth-century Boston in his autobiographical sketch One Boy's Boston; at others he could be cynical and even savage in his criticism, as in his testy review article of the work of Charles A. Beard, entitled "History Through a Beard." Intensely regional, he affirmed the superiority of the "New England way," while at the same time working to educate his readers to the world beyond New England. Committed to objective history, he nevertheless wrote with emotional sensitivity to the passage of time and remained intensely subjective in tone and subject throughout his career.

Morison's published books, articles, and lectures also revealed the rich sociology of his workplace. As a teacher and writer of history, he was influenced by many of the greatest historians of the twentieth century—Albert Bushnell Hart, Edward Channing, George Santayana, Charles Homer Haskins, Albert Beveridge, Frederick Jackson Turner, James Truslow Adams, Van Wyck Brooks, Charles Beard, Charles M. Andrews, Henry Steele Commager, and Daniel Boorstin. These diverse intellectuals influenced Morison throughout his extensive career, which spanned nearly the entire life of the American historical profession. Indeed, in perusing the bibliography of Morison's works, one is struck by the number of major "schools of thought" in twentieth-century historiography through which he passed. Attracted to the study of history in the 1890s, only several years after the founding of the American Historical Association (by his historian grandfather Samuel Eliot among others), he experienced movements with such curious and at times confusing designations as institutional history, sociocultural history, the New History, historical relativism, dialectical materialism, consensus history, historical pluralism, New Left history, and narrative revival. Morison was a guiding spirit in some of these movements; others affected him only slightly, and others he vehemently opposed. But no twentieth-century American historian other than Morison can claim to have experienced so many of the major transitions or the dominant personalities in the field of history. His life as revealed in his writings and papers constitutes a virtual intellectual history of the American historical profession from the 1890s to the mid-1970s.

Despite its diversity, Morison's career was characterized from beginning to end by a single, persistent theme—the struggle to reconcile a "professional" identity with the need to reach a larger, nonprofessional audience. Professional historians, those generally employed by academic institutions or supported by organizations such as the American Historical Association, were often identified, as was Morison, with the scholarly audiences for whom they wrote. They stressed the need for objectivity in the study of the past, formulated precise rules for scientific historical investigation, and advanced elaborate methodologies in technical monographs generally accessible only to scholars familiar with the language of the discipline. Professionals were often contrasted with so-called amateur historians, mainly journalists or men of letters who wrote for a popular audience, and who were therefore more sensitive to the need for a "usable past" and a narrative style in historical writing. Throughout his career, Morison attempted to maintain a middle ground (and even on occasion a higher ground) in the sometimes furious debates that raged between professionals and amateurs. While pursuing an academic career and writing extensively about higher education in American universities, for instance, he complained frequently about the debilitating effects of academic scholarship on historical writing. While maintaining a strong connection to professional associations (he was president of the American Historical Association, the American Antiquarian Society, the Colonial Society of Massachusetts, and the Massachusetts Historical Society), he despised professional titles, technical language, monographic literature, and formal philosophies of history. He applauded the narrative styles of the great nineteenth-century American historians like Parkman, Prescott, and Motley, but he deplored journalist-historians who sacrificed accuracy for the sake of dramatic prose and increased sales.

The contrast between Morison's professional and popular identities merely increased the mystery of his power as a writer for me. Determined to unlock the secret of his greatness, over the next several years I proceeded to read everything Morison wrote, by conservative estimations about 30,000 printed pages. In addition, I scoured archival collections containing "Morisoniana" at Harvard's Pusey Library, the Library of Congress, the Naval Operational Archives, the Naval War College, the Boston Athenaeum, the Franklin D. Roosevelt Library, Columbia University Library, the Schlesinger Library, and Harvard's Houghton Library. I interviewed Morison's friends and relatives as well, asking each to reflect on the genius of Morison's art. In the process, I feel I have come to know the late historian as few have ever had the luxury to do; indeed, I flatter myself to think that I have achieved the kind of empathy that Morison himself sought in portraying historical subjects. I have explored the nooks and crannies of Morison's Beacon Hill neighborhood, traversed the grounds of his 44 Brimmer Street residence, and hiked the paths around his beloved Northeast Harbor, Maine, retreat. I have acquainted myself with Morison's Harvard—have sat in the lecture halls he once filled with his halting but powerful voice, haunted the library stacks where he conducted his research, and visited the 417 Widener office where he wrote so much of his stirring prose. I have even risked learning how to sail—no small concession for a native midwesterner who had never seen the ocean until his young adult life and who, at the inception of this project, had never set foot in a sailboat.

What follows here, then, is not a biography, although there is much that is biographical in it. Instead, I have attempted to make a contribution to the field of historiography by describing the intellectual development of one of America's most significant historians. In the slow evolution of his art from his dissertation on Harrison Gray Otis to his final work, *The European Discovery of America*, Morison gradually developed a genius for history. In the fifteen years since his death no one has attempted a book-length appraisal of that genius; and no one has yet tried to place Morison in the context of the intellectual debates that swirled around him during his sixty-year career. This work seeks to address those gaps. In addition, I have struggled mightily to answer the riddles posed by the contrasts and complexities in the life of this Great Sphinx. In Greek mythology, the Sphinx was sent to Thebes by the Gods to ask passersby a riddle, and if they failed to answer correctly, they were devoured. In issuing this first book-length work on Morison, I ask only that readers treat me with slightly more compassion than the Theban Sphinx granted its hapless victims.

SAMUEL ELIOT MORISON'S

HISTORICAL WORLD

Historical Roots

Samuel Eliot, Francis Parkman and the Rise
of the American Historical Profession

I

A Grandfather's Legacy

One September evening in the late summer of 1898, eleven-year-old Samuel Eliot Morison read aloud to his grandfather and namesake, Samuel Eliot, as the elderly man lay quietly in his bed in their 44 Brimmer Street home in the Beacon Hill district of Boston. Recently ill, the septuagenarian had lost his ability to see well in artificial light, so members of his family had been reading to him nightly from their favorite publications. His wife usually selected articles from the *Boston Transcript* or the *Nation*, which generally elicited some response from the outspoken Eliot, but on this particular evening the grandfather seemed disinterested in weighty public matters. Sammy tried to interest him in a reading from the *Youth's Companion*, the highly sentimentalized juvenile magazine that usually stimulated Eliot's "lively sense of humor," but this too failed to evoke a reaction. Concerned by this silence, Sammy paused in his reading and stared inquisitively at his unresponsive grandfather. He had known since early summer that "Grandpa was very ill," but something in this current glance convinced him that his grandfather was "slowly sinking" away. Moments later grandfather whispered to grandson: "I've had a blessed life, a blessed life"; a few days later he was dead of heart failure.[1]

Morison's sense of loss was profound, since his grandfather had participated in nearly every phase of his development. The two lived together in the big four-story brick home Eliot had had built in 1870 on undeveloped pasture lands along the Charles River. Morison's mother, Emily Eliot Morison, was the only remaining child of the marriage of Samuel Eliot and Emily Marshall Otis, their two sons having died at young ages.[2] This sole remaining daughter had married the son of one of grandfather Eliot's college classmates, and because this son, John Holmes Morison, was a lawyer unable to afford office rent in Boston, the couple "was persuaded without much difficulty to live at 44 Brimmer Street, where the third floor became known jocosely as the 'Morison flat'. The arrangement was so mutually agreeable that it continued indefinitely." John Morison was not only busy with his career as a lawyer, but he also had political ambitions that kept him away from home a good deal.[3] Emily Morison was occupied with an endless procession of social and charitable activities.[4] They entrusted the care of their son, Sammy, to the grandfather who, by his own admission, hoped to raise the boy as a son.[5]

Eliot influenced every aspect of his grandson's daily life. Awakened each morning at half past seven by his grandfather's piano playing, Sammy tumbled out of bed, changed into his clothes, gave his hair a "lick and a promise," and was at the breakfast table in time to partake heartily of the meal of baked apples, hot cereal, bacon, ham, eggs, and fish over which Eliot always presided. After breakfast the patriarch walked his grandson to school lest his young charge be run over by the fast trotters and hacks that dashed along Beacon Street. If the traffic were not too heavy, Eliot insisted on walking in the middle of the street, since the brick sidewalks of Beacon Hill hurt his feet. "This drew jocular or snide remarks from passing wagons," Morison remembered, but Eliot cared not; he merely "beamed and waved . . . and trudged ahead." While this "occasioned no small mortification" to Sammy, he was still delighted to have "a loving grandfather always on tap to answer questions" as they proceeded to private school at Lyman house on Beacon Street and later to Miss Hudson's on Chestnut or the Shaw School on Marlborough.[6]

Sammy appreciated his grandfather's escort for other reasons as well. In the "sporty and raffish" neighborhood through which they walked to school, it was useful for a boy of Morison's social class to have an adult on hand for protection. Like other wealthy boys of his day, Morison was dressed frequently for school in the "Little Lord Fauntleroy" manner, complete with the lace collars, red stockings, and love locks of Ms. Burnett's "namby-pamby juvenile hero." On the school playground he suffered gibes, insults, and hair pullings, but the real danger to his person came from the children of "poor" Irish stable hands who eyed him suspiciously as he walked the streets of Beacon Hill. Under the watchful eye of grandfather Eliot, however, Sammy was safe from reproach.[7]

The trip home from school often took the pair past "Honest John Cotter's" tavern, which for years had proven "highly inviting to passing gentlemen with alcoholic tendencies" and whose smell became an indelible part of Morison's memories about his youth. Still more memorable was the "rich equine flavor" of the air as grandfather and grandson passed by the stables that serviced the Charles River wharf. Sammy frequently wished to linger there to listen to the fantastic "horse stories" told by the stable hands, but he was usually spirited home by Eliot so he could begin his afternoon lessons. The entire Eliot family "went in for education," Morison noted, and his grandfather literally took Sammy's education in hand. Having served as president of Trinity College, dean of the Girl's School of Boston, and superintendent of Boston Public Schools, Eliot was qualified to tutor Sammy, and tutor him he did. Morison remembered: "I was put to my books early, at the age of three, and before the fifth year came around, he started me on French." Compelled to learn by the "old fashioned method of rote," Sammy occasionally rebelled (for which he might be locked in a closet), but he ultimately came to appreciate his elder's techniques. "I was the single pupil of a man who from all accounts was one of the most inspiring teachers of his generation," Morison later noted.[8]

The weekends found grandfather and grandson together again. Saturdays meant a privileged walk to the market for groceries. On the way, they passed by the small shops of Charles Street, including De Luca's fruit store, where Eliot tried out his Italian on the owners, "with indifferent success" Morison later noted, "since he spoke the language of Dante and they were Sicilians." The pair then moved on to Faneuil Hall and Quincy Market, where the grandfather shopped for the best roast beef in town and the grandson was sure to pick up a red banana or Smyrna fig for his troubles. Morison recalled that Eliot was well liked by the "jolly red-cheeked marketmen" who admired the "gracious old gentleman with his white hair and hearty laugh." On the way home from the market the pair generally stopped by the Boston Athenaeum, where Eliot was president, and where even Miss Regan, "the stern guardian of the delivery desk, melted under his greeting." Occasionally such walks concluded with a visit to one of Eliot's many charitable organizations, including the Massachusetts General Hospital, the McLean Hospital, and the Perkins Institute for the Blind, where Sammy was once introduced to Helen Keller. "He was a trustee or director of half the charitable institutions of Boston," Morison later wrote, "and took me on some of his visits to Waverly, where I saw the feeble-minded at work with their carpentry, or to South Boston or Jamaica Plain, where the blind children greeted him as a father, and performed to my admiration, rapid feats of reading with their finger-ends."[9]

On Sundays, Eliot assembled the entire family in the 44 Brimmer Street library, where he conducted religious services and led in the singing of his favorite hymn, "Saviour, Source of Every Blessing." Sunday evenings were the occasion for the consumption of an enormous roast beef, which Eliot proudly prepared for his family and frequent guests. "I can see him carving it now . . . under the gaslight," Morison wrote decades later; "Grandma with a little lace cap on her gray hair, smiling pleasantly at the other end of the table. . . . The glass tree, with glass baskets hanging from the branches, which had been miraculously preserved unbroken since the eighteenth century, was on the table; the refreshments were 'pink and white ice cream,' cake, milk, and sandwiches."[10]

Summer meant trips to the Eliot vacation home in Beverly Farms, Massachusetts, to escape the "horsey atmosphere" of Beacon Hill, which became overpowering in the hot weather. There, Sammy and his grandfather explored the twisty lanes of West Beach in a rusty black livery stable surrey. A favorite activity was dashing up Pride's Hill to pick wild flowers for Mrs. Eliot.[11] Morison's grandfather also introduced him to local figures, including Henry James, John Jay Chapman, and Dr. Oliver Wendell Holmes. The visit to Holmes's summer home was memorable because the "Autocrat of the Breakfast Table" invited him to his fill of chocolates. These summer trips completed a yearly cycle; as fall began to descend on the Massachusetts coastal town, grandson and grandfather returned to Boston to dodge hacks and ruffians on the way to private school once again.[12]

Eliot's death, then, profoundly affected the life of his grandson. It disrupted literally every aspect of his daily routine. Morison's parents, friends, and relatives tried to comfort him with the knowledge that as a surrogate son he had been a constant source of joy to his grandfather, but Morison could not be consoled by such logic. What Sammy could not appreciate at the age of eleven was how desperately Eliot wished his grandson to learn from the mistakes he had made over a long and frustrating professional career. Nor could Morison understand the influence his grandfather had already exerted on his future development as a historian. These were matters too obscure for a small boy to grasp; he simply recognized that with the death of Eliot, he had suffered "the first great loss of his life."[13]

History as a Public Service

Had Morison been older, he might have understood better the special disappointments his grandfather had experienced in his professional life. The Eliots had amassed a substantial fortune in the shipping business in the late eighteenth century and had gained a citywide reputation for contributing to Boston's cultural institutions. Sam Eliot's relatives had endowed chairs at Harvard, helped found the Boston Athenaeum, and contributed handsomely to the Museum of Fine Arts.[14] It was expected, therefore, that Morison's grandfather would give his life over to some cultural pursuit, and because he had shown great promise in school, it was hoped he might lead a scholarly life. Enrolled at Harvard at the age of thirteen, Eliot had graduated first in a class of which he was the youngest member, having displayed a particular aptitude for historical study. After graduation he traveled extensively to expand his base of historical knowledge and to consider how he could best put his education to practical use.

A Gibbonesque epiphany while traveling in Rome in the early 1840s decided Eliot on a career as a historian. Walking among the ancient ruins of that city, Eliot was struck by the considerable role the Roman empire had played in advancing the cause of liberty in the western world. He suddenly recognized that the history of liberty might make a suitable theme for his scholarly energies, since it was a topic with "which all men are concerned and to which all events of human history are related."[15] His plan was to produce a multivolume work that traced the history of liberty from its ancient origins to its American fulfillment, and he spent many months energetically researching his topic in various European libraries.[16] On his return to the United States, he had little trouble convincing his family of the usefulness of his new work. His maternal grandfather, Alden Bradford, had been a historian of Massachusetts, and other family members had contributed to various historical institutions throughout New England.[17] In addition, a bright new generation of young historians was making a name for itself in America, and its members included respectable scholars such as George Bancroft, William Prescott, John Lothrop Motley, and Francis Parkman. Frequently associated with the golden age of American historical writing, this group of writers viewed history as a public service. As William Prescott put it, historians must be motivated by more than "selfish indulgence," "passive fortitude," or "abstract contemplation." They must live a "life of active usefulness." The goal of the historian was to "improve man" by rescuing him from "the listless, lifeless, all-devouring stupidity, idleness, inaction, ease, thoughtlessness, ennui [and] inattention" that characterized most scholarship.[18]

Perhaps the best known of this new school of historians was Francis Parkman, who shared much in common with Eliot. Parkman and Eliot had grown up within a few blocks of each other on Beacon Hill and had been part of the same social group. As teenagers they had formed a theatrical company together and staged performances in an unused barn behind the Parkman's home. The two wrote and adapted plays, printed up playbills, and invited parents and other dignitaries to attend their performances. Parkman appeared to be the more gifted of the two, and several of his dramatic efforts attracted attention beyond the respective family circles.[19] Two years Eliot's junior, Parkman followed Eliot to Harvard and then to Europe, where he formulated his own plans to become a historian. In 1849 Parkman published *The Oregon Trail* and by 1851 *The Conspiracy of Pontiac*. Although by the late 1840s Parkman's most important work was ahead of him, he was already being recognized for his special talents as a historian. Painstaking in his scholarship, Parkman set a high standard by consulting all available documentary sources before writing, paying transcribers to meticulously copy records from those collections he could not visit himself. He made it his habit as well to visit the sites of the historical events he described so that he might have a more vivid picture of the stage on which his historical subjects acted.[20]

Much of Parkman's effectiveness came from his remarkable ability to write. Striving to awaken in his readers a sense of the drama of the past,

Parkman used every literary device available to make his history come alive. He emphasized "grand themes," especially the moral conflict between absolutism and liberty. He stressed the role of heroic characters, especially military leaders, who demonstrated the place of great men in human history. He increased the dramatic power of his narratives by adopting conventions of the theater—employing rhetorical asides, Elizabethan inflections, and descriptive staging. Most of all, he accentuated dramatic action in his texts, describing with vividness and empathetic imagination the conquering of the North American wilderness by Jesuit explorers and the subjugation of the Indians by colonial frontiersmen.[21]

Eliot greatly admired the work of his friend, and Parkman, in turn, encouraged Eliot. "I hold it a great gain that American history should be presented to young and old by one, who, through education & nature . . . has the candor & ability to see and exhibit the truth," Parkman wrote. Eliot's friend admired that "in these times and in this country, [Eliot had the] heart to maintain his stand above the vortex of materialism in which the nation is surging."[22] By the same logic, Eliot appreciated Parkman's high standards as well; he dissented, however, from aspects of Parkman's historical technique, particularly his tendency to overwrite scenes for the sake of narrative effect. From Eliot's point of view, Parkman's narrative mode included too many fictive techniques and concessions to the romantic sensibilities of readers. In particular he disliked Parkman's reliance on military battles. In the preface to his work on the history of liberty, Eliot wrote that "those who love to follow the adventurous march, or hear the whizzing spear, or count the trophies of the slain" would be disappointed. "It is bad enough that wrath and bloodshed should be numbered amongst the sins of man," he observed, "without their being made the attractions of his history." He reiterated that the "teachings of history do not admit . . . the exhortatory development" belonging to the works of the literary class, "but if they be accepted with open minds," he reasoned, "they can never be regarded as indirect or vague."[23]

Eliot envisioned his history swinging somewhere between the "romantic or entertaining" and the "abstract or instructive." Appreciating "the fresh[ness] and picturesqueness of the former and the philosophical intentions of the latter," Eliot tried to reconcile the two by using the mediating force of Christianity. Christianity had played a crucial role in the progress of liberty in the western world, he argued, providing inspiring and miraculous stories for the narrative historian at one end of the spectrum while affording plenty of abstraction for the theoretical historian at the other. Christianity also had the advantage of being predictive; it allowed the historian to project the path of liberty into the future. Parkman saw the hand of Providence working through history, but he was inclined to downplay its implications for the present. Eliot viewed history as the revelation of God's plan for the present and the future. In the preface to *The Liberty of Rome* he wrote, "History is given us by God, but that it be made of any efficacy it must not only influence us in regard to the past, but console us with regard to the future . . . I have endeavored to represent the history of antiquity, as that of a period over which Providence was continuously watchful, as over our own."[24]

While Eliot worked with relative satisfaction on his historical project, it was never the success he had intended. Part of the problem was the decreasing popularity of works on ancient history. Of the six hundred works of history written by Americans from 1800 to 1860, only five were on ancient history. Americans were reading local and national histories of the sort Parkman was producing.[25] But Eliot's heavy-handed Christian moralizing and his dense prose were greater problems. Nineteenth-century readers were accustomed to some religious garnish with their historical meals, but Eliot masked the taste altogether with a too steady diet of bland religious pronouncements. He showed none of the imagination or stylistic genius of his friend Parkman. "In undertaking the history of liberty," his friend and Harvard professor Barrett Wendell noted, Eliot "mistook literary ambition for capacity." Wendell added frankly, "His earliest impulse seems to have been towards the dignified and vigorous school of historical writing which is among the most precious possessions of New England. That kind of literature demands special gifts which he never quite revealed." Eliot's history showed "neither such vivid power of concrete imagination as is essential to a notable historian, nor yet a vivid command of style. In substance and form alike it indicate[d] little creative power."[26]

Eliot was deeply affected by these criticisms and emotionally drained by the experience of writing history. "Verily this authorship hath cost me dear," he confided in his journal. "Four years, such as these past have been to me, make a deep mark upon one's life," he confessed. "The spring of 1847 found me a very different man from the one in the spring of 1851. Now I am no longer a youthful but rather a middle-aged man, whose face shows the traces of manhood over youth."[27] For the next twenty years Eliot drifted from one enterprise to the next—private tutoring, college teaching, philanthropy—unable to restore his confidence in the historical enterprise that so deeply engaged his friend Parkman.[28] Despondent and ill (Eliot seems to have been prone to various psychosomatic sicknesses),[29] he traveled to Europe once again in the mid-1860s, where he found new inspiration for his work as a historian—not this time in the ancient ruins of Rome, but in the recently developed European institutes of social science. Touring the Société d'Economie Politique of Paris and the Volkswirtschaftliche Verein in Germany, Eliot was struck by the similarities between the two programs and the kind of social application of intellectual ideas that he had been attempting for years.[30] Social science institutes taught that social relations could be scientifically engineered if enough scholarly information could be gathered on which to make intelligent choices. They employed the new historical techniques of Buckle, Draper, and Momsen, which focused on the "laws of progress" and the "social conditions of mankind." Historians were urged to elaborate social processes according to the rules of science, "by collecting facts, applying principles, and reaching the general laws which govern the social relations."[31]

Inspired by this example, Eliot returned home to help found the American Social Science Association (ASSA), a professional organization dedicated to applying scholarly knowledge to the solution of social problems and to establishing social science institutes in America.[32] The association met for the first time in 1869 in New York City to discuss the latest theories of social management, and Eliot was its keynote speaker. In his address he explained that the function of the ASSA was to "collect the data of separate efforts, and so to group them . . . [in such a way] that the general principles might be evolved, and the work of Social Science . . . might be directed and harmonized to the common welfare." Arguing that scholars in America were too often engaged in private projects, Eliot noted that the social science movement "pleads by its very name for associated, rather than individual exertions in its behalf." Eliot outlined categories of social activity in need of "combined action" from several disciplines, including health, trade, economy, education, and jurisprudence, and gave historians the special responsibility of identifying the "general laws" operating in each. If scholars could do all this, he concluded, they would be "working out social principles and framing a social code, by means of which Social Science will make such advances as it has hitherto unavailingly contemplated."[33]

Elected president of the American Social Science Association, Eliot had a wide-ranging influence on practitioners in many fields, including his own discipline of history. At the 1884 meeting of the ASSA, a young, German-educated doctorate, Herbert Baxter Adams, read a paper calling for the adoption of social scientific philosophies to the study of history in America. By the following year, Adams had initiated a meeting of historians interested in the social scientific approaches for Saratoga Springs, New York. This meeting spawned the American Historical Association (AHA), a splinter group of the ASSA.[34] Dedicated to the same philosophy of social reform as the parent organization, the American Historical Association welcomed all "historical specialists and active workers everywhere."[35] The executive council was dominated by "the academic element," men such as Andrew D. White of Cornell University, Justin Winsor of Harvard, Charles Kendall Adams of the University of Michigan, and Herbert Baxter Adams of Johns Hopkins, but a reporter for The Nation noted, "men of affairs," such as Charles Deane, were also well represented.[36] According to the Boston Herald, the goals of the AHA were to "give historical studies in this country a larger scope and purpose, and to place them upon a scientific basis" by bringing the historian "out of his seclusion" into "the wholesome air of public affairs" through contact "with specialists in the kindred fields of social science, jurisprudence, and political economy."[37]

The creation of the AHA should have been a highly satisfying event for Eliot, but from the beginning he had doubts about its intentions. At the

1884 ASSA meeting at which the creation of an independent historical association was first proposed, then president John Eaton criticized the suggestion on the grounds that "the tendency of scholarship in this country was toward excessive specialization" and that such an organization would encourage other splinter groups. Speaking on behalf of Eliot and other concerned board members, Eaton reminded the renegade historians that the ASSA had been founded so that "scholars who are working in different fields" could "compare results" and "profit by one another's labors." Social scientists should "not be organized for too narrow specialties," he argued, especially not historians, since they were charged with the important task of identifying the important "social questions growing out of history."[38]

As Eaton, Eliot, and others suspected, the creation of the American Historical Association did encourage a general splintering of the parent organization. Within a few years the American Economic Association was formed, followed by the American Political Association and the American Sociological Association.[39] As a historian of the social science movement L.L. Bernard notes, Eliot's association was a victim of its own success: "Its field of interest became so large, the volume of knowledge required to function in it effectively grew to be so immense, and the degree of specialization required of its members so extreme that these requirements finally caused it to break up."[40] The American Historical Association quickly dropped its pretensions of being a public service organization concerned with social scientific engineering. Instead, it focused on specific concerns of academic historians. Monographs became the primary means of intellectual exchange, and a precise language developed among members for the communication of historical ideas. By the 1890s, the American Historical Association was well on its way to becoming the professional organization for historians that it has become in the twentieth century.[41]

The splintering of the American Social Science Association was a tremendous blow to Eliot, because it left him once again without a means to reconcile scholarship with public service. Although Eliot joined the American Historical Association briefly, he never sympathized with its professional imperatives. After 1890 he confined most of his historical activities to the reading rooms of the Boston Athenaeum, where members of an older antiquarian bent still gathered.[42] Yet he always remained a private man, troubled deeply by his failure as a historian and his inability to transform the world around him. "I am a man of leisure," he noted toward the end of his life, "and leisure is not the brightest of earthly blessings."[43]

Those who knew Eliot best at the time of his death, therefore, admitted that there had been considerable disappointment in his life, mainly deriving from his inability to bring his considerable intellectual powers to bear on public matters. If he had had political aspirations, he might have found a platform for his philosophy, but as a patrician and a scholar he perceived himself "above politics." Instead, he wished to express himself through intellectual ideas, particularly historical ones, but he did not want to employ the literary devices that gave historians like his friend Parkman a wider influence. He assumed the paradoxical posture of a scholar dedicated to changing the masses while refusing to engage them on their terms. Arguing that such a posture was more appropriate to the "generation which preceded Dr. Eliot's," one obituary writer commented that members of his generation "were mostly placed where they must either swerve from the traditions or do their public service elsewhere than in public life." For Eliot, this condition produced the curious career "of a faithful public servant, whose service was done in the unofficial retirement of privacy."[44]

A Monument to Himself

At the time of his grandfather's death, eleven-year-old Samuel Eliot Morison was ignorant of the complex ironies and paradoxes of Eliot's career as a historian. He was likewise oblivious to the important ramifications of that career for his own future as a historian. Only years later, after he had risen to the presidency of the American Historical Association, did he realize how much that organization had disappointed his grandfather. Not until he discovered Eliot's personal journals in the basement of the Brimmer Street home did he understand how desperately his grandfather wished to make his grandson over in his own image. And not before he was a septuagenerian himself did Morison acknowledge that Eliot "probably did more to influence my decision to become an historian than anyone."[45]

Even as a young boy, however, Morison did sense that he was the special educational project of a grandfather whose interests were primarily historical. A walk through Boston rarely went by without some comment from the elder Eliot about the important part the family had taken "in historic events since the founding of the colonies."[46] The Old State House prompted stories about James Otis, the ancestor of Morison's grandmother's who had bravely opposed the writs of assistance in 1760 and led the protest against the Stamp Act in 1765. The gold-domed capitol induced tales of Harrison Gray Otis, United States congressman, mayor of Boston, and participant in the famed Hartford Convention. Eliot encouraged his grandson to browse the impressive collection of histories in the Brimmer Street library, "which included no end of illustrated books fascinating to a small boy." There he read Elisha Kent Kane's *Arctic Explorations* as well as Molly Elliot Seawell's *Decatur and Somers*, which "kindled" his interest in naval history.[47] Grandfather Eliot instilled in young Morison the feeling that he had "absorbed history from birth." [48]

After Eliot's death, his wife, Emily Marshall Otis, accepted the task of shaping her grandson's historical sensibilities. Morison continued to read history "omnivorously," particularly maritime history, which his grandmother helped him collect. A note from twelve-year-old Sammy to grandmother Eliot before one of her trips to New York City suggests the serious-ness with which he took the enterprise: "Will you bring me from New York a book called 'Under Dewey at Manilla' [sic]," Morison asked. "It is *not* '*with*' Dewey," he emphasized, and "has a red, white, and blue binding represing [sic] a sailor hoisting the flag. If you can't get it," he added, "I would like any book of the Navy."[49] Mrs. Eliot also took Sammy on several trips to Europe (where he was first exposed to the ruins of the ancient world that had so fascinated his grandfather), and on her weekly visits to the houses of Boston's most prestigious figures.[50]

Morison's reading and trappings about Boston made him intensely patri-otic about his city's history and laid the foundation for what would primar-ily be a career in New England studies. "I was proud of Faneuil Hall and the Adamses," he wrote, and "firmly believed America to be the best country and Boston the finest city on earth." He was proud of the U.S. Navy as well and boasted that "having 'licked England twice,' it could do so again, if necessary." He was delighted with Charles Carleton Coffin's *Boys of '76* and histories of the American Revolution given him by his grandmother, and he experienced unequalled pride at receiving permission from a naval officer at the Boston docks to climb "all over the full-rigged, three skysail yard ship *Aryan*."[51]

By the time he was a teenager, even Morison's friends recognized that he had the potential to become a scholar. Enrolled in the exclusive preparatory school Noble and Greenough on Chestnut Street in Boston, and later at St. Paul's Academy in Concord, New Hampshire, Morison thrived on the strictly classical curriculum that "trained his mind" and gave him "access to the best that had been written or said in Western Civilization."[52] The classes were "narrow in scope" and rigorous, Morison recalled, and occa-sioned recurring nightmares that persisted into adult life about being reassigned after graduation to Mr. Greenough to "brush up on Latin and Greek." Yet the classes "provided a broad basis for the later professional study of American history."[53] Nicknamed the "Professor" by his friends, he encouraged them to join in his incessant desire to "play at history." Each year he and his cousin "Mac" held an annual "revel day," on which they set off firecrackers and told stories about evil spirits; these stories were then recorded on parchment and buried, to be exhumed at some future date of historical significance.[54] They also endowed local figures with historical titles, punning endlessly on the name of local fisherman Hanable, making him "successively Hannibal, Hasdrubal, Hamilcar, Hanno, and the Noble Carthaginian." These pseudonyms dissolved them into fits of "idiotic laugh-ter" to the disgust of their parents but to the delight of their "adolescent wit."[55] And with another cousin, Sam Vaughan, Morison re-created scenes from his naval histories in a makeshift steamship that the boys had adapted from a discarded upright piano box. They spent hours striking the bells, throttling up and down, relaying "official" ship memos regarding enemy vessels, and citing penalties for indiscretions toward female passengers.[56] By the age of fourteen, Morison had graduated to actual sea sailing, feeling the "exhilaration, the peculiar, indescribable delight of sea transport under sail." He accounted it "the first thing he ever did well" and noted that its mastery marked his "transition from childhood to youth." For the rest of his career, Morison combined his avocation, sailing, with his vocation, writing the history of the sea.[57]

Samuel Eliot had unquestionably influenced his grandson in countless ways. If he seemed too aggressive in his efforts to make "Sammy" into a surrogate son, it was perhaps because the loss of his own two sons had devastated him so. If he seemed too anxious to push his grandson along the occupational path that he had tread, it was perhaps because he was so disappointed about having lost his way on that path. If he seemed too self-serving at the end of his life in making his grandson over into his own image, perhaps, like many, he merely wished to erect a monument to himself. Regardless of the deliberateness of the effort, Eliot's attentions bore undeniable fruit. Morison fulfilled Eliot's dreams in ways that he could not possibly have imagined as he lay on his deathbed listening to selections from *Youth's Companion*. But such fruit took years to ripen. The first real signs of its fecundity did not reveal themselves until Morison entered Harvard College as a young man in the autumn of 1904.

The Making of a Historian

Henry Adams, Charles Homer Haskins,
George Santayana and Historical
Studies at Harvard

———

2

"I Resolved to Be an Historian"

For a young man so thoroughly sculpted in the image of his grand-father, there was little question about choice of undergraduate institution. It had been understood from the time that he was a young boy that Morison was bound for Harvard, where it was assumed he would uphold the high scholarly standards of the many relatives who had preceded him there. Should he falter in these expectations, the ghost of his grandfather Eliot was there to haunt him in the person of Charles William Eliot, nephew to Samuel Eliot and president of the college. Morison was greeted many mornings by the visage of President Eliot, who strolled across Harvard Yard from the president's home on Quincy Street to his office in University Hall, looking "very presidential" in his "tall, flat-topped derby hat." Occasionally the president sought out his young freshman relative and invited him to stop by the presidential home after classes for tea; he even visited Morison in his suite, ostensibly to discuss issues of student concern with his roommates but undoubtedly also to keep an eye on his relative.[1] When Morison managed to escape the president's well-intentioned inspections, he still faced the scrutiny of another relative, Charles Eliot Norton, who was one of the college's most revered teachers and one of the Eliots' most watchful and devoted family men.[2]

In 1904, when Morison began his undergraduate education, Harvard Yard was filled with over six hundred freshmen from a variety of backgrounds; there were certainly many in his class, however, with whom he had had long association. Among these were the sons of Boston's patrician class, many of whom, Morison later remembered with disdain, were "pampered youths who batted about at night, and paid some conscientious fellow student to come and get them out of bed in time for eleven o'clock classes." Some of Morison's classmates complained that the "over-aggressive Jews or the over-aggressive Westerners or the over-aggressive sons of New England mill hands were disturbing the genteel atmosphere of the Yard."[3] These disgruntled students ate in private eating clubs that catered to sensitive palates and egos. Because of the social standing of his parents and grandparents, Morison might have socialized with this group, but he chose instead to associate with that " 'constant' of middle-class New England students" and members of his own social class who had few pretensions or prejudices regarding education.[4] These students primarily ate together in one of two dining halls—either Randall or Memorial—where ideas generally mingled with dinner in an atmosphere of democratic consumption.[5]

For entertainment, students relied on a variety of social and academic clubs. Among the most prominent was the Institute, originally a literary club, but by the first decade of the twentieth century, an exclusively social one. Morison remembered vividly, years after graduation, how, on the night of initiation into the Institute, club members used to march around the campus singing club songs and "pulling the neophytes out of their rooms with savage roars, and dragging them about in the procession." There was much in these playful fraternal antics to attract a freshman who wished to be liked, and Morison was expected to thrive in this social atmosphere. But he avoided the Institute and other such clubs because of their insistence on conformity. "[A]mbitious freshmen had to watch their steps very carefully," Morison remembered. "You must say, do, wear, the 'right thing,' avoid the company of all ineligibles, and above all, eschew originality."[6] In addition, one senses that his social "immaturity" inhibited him somewhat in these activities. Despite having waited a year to enter Harvard after his graduation from St. Paul's (during which time he traveled in Europe and spent a summer on a ranch in California), he was by his own admission "thin, weak, timid, awkward at games and not liked by most of his classmates."[7] He tried desperately to be "one of the boys": he participated in track; he applied to manage the crew team; he attempted to "make" the *Harvard Lampoon* staff; and he was one of the pranksters who chased an unlucky classmate "completely naked, out into Mt. Auburn Street and wouldn't let him back until he promised to stand drinks for all hands."[8] In general, however, Morison failed in his efforts to fit in with his classmates. He was admitted to no clubs or societies and remained "an outsider to the social life of the college." By the end of his freshman year, he made a conscious decision to stop trying to impress anyone socially. He asked only "to be let alone"; and that, he later remarked, "Harvard did."[9]

In response to this social isolation, Morison "fell back on his studies."[10] Academically he was well qualified to survive in this environment. He had excelled in classes at St. Paul's and had been admitted to Harvard without conditions. He was given advanced credit for English A, which gave him an opportunity to graduate in three years.[11] Early in his freshman year Morison decided on this rigorous path and added to his burdens by concentrating in mathematics, which required an intense battery of introductory courses. As a freshman, Morison enrolled in English 28 (British literature), German, Slavic, History 1a (Medieval Europe), and three introductory mathematics courses, including calculus.[12] Intellectually he found Harvard a "thrilling place" and his courses exhilarating, but his "inability to master the calculus knocked [his] ambition on the head."[13] By the end of his first semester, Morison was in search of a new career path.

Fortunately for Morison, the college's "elective system" gave him ample opportunity to search for other academic interests. Under the elective system a student could choose any course that interested him and that fit into his schedule; there were no assigned classes, no prescribed majors, and no requirements for graduation save the completion of any eighteen courses.[14] To Morison, trained at St. Paul's according to a strictly regimented classical curriculum, this system offered a first chance to take some responsibility for his own education. He sampled a healthy portion of Harvard's liberal arts offerings and "fairly ate up courses by the great men of the era." While Morison was as disappointed in his calculus class as its professor was in him, he thoroughly enjoyed History 1a and determined to take as many courses in the history department as he could over the last two years of his college education. The instructors in the history courses he subsequently took interested him "so profoundly" in the study of the past that by midway through his second year at Harvard he "resolved to be an historian."[15]

History 1 and the Debate over Method

The department whose courses Morison sampled with greater appetite and appreciation over the next few years had undergone some important recent changes. Throughout most of the nineteenth century there had been no department of history at Harvard at all. History had no independent status as an academic field, and it was viewed simply as a method for informing other disciplines such as philology, philosophy, and politics. With Darwin's evolutionary theories, however, a new interest in historical ideas—the origins of events, the patterns of development, the definitions of progress—evolved, as did an interest in history as an independent discipline. By 1870, history at Harvard was just beginning to differentiate itself from the "humane pursuits" with which it had been so closely associated in the past; it began, as future chairman of the history department Ephraim Emerton put it, "to fight for its life" as an independent and scientifically legitimated "member in the academic family."[16]

The move to create a "science of history" was spearheaded by the American Historical Association and the new group of "professional" historians who flocked to its membership. Many of these scholars traveled to Europe (especially Germany) to study new methods of historical research and criticism and to earn America's first Ph.D.'s in history. These *Herren Doktoren* stressed the ideals of objectivity and scientific positivism and urged historians to adopt a detached, impersonal attitude toward the past. They rejected all efforts to make history "useful"—both the romantic subjectivity and "symbolic designs" of Francis Parkman and the social pragmatism of Samuel Eliot. According to John Higham, the proponents of scientific history "distrusted imagination," avoided discussions of personality or "human character," "refrained from elucidating timeless moral verities," and embraced a scientific spirit that was "impersonal, collaborative, secular, impatient of mystery, and relentlessly concerned with the relation of things to one another instead of their relation to the realm of ultimate meaning." For them history had its own systematic, scientific prerogatives; it was accessible only to scholars with an appreciation for "the concept of cumulative, on-going change, operating through an endless chain of tangible causes and effects" and with an ability to view this change as detached observers.[17]

Some of these original American Ph.D.'s took positions in the 1870s and 1880s at Harvard, where they began to teach the first independent courses in history. Eventually they organized themselves into the "Department of History and Roman Law."[18] Henry Adams was a transitional figure in this effort. Trained informally at several German universities, Adams introduced the German seminar method to Harvard in 1870. This method encouraged students "familiar only with the dreary routine of an American recitation room" to sit down with a trained scholar "around the seminary table" to discuss "the processes of research and interpretation of history." In his seminar, Adams preached the scientific "gospel of accuracy, thoroughness, and fair-mindedness" and the German historical philosophy of *Verfassungsgeschichte*, or the history of institutional development. German historians claimed that the best way to study the evolution of human society over broad expanses of time was to examine the transformation of institutions, particularly political and legal institutions. Adams adopted this approach in his famous seminar on the origin of Anglo-Saxon law, which traced the development of legal institutions through the study of charters, constitutions, and court documents. He also attracted many able students to his two courses in American history, which outlined the growth of American political systems from Anglo-Saxon roots to national fulfillment.[19]

When Adams left Harvard in 1877, he made room for other German-trained institutional scholars, some of whom had been his students as undergraduates. In 1876, Adams student Ephraim Emerton returned to Harvard (A.B. 1871) from doctoral work in Leipzig (Ph.D. 1876) to assume a chair in ecclesiastical history. Harvard had always employed instructors in church history, but Emerton's chair was unique because it was not assigned to the divinity school but to the college. It was created in the hope (expressed decades earlier by Samuel Eliot) that "the history of the Christian church, treated not by a minister . . . but by a trained layman as a part of the general history of mankind" might attract more than divinity students to the institutional study of religion. In 1883, Freiburg Ph.D. Albert Bushnell Hart (A.B., Harvard, 1880) was hired to teach American institutional history; in the same year, another Adams student, Edward Channing (A.B., Harvard, 1878), was appointed to teach modern history. Hart and Channing collaborated in a very popular joint seminar on American institutions based on Adams's original course on Anglo-Saxon law. In 1887, another Adams student, Silas Marcus Macvane (A.B., Harvard, 1873) was hired to teach political economy; in 1888 Charles Gross was attracted from Göttingen to teach European history; and in 1893 Freiburg Ph.D. Archibald Cary Coolidge received an appointment in European and diplomatic history. All three, Macvane, Gross, and Coolidge, were trained in institutional history and incorporated Adams's seminar techniques in their courses.[20]

These professors organized themselves into a formal department in 1890 and held the first departmental meetings during the 1890–91 academic year. The secretary's minutes for these meetings reveal the extent to which they agreed on what the fundamental focus of history at Harvard should be.[21] Chairman Emerton later noted their common intellectual debt to "Maine and Stubbs in England, Waitz in Germany, [and] Fustel de Coulanges in France," historians who "initiated an eager search into the origins and development of political institutions."[22] Of the fifteen courses listed in the catalogue under "History" for the 1890–91 academic year, thirteen were on constitutional and political topics, and all followed a "rational order of progression."[23] Although the elective system prohibited the department from establishing any formal requirements for work in a given academic discipline, it could institute prerequisites for specific courses. Therefore the department of history and Roman law (later altered to the department of history and government) required that all students who wished to take advanced classes in history must follow a specific developmental program beginning with elementary classes.[24] This program began with History 1: "Mediaeval and Modern History," which was intended to provide an introduction to "the great lines of historic development . . . from the fourth to the nineteenth century."[25]

During the 1890s, History 1 became an increasingly popular course and soon became recognized as a necessary part of an undergraduate education at Harvard. Some of its success was owing to the popularity of instructors such as Coolidge who lived with the undergraduates and befriended many of them.[26] It also drew strength from the growing interest, shared by all academic disciplines, in things historical. Nearly every liberal arts department desired students to have some sense of the origin and development of institutions as a background to further study, and because History 1 was a prerequisite to all other courses in historical method, the majority of students were advised to make it an early part of their liberal arts training.

The effect was to make History 1 nearly a freshmen requirement at this college without requirements. According to the 1890–91 departmental minutes, 192 freshmen enrolled in introductory courses in the department, primarily in History 1. By 1897–98, the number had risen to 348, and by 1903, to 420. At the turn of the century, History 1 was the most highly subscribed course at Harvard. And, as enrollments in the introductory course increased, so did subscriptions to upper level history courses. In 1890–91, only 14 Harvard students listed themselves as history "concentrators." By 1897–98, however, 84 designated themselves concentrators, and, by 1903, the number had risen to 113, making history the most popular department in the school.[27]

As enrollments increased, so did money allocated to the department to provide instructors to teach them. In 1902 President Eliot authorized two new appointments in history, which were filled by Charles Homer Haskins from the University of Wisconsin and Roger Bigelow Merriman from Oxford University. Haskins, "indisputably first among American medievalists," was a man "whose energy, erudition, and character inspired the entire department to high endeavor." Merriman, whose appointment was an event regarded as "memorable in the annals of History at Harvard," was renowned as a scholar of architecture, Spanish history, British history, and eventually Latin American history. Consistent with the department's policy of giving "its best to the beginners," these newest instructors were hired to teach History 1,[28] and it was expected that they would handle the introductory course in a manner consistent with the traditions of a faculty fast earning the reputation as the "most distinguished group of historical scholars and teachers ever assembled on this continent."[29]

New appointments invited new ideas, however, and Haskins and Merriman never conformed completely to the traditions of the department. Both new professors had been trained in institutional history but both supplemented the scientific study of institutions, *Verfassungsgeschichte*, with the humanistic study of culture, or *Kulturgeschichte*. Culture in this sense referred to the study of all aspects of human "civilization"—social, artistic, intellectual, as well as constitutional and political.[30] The institutional historians at Harvard had never completely ignored cultural history understood in this way; they had, however, always subordinated culture to the larger patterns of scientific development and studied only those aspects of culture that revealed, in Hart's words, that "there is a steady progression from one condition to another . . . in the world of the mind as well as in the material universe."[31] Haskins and Merriman sought to replace this diachronic vision of history with a synchronic one; they believed that every historical moment had an importance independent of other moments, and that every historical event, even those judged incidental to the developmental standards of institutional historians, had historical significance.

The synchronic vision of Haskins and Merriman reflected a growing trend within the profession toward social and cultural history. Although institutional history was still the dominant mode of historical study at most colleges, by the first decade of the twentieth century professors such as James Harvey Robinson and Charles A. Beard of Columbia were widening the scope of history to include "[a]ll aspects of human affairs," even "common, mundane experience."[32] If Parkman concentrated on the "Great Man" in history and Adams on the "Great Institution," then these sociocultural historians sought to show how great men and great institutions were "merely the mechanism through which the Great Many ha[d] spoken." According to John Higham, historians such as Haskins, Merriman, Robinson, and Beard "broadened the subject matter of history to take in the life of the common people" and applied new scientific standards to the study of the "common folk." In recognizing the importance of "everyman" as a subject for investigation, these historians also widened the popular audience for history. Nineteenth-century students of the past experienced history by association only, through the actions of Emerson's "representative men"; whereas twentieth-century students could view their personal experiences as historically relevant.[33]

The arrival of Haskins and Merriman at Harvard was the occasion for a series of heated debates between the strictly institutional historians in the department and those willing to consider sociocultural approaches. Tensions erupted first and most forcefully over the issue of History 1. Haskins and Merriman were scheduled to take over the course from Coolidge in 1904, the year that Morison was enrolled in it as a freshman. Both believed, however, that, in its present "institutional" form, History 1 was "not helpful to the higher work of the department."[34] In a manner typical of professionally trained and scientifically inclined historians, Haskins conducted a survey of introductory courses in colleges across the country, and he published his results in an article timed (not coincidentally) for a departmental meeting called to consider the future of History 1. He concluded that although in the late nineteenth century it was common "to cover in some fashion the whole range of human knowledge" in introductory courses "large enough to give an idea of the growth of institutions and the nature of historical evolution," increasingly students seemed to want smaller courses that allowed "an acquaintance at close range with some of the characteristic personalities and conditions of the times." In particular, students desired introductory courses that allowed "time for more thorough study" in social and cultural fields. This focusing in of the historical lens could only be accomplished, Haskins noted, if introductory courses were restricted in chronological scope.[35]

In order to implement his educational philosophy, Haskins proposed to dismantle History 1 and to teach a course in Medieval History (History 1a) while Merriman taught either British history or modern history (History 1b).[36] The Haskins plan sparked immediate debate among members of the department. Some older faculty took the opportunity presented by the petition to air some long-standing grievances against History 1. Professor

Coolidge admitted he was "tired of teaching a subject" he knew "nothing about under the fire of specialists"; Professor Emerton revealed that he "had always disapproved" of the direction of the course after his retirement from it; and Professor Gross announced that students did not really "learn anything" in it.[37] Other members of the department, however, strongly objected to the reorganization plan. Silas Macvane complained that the proposal eliminated the "most valuable feature of the course" as he had taught it—comprehensiveness. Even though Professor Gross doubted History 1's effectiveness, he too opposed the plan to dismantle the course because he believed it was a "scandal to use a mild and gentle word," that Merriman's proposed History 1b would present "general historical culture" without relying on the institutional "knowledge of English history" that "seems valuable."[38] Professor Hart, however, was the most outspoken critic. He believed the proposed smaller courses would reduce History 1's effectiveness as a general introduction to the liberal arts and would thereby undercut the usefulness of the department. He reminded his colleagues of their responsibility to the large number of Harvard undergraduates who took history not to gain specific knowledge of the past but as a general introduction to other subjects.[39]

Despite these objections, there was "a certain massiveness about Haskins's character and intellect" that made "his personality the most pervasive in the department" and helped win acceptance for the reorganization plan.[40] During the 1904–5 academic year, therefore, History 1 was finally split into two introductory classes, one in Medieval and one in British history.[41] Those who enrolled in History 1a in the fall of 1904, including Morison, were presented "a cultural course" that, according to the syllabus, introduced them to the "characteristic life of the Middle Ages" in all its "action and movement and color." The new course was experimental, however, and even Haskins was apprehensive about its success. "It may be that I am attracted to this solution," he admitted, "because this is almost the only type of course I have not taught to freshmen." He remained hopeful, however, that "his confidence" in the reorganized History 1 would not "pass away with experience."[42]

Even though they had bowed to Haskins's request, dissenting members of the history department monitored the progress of History 1a and were quick to condemn its failures. Characteristic again of the professional and scientific training that professors on both sides of the issue shared, Hart conducted a detailed, developmental study over the first seven years of the course's life to determine its effectiveness. In a report filled with statistics and illustrated with graphs, Hart demonstrated with "facts" what he had predicted by intuition from the beginning—that the divided History 1 was "not so attractive to students as the old single course." From 1904 to 1912, Hart noted, History 1a had 25 percent fewer enrollments than History 1 and had lost students to other introductory courses throughout the college.[43] A Harvard History Club request for "a general course covering a larger field" than History 1a and 1b confirmed Hart in his belief that students wanted courses in broad-based institutional or evolutionary history.[44] On the strength of Hart's report, History 1 was eventually restored to its former status as the department's introductory course and History 1a and 1b were eliminated from the curriculum.[45]

The debate over History 1 revealed cracks in the history department that widened from the force of internal and external pressures. Even Haskins admitted that the reorganization had been a failure from the perspective of student enrollment; indeed, Haskins, in his capacity as chair of the department at the time of Hart's report, restored History 1 as the department's introductory course. Yet Haskins did not agree with Hart's conclusion that the drop in enrollments implied the superiority of institutional approaches to sociocultural ones. The statistics for Professor Hart's courses in American institutional history also revealed a 40 percent drop in enrollment in the first decade of the twentieth century.[46] According to Haskins, the decline of History 1a and 1b was emblematic of a campuswide retreat from history as a favored subject of study. This reflected a national trend. History as a discipline experienced its greatest usefulness to college students in a scientific age when historical laws of development seemed important to every field of intellectual endeavor. As interest in these laws decreased in the second decade of the twentieth century, and as closely related fields established their own autonomy, history lost some of its favored status as an avenue of access to a liberal arts education.[47]

This loss of status had a damaging effect on the personal and professional relationships in the department as professors competed with each other for control of the curriculum and with other departments for students. Professor Coolidge, who "made no concealment" of his growing dislike for Hart, actively campaigned to have Hart removed from the department. Hart, in turn, sought to recruit students to his courses (and away from Coolidge's), thereby justifying the truth of his contentions with numbers.[48] As faculty members in the Harvard history department struggled to reconcile institutional and sociocultural offerings, they were acting out a drama with wide implications for the profession at large. By the end of the second decade of the twentieth century, these two camps would formalize their disagreements over methodology in a battle that would cost some participants their academic lives. Young students of history, like Sam Morison, were unavoidably affected by these schisms.

"A Degree with Distinction"

As an undergraduate, Morison had little sense of these departmental battles, although they were profoundly important to his future development as a historian. He simply took the courses that interested him and gained a steady appreciation for history as a scholarly subject. He was influenced by professors on both sides of the curriculum debate, but he was affected earliest by the young social and cultural historians in the department, especially Haskins. As a freshman in the newly developed History 1a, Morison was a test case for the course's effectiveness, and his surviving student notebooks reveal a great deal about how Haskins conducted the course and about how Morison responded to it. The reading list included traditional institutional histories of the medieval period, such as George Burton Adams's *Civilization through the Middle Ages* (1896), as well as newer social accounts, such as James Harvey Robinson's *An Introduction to Western Europe* (1902).[49] Morison's notebooks also record the pattern of Haskins's lectures. For every new topic he approached in class, Haskins presented detailed factual outlines and chronologies of important political and institutional events. Having dispensed with that obligation, he concentrated in his lectures on cultural influences, devoting major portions of his lectures on medieval development, for instance, to art, literature, philosophy, and society. Morison's notebooks (an interesting combination of verbatim quotations from the lectures and cartoon sketches of Haskins) suggest that Haskins spent the majority of his time working out a program for the humanistic study of culture (*kulturgeschichte*).[50] According to Morison, this program influenced his historical development "profoundly."[51]

The influence of the sociocultural historians continued into his second year of college. In the first semester of that year he took Professor Merriman's History 27, "European History in the Sixteenth and Seventeenth Centuries," which continued Haskins's tradition of supplementing political history with social and cultural life. Morison's student paper, "The Expedition of Cadiz, 1596," was a fairly conventional treatment of the political and military struggle between England and Spain in the years after the defeat of the Spanish Armada. In the paper, he revealed his lifelong interest in nautical history by describing the size and detail of every British ship, the number of galleons in each fleet, the precise nautical position of each boat, and the direction of the sea breezes during the battle. Yet Morison also devoted long passages to a consideration of the decline of Spanish civilization, arguing that the demoralization of Spain's society, culture, and art was both cause and effect of Spain's military defeats. The battle did immeasurable harm to Spain, he wrote, "by advertising to the world [the] poverty and incapacity" not only of Spanish leaders but also of Spanish civilization.[52]

These positive experiences in the courses of Haskins and Merriman were perhaps less important in encouraging Morison's initial sympathies for the sociocultural historians in the department than the negative experience he had in the course of institutional historian Silas Macvane. In the second semester of his sophomore year he enrolled in History 16b, "History of Continental Europe since the Fall of Napoleon I," and found Macvane "one of the dullest lecturers that ever addressed a class." The professor's "dismal, monotonous delivery, broken by periods of prayer-like silence with closed eyes, took all the life of his students," Morison later recalled, and encouraged students to equate the lifelessness of his teaching style with the lifelessness of institutional approaches to history.[53] Morison's paper for this course, "The Suppression of the Paris Commune: May 20–27, 1871," was an uninspired effort; although he introduced one or two new interpretations of events, the majority of the paper was merely a repetition of the chronology of events that marked the transitions between political eras in France.[54] The fact that he did well in the course despite this lackluster effort contributed to his sense of suspicion about the intellectual rigor of institutional history.

By the end of his sophomore year, Morison's interest in humanistic rather than political and institutional history prompted him to consider participating in a new concentration in "History and Literature." Proposed in 1905 by Haskins, Merriman, and his grandfather's friend, English professor Barrett Wendell, "History and Literature" combined the sociocultural interests of historians with the new historicist philosophies of literary critics. The program was interdisciplinary and synchronic in its approaches and was part of the larger effort by younger members of the history department to expand the intellectual base for the study of the past. "History and Literature" was intended to be highly competitive and individualized; according to the program's brochure, applications to the concentration would be accepted only from those students willing to "cut across departmental and course lines" in order to design their own programs in the "history and literature of a country or of an era."[55]

Morison was among the first undergraduates at Harvard to apply to the new program. During the summer of his sophomore year he submitted an application to the program with a proposal for a "horizontal course in the 18th century."[56] Barrett Wendell was supportive of the plan, but he felt Morison needed a still more diverse background. Your proposed program "puzzles me a little," Barrett wrote, because "your only course now covering that period seems to be History 16a; and I have no memorandum of whether you can manage French or German well enough to proceed to the higher courses in the literature of these languages."[57] At the very least, Wendell warned, Morison would need a broader historical background, more English, French, and German literature, and more philosophy. Morison was also given "the then shocking suggestion" that he spend his summer vacation working through a reading list on the eighteenth century if he was serious about the concentration.[58]

Morison did not, in the end, become a history and literature concentrator (perhaps his summers were too precious), but he took Wendell's advice and filled his junior and senior schedules with literature, philosophy, and history courses.[59] The most important of these was Philosophy 10, "The Philosophy of History," with Professor George Santayana, who had a profound impact on Morison's development. Santayana, like Haskins and Merriman, was interested in the wider cultural implications of history, and he encouraged students to view the writing of history not as a science with objective rules but as a philosophical system subject to "the curious limitation and selfishness of the observer's estimation."[60] On the midterm exam, for instance, Santayana asked students to "Consider three methods of concieving [sic] and writing history."[61] The question underscored Santayana's philosophy that history "changes continually and grows every day less similar to the original experience which it purports to describe" and is therefore subject to multiple interpretations. In preparing to answer such questions, Morison studied Santayana's essay "History" in *The Life of Reason, or the Phases of Human Progress*, and copied lengthy passages from it into his notebooks for further contemplation.[62]

Morison singled out the passages in *The Life of Reason* that emphasized the "artificial" quality of historical writing. According to Santayana, historical literature was a rationalization created from the imagination to serve a psychological purpose—to help make sense of the world by giving it shape and form. Those who believed that historical writing was the objective revelation of natural laws at work in the universe (as the institutional historians did), were simply creating "an expedient to cover ignorance and remedy confusion." Santayana particularly objected to evolutionary historians who turned "harmonies into causes" and believed that the "dramatic unity" of their writings was a confirmation of the "dramatic unity" of the universe. "[P]hilosophers of evolution," he maintained, impute motives and plans to historical agents that suggest that their lives are teleological and purposeful; in fact, Santayana noted, their lives have "no dynamic cohesion" outside that which the historian creates for them through "inference," "generalisation," and "dramatic fancy." The goal of the historian should not be to explain the inexplainable forces of the past, he wrote, but to empathize and "understand" them. "Fragmentary, arbitrary, and insecure as historical conceptions must remain," he added, "they are nevertheless highly important" because they allow the historian to appreciate the humanity beating within him.[63]

In such pronouncements to students such as Morison, Santayana was challenging the prevailing scientific paradigm of history embraced by Hart, Macvane, and others. Although his ideas were more compatible with the humanism of Haskins and Merriman, he went beyond even them in proclaiming the virtues of a synchronic history. Even in their most rebellious moods, Haskins and Merriman never doubted the objectivity of history; they simply wished to apply a broader historical theory to a wider range of objective materials. Santayana argued, however, that the ideal "function of history" was "to render theory unnecessary." The historian should be "wholly devoted to expressing the passions of the dead" and to "making heroes think and act as they really thought and acted in the world." Borrowing from the "volk" traditions of the sociocultural historians, he argued that no detail was too small, no emotion too trivial for the historian's purpose of broadening the descriptive rather than the analytic base of history. In some ways, Santayana was closest to Parkman in his insistence on the nontheoretical subjectivity of history, reversing only his topical priorities. Parkman emphasized the need to recover the high public drama and emotional profiles of great men involved in great events; Santayana desired to restore "to the hero all his circumstantial impotence, and to the glorious event all its insignificant causes."[64]

Although Morison did not appreciate the subtleties of Santayana's philosophy, he made obvious attempts to employ some of it in his academic work. In his senior year at Harvard, for instance, he wrote three papers all dealing with individual historical characters and all devoted to description as much as analysis. In the spring of 1907, he wrote an essay on "The Early Travels of Peter the Great" for Professor Haskins that was submitted for honors and a "degree with distinction." In the essay, he challenged the popular notion that Peter the Great's legendary trips to Europe in 1697 and 1698 were part of a vast, purposeful education that led to political and civil reform in Russia. As Santayana had instructed, Morison concentrated on his subject's emotional character (his "lower nature") rather than on his place in the history of institutional development; he described the famed trips to western Europe as social excursions more revealing of Peter's "childness, evil temper, and repulsive cruelty" than of his political farsightedness. Peter's "neglect during the journey to study political institutions is conspicuous," Morison observed, "as being about the only thing he did not pry into." In imitation of Santayana, Morison argued that the trips were significant not as building blocks in some developmental process, but because they revealed the characteristically human confusion of a young man who could not perceive "the distant horizon towards which his steps were tending."[65]

In his senior year, Morison also wrote a paper entitled "Pope Alexander VI and the Temporal Power, 1492–1503" for Professor Emerton in History 7 ("The Era of the Reformation in Europe from the Rise of Italian Humanism to the Close of the Council of Trent, 1350–1563"). He began the paper with a concession to institutional history—a lengthy prologue outlining the effects of centralization and modernization on the papacy in the sixteenth century. Then he abandoned this analytic approach to concentrate on the character of his subject. With substantial artistry for an undergraduate, he described the slow march toward Rome of war-minded Charles of France and the consequent mental anguish of Pope Alexander, whose control over the Italian provinces was threatened by the advance. Placing Alexander at a darkened window in the deepest recesses of St. Peter's Cathedral, Morison imagined the effect that the sight of Charles's "flaring torches" and the sound of his "sinister" artillery had on his subject's emotional stability. He concluded with a description of the self-destruction of Alexander's mind at the climactic moment when Charles pierced the Vatican defenses and the Pope collapsed from psychological duress. In exposing the human frailties of a pope, Morison demonstrated a form of Santayana's historiography of passion, which directed historians to consider the essential "humanity" of all historical agents.[66]

Morison's "most ambitious" attempt to employ Santayana's philosophy came in a seminar paper on Semitic history for Professor Crawford Toy of the religion department. On first impression Toy's course (Semitic 14) seemed an unlikely place for the working out of philosophies of history. The few students who enrolled in the class at the "inconvenient afternoon hour" came mainly to "loaf," Morison remembered, while Professor Toy "chatted twice a week on the History of the Spanish Califate." One of the students took the course "because he had already written a thesis on the Cid, and hoped to use it again"; and another was a musician "who wanted to write a thesis on Arabian music," even though, as Professor Toy recognized, "there isn't any." All these students, however, found Toy "an unexpected exhilarator," and none more than Morison, who enrolled because he had "some notion of becoming an historian, and decided that he would, if the study of history made men such as Professor Toy."[67] Toy motivated Morison to spend weeks doing original research in the Boston Athenaeum on a paper entitled "The Ottoman Empire under Suleiman the Magnificent, 1520–1566," a substantial essay in the Santayanian style but influenced by the research techniques of the sociocultural historians.[68]

Morison was attracted to Suleiman because of his vast influence on the Ottoman Empire at the height of its success. Historians had overlooked the importance of the sultan to world history, Morison asserted, because they viewed the Ottoman Empire in an evolutionary way—as a baser civilization that had ultimately given way to the advances of "higher" western culture. According to Morison, however, Suleiman was "no mere passive onlooker" in history; he was an active agent of change who created a vast empire, controlled the maritime economy of the Mediterranean, determined the course of the Protestant Reformation, destroyed the Holy Roman Empire, disrupted the internal politics of France, and influenced the British defense against Catholicism. He was also a reminder that history was not deterministic. The fall of the Ottoman Empire was not inevitable, Morison argued; the Turks might have dominated Europe for centuries had not Suleiman been convinced, in a moment of human weakness, to murder his most promising successor, thus setting off a civil conflict that destroyed the empire from within. That the Turkish people have not assumed a larger role in world development since the sixteenth century, Morison added, was not the inevitable result of evolutionary forces conspiring against them; it was a tragedy of human creation. Cultures determined their own fate, he concluded, and (as Santayana suggested) history revealed no order that was not predicated on the disorder and caprice of human life.[69]

Morison received high marks for this paper (Toy "gave me an A!" he remarked with jubilation) and for his work in other departmental courses.[70] The variety of his course selections (history, literature, philosophy, and religion) suggested his commitment to the interdisciplinary approaches of his sociocultural mentors. As a bright student in a highly factionalized department, such preferences did not go unnoticed. Yet Morison was not exclusively a disciple of Haskins and Santayana; if he had been his career as a professional historian might well have been different if it had existed at all, given certain problems sociocultural historians faced over the next few decades. Instead Morison sampled other courses in the department, including History 13 ("The Constitutional and Political History of the United States, 1789–1860") offered by Albert Bushnell Hart, because "every Harvard undergraduate felt he had missed a great experience" if he did not take at least one Hart course.[71] Surprisingly, this institutional course taught by an adherent to the old school of historical study did as much if not more to influence Morison as those taught by his beloved Haskins, Merriman, and Santayana.

History 13 and the "Sprouting Seed"

Most of Morison's undergraduate courses were in European history, but in his junior year he enrolled in Hart's History 13 and was immediately impressed with both the instructor and the subject matter. Hart's classroom manner was systematic and inspiring. Morison recalled that "[a]t exactly six and three-quarters minutes past the hour" (at seven minutes students were free to leave), Hart "entered lower Massachusetts at the double-quick, bearing a huge green bag full of notes, and closely followed by a perspiring assistant, bearing an even greater bag stuffed with supplementary data."[72] His "patriarchal beard and flowing moustaches" gave him a "superb presence,"[73] and entering the classroom as he did with the "air of a Roman general bringing home the spoils," he was "generally greeted by the class with a burst of applause." Then, "[s]tacking the notes in their gaily colored jackets and manila folders on his desk,"[74] Professor Hart proceeded to deliver "with sonorous voice and impressive diction"[75] a "rapid, brilliant, and witty commentary on the subject of the day."[76]

Hart's systematic lecturing style was paralleled by the highly organized structure of his courses. For students of American history at Harvard, Hart published the five-hundred-page *Manual of American History, Diplomacy, and Government for Class Use*, which provided detailed instructions on how to approach his courses. The *Manual* advised students on how to read books, how to take notes, and how to reason historically; it listed hundreds of topics and made suggestions on how to pursue them in a paper; it provided detailed bibliographies; it outlined every lecture in each course so that students could follow Hart's presentations. The *Manual* even provided sample exam questions so that students could know in advance what they might be expected to remember.[77] For those unable to anticipate his intentions from these elaborate preparations, Hart also published general guides to the historical principles developed in his courses and systematized them into a hierarchy that reflected Hart's unique intentions for any given course.[78]

Students in History 13, for instance, were instructed to consider eight general principles at work in the course. These principles reflected Hart's preference for scientific and institutional approaches and included the following: (1) "No nation has a history disconnected from the rest of the world"; "the United States, therefore, is closely related, in point of time, with previous ages; in point of space, with other civilized countries"; (2) Institutions "are a growth and not a creation"; the Constitution, therefore, is "constantly changing with the changes in public opinion"; (3) "The source of American institutions is Teutonic" and "derived through England, thus justifying a colonial emphasis in American historical treatment"; (4) "The growth of our institutions has been from local to central; the general government can, therefore, be understood only in the light of the early history of the country"; (5) "The principle of union is a slow growth in America; the Constitution, [therefore,] was formed from necessity, and not from preference"; (6) "Under a federal form of government there must inevitably be a perpetual contest of authority between the States and the general government: hence the two opposing doctrines of States-rights and of nationality"; (7) "National political parties naturally appeal to the federal principles when in power, and to the local principles when out of power"; and (8) "When parties become distinctly sectional, a trial of strength between a part of the states and the general government must come sooner or later."[79]

Morison and his classmates appreciated these principles, not only because they saved students from the considerable task of organizing the material themselves, but because they projected the vision of a world easily reducible to fundamental laws. Even testing and grading conformed to a "rigid pattern." The evaluation process consisted of three distinct parts: hour-long midyear, and final examinations on the readings and lectures; weekly quizzes on constitutional topics; and two term papers. Perhaps because Hart was so elaborate in his preparations and so forthcoming about his expectations in his sample exam questions in the *Manual*, the hour, midyear, and final exams were not greatly feared. "It was well understood that careful lecture notes" and scattered reading in the guide books "were enough to pass these examinations with at least a gentlemanly C," Morison noted. And "for students too lazy or busy to do either, the 'Widow Nolan' offered a night-before 'seminar,' as he called it, in which most of the questions were correctly predicted and the proper answers succinctly outlined."[80]

The weekly quizzes, however, were more troublesome. They were taken in the last twenty minutes of Friday's class and were said by one future historian to be "the only torture overlooked by the Spanish inquisitors." The biggest problem with the quizzes was time. In order to cover all the material in his own rigid course syllabus, Hart frequently lectured beyond the appropriate starting time for the quiz. "[I]f the Professor's lecture went beyond 11:35" in a class that ended at noon, Morison noted, "ominous" rumblings reminded him that the fateful 11:40 was fast approaching." As

soon as Hart relinquished the floor, the teaching assistants "briskly distributed the printed questions, together with a special ruled sheet of foolscap
on which the answers had to be written." When the bell in Harvard Hall
(where Hart generally conducted the course) rang, "the assistant announced:
'Test closed' . . . and collected the papers," often before thorough answers to
the broad questions had been given.[81]

The two papers Hart assigned were the most interesting and challenging
part of History 13. One paper was always on slavery, because "Negro
advancement" was one of Hart's scholarly interests, and because he viewed
the conflict over slavery as the single most illustrative example of the eight
general principles outlined in his guidebooks. Students were asked to pick
one of "hundreds of topics relating to the facts of slavery, pro- and anti-
slavery arguments, abolitionists, the slave trade, and the Negro race in
America" listed in the *Manual*, remembered Morison. They were then asked
to write papers tracing topics within the larger institutional framework
established by *Slavery and Abolition 1831–1841* (1906), Hart's volume in
the *American Nation* series he edited. The other paper was always biographical and highly prescribed. "At the opening of the course," Morison recalled,
"each student had to fill out an elaborate questionnaire about his father's
profession, home, ancestors, etc., with a view to finding a biographical
subject which would give him personal identification with American history." Despite the fact that there were over one hundred students in the
course, Hart then "found the time to consult individual students' tastes,"
to assign them appropriate topics, and "to give them personal encouragement" in their work.[82] Many men, Morison later recognized, "owed their
start to the personal interest, friendly encouragement, and expert guidance"
Hart provided in connection with these biographical papers.[83]

Morison was a case in point. "Hearing that I was a descendant of Harrison
Gray Otis," Morison explained, "the Professor assigned me a thesis on that
forgotten Federalist." In researching the project, Morison discovered a crate
of Otis papers in the wine cellar of his grandfather's 44 Brimmer Street
home and spent an hour with Hart at his residence going over them. "He
leafed through the manuscripts with that rapid motion familiar in his
lecturing," Morison wrote, "pointed out some on the Hartford Convention
that were the most significant, and handed them back to me saying: 'They
are highly important—don't lose them.'" Morison used some of these
documents for his History 13 paper, which Hart liked so much that he
returned it with further encouragement: "Morison," he said, "you ought to
write a life of Harrison Gray Otis."[84]

Morison was overwhelmed by the suggestion. "This idea was as astonish-
ing to me, a junior in college, as if he had suggested that I should design a
cathedral or run for the presidency," he wrote. Trained primarily in European history, influenced more by humanistic approaches to the past than
by institutional ones, and unsure of his own abilities, Morison seemed an
unlikely biographer of an American statesman. But Hart had shown that

institutional history could be exciting and useful, he had taken a personal interest in his student's work, and he had encouraged an appreciation for American themes. So "the seed sprouted," Morison wrote, and before the year was out, he had committed himself to someday writing a biography of Otis and pursuing history as a career.[85] In an age of professionalism, this meant acquiring graduate training, preferably in Europe, so like his grandfather Eliot before him, following his graduation from Harvard Morison set sail for the Continent in pursuit of Clio.

The Great Triumvirate

Albert Hart, Edward Channing,
Frederick Jackson Turner and
Graduate Training at Harvard

3

"The American Centre for the Study of American History"

 s a graduation gift to his son, John Morison had agreed to finance a year of professional study abroad.[1] The question was, where to study. Hart advised Morison to enroll at the École des Sciences Politiques in Paris, where twenty-five years earlier he had done graduate work, and where he still had "connections."[2] The École had been founded privately in 1870 and had no formal ties to the Universite; its faculty, however, was primarily responsible for implanting the scientific historical tradition in the French university system and attracted "scholars with conservative tendencies."[3] Morison's recent experiences with Hart disposed him more favorably toward training in scientific and institutional history than would have been the case a year or two earlier, so he took his professor's advice and enrolled at the École.

Little of a specific nature is known about what Morison did at the École save that he studied under the French historians Albert Vandal, Charles Seignobos, and Anatole Leroy-Beaulieu and that he worked closely with political historian Maurice Caudel.[4] Members of the faculty remembered Hart, and Morison received special attention by virtue of his association with "the dean of American historians."[5] As a young aspirant with special access to his instructors, Morison was exposed to the sweeping changes overtaking the French historical profession in the first decade of the twentieth century. Faculty at the École des Sciences Politiques generally subscribed to positivist philosophies, but in the years coincident with Morison's visit many French university professors were contributing to the *Annales d'histoire economique et sociale*, a journal dedicated to dismantling institutional approaches to the past and substituting sociocultural ones. French historians of the "annal" school, as they were later known, went further even than their American counterparts Haskins and Merriman in insisting that history examine social and cultural processes; they introduced an ideological component that required historians to demonstrate the utility of their work and "to repudiate the professional historian's tendency to isolate himself from the general public under the pretext of striving for scientific accuracy and scholarly integrity."[6] Morison probably did not recognize how derivative this utilitarian movement was of his grandfather Eliot's philosophy or how reminiscent of the factionalism of the Harvard history department. But the debate over the "annal" philosophy in France certainly gave him early exposure to a similar debate that would rage in the American historical profession several years after his return to the United States and that would profoundly affect his career as a historian.

Morison's fascination with things French extended beyond historical philosophies. Upon his return from study at the École, Morison became engaged to Elizabeth Greene, an American raised in France whom he had first met several years earlier at Northeast Harbor, Maine, where his family vacationed for part of every summer. "After hearing rumors of an exotic family, the 'Paris Greenes,' " Morison recalled, "I saw a lovely girl with warm brown eyes, a pleasant smile on her lips, and a pompadour of raven-black hair." By his own account Morison was a "gangling, pimply youth of eighteen, socially immature, snubbed by the glamour girls," and too shy to propose anything but frequent sails in his sailboat. "Although I lived for those sails," he later wrote, "it was a torture that I could never say what was in my heart." One day the following year, however, "all came to a head," Morison remembered. "I told her that I loved her; she admitted she had just begun to love me," and "our whole life seemed to stem from confidences then exchanged."[7]

"Bessie" was a perfect companion for a young historian hoping to broaden his base of knowledge. "She had an amazing knowledge of French, German, and English literature, and of the fine arts and music, which were the complements to my interest in politics and history," Morison wrote. "We discussed everything."[8] Included in their early discussions were Morison's plans to continue his graduate education at Harvard and to write the biography of Otis. In both their estimations, Harvard was the "American centre for the study of American history," so in the fall of 1909 he enrolled in the Graduate School of Arts and Sciences to pursue a Ph.D. in history.[9] "Our engagement was announced and the marriage was set for the next spring, so I could first pass my 'generals' for the Ph.D.," Morison noted later, adding that "[t]hat was a mistake. So long an engagement was trying to us both."[10]

Despite the trauma associated with delaying his marriage, Morison found the first months of graduate school much to his liking. He had more of a social life in graduate school than he had in college, and he quickly made friends with several future historians, including Robert Lord and James G. MacDonald. With others, Morison, Lord, and MacDonald formed the "Star Chamber" Club, a group that met every few weeks at some member's rooms "for an evening of beer and discussion."[11] Morison also thrived on the academic life. He spent the first year of graduate school preparing for his general examinations, which (according to the department handbook) required students to "make use of Latin, as well as French and German, and to have an elementary knowledge of the following subjects: the History of Philosophy, the History of Fine Arts, Political Economy, and General History."[12] The philosophy and fine arts requirements were a tribute to the growing influence of professors such as Haskins, Merriman, and Santayana; the major requirement in general history remained overwhelmingly political and institutional. Morison's work as an undergraduate and as a student in France prepared him well in this category, and with the supervision of "Harvard's great triumvirate" (Channing, Hart, and the newly arrived historian of the West, Frederick Jackson Turner), he passed his generals in the spring of 1910 with little difficulty.[13] His marriage to Bessie followed a short few weeks later.[14]

Because Morison had already chosen a topic for his dissertation, to begin work he needed only to select an advisor. Hart was the obvious choice. The suggestion for an Otis biography had been his as had the decision to study in Paris in preparation for graduate school. In the fall of 1910, Hart encouraged the relationship further by appointing Morison as head teaching assistant in History 13. As the bearer of the bulging green bags, Morison spent many hours each week with Hart, discussing the weekly quizzes, which he was responsible for evaluating. "I used to complete the grading Friday night, ride out from Boston Saturday morning with the papers in saddlebags, tether my horse in the Yard, and place the graded papers in their proper slots," Morison recalled. In the execution of these chores, Morison found Hart an "unfailing" boss who never asked his assistant to do things he would not do himself. Hart demonstrated his devotion to his assistant in the spring of 1911, when Bessie had to undergo an appendectomy while in an advanced stage of pregnancy. "Noticing that I looked anxious and harassed," Morison remembered, Hart "asked me if anything were wrong"; when the situation was explained his mentor said, "Don't worry. Go home, stand by your wife; I'll do all your assistant's work until she is well." And Hart made good on the promise.[15]

Hart's "personal concern" touched Morison greatly, and he dedicated the remainder of his graduate career to justifying the confidence Hart placed in him. His dissertation, for instance, was a scholarly tribute to Hart's methods. Completed in 1912 under the title "The Life and Correspondence of Harrison Gray Otis, 1765–1815," it conformed precisely to the principles for historical interpretation that Hart had established in the *Manual*. "Politically and intellectually, the American people until 1815 were in the colonial epoch," Morison wrote in imitation of Hart's first principle. Therefore, "their policies" must be approached as "but a great shadow of the drama that was unfolding itself across the Atlantic." On the basis of Hart's second principle that the Constitution was a living document, "constantly changing with the changes in public opinion," Morison defended Otis for his participation in the "much-abused" Hartford Convention. Morison viewed the Hartford Convention as an exercise in the constitutional right of minority interests to air grievances against a majority government (Hart's sixth principle) and as a reflection of the tendency for national political parties to appeal to "local principles" when "out of power" (principle seven). Ultimately Morison achieved his greatest scholarly success in documenting the "trial of strength" between the Federalist and Republican parties that Hart's eighth principle insisted must occur "when parties become distinctly sectional."[16]

Morison appropriated the structure of his advisor's theories as well. In answer to the question: "Did the Federalists have a higher conception of government than the Republicans?" Hart developed a "two-handed" response. On the "one" hand, he argued, the Federalists "governed well" by building up "the credit of the country" and by taking "a dignified and effective stand against the aggressions of both England and France." To this extent, they embraced the "higher concept" of nationalism. On the "other" hand, the party failed to hold power, according to Hart, because its members clung too tenaciously to "a government by leaders" while the Republicans "represented the rising spirit of democracy."[17] Morison borrowed this exact strategy for his discussion of the Federalist party. In the "Life and Correspondence of Harrison Gray Otis," Morison argued that the Federalists organized the Union "on a basis of efficient government and sound finances" and safeguarded the nation against "the extraordinary failure" of the Republicans to see that their foreign policy "tended inevitably to make their country a foreign dependency." The Federal party failed, Morison added in imitation of his advisor, because of a "fundamental defect"—the "failure to respect the ideals, the jealousies, and the prejudices of a free people."[18]

Morison also duplicated the language of his mentor. In discussing the constitutionality of the Alien and Sedition Acts, Hart had written that (from the Federalist point of view), the Republicans "seemed leagued with France in an attempt to destroy the liberties of the country." The Federalists devised the acts, therefore, to "punish American-born editors who too freely criticised the administration." Their main purpose was "to silence the Republican journalists," Hart noted, by illegally declaring the "publishing of libels upon the government . . . a crime." Yet, according to Hart, in doing so the Federalists "violated the freedom of speech and served only to destroy [their] own party."[19] Morison similarly argued that the Alien and Sedition Acts were motivated by fears "of French plots to subvert the Union," which convinced the administration that it needed to "preserve and defend itself against injuries and outrages which endanger its existence." The acts were intended to protect the Federalist party, he wrote, "to muzzle the opposition press" by making "political opposition to the Federal party a crime." The effect was the opposite, however, since the acts threatened "freedom of speech." From "a political point of view," Morison concluded, the measures were "suicidal."[20]

Inasmuch as "The Life and Correspondence of Harrison Gray Otis" was a doctoral tribute to the History 13 method, there was little doubt that Professor Hart would approve the completed manuscript. " 'The Life of Harrison Gray Otis' obliges you henceforth to give laborious nights and days to the extension of our knowledge of American history," he wrote his student.[21] Yet Morison was concerned that his second and third readers might be more rigorous in their standards and intolerant of Hart's indelible influence on the work. He was especially anxious about the reception his work might receive from the other two triumvirs of American history at Harvard—Edward Channing and Frederick Jackson Turner.

The Search for a New Parkman

Edward Channing had never made much of an impression on Harvard undergraduates. His courses were generally undersubscribed because he had a reputation for being a disinterested professor. "As a teacher of undergraduates," Morison later wrote, "Channing was not so conspicuously successful." Unlike the flamboyant Hart, Channing ("short, round, and smooth-shaven") sat down at the podium and "had a one-sided conversation with his students." This method proved an impediment to student learning in an age when spirited lecturing was considered an essential professorial trait. "History never ran smooth from Channing's lips to the student mind," Morison remembered, and because Channing had "a great contempt for the 'finished lecturer' beloved by lazy students and women's clubs," he remained unpopular throughout most of his career.[22]

Edward Channing was the unfortunate son of the renowned New England poet Ellery Channing, whose habit it was to embark on trips without the "formality of saying good-bye to his wife and children, or making any provisions for their support." His mother died three months after he was born, and his poet-father, unable to handle the responsibility of the child and his four siblings, abandoned them completely for the remaining forty-five years of his life. Channing only saw his father once. After moving to the home of his grandfather, Channing became a "lonely boy with a passionate love for companionship which was never satisfied." This insatiate but unfulfilled desire to be liked soured him to most undergraduates who found his manner too "crusty" and resented the way he "gruffly boxed" them "into the paths of historical rectitude." He was a "terror to the lazy," since he did not "suffer fools gladly," and he even alienated the brilliant but pretentious Harvard students, deflating them "by piercing sarcasm." Among graduate students, Channing had a reputation as a domineering advisor who was all too frank in his assessments of vulnerable graduate students.[23] It was rumored among Morison's graduate classmates that "Hart picked out and encouraged promising young sprigs, then sent them to Channing to be growled at and discouraged; if they survived that, they might do."[24]

Under the circumstances, most graduate students chose to work with Hart and avoid Channing if they had the opportunity. Morison was no exception, although he had never experienced Channing's "cantankerous side." In fact, there were early indications that this unliked professor liked Morison and that Morison liked him. As a rule Channing encouraged "the shy boy who had good stuff in him," and being by his own admission just such a student of history, Morison found favor with the professor. Channing may well have seen some of himself in the young graduate student. Like Morison, Channing had been a rather frail, tall, and thin boy, unable for these physical reasons to excel at rigorous sports. As a Harvard undergraduate he too had been socially immature, had had few friends, and had been snubbed by the social clubs. In turn, he devoted himself to his studies, distracting himself only with long sails up and down the New England coast. Years later Morison described these "lonely longshore cruises" as "most useful" to Channing's historical work and cited them as the inspiration for his own later efforts to make sailing "serve Clio."[25]

Morison was one of Channing's few supporters among the graduate students. Noting that Hart "followed the British method of turning graduate students loose to sink or swim" while working on their dissertations, Morison was glad to have occasional advice from Channing, who let his few favored students in "on the workings of the maestro's mind." Channing was also "the better scholar of the two," Morison believed, since Hart's many teaching and editing projects "dissipated his energies" and reduced his time for scholarship.[26] Channing's abrupt personality and sometimes inadequate teaching was offset in Morison's estimation by his commitment to the profession. Channing's rise as a scholar had coincided exactly with the exciting first years of the historical profession in America. As a Harvard undergraduate, Channing had been a student in Henry Adams's famous seminar on medieval institutions and later became his research assistant.[27] Channing had had the honor of reading the first paper before the newly founded American Historical Association in 1886.[28] His dissertation, "Town and Country Government in the English Colonies," had been published in the important *Johns Hopkins University Studies in Historical and Political Science*.[29] He had been elected to the Massachusetts Historical Society at the unusually early age of twenty-six, and by the turn of the century, he was recognized as one of America's foremost authorities on colonial New England.[30]

During Morison's years as an undergraduate and graduate student, Channing was preoccupied with his "Great Work," a multivolume history of the United States from the colonial period to the Civil War.[31] This "Great Work" had been in conception since the 1870s and owed much to not only the panoramic narrative histories of Parkman and Prescott but the multivolume surveys of amateur historians such as James Ford Rhodes.[32] Like his amateur predecessors, Channing deplored the tendency of professional historians to write monographs and to train themselves as specialists in restricted areas of American history. Channing differed from Parkman and Rhodes, however, in his desire to employ scientific and institutional principles in the service of metahistory. Trained as a professional, Channing insisted on scholarly detachment and objectivity. He was a member of the evolutionary school of institutional historians and urged readers of his history to remember that all great nations owed their development to humbler versions of themselves. The "Great Work," Channing informed readers, was devoted to suggesting that America was as much a borrower and an adapter as a creator.

Channing also argued that "the most important single fact" in American history was the "victory of forces of union over those of particularism." American history since the revolution, according to Channing, was the story of threats to the homogeneity of American culture, to the preeminence of nationalism as an operating principle in politics, and to the necessary submission of states rights to federal authority. The Civil War was for Channing a great legitimizing event in American history, because it confirmed the victory of unionism over sectionalism. Flirting with a "progressive" philosophy not unlike Samuel Eliot's, Channing noted that his volumes told "the story of living forces always struggling onward and upward toward that which is better and higher in human conception." He retreated from the full implications of this statement, however, by adding a professional caution. Such "a notion of progress should not obscure the past," he wrote, "nor make the inhabitants of the historical landscape subject to higher, present standards." To estimate past figures "by the conditions and ideas of the present day," he warned, would do them an injustice. "[T]he time and place of one's birth and breeding," he argued, must "affect the judgement."[33]

By 1910, Channing had produced three volumes of his series and planned three others for the years ahead. "Although Channing never slighted his duty as a teacher," Morison later wrote, he "frankly considered his *History of the United States* the most important part of his work for the University and for posterity."[34] Its standards were the example students and colleagues were expected to follow in their own work for him, and Channing was outspoken about his disappointment in their inabilities to do so. In his estimation, the majority of American historians were mediocre scholars. "In looking about for writers of history in this country at the present moment," complained Channing in 1910, "the seeker is met with greater disappointment than would befall him in almost any other path of original research. Let anyone turn the matter over in his mind," he challenged his students, "and see if he cannot count the really first-class works of American historical writers within the last twenty-five years, on his fingers."

Without a substantial change in attitude and method on the part of students of American history, Channing warned, the once noble art of historical writing might be lost to the nation.[35]

Channing treated all of his classes to some version of this jeremiad, but he also expressed his hope that a few of his best students might reverse the trend. "Scholarship is momentarily at a very low ebb," Channing wrote, "because it is not valued throughout the country at large." But someday, he predicted, "the wheel will turn around; scholarship will again be valued as a national asset; and a new Parkman will arise."[36] This "new Parkman" would resemble the original master in literary style and epic scope but would adhere to professional standards established by the American Historical Association and would appreciate the need for scientific objectivity. Channing was obsessed with scholarly detail, and he felt nothing but "scorn for slipshod or dishonest work," of which he believed there was much in American history. His new Parkman must, in short, be both a gifted writer and adhere to the highest standards of academic scholarship.[37]

Channing had once had hopes that he would become the new Parkman. Early in his career, he was certainly filled with a sense of his own potential greatness. A story circulated around Harvard while Channing was still a junior professor to the effect that he had been approached one day by a well-meaning undergraduate who wished to know if he was the son of the "great" Channing. The student was referring to the transcendental poet, of course, but Channing simply peered over his wire-rimmed glasses and with disdain in his voice replied, "I am the 'great' Channing." By 1910, Channing began to sense that his career would not eclipse that of his reprobate father, primarily because, as Morison later noted, he had "no knack of vivid narrative or description" and because "his method of dictating rather than writing resulted in a rather formless . . . style." This recognition caused Channing to project his hopes onto his students; he admonished them with uncharacteristic modesty to use Parkman and not Channing as their stylistic model.[38]

Morison was one student who worked hard to fulfill his professor's expectations. Enrolled in Channing's History 23, a seminar on research methods, Morison attempted to satisfy the conditions for the new Parkman by demonstrating his abilities to write and organize materials. The seminar began each term with a series of lectures in which Channing discussed methods, "interspersing the solid matter with shrewd, witty, and original comments on persons and events." Students were then expected to research a topic and present written and oral reports. The oral report had to be "presented in the form of a lecture, with only an outline, or a few notes on slips," Morison remembered, "and the speaker must submit to interjectory comments and discussion by the master and other members of the class." Morison took advantage of the proffered "right to as much of Channing's individual attention as he wanted" and produced work that ultimately garnered for him the coveted History 10 teaching assistantship, awarded to the "top student" in the seminar.[39]

Morison's efforts to meet Channing's high standards put a strain on his young marriage. "Serious and ambitious" in his desire to become the new Parkman, Morison later admitted that "the first two years of marriage were made unnecessarily hard." "[W]ith the pride of youth," he wrote, "I endeavored to bend [Bessie's] personality to mine, even to make her a secretarial drudge." He provided her with reading lists from his graduate seminar so that she could discuss professional matters with him. He recruited her to copy documents, to translate German, and to type the manuscript for his dissertation. She performed these tasks for a while, but eventually she "struck, and rightly too," Morison noted. "No scholar should make a secretary of his wife," he concluded, not even for the sake of his scholarly reputation. "[I]f she had not been the kind of woman who gives her love once and for all, our marriage might have gone on the rocks during the first few years," Morison added. "Would-be wreckers were not wanting."[40]

Despite his concerns that he might not meet Channing's high standards, the latter approved his dissertation as well: "I wish your father had lived to see [this work]. It would have made him very happy," Channing said. Channing was most impressed with the quality of Morison's original research in primary documents and his willingness to characterize the Hartford Convention as a national rather than a sectional affair. The best indication of Channing's approval came several years after the dissertation was completed, when the professor cited Morison in the fourth volume of the great work.[41] To be " 'embalmed in a footnote' of the 'Great Work' was deemed a great honor by his students," Morison later noted, particularly since students understood the tendency among many historians to exploit their graduate students by turning the historical seminar "into a sort of sweat-shop in which the students save the professor time and labor by working up material which he can use."[42] Greeting his student at the beginning of a fine career, Channing expressed his hope (for reasons that would later appear a bit self-serving but that at present flattered the young scholar), that the two might one day work together as colleagues.[43]

The Frontier Thesis and Sectional Conflict

The prospect of becoming the new Parkman certainly appealed to Morison and his fellow graduate students, but there was no universal agreement that Channing's principles would lead them to achieve the title. Some graduate students believed that a "new Parkman" of a different sort already existed in the person of an exciting young historian from the University of Wisconsin, Frederick Jackson Turner. Born and raised in Portage, Wisconsin, in the 1860s, Turner had witnessed the progression of prairie "schooners" carrying "emigrants" through Wisconsin on the way to the Dakotas and had observed the idle wanderings of the few remaining Indians who refused to go to the reservations. Like Francis Parkman, he had been inspired by stories of the frontier wilderness and devoted the better part of his career to illustrating the importance of that wilderness for American development.[44] Unlike Francis Parkman, however, Turner was not trained in the narrative tradition. Under the tuteluge of William Francis Allen at the University of Wisconsin, Turner was trained as an institutional historian, and because of his considerable talents he was encouraged to study for the Ph.D. at the Johns Hopkins University under Herbert Baxter Adams.[45]

One of the original founders of the American Historical Association, Adams had established Johns Hopkins as the most prominent of the several American universities awarding Ph.D.'s in history in the 1880s and 1890s. He taught the institutional method of the scientific historians and placed a heavy value on the importance of politics in national development. Students in his famous seminar were greeted with the words "History is Past Politics and Politics Present History" as they entered the classroom, and they were subjected to a large dose of congressional and presidential material. In addition, Adams was a proponent of the "germ" theory of American history, which traced the roots of American institutions to the Teutonic "tun" (town) of medieval Germany and the Anglo-Saxon village. According to this theory (which Albert Hart was simultaneously introducing at Harvard), American development was inextricably linked to medieval Europe.[46]

Although Turner admired Herbert Baxter Adams as a teacher, he chafed at Adams's theories almost from the moment he arrived in Baltimore to begin his graduate studies. He especially disliked the "tun" theory, because in emphasizing the determinacy of the medieval past it ignored the considerable role the American environment played in shaping the American character. Internal social and economic pressures working independently of European (and particularly medieval) precedents were responsible for the uniqueness of the American people, Turner believed, and it was the frontier and not the German tun that gave American institutions their unique character. Turner raised his objections, cautiously at first, to fellow Ph.D. candidates at Hopkins, such as Charles Homer Haskins, who seconded them, and Woodrow Wilson, who did not. More confident than ever of the validity of his beliefs by the end of his graduate career, Turner urged Adams himself to abandon his "eastern" prejudices and to reconstruct American historiography in the light of western influence.[47]

At the University of Wisconsin, where Turner received his first teaching appointment, he began to refine his own principles of western and environmental determinism. These ideas were articulated in his famous address, "Significance of the Frontier in American History," which he delivered at the 1893 annual meeting of the American Historical Association held in conjunction with the World's Columbian Exposition in Chicago. In this address Turner introduced his thesis (later expanded and embellished) that

American democracy had come "stark and strong and full of life out of the American forest" rather than from the European village. Americans created a unique wilderness personality that they renewed in each successive era of American history on a frontier that stretched ever westward with time. The "great American West," wrote Turner, "took them to her bosom, taught them a new way of looking upon the destiny of the common man, trained them in the adaptation to the conditions of the New World, to the creation of new institutions to meet new needs."[48]

By the end of the 1890s, Turner's "frontier thesis" had changed the way Americans viewed their past. Years later Morison remembered the impact the thesis had on graduate students and scholars in the American field. "It stimulated study and interest in American history," he claimed, "served to differentiate our history from that of other lands, removed the inferiority-complex of the West and made that section proudly conscious of her immediate past, struck at the intellectual complacency of New England and the romanticism of the South . . . and gave young westerners topics for books that they could integrate with their environment."[49] Part of the power of the thesis also derived from Turner's ability to use the new methods of scientific analysis to make understandable themes that had operated just below the surface of American life. Employing graphs, charts, demographics, and statistics, Turner buttressed his developmental frontier theory with a vast body of technical research that gave his work the appearance of incontrovertible fact. Although he had none of the narrative genius of Parkman, Turner extended the life of Parkman's wilderness thesis by lending social scientific credibility to its already considerable reputation as a form of mythic explanation.[50]

So great was Turner's impact on American historiography that members of the Harvard history department felt they must claim him for their own. Charles Homer Haskins was at the forefront of the movement to recruit Turner, not just because he was Turner's former classmate but because he saw in Turner an ally in the methodological battles he was waging with his colleagues. In his efforts to find a balance between sociocultural and institutional approaches, Haskins embraced the frontier thesis as a potential mediating device, developmental in its outlines but instructive of the social and cultural character of the American people. After several sessions with newly elected Harvard President A. Lawrence Lowell and the Board of Trustees, including one in which Coolidge offered to pay for Turner's appointment from his own salary, Turner was offered a professorship. Several more months of cajoling convinced Turner of the advantages of the move, and in the fall of 1910 Turner arrived in Cambridge in time to serve on Morison's oral examination committee.[51]

Harvard students rejoiced that "perhaps the strongest professor of history in the United States outside of Harvard" was now on the faculty.[52] Although by Morison's recollection "Turner delivered painstaking lectures, illustrated by charts," students appreciated "how his eyes lit up when he spoke of the

Great West!"[53] In his first lecture for History 17, "The History of the West," Turner guided students "over western trails" with an active whip. Leading them "deep into the wilderness that morning," biographer Ray Billington has written of the occasion, Turner assigned "a terrifying battery" of materials at the end of class, including his own essay, "The Significance of the Frontier," an article on the legacy of the pioneers, a book on American democracy, a philosophical piece on the economic foundations of society, and a series of maps from the census atlas of 1900. Nevertheless students responded. "It is not too much to say," one noted later, "that Turner's class in the History of the West opened to me a new heaven and a new earth."[54]

Morison was enrolled in Turner's first seminar at Harvard on the election of 1836 and was as delighted with the new instructor as were most of his fellow students. Because Turner viewed doctoral candidates as "fellow investigators" and treated them "with all the sympathy of a kindly father," Morison never felt intimidated by him as he sometimes did with Channing. Meetings of the seminar were always good-natured affairs, with Turner offering theoretical insights as well as practical advice about how to chart demographic trends or map election returns. Turner was also willing to cater to his students' intellectual needs. When he sensed that Morison and his fellow graduate students viewed the election of 1836 as too restricted a topic for a seminar, he broadened the course the following year and adopted the more appropriate rubric "Selected Topics in American History." Subsequent seminars investigated not only the Van Buren administration but also Jacksonian America, the Age of Reform, and America in the Era of Good Feelings.[55]

Not everyone at Harvard was delighted with Turner's presence on campus, however. Albert Hart "was generally cordial and did his best to be friendly" to the newcomer, but he had "no time for companionship."[56] Edward Channing had the time but not the desire. Channing had been a critic of Turner's work while the latter was a professor at Wisconsin, and he was strongly opposed to the Harvard appointment. The difficulties between the two first developed when, in 1898, Channing wrote a short volume, *A Student's History of the United States*, which he intended to market as a textbook for college survey courses in American history.[57] Asked by the *Educational Review* to review the work, Turner attacked Channing's methodology with unusual aggressiveness. His major complaint was the parochialism of Channing's selections, which heavily favored New England institutions to the exclusion of other sections of the nation that had made crucial contributions to national development. The conspicuous absence of the role of the West led Turner to conclude that Channing's book was so one-sided "as to be misleading, if not entirely incorrect."[58]

Channing was too sensitive to criticism to allow this attack to go unnoticed. He defended his selection process by noting that constraints of time and space had prevented him from subordinating the rich legacy of the East to the relatively new and unhistoried West. His more comprehensive "Great

Work" would address the issue of western influence and affirm the importance of unionism over particularism, he promised. While acknowledging
the role of the West in American development, however, the first volumes
of the *History of the United States* downplayed the importance of the
frontier thesis. Channing mentioned Turner's theory by name in only three
footnotes, and a single chapter on "The Westward March" traced the
influence of New England families on the Midwest rather than vice versa.
Channing went so far as to "tease" Turner by denying him even the most
accepted of his assertions—that the election of Andrew Jackson in 1828 was
a victory for frontier egalitarianism. By Channing's account, the election
was a coup by the South "having nothing to do with frontierism."[59] In
addition, Channing was quick to note the ironic limitations of Turner's
thesis for a postfrontier age. Turner had begun his famous 1893 address,
"The Significance of the Frontier in American History," with the disturbing
revelation that as of the census of 1890 there was no longer a frontier line
in America. "This brief official statement marks the closing of a great
historic movement," he acknowledged. "[T]he advance of American settlement westward," so crucial to explaining "American development," had
been halted; therefore, Americans could no longer expect to experience in
the present what had made them so distinctive in the past.[60] Could Americans afford to build a historiographic tradition around a thesis with rele-
vance only to the first 120 years of American development? Channing
presumed not.[61]

While Channing and Turner were on different college campuses twelve
hundred miles apart their disagreements remained esoteric. With Turner's
arrival at Harvard, however, their differences became highly personalized
and visible. Each attempted to sabotage the other's career. Turner had always
been slightly sensitive about his lack of scholarly production. Despite his
being recognized nationally as one of America's preeminent historians, he
had only produced one book, and this only under the persistent threats of
his editor, Albert Hart.[62] Channing made a point of reminding colleagues
and graduate students of this sparse output. "Turner is a dear fellow,"
Channing would say, but "he has no idea of the value of time. He has never
written any big books."[63] Turner, in turn, capitalized on Channing's sensitivities about his idiosyncratic manners. In private he referred to Channing
as "Porcupinus Angelicus,"[64] a phrase he reserved for "prickly, hedgehoggy,
unadulterated Bostonian Yankee[s]" and men who must "speak from a
higher attitude toward [their] fellows."[65]

Graduate students such as Morison who had to deal with both professors
on a nearly daily basis tried to satirize the situation. In one particularly
inspired action, members of the "Star Chamber" Club circulated a fake
letter, purportedly written by Channing, that blamed Turner for trying to
destroy the sound structure of American historiography recently con-
structed in the fourth volume of his own "Great Work." The letter focused
on the issue of sectionalism and its apparent threat to Channing's thesis

concerning the superiority of unionism to particularism. "He treats my American history as an amoeba," the lampooned Channing began, "capable of unlimited division" into "Old West, New West, Middle West, North West, South West, and Far West." A copy of the letter "accidently" slipped into Turner's possession, and he recorded correctly in the margin: "Hazing me."[66] But the letter primarily hazed Channing, who was doubtless as hurt by it as he was by several subsequent cartoons in various Harvard publications that pictured him with a hatchet "or some other instrument of destruction" aimed at theories of history opposed to his own.[67]

Joking about the rift could not relieve the tensions it created for graduate students working in the American field. Morison felt these keenly, since he was a favorite of both Hart and Channing, and was firmly committed, at least for the purposes of obtaining his doctorate, to their institutional approaches. Yet Turner and other sociocultural historians from his undergraduate days, such as Haskins, Merriman, and Santayana, did exert some influence on his dissertation. In one noteworthy chapter entitled "Oratory, Law, and Personality," for instance, Morison momentarily dropped his institutional approach to consider the personality and passion of Otis the man. Urging his readers "to abandon for a time the political viewpoint" and to "glance at [Otis's] personality and non-political activities," Morison considered his subject's "tact, affability, and consideration" and the significance of his "sunny, genial nature," which earned him a place in "the affections of the people." In an inversion of Hart's logic about the private histories of public figures, Morison also concluded that "Mr. Otis" the "prominent citizen of Boston, is quite as interesting a person as the Honorable Harrison Gray Otis, politician and statesman."[68]

Not only because of these concessions but because of the fine general worth of Morison's work, Turner accepted "The Life and Correspondence of Harrison Gray Otis, 1765–1815" in the spring of 1912. Channing and Hart added their signatures, as did the dissertation's outside reader, the redoubtable curator of the Library of Congress's Historical Manuscripts Division, Worthington C. Ford. In his comments, Ford noted with appreciation Morison's rare ability to reconcile "political history and social conditions." Although he believed that the style of "The Life and Correspondence of Harrison Gray Otis, 1765–1815" was a bit too "adjectival" and that the entire manuscript needed "pruning," he recommended it for eventual publication.[69] Turner confirmed this judgment, noting that the dissertation could "stand some reduction profitably when printed" but on the whole asserting that it was worthy of publication.[70] In June 1912, Morison received his doctoral degree and immediately began to prepare a manuscript for review by Houghton Mifflin Company, a Boston publishing company.

Turner's influence was especially pronounced in the published version of the dissertation, which was produced by Houghton Mifflin in 1913 as *The Life and Letters of Harrison Gray Otis: Federalist, 1765–1848*. Morison had ended the dissertation with the final defeat of the Federalist party at the national level in 1815; Otis, however, lived three decades longer and enjoyed a full social life. Morison's decision to end the dissertation at the end of Otis's political career, rather than at the end of his life, suggested the influence of Hart and Channing. The published version continued the narrative to Otis's death in 1848, thus making the rise and fall of the Federalist party but a chapter, albeit an important one, in the life of a complex man. Otis's talents were not only political but social and intellectual, Morison now acknowledged. "I have not confined myself . . . to political biography," Morison wrote in the introduction to the published version, "for, in addition to being a politician, Otis was an orator and a lawyer of the very first rank, a leader in social life, and a man who did much to influence the community in which he lived."[71]

The published version of Morison's dissertation was also filled with anecdotes that revealed the private side of Otis. Reviewers of *The Life and Letters of Harrison Gray Otis* found these touches either a strength or a weakness depending on which school of history they preferred. A reviewer for the *New York Times* praised the personalized quality of the work: "It is not only as the biography of an important figure in public affairs . . . that this work arouses interest," he noted, "but also as a running commentary upon the social life of the early administrations."[72] Another extolled the biography's "intense human interest."[73] Yet others criticized the work's concession to social history and attacked the book "as containing too much trivial and frivolous detail." One called it "a chronicle of small beer," and not surprisingly, Morison's *"cher maître"* at the institutionally minded École Libre des Sciences Politiques, Professor Caudel, wrote to scold him "for including anecdotes *un peu grises*."[74]

Morison later attributed the redirection of his dissertation to the growing influence of the "new school of social history" and to the revival of appreciation for the literary art and passion of Francis Parkman. In 1912, the day after his defeat in the election for president of the United States, Teddy Roosevelt delivered a presidential address before the American Historical Association meeting at Symphony Hall in Boston. His speech, entitled "History as Literature," inspired Morison and other recent Ph.D.'s in the audience to "rise above the stiffness of Ph.D. dissertations and write history that people would read." Noting that Roosevelt had dedicated *The Winning of the West* to Parkman, Morison determined to strengthen his commitment to Parkman as a model.[75] While the German doctoral model on which his dissertation was based had allowed him to make a "contribution to knowledge, honest and thorough," he reflected after Roosevelt's speech, it had also contributed unhappily to the production of a history "devoid of wit, color, or anything calculated to suggest that the past had been shot through with passion." Increasingly interested in things like "wine and song," Morison came to believe that "no detail of how people lived is inconsequential." While Caudel and Hart considered such ideas "tendentious," by the second decade of the century it was becoming increasingly clear that social history was gaining acceptance and even dominance in American historical circles. Morison agreed with Haskins, Turner, and others that historians had to "do something besides print documents, dig out facts, and marshal them in sober prose."[76]

As pleased as Morison was with Hart's and Channing's positive responses to his dissertation, he must have been still more satisfied with Turner's assessment of his *Life and Letters of Harrison Gray Otis*. Turner wrote Morison that his "contribution" was "a real one," and he expressed his special delight that Morison had shown no sectional bias in his handling of the Hartford Convention.[77] While Henry Adams had treated the convention in the spirit of "grandpa was right,"[78] and Channing viewed it as an unfortunate reaction to western pork barrelling, Morison's treatment vindicated the frontier thesis, as far as Turner was concerned, because it highlighted the conspiracy of "a union of the old 13 against, or aside from, the West." Morison's handling of the Hartford Convention proved, according to Turner, that the West had saved America from a secessionist movement in the East. "I am confident that as a force . . . in American politics," Turner continued in his letter to Morison, "the West needs more intelligent study than it has received by most scholars, especially in the East."[79] He might have added, especially among students of Channing.

The Academic Marketplace

Although "their personalities were about as different as those of any three scholars in a similar field could well be," Hart, Channing, and Turner each influenced Morison's scholarship in important ways.[80] They had a similar impact on his teaching career. After the publication of *The Life and Letters of Harrison Gray Otis*, Morison took a vacation to Europe and the Balkans with his wife to relax and to consider his future career plans.[81] During his absence, his mentors at Harvard kept an eye out for possible job openings in American history for the 1914 academic year, since they felt he had a future as a professor and scholar. Professor Hart, for instance, recommended his former student for a summer position at the University of California, Berkeley, advertised by his friend and fellow historian H. Morse Stephens. Morison soon discovered that "to have been [Hart's] pupil was enough recommendation for a young scholar to a university post,"[82] for on his return from the Balkans in February 1914, he found the following communication from Stephens: "INVITE YOU TO SUMMER SESSION UNIVERSITY CALIFORNIA JUNE TWENTY TWO TO AUGUST FIRST [stop] HONORARIUM THREE HUNDRED FIFTY [stop] IF YOU CAN ACCEPT SEND DETAILED ANNOUNCEMENT OF YOUR TWO COURSES AND BIOGRAPHICAL STATISTICS BY MAIL AT ONCE [stop]."[83] Several weeks later the offer was increased to six months and six hundred dollars for an additional two courses in American history during the fall semester.[84]

While Morison was considering the Berkeley position, a second offer came from Wellesley College in Massachusetts to teach American history during the 1914–15 academic year.[85] Despite his friendship with Stephens and his efforts to recruit Morison for Berkeley, Hart favored the Wellesley job, since, as Morison pointed out to him, there were a number of definite disadvantages associated with the Berkeley position. To take the job, Morison noted, "I shall have to bring my wife and family to California, for I cannot be separated from them for so long a period." Furthermore, the money at Berkeley was inadequate, as he pointed out to Stephens. "I think I am worth more than $600 for such a position. . . . I am glad to come to summer school for bare expenses, but I doubt whether in justice to myself and my profession I ought to continue . . . with you on anything less than a paying basis."[86] There were also "some obvious conveniences" to Wellesley: it was not a replacement position, it required no move, and it was near Harvard. Hart pressed him to pursue the position. "Your friends at Harvard are very much interested in finding a proper opportunity for you next year," Hart argued, and the Wellesley job "seems an excellent opportunity for a man to show his mettle."[87]

Yet a third offer came while Morison was mulling over his decision, and this was one that seemed impossible to refuse. Late in the spring of 1914, a position as tutor in the newly formed government department at Harvard was created, and Hart nominated Morison to fill it. That Hart should have been involved in the search for a government tutor was itself the result of his own changing job description. The tensions between sociocultural and institutional historians that had been incubating in the history department for years erupted in 1914 when an arrangement that was supposed to have been temporary became permanent. In 1909, after nearly forty years of service, Charles Eliot resigned as president of Harvard College, and he was replaced by A. Lawrence Lowell, a member of the history department and holder of the Eaton Professorship of Government.[88] When Lowell vacated his chair, it was awarded to Hart, whose interests were as much political as anyone's in the department. This set into motion a series of events that ultimately forced Hart out of the history department. First, Professor Coolidge put forth a motion to the faculty to create a new department, government, based on the political science offerings in the history department. This change had been long anticipated, since political science had been gaining recognition as an independent discipline in colleges and universities across the country. Second, and a move that was not anticipated, Coolidge proposed that the Eaton professorship be transferred to the government department. Over Hart's objections this motion passed, and he was obliged either to switch departments or resign his chair. Hart's eventual decision to migrate to the new department of government gave the sociocultural historians practical control of the history department.[89]

Hart remained unhappy with the arrangement and did not profit by it. He continued to believe that the study of political and institutional matters belonged to the history department, and he tried to maintain a presence there as long as possible. His courses were included in the college catalogues under the government department listings, but their names, descriptions, and content were essentially the same as those previously offered through history. Hart insisted as well on continuing to teach his favorite History 13 in the history department. This he managed to do until 1913, when he was cheated out of even this slim affiliation with the department by what Morison called a "rather sorry academic intrigue." Professor Channing had long coveted the course, which overlapped with his research for the "Great Work" on the colonial period, and he petitioned the department to let him teach it. Anxious to be rid of Hart completely, the sociocultural historians awarded Channing the course. Hart protested, but under pressure from Channing, who began "to make malicious comments" about Hart "in the presence of his students," Hart finally relinquished the course. He did so, however, only under "the rather touching condition that the name and number of his famous course, which he had given for thirty years, should be used by no one else." Channing changed it to History 10.[90]

Hart tried to make the best of a bad situation, and he hoped to enlist Morison's help in doing so. In 1914, President Lowell introduced a system of tutors throughout the college who were to serve as general advisors and instructors to groups of undergraduates in new concentrations that were the precursors to majors.[91] Hart had nominated Morison for the head tutorship in the government, economics, and history concentration, which was administered through the government department. In an effort to recruit Morison, Hart jotted down several compelling reasons why he felt his young charge should accept the position. As a tutor "you will find yourself a fellow with . . . a good crowd engaged in good work," Hart noted, and "I should like very much to see you associated with it." With an emotional appeal to their long-standing friendship, Hart compared his own career beginnings to Morison's: "I remember very distinctly, in 1883, receiving a letter from President Eliot offering me a small instructorship at Harvard for the following year," Hart wrote. "The pay was not significant, but the opportunity was a great one—it opened the door to a lifetime of work which has been exactly to my mind."[92]

Morison turned down the offer, however, in part because he viewed it as part-time employment outside his area of specialty. The appointment carried some responsibilities in history, but because it was monitored through the government department, Morison correctly assumed it would require particular attention to the areas of political science and economics, and he was dissatisfied with this prospect. "I think it would be a technical error on my part to take up another line of historical work," Morison wrote Hart. "I might fail to make good—and thus blacken my record." And, he added, the position offered him no security. The tutorial appointment represented a descent "to the submerged level of the profession," he noted.

"I might have to wait ten years before there would be a vacancy in the Department," he added, "or might be passed over in favor of some other."[93]

Morison's reluctance to teach in the government department, despite the attractive opportunity it provided him to work at Harvard with his old mentor, suggests how thoroughly he had been influenced by Hart's adversaries in the history department. The sociocultural historians, especially Turner, had played an important role in his decision. Turner, who would himself one day leave Harvard for Berkeley, advised Morison to take the job in California. Western universities were competing with Harvard "as a producer of teachers and scholars," he maintained, adding that it would be useful for a student of Morison's east coast background to experience education in other sections of the nation. Glad of the opportunity "as a son of the West" to advise "a son of New England," Turner persisted in his belief that no American historian could be considered adequately trained until he had a full appreciation for the influence of the West on American development. Teaching at Berkeley would provide an opportunity for just such an awareness.[94]

Morison eventually accepted the Berkeley position, and in the summer of 1914 he moved his family to California to begin his teaching career. As one might expect, however, Edward Channing was not willing to stand idly by while his former student was unduly influenced by Turner. He too recognized Morison as a rising star and hoped to guide his career path. In the summer of 1914, therefore, Channing offered Morison the position of head teaching assistant for History 10, which he had recently acquired from Hart. Morison was an obvious choice for the job because it required, in Channing's words, someone who was "persona grata" to the students, and Morison had been the head teaching assistant for the course when it was History 13.[95] Morison turned down this offer, however, on the same grounds as he had Hart's—it was below his station. Channing seemed to expect the rejection. "Sammy's head is too large to jam through the yoke, or under it," he told fellow professor and family friend Barrett Wendell.[96] According to Channing, however, Morison had not rejected an appointment in the history department outright, by which Wendell assumed Channing meant, in his "odd terms," that "the work in question is not important enough for Sam and that when something better is in sight his chances are good."[97] Channing joked that for a time Morison had "escaped the despot."[98]

Channing next offered Morison an instructorship in history for the fall of 1914 with responsibility for co-teaching History 10. He reminded Morison that "[i]t is not a bad thing to have to do with an assemblage of Cambridge hermits," and that "intercourse with the pesky young is rather stimulating to the literary faculty."[99] Despite the plea, Morison also rejected this offer. He claimed that since he was already teaching at the University of California, "it would be hard to start in medias res" at Harvard.[100] But the strong-willed Channing was not satisfied with the explanation. If the offer "comes to you again," he warned, "I would consider it carefully." Channing had very personal reasons for pushing Morison so hard to accept a position with him. His health, which had never been good, was deteriorating, and he was considering an early retirement so that he might dedicate himself completely to the "Great Work." He hoped to groom Morison as his successor. Reiterating his plea some months later, Channing used a nautical analogy to hint at his intentions. "I wonder if you ever read 'Tom Cringles Log,'" Channing lectured, referring to a popular fictional sea narrative from British literature that Morison surely had read as a boy. Tom Cringle "looked askance at the offers of the command of a little schooner," when they came, but someone who was interested in him assured him that he need not feel offended, because "if the climate carried away his superior officers he might find himself on the weather side of a corvette's quarterdeck before very long." With obvious reference to himself, Channing added, "[s]o possibly, if anything should happen to one of the post captains here, the commander of the little schooner anchored near might get a whack at his job."[101]

The pull of this logic was great, but it was not until Morison was offered an instructorship with sole responsibility for teaching History 10 that he agreed to return to Harvard.[102] Such a position would allow him to follow in Channing's footsteps without walking consistently in his shadow. It also promised some future security if Channing retired. Most of all, it allowed Morison to pursue the kind of history he desired. Although the history department was now dominated by sociocultural historians who acknowledged the need to provide alternatives to traditional institutional history, Channing was still of the old school. Never as anathema to Haskins and Coolidge as was Hart, his diachronic approaches still aroused the suspicions of his younger colleagues, and his personal war with the popular Turner alienated him from them. Had Morison accepted a position as Channing's co-teacher, he might have been too closely associated with a sinking academic ship (to complete Channing's nautical metaphor) and might have been forced to go down with its captain. By waiting for Channing to abandon History 10 altogether, Morison assured himself a necessary autonomy in making choices about historical method. As Morison reminisced to the Massachusetts Historical Society years later, Channing recommended: "Let Sammy do it, and Sammy did."[103]

There was an irony associated with Morison's appointment that was doubtless not lost on him. As instructor for History 10, he was now teaching the course from which his former mentor Hart had been relieved several years before. Motivated by his desire to become Channing's "new Parkman," yet heavily influenced by the sociocultural techniques of Channing's adversary Turner, Morison was a strange polyglot. His twisted progress along a path that led him from student to head teaching assistant and finally to instructor of the same course reflected the larger alternations in the journey of the department and the profession from 1904 to 1914. The conflicts between institutional and sociocultural historians, between westerners and easterners, and between political science and history departments forced

Morison to make uncomfortable decisions among differing methodologies and irreconcilable personalities. Yet years later Morison was still able to say, with unqualified pride, that his training under fire had been worth it. "I am telling the plain unvarnished truth," he wrote, "when I say that never have I encountered such a remarkable body of gentlemen and scholars as the members of the Harvard History Department between 1904 when I entered as a Freshman, and 1913 when I took my Ph.D."[104]

The "Usable Past"

*Carl Becker, Albert Beveridge, Woodrow Wilson
and the Politics of History*

4

Everyman His Own Historian

Morison's appointment to Harvard indicated that his former teachers believed he had a rich future as a historian. The scholarly reception of *The Life and Letters of Harrison Gray Otis* justified this confidence. The work received glowing reviews from historical journals such as the *American Historical Review*, whose reviewer called it the "most important political biography that has lately appeared."[1] On its strength, Morison was elected a member of the Massachusetts Historical Society and the American Antiquarian Society before his thirtieth birthday.[2] The book opened other professional opportunities as well. Channing was contracted to write a volume on Massachusetts for the American Commonwealth Series, but his commitment to the *History of the United States* and his recent fallout with the series' editor, Albert Bushnell Hart, hampered his progress.[3] Channing eventually turned the project over to Morison, who, by virtue of the assignment, found himself in touch with a group of impressive young scholars, including Marcus W. Jernegan, Kenneth Murdock, Lawrence Mayo, and his old friend Robert Lord. His association with these authors helped confirm the impression conveyed by his Harvard advisors that he was one of America's finest aspiring professional historians.[4]

Morison did not share entirely the confidence of his mentors, however. For one thing, he was suspicious of his teaching. At Berkeley he had been unable to communicate his ideas to students. He blamed the "wretched secondary system of education" in California,[5] which produced mediocre college students and made the work of "getting up 5 new lect[ure]s a week" a chore.[6] He also blamed himself. "I do not feel I am being the success with the students that I should be," he confessed to Professor Wendell during his summer session at Berkeley. "As the weeks go by, the teaching becomes less of a novelty and pleasure, and more of a burden."[7] Teaching at Harvard proved no more fulfilling. Preparing lectures was still "boresome," he noted, and students continued to disappoint.[8] Morison was particularly disappointed with the women at Radcliffe, whom he refused to continue teaching after he discovered that they were recording every word of his lectures, even his jokes, with indiscriminate accuracy.[9]

Nor was Morison completely happy with his teaching situation at Harvard. Responsible not only for History 10 but for the History of Massachusetts, tutorials in history, as well as grading in upper level history courses, Morison was innundated with work before his position officially commenced in September of 1915. The work in preparing lectures for History 10 alone was overwhelming, and after working all summer on his notes, he still had not progressed beyond the first few classes.[10] This teaching burden also affected his scholarship, and he complained to Channing about it. Channing sympathized with his student, admitting that "it is pretty tough work teaching and writing at the same time," but he added, "I have done it for years and am able to stagger along."[11] Morison did not wish merely to "stagger along," however, in the manner of his unpopular advisor. He wished to make a mark as a teacher and as a scholar by balancing both identities, and this he found increasingly difficult to do under the conditions Channing had established for his employment.

Morison's frustrations were increased by the knowledge that his courses were populated with ex-Channing students who found the elder historian's lectures a "wretched experience" and his classroom delivery "profoundly disappointing and disillusioning." One student, a future professor of history, noted years later that Morison's presence on the Harvard campus as an alternative to Channing influenced his decision not to transfer from the college. "I ambitiously enrolled . . . in Channing's 'History of the United States since 1865,' " remembered Kenneth Porter of his freshman year. "I did not care for Channing," however, for his lectures were "full of prejudices against the West" and "anything savoring of liberalism." After the chilling experience with Channing's course, Porter "had considerable doubt" as to "whether Harvard was the place" for him. The next semester, however, he enrolled in Morison's colonial history course, and "everything changed. . . . I used to wake up in the morning with a feeling of pleasurable excitement," Porter wrote, "as if this was the day that I had tickets to the second balcony for the performance of some play to which I had long looked forward." When he asked himself the reason for this feeling, the answer would be: "This is the morning of one of . . . Morison's lectures!"[12]

Porter's comments suggest that Morison was perhaps more successful with his students than he himself perceived, but they also reveal how many of Channing's responsibilities Morison was assuming so that his former mentor could finish the "Great Work." Morison's fears in this regard increased when Chairman William Ferguson of the history department notified Morison that his suggested courses for the spring of 1916 were being modified with an eye toward "draw[ing] the greater part of Professor Channing's constituency."¹³ Determined not to be a mere academic pinch hitter, Morison devised a plan at the end of his first year at Harvard to allow himself a half-time teaching load at half pay, so that he could devote the remainder of his time to scholarship. Hoping to live off an allowance from his mother and the income from a half salary, he proposed to teach colonial history and the History of Massachusetts one term a year with a second term free. He received support within the department from Turner, who wrote with self-conscious honesty: "Far be it from me to protest against a man's finding the time to do his writing. My own opinion," he ventured, "is that you are wise, if you can adjust your own and the university's interests to half time and I shall do what I can to see that it is possible." Furthermore, he added, "I have already intimated my belief that your feeling that you should have a higher salary is justified."¹⁴

Morison's plan was never realized, however, in part because it was opposed by Channing, who in all likelihood recognized that it might mean more teaching for him. Its failure intensified Morison's anxieties and exaggerated the effect of several other disappointments Morison experienced with his scholarship. Although professional historians praised *The Life and Letters of Harrison Gray Otis*, for instance, it sold poorly. Published in a small edition of under one thousand copies at the expense of Morison's family, it had sold only three hundred copies after three years, mainly to libraries and friends.¹⁵ Morison complained to his editor, Ferris Greenslet, about the publishing company's marketing techniques, but there was little the editor could say. Greenslet reminded Morison that academic books seldom have a large immediate circulation and counselled patience.¹⁶ When Houghton Mifflin "plugged the remainder" of the volumes and destroyed the plates, however, Morison feared his Otis biography was destined to obscurity.¹⁷

Other scholarly projects floundered as well. On his postgraduate trip to Europe, Morison had begun working on a new book, tentatively entitled "The United States and the French Revolution." After a year's work, however, he was "scared off" the project by Professor James A. James of Northwestern University, who alleged a prior claim to the topic. James never completed the volume, and years later Morison vented his frustration by using James as an example to warn students never to give up on scholarly projects because of the territorial claims of their professional elders.¹⁸ The *American Commonwealth History* also lingered. By 1915 Morison had drafted several sections of the volume on the early history of Massachusetts, but he received negative feedback from nearly all his manuscript readers, one begging him (for the sake of his career) not to consider publishing any part of the unworthy chapters he had written. This critic was a colleague of Morison's at Harvard, Professor of Divinity James A. Ropes, whose original comments on the chapters were so critical that his wife and friends would not let him deliver them. Ropes was particularly unhappy with Morison's essentially negative portrait of the Puritans, which he found "needlessly contemptuous and irritating," and which was "merely a repetition of the familiar commonplaces of anti-puritan polemic." Reminding Morison of the important role the Puritans played in the founding of Harvard, Ropes linked the need to "make the Puritans appear respectable" to Morison's chances for advancement at the college. "I can only beg you not to publish it," Ropes concluded, since "you've done a piece of work not worthy of you and the expectations we all have for you."[19]

Morison apologized to Ropes for his "sloppy and incoherent" work and dismissed the project as only "a bit of hack-work" undertaken to "earn a little money."[20] But Ropes's comments so troubled him that by the fall of 1917 he had written nothing further and showed no signs of moving ahead with the project. Professor Hart and the editors of the American Commonwealth Series sent periodic letters asking whether the volume would be ready for publication on this date or that, but in response they received only apologetic forestallings along with vague promises that he would finish the work by 1919 or 1920.[21]

Morison's frustration with teaching and scholarship also derived from his doubts about the value of his work. The Otis biography reminded Morison of the political and social influence of his ancestors and invoked the memory of his grandfather Eliot, who first inspired his interest in the topic, and whose life as a historian was marked by consistent public service. Friends and relatives frequently reiterated to Morison the responsibilities commensurate with his family name, and even fellow historians urged him to play a more active role. He will "take his proper place in a long line of faithful public servants which his family has given the State and the Nation during the past two hundred years," predicted one associate, "for he has in his veins the fighting blood of the Otises."[22] When Morison expressed his doubts to historian Ellis Oberholtzer about whether he was exerting any "pull" or "personality" on public affairs, his colleague reminded him that he must be different from the majority of his scholarly peers who were by and large "hampered through life" by a tendency to "withdraw from the turbid stream of our modern life." He must be a historian with public ambitions.[23]

Many other professional historians in the first and second decades of the twentieth century also shared doubts about the usefulness of their historical scholarship. Morison had heard some such apprehensions voiced by the burgeoning "annal" historians in France, but his first real exposure to an American dialogue on this issue came from Carl Becker's seminal article "Detachment and the Writing of History." First published in the *Atlantic Monthly* in 1910 by an as yet relatively obscure professor of history at Kansas University, this article launched an attack on the "objectivists" within the historical profession who insisted that the historian, like the scientist, must be detached and distanced from his subject matter and must disavow any practical intentions for his work. In making the assumption that a historian should or even could "separate himself from the process which he describes," Becker believed professionals were losing sight of the relativity of all knowledge. He called for a new attitude toward history, one that recognized the responsibility of the historian to rewrite the past according to current social needs. His article inspired a group of historians to establish within the profession a new school unhappily labelled "New History." Some of its members were sociocultural historians such as James Harvey Robinson, Charles Beard, and Charles Homer Haskins who had been alienated from the institutional historians in their respective departments. Others joined for ideological rather than methodological reasons; they approved of the presentist emphasis of New History and its "predictive value" for solving contemporary dilemmas. In short, they called for a "usable past," one not unlike Samuel Eliot's vision of "practical scholarship" in which the techniques of the professional historian could be applied to the pressing concerns of contemporary society.[24]

No one articulated this position with greater meaning for Morison than Turner. Finding labels personally repugnant, Turner nonetheless conformed nicely to the utilitarianism of the New History outlook. As a professor, he frequently reminded students such as Morison of the functional value of knowledge.[25] In his 1910 presidential address before the American Historical Association, for instance, Turner acknowledged that younger historians were justifiably "on the point of rebellion against the traditional interpretation of the past" because they recognized the urgent need to convert history "into an instrument for the transformation of society." History is "not planted on the solid ground of fixed condition," Turner noted, but must be reworked again and again "from the new points of view afforded by the present." Turner urged a new generation of professionals to play active roles in reform movements and to view the historical events they inspired as expressions of "deep-seated forces" rather than "fragmentary and sporadic curios for the historical museum."[26]

Moved by the appeals of Becker and Turner, Morison attempted to supplement his teaching and scholarship with an increasing number of public service projects. He agreed, for instance, to become editor of the Old South Church Leaflets, a series of pamphlets devoted to introducing school children to the rudiments of American history in a readable and contemporary style.[27] He contracted to write a history of the Constitution of Massachusetts for the State Printing Office with the purpose of popularizing democratic principles and circulating historical documents for use by the general public.[28] He volunteered to teach night courses in history and government to electricians and plumbers at a local trade school as his grandfather Eliot had done for adult laborers seven decades earlier.[29] And he helped organize the New England History Teacher's Association, a civic-minded group of primarily high school teachers who experimented with pedagogical techniques in an effort to make the past more serviceable to the present and future needs of students.[30]

Morison also became more politically active. With his friends Smith Dexter, Ted DeFriez, and Lucien Price, he formed a political study group to consider current world problems. "All four were progressives of the 1912 vintage," remembered Morison, "sanguine, liberal and democratic." They worshiped Thomas Jefferson, discussed "Graham Wallace, took in *The New Republic*, and loved Romain Rolland."[31] In their company, Morison became, in the eyes of one student, "a political idealist who took an intense, even partisan, interest in public affairs."[32] Along with his "progressive" friends, Morison volunteered for community work, especially municipal politics. The group spent long hours in 1917 helping create a new housing code for the city of Boston and were active in fighting teacher loyalty oaths.[33] And, although he had no political aspirations of his own, Morison did campaign work for various politicians in the Boston area, lobbying consistently "against an increasingly rigid Republican party," one student remembered[34] and supporting third-party candidates such as Eugene Debs when no suitable Democrats presented themselves.[35] "All wrongs would soon be righted, all crooked ways set straight," Morison naïvely believed, if history could become the handmaiden of reform.[36]

History as Politics/Politics as History

During this period of increased political activity, Morison was first introduced to Albert J. Beveridge, a former senator from Indiana whose life had been given over almost exclusively to public service. Beveridge had a reputation as a progressive Republican reformer who backed big business against the interests of labor but worked for anti–child labor laws, conservation of natural resources, direct election of senators, and government regulation of public utilities. A visible and popular senator, he had had a falling out with Republican President Howard Taft over trusts and was eased out of office by the Republican machine in 1911. He joined Theodore Roosevelt's Bull Moose campaign in 1912 and ran for reelection to the Senate as a Progressive in 1914, but he was defeated. At the time of his first meeting with Morison, Beveridge was ostracized from and disgruntled with politics.[37]

As a form of relaxation and escape, Beveridge read and wrote history. After his political defeat for reelection to the Senate, he began work on a biography of Chief Justice John Marshall, one of his boyhood heroes. Beveridge's formal training in history was limited to a topics course in college, "readings in history," taught by the spirited author of a popular history of the world, John Clark Ridpath, who was shunned by most professional historians because his "facts" were considered thinly researched and unsubstantiated.[38] Beveridge "had no more idea of the methods and obligations of historical scholarship than the average casual reader," his biographer Claude Bowers has noted.[39] To compensate, Beveridge made it his habit to seek out scholars in his field and to consult them on theoretical and practical matters. "I would like to get a whole lot of you 'history sharps' . . . together," Beveridge kidded one correspondent, "and make you professionals look up the sources, write the book, in short, do the whole bloody work and then bring it out under my name."[40] Morison was introduced to Beveridge in this way, through a letter of inquiry about his characterization of Marshall and the Federalists in *The Life and Letters of Harrison Gray Otis*. From these simple beginnings blossomed a friendship that had lasting implications for their work.

Morison and Beveridge had much in common. Both were students of the early national period, and both were interested in political biography and political history. Morison had studied Marshall's judicial rulings in connection with his research on Federalist politics in the 1800s, and Beveridge consulted Morison's *Life and Letters of Harrison Gray Otis* in preparing his biography of Marshall. Both owned property in Beverly Farms, where together they enjoyed "all that makes life worthwhile," as Beveridge described: the "normal living, the walks through the forests, the regular hours of refreshing slumber, the new birth of mental and physical vigor."[41] And both had an appreciation for lively historical prose. Morison found a chapter on the Burr conspiracy in Beveridge's Marshall biography "so engrossing" that he "sat up till 1:30 A.M. reading it." He was especially impressed with Beveridge's descriptive power. "The narrative is full of color," he complimented, and the reader is "carried along with it."[42]

Morison and Beveridge disagreed, however, about the value of a scholarly life. In fact, in 1917 the two were moving in parallel but opposite directions on this issue. Morison was dabbling in politics as a way of making his historical work more useful, whereas Beveridge had taken up historical writing as an escape from politics. Of the two, Beveridge was far more enthusiastic about the power of isolated scholarship. "As I feel now," Beveridge wrote a friend, "I consider it a Godsend that I am out of politics. It has furnished me an opportunity for quiet, for study, and for thought which political activity utterly forbids."[43] Beveridge's philosophy of history comported nicely with this detached life-style. Out of sympathy with the New Historians, he argued that historians must be objective and avoid ideological entanglements. On this point, he drew his philosophy and language expressly from the scientific historians of the late nineteenth century. "The writer of history or biography has no more business with a prejudice or fixed idea than the chemist, the biologist or the astronomer," Beveridge argued, adding that historical work required an attention to detail that went beyond anything he had ever experienced in previous vocations.[44] "[A]ll the work you ever saw me do in the law or in getting up a speech,— the long, hard, toilsome hours of investigation so as to get the facts correct,"

Beveridge told friends, "all that was nothing at all compared to this pains-taking and brain-racking scholarly labor."[45]

Influenced by Becker and Turner, Morison took issue with Beveridge's positivistic philosophy. Arguing that no historian could write truly "objective" history, Morison insisted that the best students of history were those who were sensitive to their own predispositions and used them to affect a specific political and social agenda. Citing himself as an example, Morison wrote: "I . . . was born into the most respectable Federalist-Whig-Republican tradition of Massachusetts, and it was only after writing my first book that I came to see the hollowness of that political creed." Having discovered the "stupid, narrow-minded, and local" character of this tradition, Morison added, he was now in a position to use the insight in the service of contemporary reform.[46] His attacks on the Republican party were a part of that strategy. Having every reason to resent the strong anti-Republican implications of Morison's words, Beveridge nonetheless resisted the temptation to reduce history to politics, a policy consistent with his philosophy of history. Despite having been active all his life in the Federalist-Whig-Republican tradition ridiculed by Morison, Beveridge believed his portrait of Marshall could be (and was) detached, impartial, and apolitical.[47]

Morison begged to differ. Beveridge's biography was a perfect advertisement for the New Historical claims against objectivity, he noted, because it was an obvious political assault on Jeffersonian principles and the Democratic party. To prove his contention, Morison cited Beveridge's description of Jefferson during the treason trial of Aaron Burr over which Marshall presided in 1807. Burr had been accused by several co-conspirators (William Eaton and James Wilkinson) of planning a revolt in the newly acquired Louisiana Territory; the purpose of this revolt, Jefferson contended, was to establish himself as president of a rival country to the United States. In pursuing the case against Burr, Jefferson acted with contemptible vindictiveness according to Beveridge's narrative, going so far as to obstruct justice by pressuring Marshall to return a guilty verdict against Burr. When Marshall refused to do so, Beveridge's Jefferson turned his fury on the chief justice and tried to remove him from the bench.[48] Such a portrait, Morison argued, was not only skewed but politically charged. What reason had Jefferson "to go after Burr's scalp after 1804" considering that by that time Burr and Jefferson "were pretty well quit?" asked Morison. "Is it not possible that T.J. was sincerely convinced by Eaton, Wilkinson, and Co. that Burr was [a] traitor?" If so, could the subsequent "vindictiveness" of Jefferson be simply "a matter of government prestige?" Or, concluded Morison with reference to Beveridge's partisan politics, "will you not admit that T.J. could be sincere?"[49]

Beveridge would not admit the possibility and lashed out at Morison for giving Jefferson the benefit of the doubt. Jefferson was a demagogue with an "abnormal and almost insane love of popularity," Beveridge believed, and had "an implacable hatred of anybody who antagonized him."[50] In dealing with Marshall, Jefferson allowed his pathological paranoia to distort his reason, and he frustrated the work of America's greatest legal mind. Beveridge contended that his assessment of Jefferson was not politically motivated; historical research, scholarly and objective, compelled the judgment. The "careful reading of [Jefferson's] letters and study of his career has disillusioned me," Beveridge confessed. "I am sometimes almost sorry that I ever made the investigation of Mr. Jefferson."[51] To the suggestion that "Marshall could talk rot just as clotted and dishonest as Jefferson,"[52] Beveridge added the caveat that Marshall's rhetoric was in the interest of the country; Jefferson's was not.

Morison admitted that Jefferson had failings, but these did not exonerate Marshall of his many faults, faults that Morison claimed Beveridge had ignored for political reasons.[53] In a review of Beveridge's biography in the *Atlantic Monthly*, Morison conceded that Marshall had made judicial decisions that saved America from internal destruction in the perilous first years of nationhood. But, he added, Marshall carried to the Supreme Court "opinions which, until the end of his life, were at variance with those of the American people as a whole," and he did not hesitate to impose those opinions against the will of the people when *he* thought it necessary.[54] Beveridge justified this autocratic propensity on the grounds that "the country was in desperate case" in the last decades of the eighteenth century, with "bitterness, fraud, poverty and wretchedness" prevailing throughout the nation. The "history mutt" who "put over the phrase 'The Era of Good Feeling,'" he ridiculed, did not understand that "this great and glorious republic was in a devil of a mess." At this pivotal moment, Marshall "called forth four or five of those great state papers . . . as Chief Justice, that saved the nation."[55]

Despite the strong tone of some of these remarks, Beveridge and Morison became good friends and frequently made light of their political and historiographic differences. Morison once sent Beveridge a "playlet," for instance, entitled "The Education of John Marshall; Act I, according to Senator Beveridge; Act II, as it really happened." The first act of this parody, "according to Senator Beveridge," begins in 1774 with a quaint scene at Marshall's Virginia home, "Oak Hill." John Marshall's father, Thomas, entering his home in "well-fitting but mud-bespattered travelling costume," is besieged by the colored maid welcoming him back "from de 'sembly" and by his wife and "5 or 6 children" who greet him with "effusive reunions, kisses, etc." Thomas Marshall brings news that the British have "dropped the mask of conciliation and displayed the horrid countenance of tyranny! Boston is blockaded." Upon hearing the news, young John marches to the mantelpiece, takes the musket down, and comes "to parade rest." In melodramatic manner his parents exclaim, "My child! Must it, will it, come to this!" Knowing that it must and hearing the far-off notes of a bugle playing the assembly, John grasps the powder horn and his "coon-skin cap" and races to begin a revolution. The scene ends with the rest of the Marshall clan weeping and the orchestra playing the "Star-Spangled Banner."[56]

The second act, "as it really happened," opens with Thomas Marshall, dressed in hunting shirt, buckskin breeches, and moccasins covered with mud, bursting into his "rough, one room, earthen floor board cabin" and sinking "wearily and gloomily onto the bed." The children look on "speechless from apprehension," while Mrs. Marshall, spitting into the fire, scolds her "lazy, no-count politician" husband for forgetting the household provisions from Williamsburg. Blaming his absentmindedness on the troublesome news of a blockade in Boston, Thomas Marshall proceeds to discredit the revolutionary effort. Patrick Henry is nothing but a "wind merchant," he proclaims; George Mason can only spout meaningless latinisms and talk about the "Magner Cyarter." "I'm through with the whole lot" and their "patriotic blatherskate," asserts Tom. When John approaches his father to propose joining the revolution as a step to subsequent election in the Assembly, Thomas's response is final. Now "see here, you young lout," warns the father. If "you ever so much as whisper of going into politics, I'll break every bone in your body. [I would] ruther yo'-all steal horses for a livin."[57]

Beveridge thought the parody a "smasher." According to the ex-senator, it revealed "another, and a most attractive phase" of Morison's mind and character. "Who on earth ever would have imagined that your cold, scholarly New England mind with its Harvard discipline could contain such an hitherto hidden fountain of humor?" he kidded.[58] Humor aside, however, there was a more serious aspect to these historical disagreements, since, according to Morison, Beveridge's depiction of Marshall, Jefferson, and party politics was having a direct impact on a nation near the brink of war. In 1917, when the first two volumes of Beveridge's biography of Marshall were published, Americans were faced with hard choices about neutral shipping, European warfare, and isolationism. Many readers searched Beveridge's biography for clarification of these issues and sought (in true New Historical fashion) precedents that might aid them in formulating current policies. Beveridge was not only naïve in his assertion that his biography was apolitical, Morison argued, he was irresponsible in assuming so, since Marshall's foreign policies implied some dangerous things for American policy. Beveridge's failure to recognize his political bias or to acknowledge the presentist implications of his historical conclusions might embroil him, unwittingly, in the single most important political event of the century—the Great War.

Historians at War

Almost as soon as the first two volumes of *The Life of John Marshall* were published, Beveridge received mail from readers anxious to draw parallels between 1815 and 1915. Some readers found connections between the conservatism of the Court during the foreign policy struggles of the early 1800s and the isolation of the Republican administrations of the early twentieth century. Beveridge's friend Charles Beard, fresh from his own New Historical study of the Court's conservatism (*The Supreme Court and the Constitution*, 1912), was convinced that the biography was a political defense of the beleaguered bench.[59] One reader hoped the book would have "a steadying effect on the minds of thoughtful men in these days when . . . [w]e may be mixed up & ruled by the politicians and diplomats of Europe." We need "a Marshall in this critical period of our national life," he noted.[60] Others were disturbed by the isolationist implications of the Marshall portrait and questioned their accuracy. A. C. McLaughlin warned readers of the *American Bar Association Journal* that Beveridge's portrayal of Marshall's attitudes toward war was "not balanced."[61] In the *Virginia Law Register*, L.C. Bell claimed that Beveridge was "a biased biographer" whose "inordinate political partisanship" rendered it impossible for him to present foreign policy issues with "the judicial claim and impartial point of view necessary" to "the office of historian."[62]

Between the lines of *The Life of John Marshall*, Morison perceived an attack on the Democratic party and Woodrow Wilson. Wilson had become somewhat of an idol and even a role model for Morison since 1912. Not only did the president embrace the Jeffersonian principles to which Morison was ideologically committed, he was a former historian who had dedicated his life to public service. Trained in history at the Johns Hopkins University with Turner, Wilson wrote his first book, *Congressional Government* (1885) with a dual purpose that Morison very much admired.[63] On the one hand, Wilson wrote in the introduction, he hoped that his account of the usurpation of power from the executive by the legislative branch would "stand as a permanent piece of constitutional criticism by reason of some depth of historical and political insight." On the other hand, he intended the book "to catch hold of its readers' convictions and set reform a-going in a very definite direction."[64] Wilson brought his historical propensities to bear on practical problems, and his success as a politician and a statesman vindicated the New Historical technique. Morison trusted Wilson, he noted, because the president knew the "national experience which [he], as an historian, had made a part of himself."[65]

Morison was enthusiastic, therefore, when Wilson proclaimed to the Senate on January 22, 1917, that the United States must involve itself in diplomatic efforts to restore lasting peace to Europe. The president announced the formation of a special committee, the Inquiry, to investigate peace alternatives and to consider plans for a "super-national organization" for the promotion of a "new world order," the future League of Nations.[66] The suggestion lit a fire in Morison. "I shall never forget the exultation this address of the President to the Senate gave the ardent young men of my generation," he wrote. The concept of a peacekeeping organization "opened up a new and wonderful vista beyond the war" and gave promise for active scholarship in the years to come.[67] The Senate speech reminded Morison that "no President since Jefferson had been able to turn an intellectual equipment to public service," but that Wilson had now done it in "words and phrases that sang in our hearts."[68]

Given his support of the president, it is small wonder that Morison chafed under the impression that the *Life of Marshall* was a thinly veiled political attack on the Jeffersonian tradition. Beveridge's personal dislike for Wilson and his tendency to compare Wilson to Jefferson only increased Morison's suspicions. Wilson is "the most adroit politician the country has ever seen since Jefferson,"[69] Beveridge noted, and, like Jefferson, uses his "amazing gifts as a politician" to fool people.[70] "I can only account" for the disturbing similarities between the presidents, he said, "on the ground that Wilson has been a profound student of Jefferson the politician."[71] Despite these outspoken attitudes, however, Beveridge insisted that *The Life of John Marshall* was not political propaganda but objective history. He claimed to have presented the facts as they existed; readers were free to interpret those facts as they saw fit.[72] Friends reminded Beveridge that, at a time when "all men who have any patriotism and anything to say must take their place on the political firing line," the Marshall biography had increased the ex-senator's "standing as a leading public man."[73] Some even hoped that the Marshall biography was a subtle indication that Beveridge intended to lead an anti-Wilson campaign on behalf of the Republican party. Beveridge, however, affirmed his commitment to objectivity and his disdain for "history according to propaganda-made plans."[74] The historian "who is a partizan [sic] merely for the sake of a party name," he reaffirmed, "is a ghost of the past among living events."[75]

Beveridge was so committed to the ideal of detached scholarship that he isolated himself in his bungalow in Beverly Farms and vowed to continue uninterrupted work on the last two volumes of his Marshall biography despite the rumor of war. In the back of his property was a small, one-room stone house with a fireplace, which he adopted as his study. There he continued to work all day and into the night in privacy on the biography. One visitor to this cloistered environment remarked, "while he worked it was impossible, physically, to enter the study, for he had books, pamphlets, Government documents he was using spread all about him on the floor."[76]

Beveridge urged Morison to isolate himself from the war and politics as well and to press on with his scholarly work. "I trust you are going right ahead with the history of Massachusetts," he wrote Morison, adding with encouragement, "[it] is, I know, a prodigious task, but it must be done."[77] Morison, however, was too distracted by political events to think of writing. The book would have to "await the end of the war," he wrote Beveridge, because he found it "impossible to sit down to steady writing in these times."[78] He found it still more difficult to resist drawing historical parallels between contemporary and past events. Impressed by Wilson's speech and committed to relating scholarship to public affairs, Morison took time from his final lecture in the survey of American history to state how significant he thought Wilson's ideas were for the future of America. Declaring the January 22 speech "the biggest thing since the Monroe Doctrine," Morison encouraged his students to draw parallels between the courage of the founding fathers and that of Wilson.[79] If a president of such "great character" as Thomas Jefferson "could not keep out of a war in which [American] interests and emotions were involved," Morison reasoned, Wilson, his successor, must not be expected to do so either.[80] Channing, who thought Wilson's speech "all stuff," "reproved" Morison for making such a blatant interventionist statement,[81] but Morison was too enamored of Wilson and of the potential for New History in the classroom to back down. "We are in some of the most momentous years of human history," he responded. "The pros and cons ought to be thoroughly ventilated in college lecture halls."[82]

If Morison was moving closer and closer to a politicized history, he did not at first go the full distance with some of the New Historians who were becoming actively involved in the war effort, especially Turner. In February of 1917, Turner decided it was time for him and his colleagues "to assess ourselves or bear the stigma of servitude." In April he invited the Harvard faculty to a national gathering of historians in Washington, D.C., to form an organization of historians to support the war effort. Two days later the National Board for Historical Services was created with the expressed goal of channeling "historical activities throughout the nation in support of the war."[83] Turner expected most of the department to sign on, as his letters to board co-founder J. Franklin Jameson attested. Coolidge "will be friendly," Turner noted, and Ferguson "will be satisfactory to the board I know." Haskins "is busy finishing his book," he added, "but is giving the enterprise expectant treatment." But Channing, he warned, would remain strongly opposed to the idea. "Channing is, of course, settled in his conviction that it is futile and superficial to try to apply past precedents to present predicaments," Turner complained.[84] Persistent nonetheless, Turner approached Channing with the proposal; as he predicted, he was treated to a lecture on the ahistorical tendencies of New History.[85]

Reluctant to take an active part in a movement so likely to force him to choose between his former mentors, Morison was evasive at first when Turner approached him to help with the manifesto for the board. "Sammy Morison is of the opinion that if there is any writing to do I ought to set the example," wrote Turner to Jameson, "and there he spiked my guns."[86] Morison's response was a safe one, for he threw the challenge back at Turner, who was haunted by Channing's accusation that he was incapable of putting his ideas in writing.[87] But Turner would not be put off so easily. Morison "will help," he concluded, "if he is shown the way."[88] Turner was right, for although Morison never joined the National Board, he joined the staff of Wilson's Inquiry committee before the year was out. Morison was assigned the task of writing position papers for the settling of potential boundary disputes in the Balkans and the Baltics. After long days of teaching classes at Harvard, he labored well into the night drawing maps of Serbian railway routes and studying Austrian staff publications.[89] He made studies of diplomatic history, international law, and the various territorial and racial questions likely to be addressed at a peace conference.[90] He also supported efforts to create "a favorable public opinion for a just peace" by organizing a four-day conference (with a "three-ring circus of speakers") in his new hometown, Concord, Massachusetts, where he had moved with his family earlier in the year. Although few "constipated Concordians" (as Morison dubbed his apathetic neighbors) participated in the event,[91] he reported with satisfaction that "I have used my tongue and pen, to the best of my ability, to support the war and the government."[92]

Morison's real commitment to contemporary political events came in July 1918, when he decided to enlist in the Army. It was a decision that reflected some of his frustration with teaching. In a letter to President Lowell requesting a leave of absence from his classes for an indefinite period of time, Morison hinted at his dissatisfaction with his current position. Describing himself as Channing's "assistant" and "substitute," Morison argued that he would be far more useful working for the war cause than at Harvard as a mere understudy to his former professor. After receiving Morison's request, Lowell summoned Channing to the presidential offices for an explanation. Channing claimed to be "greatly shocked" at the inference that Morison was merely his "assistant," and he reaffirmed Morison's vital role as his successor. Channing and Lowell then tried to convince Morison of his importance to the university and recommended that he stay at Harvard to teach a course on modern European history and the coming of war.[93] But Morison had made up his mind to abandon the isolated halls of academia to take an active role in contemporary events. He had decided to become a soldier.

Morison's stint in the Army was not as important to the war cause as he had hoped, however. He was sent to Camp Devens, Massachusetts, where he expected to be accepted in the field artillery officer's training camp on the strength of his Harvard background. But there were objections made to his candidacy, and in late August Morison discovered that "serious charges" had been raised against him.[94] The Army wished to keep him at Camp Devens under surveillance at the rank of private, and Morison was outraged. "I cannot conceive what basis they can have for charges against me," he protested to his mother, and he asked President Lowell to get his "record cleared" and "have the person responsible for this cowardly stab in the back properly punished."[95] In the end, it proved to be a cousin by marriage, an amateur spy hunter, who had denounced Morison as pro-German because of remarks he had made in a casual conversation. By the time the charges had been cleared, the war was nearly over.[96]

Undaunted, Morison attempted to join the Army's historical staff, charged with writing the history of the war, and, when this failed, he tried for the peace commission.[97] After numerous rejections, he was finally referred to Henry White, former ambassador to France and a member of the U.S. delegation to the Paris peace conference scheduled for early 1919. Morison asked White if there was "the bare chance" that he might "have some use" for the services of a Harvard scholar. "It is my desire to put my knowledge to some practical use in the peace negotiations," he announced.[98] In January 1919, two months after the end of military hostilities, word arrived that White had secured him an appointment to the Russian division as a minor secretary. Morison registered his "Great excitement!" by packing in a matter of hours, making quick arrangements for his family, and reporting for duty in New York early the next day. He even found time to purchase a diary to preserve a written record of the important events in which he expected to participate.[99]

Morison's diary of the peace conference is a remarkable account of the trials and tribulations of a New Historian. The first installments record only frustrations. The Army was reluctant to part with personnel, and Morison, who had enlisted only four months earlier, was temporarily denied leave for the conference. "It was considered a great joke at army headquarters that a 'Harvard Professor' couldn't get out of the army in time to help make peace," remembered Morison. But he pestered officials until he got his way. By January 1919, he was steaming to Europe aboard the *Lapland*.[100] There he met many other scholars who had also committed themselves to active scholarship, including many of his Harvard associates. The Russian division to which Morison was assigned was headed by Robert H. Lord, then professor of modern European history at Harvard; Joe Fuller, a Harvard teaching assistant, was personal secretary to the division; Archibald Coolidge was a special assistant on the Central Territorial Commission; Charles Homer Haskins served on the Council on Foreign Affairs; and Roger Merriman was assigned to the U.S. Embassy in Paris.[101] They were optimistic and eager scholars who, according to one observer, "would humanize even a peace conference if it were possible."[102]

Morison viewed his assignment to the Russian division as fortunate and important since the success of the treaty rested in large part on how the Allies handled the question of the Soviet Union. Nicknaming themselves "The Soviet," Morison and the Russian division plunged headlong into their special assignment—to determine U.S. policy toward the Russians and to consider the applications for independence from various Baltic states. This was no easy task, for Russia had undergone a series of revolutions during the war. The czar's power had been eroding since the turn of the century, and fighting on the Eastern front had demoralized his authority. In February 1917, a military and labor uprising forced the czar from his throne, and he was replaced by a moderate socialist provisional government of quasi-democratic and western affinities, headed by Aleksandr Kerensky. In October 1917, however, Kerensky was overthrown by the more radical Bolsheviks under Lenin and Trotsky. This takeover pitched Russia into a civil war.

Moderate "white" socialists fought radical "red" socialists, and both fought remnants of the czar's supporters. During the confusion, several provinces on the Baltic Sea attempted to establish themselves as independent countries. Hence, by the end of the war, it was not clear who represented the interests of the Russian people, who should be recognized at the negotiation table, and whether the Baltic states had a legitimate claim to independence.[103]

Morison's special assignment was the Baltic problem, which required him to take a position on the Russian Revolution. Characteristically, he brought historical insights to bear on the question. "What I attempt to do," he said of his method, "is to judge every question foreign and domestic on its merits, in the light of history and common sense."[104] In the Russian case, history and common sense suggested a guarded policy as far as Morison was concerned. On the one hand, he acknowledged that "[n]either I, nor (I venture to say), anyone at present in the Department of State has enough trustworthy data on internal conditions in Soviet Russia during the past year to justify conclusions."[105] Whether "Bolshevism is a success" even "from the peasant laborer's point of view" no one could yet say. On the other hand, Morison believed that the Kerensky government was corrupt and incompetent. On the basis of conversations with American visitors to Kerensky headquarters and on the basis of the "many relations" he had with Kerensky's military advisors, Admirals Kolchak and Denikin, Morison concluded that even if Kerensky could achieve a complete military victory over the Bolsheviks, it "would only postpone a settlement of the Russian question, and prolong the agony of Russia." In his mind "these men and their supporters" were "incapable of governing Russia."[106]

Therefore, Morison urged strict neutrality toward the different Russian governments and factions. Finland, Estonia, Latvia, Lithuania, Georgia, and Armenia, however, were not Russian governments in his mind and should be assisted in their efforts toward liberty.[107] Morison based his Baltic policy on his Jeffersonian belief in democratic liberalism. Americans were "once foremost in extending fellowship to people who have freed themselves," he wrote during the conference, and "[i]t is high time that these heroic peoples, who have had to fight both German and Russian for a full year after the Armistice, received recognition from the United States Government."[108] In a few instances the United States did give official recognition to these governments, justifying Morison's faith in America's Jeffersonian ideals. On May 6, 1919, for instance, Morison recorded with delight in his diary that the United States had recognized Finland as an independent nation. More often than not, however, Morison felt increasingly helpless in bringing about the kind of postwar world he desired. On May 7, 1919, the day after his recorded excitement over Finland, Morison's diary notes, "the temperature dropped." On that day an advance copy of the war treaty came into Morison's hands, and he discussed it over dinner with "the Soviet." He and his associates were appalled by the treaty and its compromise of Wilson's peacekeeping aspirations as announced in his speech on January 22, 1917. "We are indignant, and our indignation grows as we continue reading," the diary noted. Later Morison added: "I well remember our sitting around as one of us read selected clauses aloud, and the comments—'the bastards!', 'son-of-a-bitch!', etc. We had all gone in whole-heartedly for the war on Wilsonian idealism and felt the old man let us down." The document "was a blow," Morison noted, because it suggested just how little sound intellectual ideas from trained historians had contributed to shaping the course of events at the conference.[109] "We all saw then, that very evening, what everyone knows now," he concluded, "that the treaty (as the French say) was *'plus qu'une crime, c'était une faute.'* "[110]

Morison's frustrations grew as the Big Four announced its Russian policy. From the beginning of the conference Wilson and the Allied leaders had courted the Kerensky government because of its professed democratic tendencies. Hoping to aid the white Russians against the Bolsheviks, the Allies proposed a blockade of red cities and considered armed intervention in Russia's civil war. The effect of this action, Morison warned throughout the conference, would be "to rally Russians around the Red flag" and to "stamp Bolshevism in, instead of stamping it out." He was skeptical of Kerensky and believed that bolshevism was "a great social and political force, now too strong to be forcibly suppressed." He argued that the Allies could deal from a stronger position if they opened up a dialogue with the Bolshevists and sent supplies to the war torn people of Russia. "People must get out of their heads that Bolshevism is a disease to be treated as such," Morison concluded.[111] The Big Four, however, feared the prospect of a worldwide Bolshevist revolution and instead instituted a blockade with some very disturbing features. According to Morison, relief organizer Herbert Hoover was withholding stockpiles of food from the Russian people "as a sort of bait to the Russians to 'throw the Reds out.' "[112] The use of food as political currency disgusted Morison and dampened still further his belief in the idealism of the peace efforts.[113]

The final blow to Morison's New Historical aspirations came when the Allies formalized their position on the Baltic states. Morison had proposed to Wilson a procedure for the recognition of those states that he believed was "framed in such a way as not to preclude an eventual reconciliation with a democratic Russia."[114] But the Allied leaders rejected the proposal on the grounds "that it would constitute a dismemberment of Russia" and would undercut Kerensky's power. They then "adopted the ridiculous step," Morison noted, "of recommending to Admiral Kolchak (already in retreat to Siberia!) that *he* grant autonomy to the Baltic States!"[115] When, on June 12, 1919, Kolchak replied "amiably and evasively" and the Allies accepted his request for a postponement of the issue, Morison was devastated. His diary for that day records the result: "On Boulevard de la Madeline was stopped by L. Steffens who says R. S. Baker had just announced that the Four have accepted Kolchak's reply as satisfactory, and will continue to support him.

Decide *sur-le-champ* to resign."[116] His letter of resignation was submitted three days later. Explaining that he felt the Baltic commission was a "farce" and his presence "useless," he left the Russian division for the sake of "honesty and self-respect."[117]

Morison's fellow historians on "the Soviet" admired his courage. At his farewell dinner, they presented him with a mock letter bestowing on him honors associated with the various Baltic independence movements. He was awarded "the Grand Cross of the Esthonian Solid Ivory Elephant," along with "the Rank of Lieutenant General as 251st Assistant Chief of Staff in General Yudenitch's indomitable command," and was made "the Grand Rabbi of Vilrio."[118] But despite these embellishments, Morison believed there was "nothing heroic" about his resignation.[119] Nor was he treated as a hero. On his return from the peace conference, the *New Republic* and the *Nation* ran articles condemning him as a reactionary because he "assisted the recognition of the white but democratic government of Finland." Others "are calling me a Bolshevik because I cannot stomach Kolchak and company," complained Morison. "We liberals are getting it from both sides."[120] He left Europe disillusioned with his attempt "as one poor cog" to "stop the big machine."[121]

Reversals

Morison held one last hope for the peace conference—Wilson's League of Nations. In 1917 Wilson proposed the League as a permanent institution against the prospect of future world wars. Morison believed that a League of Nations "with the United States as a leading and active member" could "remedy the major injustices of Versailles." Arguing that America "had a duty to put together the pieces she had helped to break," he applied his scholarship to defend the League proposal.[122] In a series of articles for *New Europe*, a journal dedicated to the reconstruction of the Continent after the war, Morison advocated the creation of a peacekeeping agency to safeguard the rights of the Baltic peoples. "[T]he time has come . . . to admit the Finnish Republic to the League of Nations,"[123] he wrote, and to desist from the Russian view that a "League of Nations will only be called upon if the border peoples prove recalcitrant."[124] The League must be established, instead, to protect border states from Russia. Opinion turned almost immediately against the League, however, and Morison held little hope for its ultimate establishment. If "W[oodrow]. W[ilson]. is able to get a just peace out of this welter of hate, jingoism, toryism, and nationalism," he asserted, "he is greater than G[eorge]. W[ashington]."[125]

Ironically, Albert J. Beveridge was one of the greatest obstacles to Morison and the League. He had promised to remain aloof from politics for the duration of the war so that he could complete the remaining two volumes of his Marshall biography. The League of Nations controversy, however, aroused his party loyalties and brought him out of retirement. Claiming that the Democrats were trying to play a "skin game" on "Uncle Sam," he told fellow historian and friend Clarence Alvord that he had not been "so 'het' up about anything in [his] whole life."[126] After having promised to keep America out of war in 1916, Beveridge argued, the Democrats not only broke their promise, but they now threatened to implicate Americans in the future wars of Europe. Such a blatant violation of the American trust demanded immediate response from the Republicans. In a series of private consultations, he urged presidential candidate Warren G. Harding to press not merely for revisions in Wilson's League proposal but for rejection of the League altogether.[127]

These actions encouraged some Republicans to promote Beveridge as a possible running mate for Harding. Beveridge was not interested in the vice presidency and informed party leaders of as much. He was interested in the position of secretary of state, however, and he allowed his name to circulate as a possible candidate for that post. To strengthen his claim, Beveridge joined Henry Cabot Lodge on the campaign trail against the League.[128] In a series of speeches in Boston before packed audiences, Beveridge hammered out an anti-League platform, using the kind of historical analogies that had made readers of the first two volumes of the Marshall biography suspicious of his political motives. "What a fool John [Marshall] was after all to waste his time upon so important a thing as the building of the American Nation," Beveridge proclaimed, when he was "too shortsighted" to see that one day "our friends from overseas and a lot of internationalists among us" would "propose to abolish the whole thing and go in for the 'brotherhood of man and federation of the world,' and all that sort of thing."[129]

Beveridge's campaign against the League placed him in direct conflict with Morison, who was campaigning in Boston in support of the organization. Morison expressed open chagrin at his friend's actions. If "the American people as a whole" were "as devoid of moral sense as Henry Cabot Lodge," he wrote Beveridge in a strongly worded note, that is, if "we all had the moral outlook of a louse," such politicking might be accepted "with cynical detachment." "[S]elfish" and "dastardly" attacks were being made against Wilson, Morison complained, and the League was being "emasculated" by "one of the most vicious campaigns of political revenge and wilful misrepresentation in our history."[130] Failing to "denounce" the real mistakes of the administration, Morison argued, the Republican party concentrated political attacks on a proposal for world peace that should stand above politics. According to Morison, Beveridge's complicity in such blatant partisan politics meant he was "sinning against the light, against the national conscience."[131]

Despite Morison's best efforts, Lodge won the battle over the League. Yet the victory was bittersweet for Beveridge. He had campaigned well for the Republican party and for Harding, who won handily over lackluster Democratic opponent James Cox and his young vice presidential candidate, Franklin D. Roosevelt, but Beveridge was passed over for the secretary of state position (which went to Charles Evans Hughes), and the consolation prize of an ambassadorship in Japan did not interest him. Furthermore, Beveridge had alienated some of his close political friends by questioning their integrity on the League issue. His accusation that members of his own party were "higgling, piddling, side-stepping and shifting" fools for refusing to come out fully against the League produced "a pretty ugly feeling" between him and several leading Republicans.[132]

Furthermore, by reentering the political arena, Beveridge had broken his vow to keep politics and scholarship separate. He was nervous that his use of history in support of "the cause" might prejudice readers against the final two volumes of the Marshall biography, and his fears were confirmed when friends returned the first drafts of the remaining volumes of the Marshall manuscript. "I have been reading recently in manuscript the product of a brilliant young history writer in which he says something like this," Clarence Alvord wrote: "The worst pest of democracy is the ignorant politician who lashes into a fury the passions of the people and then maintains his political position by pandering to them." Teasing Beveridge, Alvord continued, "You may have heard of him. His name is Albert J. Beveridge." This Albert is "not to be identified with his brother, the politician," he added, "who seems to me to be engaged in a somewhat similar operation at present by associating himself with an absolutely misguided senator [Lodge] of the republican party." Historians "have to earn bread which is the chief business of life," Alvord concluded sarcastically. So, "go on my friend and lash to 'fury the passions of the people,'" for in this way "the republican party will be saved and its security in the future assured."[133]

These comments found their mark. Beveridge, who had once written that "no man alive can pursue a political career and pursue a definite work of history at the same time," now began to doubt whether he could ever finish his Marshall biography.[134] He found it "exasperatingly difficult"[135] to work after the election since politics continued to take so much "precious time" from his day, and, nearing the age of sixty, he worried he would not "be alive" long enough to finish his biography.[136] "If I am," he told Alvord, "it is pretty certain that a jack rabbit in the month of March will be a sane creature compared to me."[137] Still more disturbing was his tendency to speak as if he would never write history again. "I am still toiling—toiling is the word, on my *Marshall*," he wrote constitutional historian Edwin Corwin. "When I get the old boy buried, you can bet all you are worth that I never will again undertake to do such a job."[138]

Ironically, Beveridge's return to politics was the occasion for Morison's first real impact on American politics. Affected by the "strain of confinement," Beveridge felt uninformed about certain political issues associated with the campaign of 1920 and turned to Morison for advice. "I wish you would call my attention to any books or articles of real value on questions of present importance," Beveridge wrote Morison. "I fear that I am not advised of the best, most thorough and latest discussions of real social and economic issues that affect living people." Beveridge's fears intensified as the issues in the election of 1920 became "muddier and muddier." He needed no advice from Morison on the League question, of course; on that issue Beveridge had settled his mind in opposition to Morison. He was concerned about domestic issues, however, and he made an informal practice of submitting his political speeches to Morison for review. "I wish most earnestly that, if you can find the time, you would point out to me just where I am wrong in that speech," Beveridge requested of one such effort.[139]

Beveridge's dependence on Morison grew as his involvement in the Republican campaign intensified. In January 1920 the ex-senator was nominated as the keynote speaker for the Republican party convention. In drafting a speech for the nominating committee, Beveridge made use of a comment of Morison's to the effect that Americans must keep all (not just some) American institutions honest to the principles of the Constitution. Beveridge asked if he could "crib" the idea for the convention speech.[140] Morison gave him permission, only to find that Beveridge had still bigger plans for it. After testing it on various audiences, Beveridge printed thousands of copies of a speech centered on Morison's comment and distributed them as part of the campaign literature for Republican candidates.[141] "You will find that the next Republican platform will not be much, if any different" from what is in these speeches, Beveridge told Morison. The pair even joked about Morison's possible conversion to the Republican standard and his potential appointment as "ambassador to Finland" under the watchful eye of Secretary of State Beveridge.[142]

Previously Morison might have been flattered by the thought that his ideas were to have such a direct effect on national politics; he had worked hard before the war to achieve just such an influence. But he had become disillusioned with politics and was personally devastated by the war. The failure of the League was "a blow to my millenial hopes" for a world without militarism, Morison noted.[143] "After six months on the Peace Commission," he wrote Beveridge, "I return a sadder and (I hope) wiser man." He had devoted the previous few years of his life to public causes that had borne no fruit, and he was depressed over the prospects for future projects. Understandably, then, he was reluctant to accept too much credit for political platforms, let alone a Republican one. "I am glad of your assurance that some of my ideas are in [the platform]," Morison wrote to Beveridge, but he added, "I must confess I did not recognize them." Besides, he claimed, "I remember your saying the same thing over a year ago."[144] In addition, Morison began to retreat from his ardent New Historical beliefs. Disturbed that the "world since 1914" had "gone very contrary to [his] youthful dreams," Morison blamed himself for falling prey to so naïvely optimistic a philosophy as preached by Becker and Turner.[145]

The extent of Morison's despair over the failure of political and historical reform can be measured in his "Memoranda of 1920," written as a private summary of his experiences with the peace commission. "A year of disillusion," the memoranda begins. "I found a group of ardent young intellectuals who like me had staked all their hopes on Wilson's getting away with it, and like me were sad and disgusted with it." All "idealism and unselfishness" are gone, he complained, and "the Treaty and League attacked—but by what arguments?" America had degenerated into an "orgy of extravagance, profiteering, and soaring cost of living" as well as "intolerance, hypocrisy, cruelty to foreigners, shortsighted persecution of Reds," in short, "white terror."[146]

Morison had begun the year confident that he could change the world but had returned home reeling with confusion. "Where are we going?" he asked; "What shall I do? I cannot discover, nor has anyone given me the clue." How could scholars with intellectual ideas effect change in the world? "[H]ow change this miserable system short of revolution?" he wondered. Bolshevism was not an option, for he had "learned too much of it in Paris." Perhaps "the best thing is to . . . let the world go by and trust the reactionaries to hang themselves," he suggested with resignation. As for him, there seemed nothing left to do but "cultiver le jardin." He had failed to gain recognition for the Baltics, failed to persuade Wilson of bolshevism's hold in the Soviet Union, failed to rally support for the League, and failed to write any works of history. "O year of disillusionment," he cried, "May you be the bottom of the curve."[147]

Historical Relativism

*Van Wyck Brooks, Albert Beveridge,
Lord Harmsworth and the
Historian as Expatriate*

5

The University under Attack

Morison was not the only reform-minded historian to experience feelings of disillusionment and despair in the postwar period. Many New Historians felt deceived and misled, and these feelings of betrayal were intensified by the knowledge that one of their own, a professionally trained historian, had forsaken them.[1] Woodrow Wilson's failure at the peace conference soured many historians to his vision of a progressive world and, simultaneously, to a progressive historiography. In opening the historical sessions for the Congress of Arts and Sciences at the St. Louis Exposition in 1904, Wilson had pronounced, "We have seen the dawn and the early morning hours of a new age in the writing of history, and the morning is now broadening about us into day."[2] By 1919, Wilson's bright vision for progressive history had been blackened considerably by a pessimism about historical events created, ironically, by his own failures. "[A]ll the spawn of hell roamed at will over the world and made it a shambles," wrote historian Clarence Alvord of the postwar climate, and the "pretty edifice of . . . history which had been designed and built by my contemporaries was rent asunder."[3]

Morison felt the full effect of these deflated hopes when he returned to his civilian duties in the fall of 1920. According to an autobiographical sketch, the high idealism he enjoyed prior to the war turned "sour," and he experienced the most "spiritually . . . difficult" years of his life. "We felt out of touch," Morison wrote on behalf of Bessie and himself, "repugnant alike to high finance capitalism and to communism, toward which the world seemed to be slipping."[4] Reflecting the disillusionment that compelled a "lost generation" to create a literature of rebellion, Morison described America of the early 1920s as filled with "persecution, materialism, and corruption."[5] He was especially disturbed by the conservatism of the Republican "back-to-normalcy" campaign, which encouraged Americans to turn their backs on the postwar European settlement problems on which he had worked so futilely as part of the peace commission. Bessie "could listen with an amused and serene tolerance to the mischievous political nonsense indulged in by American reactionairies," Morison later wrote, but it "aroused me to a cold fury." She felt "sorrowful, not indignant, over her contemporaries who were hagridden by fear of the future or endeavoring to escape into the past."[6] He felt only "disheartened and disgusted" by them.[7]

Feeling that he "did not ha[ve] the ability to do anything" about such conditions, Morison abandoned his public service activities.[8] The decision to do so was not made easily. He heeded to Bessie's suggestion that he give up extraneous activities and spend more time with her and the children (who now numbered three, two girls and a boy), but Morison found it difficult to suppress "the obligation to attempt a certain amount of political or social work."[9] He spoke with his father confessor and friend Smith O. Dexter about the problem. Dexter was pastor at the Episcopal church in Concord where Morison attended services and had been an important source of inspiration for Morison's prewar public service activity.[10] Under Dexter's influence, "in the spring of 1917 . . . a great rush of belief came over me like the conversions of old," Morison wrote. A veteran of reform causes, Dexter had exhorted Morison "to show by deeds, not words" that he was concerned with his fellow man.[11] It was with a great deal of apprehension, therefore, that Morison confessed to the pastor that he was tired of public reform. "Oh, those boring evenings working out a housing code for Massachusetts that the legislature refused to adopt!" he complained. "Alas, those exhausting efforts to interest young plumbers and electricians in Andrew Jackson and Daniel Webster." These public services had been motivated by "an attenuated Puritan conscience," Morison admitted, which had made it "incumbent" on him "to take part in various causes." He now neither liked the work nor believed in its effectiveness, and this new attitude concerned him.[12]

To his surprise, Morison found Dexter sympathetic. God "has given you a great gift and vocation," the pastor said. "[C]oncentrate on it, and don't wear yourself out working for good causes."[13] Bessie concurred that "the best use I could make of my life was to cultivate my natural gifts,"[14] Morison noted. Such advice shocked him into a reconsideration of his historical epistemology. For Morison the New Historian, reform activity was essential for the creation of a "usable past"; for Morison the disillusioned postwar historian, it was merely a distraction. Vowing to spend no more "long unprofitable evenings sitting on committees," Morison renounced his New History tendencies and "simply worked harder at his profession."[15] He found that his wartime reform activities had not jeopard-

ized his career too much. "President Lowell and . . . my academic supervis-
ers may have thought me a damn fool," Morison recalled, "but as long as I
did a good job teaching they were much too liberal to hold the [peace
conference] resignation against me."[16]

Yet Harvard proved frustrating. In the first place, he confronted the same
personality conflicts in the history department as had existed before the
war. In his opinion, Channing continued to overshadow him. While Morison
and the rest of the department were in Europe, Channing had been obliged
to increase his teaching load, and he was unhappy about it. Wondering aloud
whether the "Great Work" "ever will be done," he sent letters to Morison at
the peace conference attempting to lure him back to campus. Part of his
strategy was to keep Morison informed about the health of various department members, tempting him with the possibility of openings for a full
professorship in the near future. Hence, Channing confided to his young
charge at various times: "Turner is looking thin,"[17] or "Bushnell Hart
appears to be ageing very rapidly," or "Abbott goes around enveloped in
overcoats and silk scarves as if he were tottering on the brink."[18]

Wilbur Abbott, a student of English history who had been called from
Yale to fill a spot vacated by Harold Laski, was one of two new members in
the history department.[19] Laski's short and controversial tenure at Harvard
had begun in 1916 when he came from Oxford to teach political science.
Having earned his doctorate at the age of twenty-three, Laski was filled with
youthful enthusiasm for the job and attempted to graft some of Oxford's
open-minded liberalism onto the Harvard curriculum. "Laski had a provocative influence on many undergraduates," Morison wrote. "At his house
could be heard some of the best conversation in Cambridge," while "his
experiments in academic freedom furnished much of the conversation
elsewhere." When the Boston police strike of 1919 occurred, Laski addressed
a crowd of strikers' wives, praising "their husbands' contribution to political
science in philosophical language" tinged with radicalism. "Then, things
broke loose," according to Morison. President Lowell had spoken against
the police strike and had even authorized two hundred students to join the
temporary police force. "Laski was a traitor and a Bolshevik," the alumni
declared, and pressure was put on the president to dismiss him. Despite the
fact that the British scholar was persona non grata to him, Lowell "stood
firm" behind him; but frustrated with the efforts to stifle "free expression"
in America, Laski eventually left Harvard of his own accord for the University of London.[20]

If Channing's comments about Abbott's health reflected an insensitivity
toward Abbott's situation, his remarks concerning a second new member of
the department were still more callous. During Morison's absence in Europe, a graduate of the University of Wisconsin, Frederick Merk, had been
hired to help in American and European history.[21] Merk was a favorite of
Turner's, and rumor had it that Turner was pushing for his rapid promotion
so that he might accede to the next vacated departmental chair. Channing,

who was likely to be the next retired chair, reacted predictably. Not only did he take an immediate dislike to Merk, he sought to sabotage his career by advancing Morison's name wherever possible when promotion and tenure decisions were being made. This placed Morison in the awkward position of seeming in competition with Merk, thus not only straining Morison and Merk's relationship but also Morison's relationship with Turner.[22]

The strain between Morison and Turner became apparent within the first months of Morison's return to Harvard. Because of his recent experience with postwar conditions in Russia, Morison was invited to attend a discussion group for graduate students led by Turner on the Bolshevik revolution. Arguing for the merits of democracy over communism, Turner cited cornhuskings on the American frontier as proof that mutual help tendencies had democratic rather than communist origins. Morison, who later claimed that Turner had asked him to attend "in order to heckle him and start discussion," came "loaded to the bear" by his own account and "discharged two shots, one of which went home." Morison noted that Prince Kropotkin of Russia had cited the cornhusking activity in Provence as proof of "the ineradicable communism of human nature" and added with mock condescension, "I think you [Turner and Kropotkin] are both wrong, and that the determining factor is the ear of corn that has to be husked."[23] Turner "didn't like that at all," recalled one student, and in his rejoinder Turner "tried to cast ridicule on Prince Kropotkin's communist cornhuskers."[24] It became painfully obvious to the audience, in the process, that Turner had never heard of Provencals or their cornhusking activities. He was greatly embarrassed by the entire affair. Morison claimed years later that "the incident never in the least disturbed our friendship or my admiration for Turner," but one student who attended the discussion remembered that Morison clearly "baited" Turner, and that Turner was visibly angered by the exchange.[25]

Even Morison's relationships with normally steady colleagues faltered. On January 6, 1919, Teddy Roosevelt died, and Morison invited the late president's "avid supporter" Albert Bushnell Hart to speak to History 32 (Survey of American History).[26] "As Bushnell was a great friend and follower of Roosevelt," Morison noted in his diary, "I asked him to do this, and it was quite impressive," he added. Hart took as his theme the "greatness" of Roosevelt and developed a quasi-deterministic philosophy to suggest that the exceptional qualities of his subject were evident from his earliest days and came to fruition in college. "[I]t annoyed me personally," Morison wrote, "as he told the boys in effect that if they weren't popular and prominent in college like T.R. they were not likely to succeed." Distinctly unpopular as an undergraduate, Morison was sensitive to these remarks, and his sensitivity was heightened by the unique conditions under which the course was being conducted: "I was giving the course in my private's uniform," he noted, "and was much embarrassed as there were a number of junior officers in History 32."[27]

Morison angered other colleagues by refusing to play an active role in departmental affairs. "Rarely did Sam speak" at departmental meetings, and he "assumed no major administrative responsibilities," remembered one associate.[28] He was "stiff, unbending, and rather taciturn" and "showed no desire for intimacy," recalled another.[29] And he rarely socialized with his colleagues or invited them to share his private life.[30] But most disturbing of all, his teaching was suffering. One former pupil noted that "Morison kept students at a distance both by his manner and teaching style, lecturing more and more from typed notes in a fluent but uninspired" way. Where once he had excited students, he now did little to inspire "student awe and worship."[31] He paid still less attention to graduate students. Whereas some of his colleagues prepared a large number of graduate students, Morison encouraged very few and could not always recall the names of those he did. This undoubtedly created a resentment on the part of Morison's colleagues, who, by process of elimination, were forced to accept students whose dissertation topics were more suited to Morison, but whose temperaments were not.[32]

Morison's indifferent attitude in the classroom was a reflection of his disappointment over the apathy of postwar students on the one hand and his inability as a frustrated New Historian to do anything about it on the other. "The student body, deeply affected by post-war disillusion and the decline of moral standards, in part took refuge in work, in part in dissipation," Morison noted later, and this caused a kind of philistinism to arise among them. Many of them should have gone straight into business, he added, since they will be "no better businessmen or citizens for having attended college. Having their business careers unreasonably postponed, they try to make a business out of College activities," he complained, "and succeed only too well."[33] Other disaffected intellectuals in the 1920s agreed with Morison's assessments. In 1922, Upton Sinclair published *The Goose Step: A Study of American Education*, in which he charged colleges with being "subservient supporters of capitalistic society, purveyors to Wall Street, recruiters of reaction, [and] obstacles to democratic progress." Professors, according to Sinclair, were powerless to resist the large business interests that were inveighing on traditional academic freedoms; they had no choice but to "fall into step" or lose their jobs.[34] Morison noted in sad concurrence that at Harvard "a vociferous minority felt that he who pays the academic piper should call the tune—that, if private capital provided the money for our academic band, they must play nothing but patriotic songs." Harold Laski was a victim of this reactionary climate, Morison noted, as were other professors across the country.[35] Columbia University had dismissed two professors with pro-German sympathies during the war, which prompted the resignation of a third in protest, New Historian Charles Beard.[36]

Increasingly, frustrated historians argued that scholarly work of integrity could not be done in universities. New Historians who had once believed so ardently in the possibilities of effecting change in the present by educational investigations of the past, now eschewed America's colleges as "literary annexes to Wall Street."[37] They called for a new, "New History," one based outside the university and in distinct challenge to it. Van Wyck Brooks, a classmate of Morison's at Harvard, led the attack. In a seminal article entitled "On Creating a Usable Past," Brooks argued that American universities were too responsive to foundations and private organizations that (largely through contributions to endowments) promoted "commercialism" in American education. These groups encouraged professors to produce dull monographs on specialized and self-serving topics, making little allowance for "clarity and pungency of expression" or the needs of the popular reader. In Europe, Brooks noted, "the professor is free from these inhibitions; he views the past through the spectacles of his own intellectual freedom," while in America restrictive tradition teaches him to put "a gloss upon the past that renders it sterile for the living mind." And, according to Brooks, no university was more prone to such professional materialism than Harvard.[38] In "Harvard and American Life," written shortly after his graduation, Brooks had argued that commercialism and specialization were gradually causing Harvard intellectuals to "mistake 'getting a living' for living itself."[39]

Other intellectuals joined Brooks in this attack against university professors of history. Journalist and historian James Truslow Adams wrote that the fundamental idea underlying our civilization is "business profit." One need only read the works of college professors, he noted, "to see how the new leaven of the business ideals of profits and 'service' are working in our academic minds." Harvard, in particular, led the way in giving "scholastic benediction to business."[40] Adams, who had been a Wall Street executive before becoming a man of letters, was offered teaching positions at several American universities (including Harvard) during his career, but he turned them all down.[41] He preferred to identify himself with a new group of "amateur" historians who worked outside the university and maintained an adversarial relationship to all institutions of higher education. The successful careers of journalist-historians such as Bernard De Voto, Frederick Lewis Allen, Henry F. Pringle, Marquis James, and Claude Bowers confirmed his belief that noteworthy work in history could be conducted independent of commercially minded colleges.[42]

This antiestablishment logic revived Morison's lingering suspicions about his place in academics and encouraged him to resuscitate plans to either teach on a part-time basis or to give up teaching altogether and write history unmolested by tenure committees and professional reviewers. Nowhere was this rejection of professional identity more obvious than in his attitude toward the academic projects on which he had been at work for many years. In 1920, Morison confided to his friend Albert Beveridge that he was having trouble writing in the academic climate of philistinism in which he was both victim and participant. "The History of Massachusetts is going on," he noted, "but one has to work so hard these days to keep one's head above the cost of living, that I do not know when I shall get it done."[43] Different explanations went out to his professional colleagues who were beginning to question the "long gap" in his scholarship, but the bottom line was that he had not completed a major history for professional consumption in seven years, and he showed signs of a permanent inability to work effectively within university walls.[44]

History for "He-Men"

Postwar disillusionment influenced not only where New Historians chose to work (outside the university), but what they chose to write. Even in their attacks on the "detached facts" of scientific historians, New Historians had never abandoned faith in objectivity; they simply wished to employ facts in the service of contemporary reform. But in the postwar period, a growing number of New Historians began to doubt even the objectivity of the past. Carl Becker admitted in 1920 that he had "always been susceptible to the impression of the futility of life," and, in light of the war, was now "easily persuaded to regard history as no more than the meaningless resolution of blind forces which struggling men . . . do not understand and cannot control."[45] James Harvey Robinson echoed Becker's skepticism in a retrospective piece on the New History movement. "History does not seem to stop any more," he wrote in his article "After Twenty Years." It is as difficult "to tell where to start as where to stop," and "all the historian can do nowadays is to leave off, with a full conviction that he may have played up merely specious occurrences and have overlooked vital ones." In a confession revealing the important transitions occurring within New History, Robinson concluded, "I have come to think that no such thing as objective history is possible."[46]

Given this rejection of objectivity in history, it is not surprising that New Historians in the 1920s turned gradually toward a form of "historical relativism" in their writings. Drawing its title ironically from a paradigm revolution in the sciences (created by Einstein's "Theory of Relativity"), historical relativism emphasized the "relative" or subjective quality of all intellectual traditions, including history. According to this new philosophy, an appreciation of the "point of view" of the observer of history was not only necessary for a valid interpretation of the past, it was unavoidable. Objective, absolute history was a chimera; all history was conditioned by the "climate of opinion" in which the historian worked. An elaboration of the presentist tendencies of the New History movement, therefore, the "relativist" outlook acknowledged the plurality of historical interpretations. In addition, historical relativism comported nicely with criticisms of the exclusivity of university historians, since it claimed that "everyman" (to borrow Carl Becker's phrase) should become "his own historian." In an age in which the personal point of view of the observer carried as much weight as what he or she observed, academic training conferred no special status on the observer.[47]

In its most extreme form, this "subjectivism" implied that history was a product of the imagination and had no ontological significance outside the perceiver's mind. For Van Wyck Brooks, for instance, history was a creative act subject to constant revision depending on the mood of the historian. If the history "our professors offer us is too sterile and unusable," Brooks wrote in "On Creating a Usable Past," then the "past should be rewritten. . . . If we need another past so badly," he added, "is it not conceivable that we might discover one, that we might even invent one?" Although the notion of "inventing" the past made many historians nervous (what, they justifiably asked, would separate them from writers of historical fiction?), Brooks's radically subjective vision convinced some to expand their conceptions of what qualified as important for the study of history. In particular, the call for a new appreciation of "everyman's" perspective (especially those outside universities) awakened some to the need for a similar open-mindedness toward the past. "Look back and you will see, drifting in and out of the books of history, appearing and vanishing in the memoirs of more aggressive and more acceptable minds," Brooks wrote, "all manner of queer geniuses, wraith-like personalities that have left behind them sometimes a fragment or so that has meaning for us now." These undervalued figures, ignored by academic historians and living in "a limbo of the non-elect," deserved to have their interests served according to Brooks. They merely required the services of a new breed of social historians with an appreciation for history's voiceless "little people" and with the courage to act as so many Davids against "the Goliaths of . . . philistinism" and established academic convention.[48]

Perhaps no one had conveyed the potential rewards of writing from a personal perspective outside the university more than Morison's friend Albert Beveridge. Although he considered himself an objective historian, Beveridge as a former politician still prided himself on understanding the "common man," and he attempted to make the figure of John Marshall accessible to the average reader. He did so by attempting to elaborate the hidden contexts of history, by "ascertainment of all the facts, little and big, concerning every character, great or small; and more than that—these facts must include the manner of living of the masses of the people."[49] This attempt to re-create the "color and atmosphere" of the eighteenth century, to be "truthful" yet "entertaining" in conveying the social history of Marshall's era, paid rich dividends. To Beveridge's great delight the last volumes of the Marshall biography received the Pulitzer Prize for biography in 1920.[50]

No one was more pleased and envious than Morison. Congratulating Beveridge on his success, he asked his friend to what it could most be attributed. The professed "scientific" historian offered advice ironically reminiscent of Brooks's philosophy of historical relativism: do not write to satisfy an academic audience but the general public; write what you feel in a language that the great reading public can understand, Beveridge explained, and success will follow. "The trouble with you professors," he told Morison, "is that you write for each other. I write for people almost completely ignorant of American history" who share interests in law and judicial decisions. Beveridge chose Marshall as a subject, he explained, because his own experience in the law made the chief justice personally appealing to him. This personal enthusiasm for the subject matter of history undoubtedly transferred to the written page, he concluded, and it was enthusiastic prose, not prose written from a sense of duty, that sold books.[51]

Beveridge urged Morison to consider dropping his academic pretensions and writing the kind of general history in which he, Adams, and Brooks were engaged. Morison had little to lose. The editors at Houghton Mifflin were still waiting, impatiently now, for the manuscript of his *History of Massachusetts*.[52] The work had languished for five years and the few chapters that had been circulated to readers at Harvard had gone unappreciated. On the basis of Beveridge's suggestion, therefore, Morison proposed a new direction for his volume, one based on more personal considerations. Since his boyhood, Morison informed his editors, he had had a "deep, almost passionate" love of the sea, one of Massachusetts's most valuable assets.[53] Would it be possible, he asked, to replace the scholarly history of Massachusetts he was currently writing with a more popular maritime history of the state?[54]

To his surprise, the editors agreed, and Morison immediately began work on a new volume for popular consumption. He described the effort to Beveridge as an experiment with far-reaching implications for his career. It was an attempt to "dish up a bit of unwritten history in a form and style that the dear reading public—especially 'he-men' would come to read," he said. "If they take the bait, I shall go ahead along the same line," he added, "if not, I shall return to the small clientele which appreciated my first book."[55] Its success or failure might determine whether he continued in academics and at Harvard or whether he pursued a career independent of the university and in the literary tradition of the disaffected historical relativists.

The Maritime History of Massachusetts, 1783–1860 (1921) eventually validated Beveridge's advice. "Written in one swoop, on a wave of euphoria," Morison noted, the book took only eleven months to complete. It had a magical, "strange career," according to friends, "bordering on the weird." For five years Morison had labored in vain to find appropriate sources for the kind of political history of Massachusetts he felt he was expected to write. When he began writing a maritime history, however, obscure references materialized in unexpected places. Searching the North Shore of Massachusetts for customs records and ships' logs, Morison would happen upon "some ancient mariner's sea chest painted robin's-egg blue in the garret of some old white house." Although the chest might not have been opened for a hundred years, marvelled one witness, "the first or second log book or loose-leaf document his hand touched would be the one he wanted." He "made no pretense of understanding these strange happenings," but they contributed to the pleasure and ease of the enterprise.[56] Nor was the actual writing difficult. When "inspiration lagged," Morison noted, "I would take one of my books of printed sea chanteys to the piano, where Bessie banged out the tune while I bawled 'Blow the Man Down' or one of the other deep-sea classics."[57]

If *The Maritime History of Massachusetts* seemed to write itself, it was perhaps because Morison expressed long-repressed feelings in it. Since his adoption of the New History philosophy, Morison had undertaken historical projects with only demonstrable political or professional applications. His frustration with "good causes" in the postwar period ended his personal commitment to reform, but lingering New Historical sensibilities and confusions over his professional identity created a paralyzing guilt. It is not coincidental that Morison overcame this paralysis at a time when Freudian psychology was influencing every aspect of American intellectual life. Historical relativism owed much to the application of Freud's principles of ego development and id enhancement, and the subjectivity professed by Brooks and others was nothing more than an acknowledgment of Freud's psychoanalytic advice to "listen to the voice within."[58] Beveridge's counsel that Morison should forget what he thought he should feel and write what he did feel, justified a "self-indulgent" behavior that eventually liberated his art. For the first time in his career, Morison followed the "impulse" to write "from within," and the results converted him wholeheartedly to the historical relativist standard.[59]

"Within" Morison felt despair for his age and nostalgia for a time when war was not so frightening, materialism not so pervasive, and political idealism not so impotent. Written with sentimental rather than practical intentions, *The Maritime History of Massachusetts* tells of a better day when Morison's region and his family were at the height of their prosperity. For Massachusetts, "better days" meant the great age of shipping from the Revolution to the Civil War. According to Morison, between 1783 and 1860 Massachusetts achieved a great victory over geography. "Nature seemed to doom Massachusetts to insignificance," he wrote, "to support perhaps a line of poor fishing stations and hardscrabble farms, half-starved between the two hungry mouths of Hudson and St. Lawrence." Through a "miracle of human enterprise," however, Massachusetts residents created a thriving maritime economy. Her codfishermen exacted "tribute from the Banks" and fed the world, Morison wrote; her whalers pursued "their 'gigantic game' around the Horn"; her merchants discovered "new, virgin markets and sources of supply in the Pacific"; her trading vessels opened Atlantic homes to the delicacies of "the Canton market"; and her shipbuilders created the most majestic sailing vessels the world has ever known. These years also constituted a golden age for Morison's family, a period when Eliots actually influenced rather than merely reminisced about public affairs. Both the family fortune and the family appreciation for the sea, Morison acknowledged with self-indulgent pride, were "inherited from remote ancestors in the old China trade." Morison grew up with reminders of the lucrative China trade all around him in his 44 Brimmer Street home, and the stories he heard exchanged there of the once busy wharf life, when Eliot family members gathered with other prominent merchants at the lunch hour to socialize and count their cargoes, figured prominently in the book. These developments ushered in a great era of prosperity and pride, which, from the vantage of 1921, seemed the state's "Golden Age."[60]

The importance of maritime culture for his region and his family made the writing of *The Maritime History of Massachusetts* an intensely personal experience for Morison. An attempt to recover an aspect of his lost childhood, the work required a special persona appropriate to that need. The attitude of the scholar was unhelpful, since scholars traditionally overvalued "literary" genius and, in the case of New England, studied only established writers such as Emerson, Thoreau, and Hawthorne. Another genius, a more pervasive one according to Morison, was expressed by the "Yankee" mind. That mind "open[ed] up new channels of trade, set new enterprises on foot, and erect[ed] a political system to consolidate them," thereby producing the kind of thought by which "the grist of history is ground." To understand Massachusetts properly in the period between the Revolution and the Civil War, Morison noted, one must understand the "tough, tenacious but restless race" of Yankees who farmed her seas. Accordingly, Morison adopted a Yankee persona to tell his story, dropping all scholarly trappings that might diminish the effectiveness of his gruff and candid Yankee voice. Hence, he described in vivid detail the rough, dirty, and dangerous aspects of seafaring—the brutality of "cold-blooded, heartless fiends" who stalked the quarterdeck, the "meanness and rascality of skippers," and the nauseating effects of a steady diet of "hard-tack, molasses, and 'salt horse.' "[61] Morison's "whaleboats stink and his fishermen sweat" one reader aptly noted.[62]

The Maritime History of Massachusetts revealed how far Morison had strayed from the New Historical impulses that had attracted him to the project in the prewar period. No longer enamored of political idealism, Morison now measured a government's worth by its ability to maintain sea culture and commerce. Hence he attacked his favorite Jefferson for the Embargo of 1807, because it "sacrificed the commercial profits of Massachusetts and her good-will" without achieving its expressed aim of "coercing the belligerent nations." Jefferson's defense of the principle of law in the face of its ineffectiveness was even more damaging to his reputation in *The Maritime History of Massachusetts*. The embargo was so unworkable "as a measure of coercion," Morison wrote, that "Jefferson's persistent faith in it could be explained only by enmity to American shipping, or by pathological causes." The Yankee perspective also encouraged a new respect on the part of Morison for John Marshall, who was described as having understood perfectly the irony of an embargo declared in the name of "free trade and sailors' rights" by "men who rarely ever saw a ship or sailor." Given the misplaced idealism of the embargo, Morison asked, "[i]s it surprising that . . . maritime Massachusetts followed Chief Justice Marshall" rather than the party of Jefferson?[63]

The very language of The Maritime History of Massachusetts revealed the extent to which it was a work of liberation and escape for its author. When read in the psycholiterary terms popular in the 1920s, the project represents a return to the comfort of a prepolitical time in Morison's life, a retreat to a boyhood in Boston and the maternal breast of the "ocean mother." The Oedipal language of Morison's writing suggests the ambivalence of this return. On the one hand, Massachusetts is a "great nursery" where the "ocean mother" (that "old husky nurse"), "suckled" her sons until it was time for them to follow the sea. Maine is her "first-born," Connecticut her "offspring," and in her "lap" sprawled Boston, "long since outgrown the small rocky peninsula of her birth, and ever in need of a new suit of clothes." Her fledglings, the Elizabeth Islands and Martha's Vineyard, surpassed even "their mother state" for "sir[ing]" sons of the sea. On the other hand, Massachusetts is a temptress, a sexual earth goddess, whose "flattish curves" and "gentle contours" force sailors to do her bidding. Cape Cod and Cape Anne are "two giant limbs thrown seaward . . . to guide seaborne commerce into Boston's fruitful embrace." The "long sandy finger" of Plum Island "reached out seaward" to "beckon" into "her deep, landlocked inner harbor" those who escaped these arms. "Neither imposing nor spectacular," Morison noted, the Massachusetts coast had a "subtle charm" that could be deadly. The "perfumed breath" of Boston harbor lured farm boys to the sea, where they either lost their lives or returned more mature and permanently "cured" of "wanderlust." Even experienced captains who "dared approach" too close to the seductive shores of Massachusetts found themselves in peril. "A mistake of a quarter-point fetched up many a good ship on Cohasset rocks or the Graves," Morison wrote.[64]

This ambivalence toward the sea, suggested by the mixed imagery of mother-protector and mother-destroyer, reflected a conflict at the heart of New England economic life. On the one hand, New Englanders recognized "their dependence on the sea, which, for two hundred years . . . was the sustenance of Massachusetts." On the other hand, the Yankee reliance on sail caused New Englanders to adopt an "ostrich-like" attitude toward the development of steamers, which eventually replaced sailboats as cargo carriers. In the clipper ships, "the long-suppressed artistic impulse of a practical, hard-worked race burst into flower," Morison noted, but these vessels proved as ephemeral as "monuments carved from snow." As the commercial center of water transport changed from the east coast to the Midwest and steamboats raced up and down the Mississippi River in defiance of winds and currents, New England wind-aided vessels became increasingly obsolete. Out of sheer stubbornness many Yankee seaman "remained faithful to sail for the rest of their lives," but the majority, Morison noted, eventually abandoned the sea to follow prevailing westward winds to the farmlands of the Great Plains.[65]

In his portrayal of the decline of the clipper ships, Morison demonstrated the power that subjective writing could have. The sleek, square-rigged vessels these merchants once piloted, whose hulks still rotted in Boston harbor, came alive again in Morison's prose, in nostalgic, dreamlike visions recovered from the past through squinting, clouded eyes. Morison concluded his work thus:

> Out of the mist in Massachusetts Bay comes riding a clipper ship, with the effortless speed of an albatross. Her proud commander keeps skysails and studdingsails set past Boston light. . . . Colored pennants on Telegraph Hill have announced her coming to all who know the code. . . . The 'old man' stalks the quarterdeck in top hat and frock coat, with the proper air of detachment; but the first mate is as busy as the devil in a gale of wind. . . . A warp is passed from capstan to stringer, and all hands on the capstan-bars walk her up to the wharf with the closing chantey of a deep-sea voyage.[66]

From his imagination, Morison reconstructed the "effortless" clipper ship, sustaining an impression of its timelessness by collapsing the distinctions of time and place. This tendency reflected his new attitude toward history—one that catered to his own sentimental attachments and those of his audience. If clipper ships could not be physically resurrected in the twentieth century, at least they could be figuratively revived through the agency of historical relativism. Adopting the realist writer's pursuit of the "inner psychology" of his subject, Morison's brand of historical relativism was aphilosophical; it provided no usurping ideology or moral system by which to judge events. Filtered through a complex matrix of intentions and deep psychological influences, knowledge remained fragmentary, scattered, and impressionistic. Subjectivity displaced objective order; emotion precluded rational analysis.

Morison's experiment in "historical relativism" paid off nicely for him. *The Maritime History of Massachusetts* was praised as a "fresh, sparkling" contribution to nautical literature, with the "odor of the sea" about it.[67] It was geared for "old salts living on . . . beached keels in New England's seaports," recognized one reviewer, who applauded the "novelistic" devices that "brought back to [average readers] the days of their youth and glory." The "highly visualized descriptions," the weathered "portraits of people," the narrative "that raced like tall ships," and the authentic "dialogue" all contributed to the effect. The work was pleasurable, readable, personal, and nonideological and attracted the sort of national audience Morison had long desired.[68] A large-paper limited edition book at fifteen dollars a copy was sold out before publication. The trade edition at five dollars a copy went through numerous reprintings and netted over ten thousand dollars in royalties.[69]

Morison had many people to thank for the reception of the book. Supreme Court Justice Louis Brandeis undoubtedly contributed enormously to its success by referring to it as "the best little history ever written by an American."[70] But Morison had Beveridge to thank primarily. "The book is written . . . under your inspiration," he told his friend. "[Y]our advice 'Don't write for fellow-professors!' has been ringing in my head ever since."[71] If Morison did not "cramp" himself with political or scholarly obligations but wrote with "fairness, accuracy, and proportion," Beveridge predicted, his work would "sell very well indeed."[72] He was correct in his assessment and only failed to anticipate the negative reaction of professional journals, who either ignored it as not suitable for review or criticized its technique. The reviewer for the *American Historical Review*, for instance, cited Morison for carelessness in his use of Federal shipping statistics and in his interpretation of several maritime statutes.[73]

In light of the book's popular readership, a few negative reviews by professionals could be dismissed as scholarly nit-picking. The success of the work confirmed Morison in his belief that his future as a writer of history might lie outside the university. He began to fantasize about resigning his post at Harvard to write history exclusively in a personally designed bungalow on the coast of Maine. "I'd build me a house of field stone . . . sheltered from the northerly winds by the high wood cape, with a library two stories high and tall French windows looking down Blue Hill Bay to Isle of Haut," Morison told his friend Lincoln Colcord. "I would keep an auxiliary ketch or schooner to go to Boston in twice a year, and to cruise in when I felt like it," he added, "and have complete immunity from motor cars, jazz, radio, etc. etc. Thousands of people situated like me in Europe have done just that," he concluded optimistically.[74]

Historian in Exile

Morison's escapist fantasies were not unique among historians in the postwar period. Disillusioned New Historians not only withdrew from universities and retreated into highly relativistic forms of writing, they also sought to escape the very society they had once struggled so tirelessly to reform. Many of these "expatriates" went to Europe, where they joined other disillusioned writers and poets in a culture of renunciation. In Paris, Harold E. Stearns in 1921 edited a symposium entitled *Civilization in the United States*, which Morison later described as: "one long moan by thirty solemn young men on American mediocrity, sterility, conformity, and [the] smug prosperity" of American academic life. Van Wyck Brooks took an active part in this expatriate project, as did other historians without academic affiliation, such as James Truslow Adams, Malcolm Cowley, Lewis Mumford, and H.L. Mencken. Speaking on the decline of history in American universities, Hendrik Willem Van Loon argued that Clio had been afforded no special place of prominence by American universities interested only in "the practical sides of life." Because he believed that scholars had failed to recognize that history "like cooking or fiddling is primarily an art" that "embellishes life" and "is without the slightest utilitarian value," Van Loon urged them to quit their academic posts and travel to Europe to escape the "scientific historical machine" that was destroying "popular interest" in history in the United States.[75]

Morison was not immune to this argument. His success with *The Maritime History of Massachusetts* convinced him that history was primarily an artistic endeavor, and his disgust with teaching at Harvard made him ever receptive to alternative employment. Unlike Van Loon, Brooks, Adams, and others, however, Morison could not drop out of the mainstream completely. He had a family to feed, and he was still very concerned about his career. But in 1921 an opportunity presented itself that seemed ideal for Morison's purposes. That year Oxford University announced that an endowed chair of American history had been created under the supervision of Lord Rothermere in memory of his son Harold Vyvyan Harmsworth, who had been killed in the war. The Harmsworth chair was to go to an American citizen capable of giving lectures on American history. Morison's name was one of many placed in nomination by a committee of American university presidents, and he was asked by George Harvey, the American ambassador to Britain, if he would consider applying.[76]

Oxford was an attractive opportunity for several reasons. In the first place, it represented a convenient way to escape the petty materialism of American intellectual life in the 1920s and to participate in the rich alternative tradition of expatriatism in Europe. In the second place, it was an easy way to escape the American university system without abandoning academics. Oxford had a reputation as a "university where learning is no mere handmaiden to church or state or business, but a proud and independent goddess."[77] Indeed, many disaffected intellectuals in America were actively campaigning to reform the American university to conform with the Oxford educational system. Led by Frank Aydelotte, a former Rhodes scholar at Oxford and professor at the Massachusetts Institute of Technology, this crusade attempted to substitute Oxford's tutorial system of learning for the utilitarian, German-based pedagogical methods prevalent in American universities. In particular, the tutorial system at Oxford required students to take responsibility for their own educations by deciding what was to be read, in how much detail, and from what point of view. By throwing students "largely on [their] own resources," the Oxford system increased their confidence in the relevancy of their opinions while developing respect for the relativity of knowledge. "In an American university [students take] courses," Aydelotte concluded; "at Oxford [they study] a subject."[78]

Neither were Oxford professors subject to the kind of pedagogical scrutiny that had haunted Morison's colleague Laski at Harvard. "No heresy hunt, or Red raid, or efficiency expert disturbs the Oxford professor," Morison wrote in appreciation of the university. At Oxford, one could write and lecture on topics of personal even idiosyncratic interest without fear "from the unreasoning and malicious criticism that every American university has to bear from Press and public." And at Oxford Morison would have an opportunity to reduce his academic workload and thereby create the time he needed to write what he wished. The "beauty of the Oxford system," he noted, is that "Oxford chairs are usually given to men who have outlived the desire to teach undergraduate students," and to those who wish to retire to the relative obscurity of an academic position. While American professors taught for thirty or thirty-five weeks a year, the Oxford don taught for only twenty-four, spending the remainder of the year on personal projects. "The only chair I ever used at Harvard was a desk-chair in my office, between lectures," Morison noted, but at Oxford, the endowed chair had "evolved into a well-upholstered sofa, which the professor is forced to leave only 42 times a year, to deliver his statutory minimum lectures."[79]

All these perceptions influenced Morison's decision to apply for the Harmsworth chair. The tenure of the position was peculiar and the subject somewhat superfluous to the Oxford curriculum, so (as Morison put it) "all the eminent American professors who were approached declined with thanks."[80] As his name rose to the top of the list of those being considered for the position, Morison requested that Albert Beveridge send a letter to George Harvey (Beveridge's close friend), "intimating that I am-kind-er-willin."[81] Beveridge gladly wrote the letter of recommendation, calling Morison "the finest type of American manhood," a brilliant scholar, and the future head of his profession.[82] He warned Morison privately, however, that he must not completely abandon his Americanness or become subsumed by British ideas. He feared that Morison would "desert" Americans to "become a cog in the elaborate machine of British propaganda,"[83] and, that as a result, he would be Anglicized like so many American expatriates before him had been. For "God's sake," Beveridge advised, "don't let them infect you with their famous 'common race' virus."[84]

Morison assured Beveridge that he had little to fear from British propaganda. "I grew up in the stale Victorian atmosphere of the Back Bay," Morison noted. "I have traveled in England, studied in England, lived in England, visited the houses of the great in England." And yet, "at an impressionable and uncritical age I remained a gen-u-wine Amurrican." Therefore he asked, "what in God's name could make me a Johnny Bull now?"[85] All he wished to do at Oxford, he asserted, was to teach and write "some honest American history of sufficient excellence to stand the test of time."[86]

After several months of waiting, Morison received confirmation late in 1921 that the appointment was his. He telephoned Beveridge to thank him for his support and then informed his academic superiors that he would once again need an indefinite leave of absence from Harvard.[87] Lowell was cautiously supportive, but Channing was not. Assuming that Morison was still disgruntled with his status in the department as an "assistant," Channing offered to allow Morison to teach "anything" he wished. "I have a sort of idea that you are a little tired of History 23: The History of Massachusetts and would like to do something else," he wrote. "If I am right, please say so . . . ! [O]pen your mind fully and freely to the 'Old Man,' " he added paternally, "and do it at once."[88] When it seemed clear that Morison was determined to go, however, Channing tried to discourage him about the virtues of an expatriate life in England. "You will have a nice time for a couple of years," Channing predicted, "but the English are insular and have slight interest in the U.S.A.—except from a money point of view." He reiterated that professional opportunities might soon be available in the department, and Morison needed to be nearby to take advantage of them.[89]

Although such logic had been persuasive enough to attract Morison to Harvard from Berkeley before the war, it could not now keep him from sailing for England. Determined to escape Harvard, to pursue his own brand of subjective history, and to join America's intellectuals abroad, he set sail for Europe in the spring of 1922. On his arrival he was met by officials from Oxford, who welcomed him with a reception and settled him comfortably in his lodgings at Christ Church. At the age of thirty-four, he was the youngest full professor at Oxford and the most optimistic about the advantages of his position. "Compared with the strenuous academic life of America," he wrote friends, the Oxford chair would be his "bed of roses."[90]

The Retreat from Relativism

*Albert Beveridge, Charles Beard,
Edward Channing and
the Debunking Mode*

6

The Oxford Interlude

Morison never forgot his first "soft and sheltered days within Oxford walls."[1] He informed friends at home that "Christ Church was a revelation of what academic life might be at its best," and he quickly came to regard Oxford "with deep affection as a second *alma mater*." He especially loved the "mellow social life of the University," including "history luncheons where everything but history was discussed" and conversations with "the most humane and intelligent group of people" he had ever known.[2] Invited to participate in a wide range of social activities (folk festivals, dances, even fox hunts), Morison adjusted quickly to the peculiarly British ways of doing things.[3] Bessie had a somewhat harder time, since, as Morison later remarked, the social life was "geared to men, who were generally too much absorbed in scholarship, teaching, and academic politics to appreciate a beautiful and intelligent woman." Yet even she adjusted well enough to produce a series of sketches entitled "Oxford Days," which proclaimed the "unending attractions" of the British university. To both Morison and his wife, Oxford "seemed a dwelling place of light."[4]

Morison's first academic responsibility as the Harmsworth Professor of American History was an inaugural address, which he delivered in May 1922. Entitled "A Prologue to American History," it was presented to an expectant crowd, presided over by the Vice Chancellor of Oxford, Dr. Lewis Richard Farnell, who "took a very dim view" of the Harmsworth chair. The hall was sparsely filled with a handful of American students, who "felt it a duty to rally round a compatriot," a "sprinkling of English students and dons who hoped to be amused but feared the worst," and a smattering of

"good ladies who attend every free lecture at Oxford." He began by addressing the fears of Beveridge, Channing, and others that he might use the chair
to revive some of his New History concerns, such as an Anglo-American
sponsored League of Nations. Acknowledging that it would be "easy and
pleasant" for him to devote his lectures to the development of Anglo-
American relations—studying the Great Lakes disarmament, Daniel Webster and Lord Ashburton, John Hay and Lord Pauncefote, and World War I—
he warned that such would be a "primrose path of dalliance for an American
historian in England." To be truthful to the historical record, Morison
argued, he must stress the differences rather than the similarities between
the two countries. To do otherwise, "would give a distorted view of the past,
and lead to false hopes and expectations."[5]

Having disavowed any New History purpose, Morison introduced his
audience to the philosophy of historical relativism that had dominated his
thinking since the war. "The study of the history of a people other than
one's own can hardly fail to be of value, in broadening sympathies, dispelling
prejudices, and fitting one for enlightened citizenship," he admitted to his
Harmsworth audience, but the "vast majority" of those who have read or
written history have done so "not for any practical reason, not to improve
anyone" or to be improved, but "because they liked it." In fact, Morison
argued, "much of our talk about the value of history . . . is a mere
rationalization of the intense pleasure we take in reading history." Far from
a pragmatic tool for the pursuit of change, history was a "necessary defense"
against pragmatism. It was a form of entertainment, Morison announced,
and as a self-proclaimed "historical hedonist," he intended to make his
lectures as pleasurable and artistically compelling as he could for both
himself and his audience.[6]

This opening lecture set the tone for the kind of work Morison set out to
accomplish in his first months at Oxford. The Harmsworth chair was
completely new and entirely his to organize, and he intended to put his
personal stamp on it. Recognizing that undergraduates at Oxford have a
"taste for good books," he decided that "a well-equipped lending library"
would be "the best sort of bait" to interest them in American history. He
solicited friends in the United States as well as new acquaintances in
England and expatriates throughout Europe for money and books, and
within weeks he had collected thousands of volumes.[7] Schematizing them
according to his own personalized vision of American history, Morison soon
discovered that he was effecting a cataloguing revolution in England. He was
"fairly deluged" with letters from British librarians asking for advice about
how to begin collections in American history and by what philosophical
system to organize them.[8]

Morison also worked hard to establish his own unique identity as a
teacher of undergraduates. He was particularly interested in making a mark
on the honors college, the gem in Oxford's educational crown and "the best
system of undergraduate instruction in the English-speaking world" accord-

ing to Morison. In the honor schools there were no courses for a professor
to give and no explicit requirements for a student to fulfill on the way to a
cumulative degree. Students received a Bachelor of Arts degree based solely
on an honors examination, which lasted six hours a day during ten consec-
utive weekdays at the end of the student's third or fourth year. Each student
is "prepared for this agony," Morison wrote, by tutors who advise him what
lectures to attend, what books to read, and how to prepare for individual
examination areas. Morison agreed to help several students who were trying
for high honors in history by preparing them for an optional examination in
American history. He found this work "highly satisfying," since his honors
students were "at home among ideas" and "wrote so well that it was hard
to find a crack wide enough to admit a critical knife." One of his students
studied the Virginia Convention and discovered "underneath the flow of
words what the orators were really driving at." Another traced the political
philosophies of Adams and Jefferson back to Plato and Aristotle and
sketched their consequences down to the present.[9]

Morison's attempt to influence the training of students in the honors
college surprised some Oxford dons and underscored the reduced workload
of the Oxford professor. "My new colleagues were somewhat astonished at
my desire actually to teach my subject to undergraduates, and did not quite
know what to do about it," Morison acknowledged. But his actions were
calculated to increase his influence and that of American history on the
curriculum of the honors college. British students "have a history that starts
about a thousand years earlier than ours," Morison noted, and the classical
system of British secondary education "makes the history of lands over
which the Roman legions have not tramped seem strange and inchoate to
English historians." In an effort to alter the curriculum, therefore, Morison
attempted to make American history a "special subject" for examination in
the honors college. The tutors kindly consented to consider the proposal,
"with the understanding that they washed their hands of all responsibility
for teaching it," Morison noted, "and some of them cooperated in sending
me their best pupils."[10]

In addition, Morison hoped to spark an appreciation for American history
by writing a textbook for his students. Most survey textbooks on the United
States were written almost exclusively by Americans for Americans and
took "so much for granted that is fundamental," Morison noted, as to be
"incomprehensible or uninteresting to British readers."[11] Even those textbooks that were understandable were often inaccurate or biased in some
manner by the "tendentious people" in the American publishing world and
on boards of education who monitored opinions expressed in them. The
result was that American historians tended to write only "dull, colorless
compendia of history" whose tedious effects were multiplied and exaggerated on foreign readers. Whereas Morison's Oxford colleagues viewed writing textbooks on British history as part of their "duty" and were facilitated
in their efforts by the British government, no equivalent aid was extended

to writers of foreign subjects.[12] Consequently, Morison petitioned the editors at Oxford University Press to consider publishing a textbook based on the questions asked by his English friends and pupils. British readers have been introduced to the "high peaks of American history" by European historians such as Charnwood, Henderson, and Trevelyan, Morison argued, but they needed someone "to guide their countrymen, as it were, through the valleys into the plains: to tell a story of intrinsic interest which may also serve to explain the United States of today."[13]

The executors of the Harmsworth chair were very pleased with the enthusiasm and initiative of their new recruit. At the end of his second year at Oxford, the committee offered to extend his appointment to ten years and held out the possibility that he could retire at the university.[14] Morison considered the offer carefully. When he had left Harvard in 1922, he had promised President Lowell that he would stay only two years.[15] The history department was operating under the assumption that he would be returning for the 1924–25 academic year, and Channing had been writing him letters almost from the moment of his departure urging him to return still earlier.[16] Rumor had it, Channing revealed in one of these letters, that Turner was planning to retire from Harvard in 1924 and that Frederick Merk would be his successor. "Merk has done very well, and can go right along with 32a [The History of America], if you don't want the job," Channing prodded Morison. "Whisper it not," he added with paternal affection, "I would like you [to do it.] No one would be more delighted to see you [reestablish] the study of colonial history in this University," Channing concluded in an obvious attack on Turner and his disciples. "We need it."[17]

After leading Channing to believe he might come back, Morison's head was turned by the offer of an extension of his Harmsworth position, and he delayed a decision about returning to Harvard. Consequently, Merk was given a full position in the department, and Channing was upset. "I only wish that you had made up your mind before I used up several half hours of eloquence in arranging matters for you," he complained.[18] Still more troubling to Channing was the news that the department had hired another American historian in Morison's absence, Arthur Schlesinger from Iowa. Schlesinger was not only a midwesterner, but he was also a social historian, a student of Charles Beard, and author of New Viewpoints in American History, a historical manifesto that specifically challenged the historiographic tradition of Channing's "Great Work."[19] Hinting that he could only safeguard Morison's position against departmental overcrowding for "one more year," Channing concluded, "Whenever you feel like coming back to the U.S.A., I make no doubt that there will be a place open for you at Harvard." But, he added threateningly, "what that job will be, one cannot say."[20]

Friends advised Morison to stay at Oxford despite these professional pressures. "If you like the place and it likes you, why not stay in it and make yourselves and others happy?" wrote Lucien Price, his friend and a

Boston Globe editor. "Forget the New England conscience," he added with a note of pessimism; "after you have been here awhile, you will be all the more willing to return."[21] With an agenda before him and a desire to exert a real influence on American historical perceptions in England, Morison needed little convincing from friends. In 1924 he drafted a letter to Lord Harmsworth informing him that he would like to stay on in the position for at least one more year and perhaps longer.[22]

Exile's Return

As long as Morison believed he could pursue his own subjective brand of history and continue to exert an influence on his students, he was content to remain an expatriate. Difficulties that affected his ability to achieve these goals emerged in his third year, however. For one thing, his plan to introduce American history as a "special subject" in the honors college faltered. Some of the "hard-worked" and unappreciated tutors, as Morison described them, justifiably argued that if American history were added to the list of twelve "special subjects" for examination, one of the current subjects should be dropped.[23] The discussion of which subject might be sacrificed set off a debate in the department that revealed some long-standing tensions. Morison proposed that a study of "Imperial and American History" be made optional to the "first English political period" (the medieval period) for purposes of examination. Regius Professor H. W. C. Davis agreed, explaining to the board of regents that while "it was desirable to have a continuous study of English history in the Honour School . . . other things might be more important." Arguing for breadth of knowledge rather than depth and for a bias in favor of modern subjects, Davis noted that "in three years one cannot give a complete education to everyone."[24]

Morison's motives for the proposal were both personal and philosophical. From a personal point of view, Morison hoped to attract more students to his lectures. Oxford students who wished to attain honors in history were required to be examined in all phases of British political, constitutional, and economic history and on much of the institutional development of western and central European history. An occasional student might get "a dash of Near East, a shot of Latin America, and a dose of America," Morison noted, but most could not afford the time needed to learn these fields. His lectures, he recognized, were an "intellectual luxury" that few could justify.[25] "It would be like taking an extra course, not counting toward a degree, at an American university," he noted. Consequently, his lectures were poorly attended. His efforts to introduce a variety of American courses in foreign policy, representative government, and the Civil War did little to alter the situation.[26]

From a philosophical point of view, Morison's campaign to introduce a special subject in American history reaffirmed his commitment to historical relativism as a pedagogical methodology. Arguing that the "honors college" was too restrictive in its requirements and too traditional in its institutional approaches, Morison wished the honors student could "mix his own drinks from the Pierian spring." Reviving the relativistic belief in the plurality of perspectives, Morison noted that British students could benefit greatly from an appreciation of an outsider's point of view. This was particularly necessary in England, Morison added, where superiority over a vast colonial empire had rendered British citizens particularly insensitive to the autonomous beliefs and attitudes of different civilizations. "This may explain why Oxford, for all its hospitality to American students, is rather unreceptive to American history," Morison commented. "Even the history of the British Empire is still on the threshold, with one foot in the door."[27] Nonetheless, members of the department were resistant to the Morison plan for equally philosophical reasons. Fearing that the scheme would divide the modern school "into a Mediaeval and Modern side," one member of the governing board concluded that it would be disastrous "to tempt undergraduates to elude Mediaeval history." Reviving the argument that members of the Harvard history department used against the separation of History 1 into 1a and 1b, he added that medieval history was absolutely necessary for "historical training," since "there was more spade-work to be done by scholars" in the medieval field, and since "[t]here was no other field, the study of which, gave scope to the best historical work."[28] Another asked "where we were to stop if we began having special papers on the outlying subjects," noting that "Ecclesiastical history and the history of Art were certainly as important as Colonial and American history."[29]

Morison attempted to exert pressure on the tutors and younger members of the department by appealing to their presentist sentiments. In contradiction to what he promised in his "Prologue to American History," Morison even momentarily unsheathed his new historical axe and ground it on the whetstone of postwar internationalism. "[T]he young men going through Oxford ought to have a chance to study their own empire and the United States considering how close relations now are," he argued during the departmental debate. But Morison knew full well that his argument would "not make the least appeal" to an honors college whose members prided themselves on apolitical, subjective, eclectic approaches to history. "In fact," Morison discovered, "such a proposal antagonizes them, because they look upon history as partly a science, partly an art, entirely divorced from the practical world; and they are very resentful of any suggestion of political pressure being put on the University." Nor did "wheedling or scolding the British public" to exert pressure seem to do any good. "Your Britisher is as impervious to propaganda as a porcupine."[30]

Not surprisingly, Morison's proposal was defeated. As Morison suspected, Oxford dons would not permit any political or relativistic argument to inveigh against honors college tradition. He was disappointed with the rejection of his plan, however, because he realized the implications of that vote for his larger agenda beyond the walls of Oxford.[31] A survey of British secondary institutions undertaken during Morison's stay at Oxford revealed that American history was only taught in three British high schools. "[I]t was not likely to spread much," Morison added, "until future masters in the public schools were given more opportunity to study American history in their universities." At present, he noted, the alternative was the un-healthy absorption of American culture through extrahistorical and even ahistorical media: most English children got their American history through films, which created a "very distorted" view, since American films shown in England portrayed a country "mainly concerned with sex, crime and getting rich."[32] Films about America produced for American consump-tion provided harmless "romantic compensation for the humdrum life of Main Street," he acknowledged, but "[t]heir effect on the people of a country with a different background was . . . unwholesome."[33] Even the old "penny dreadfuls" or the "Fenimore Cooper, Mayne Red, and Diamond Dick school of fiction," Morison argued, were better than the "Wild West stuff in the movies of today."[34]

American expatriates with whom Morison had felt previously such a camaraderie served only to worsen matters. Excessively critical about Amer-ican culture, they wrote little to inspire British citizens to study it. In trips to the Continent, Morison found "scores of [expatriates] in certain Parisian cafés declaring to anyone who would listen, that America was 'finished'" and was now "an 'impossible' place for a 'cultivated man' to live."[35] While Morison understood this point of view, even felt it himself to some extent, he believed it was inappropriate and detrimental to the intellectual study of the American past. Historical relativism demanded a variety of points of view, and the pervasiveness of the expatriate denunciation of America made this impossible. Some literature of renunciation was necessary, Morison wrote, but European readers did not understand what a small and dispropor-tionally vocal part of a diverse American culture the expatriates were.

In particular, Morison objected to the "debunking" mode, fashionable among expatriates in the 1920s. Deriving from the term coined by William E. Woodward in his 1923 novel *Bunk*, "debunking" consisted of the icono-clastic tendencies of disaffected intellectuals who hoped to expose and ridicule American institutions in order to call attention to their shallow-ness. "In this era," Morison later observed, "the peculiarly American form of . . . *la trahison des clers*, was to attack American traditions." Nearly every American hero "from Columbus to Coolidge was successfully 'de-bunked,'" and Woodward himself did it to Washington, Grant, and Lafay-ette. Charles Beard's *Economic Origins of the Constitution* (1913) "paved the way for a host of writers who maintained that the Federal Constitution was the work of wealthy tricksters to keep democracy down," Morison remarked, while Beard's textbook *The Rise of American Civilization* (1927) was written "to prove that there were no heroes or even leaders in American history," only antiheroes and deceivers. The greatest offender in this regard, however, was H. L. Mencken, whose descriptions of the American "booboisie" did more to confuse impressionable British readers about the United States than any other writer of the 1920s. Mencken's "cynicism might have broken down American smugness if that had been his objective," Morison wrote, "but he had no objective."[36]

Morison failed in his efforts to provide a more unified and esteemed recognition for American history in England in part owing to an ironic feature of his own relativistic philosophy. Having committed himself to accepting a multiplicity of views on any intellectual subject, he had to face the irritating fact that no one interpretation had any prerogative over any other. A professor at Oxford might have no more voice in determining attitudes toward American history than a romantic filmmaker or a disaffected literatus. Furthermore, in having proclaimed the right of the historian to emphasize intrinsic and subjective values, he was, according to critics of relativism, inevitably bound by them. Relativism, in its extreme form, left one with no objective standards by which to prioritize judgments and no system of measures for evaluating statements or legitimizing contentions. This "relativist dilemma" made it difficult for Morison to "step off his own shadow" or to advance his claims with any authority against those standing on longer and wider shadows of their own.[37]

Morison's inability to exert the influence he wished on British attitudes toward America caused him to reevaluate his position at Oxford at the end of his third year. "My three years at Oxford" have been a "harvest season for me," he noted, "but only a plowing season for American history."[38] Personal factors intervened to reduce the bounty even of his private harvest. As idyllic as life was at Christ Church, he began to feel isolated and slightly homesick. At Oxford, Morison realized, a "newcomer either remains isolated, within a little wall which he alone does not see, or he is absorbed into the tepid current of donnish life, and the world knows him no more."[39] Disconnected from his New England roots, he began to experience the "separation anxiety" that so many other expatriates felt in the mid-1920s. Letters from his friend Lincoln Colcord about New England in the spring filled him with nostalgia. Colcord's descriptions of the "[i]ndigenous life" of the Maine coast, which "springs easily from our clay, loves the wet fog and the cold breath of the sea, [and] fills woods and fields with a richness of growth such as the dry sands of the south have never known," resonated with startling incongruity in foul-weathered Oxford.[40] "Your description of the Maine spring strikes me all in a heap, like the first whiff of spruce one gets from the Bangor boat at Rockland before sunrise, passing Owl's Head," Morison wrote Colcord. "For over thirty summers now I have come up that way, and as far back as I remember Maine has thrilled me as nothing else in nature has." "You need not envy me my Oxford spring," he added: "Icy blasts, squalls and hailstorms; and then a settled dull cold, never up to 60 even."[41]

Furthermore, Morison had Bessie and the children to consider. "[W]hen I broached the subject to Bessie" of staying on at Oxford, Morison contended, "she imposed a firm veto, for the sake of the children." As the "child of an expatriate" herself, Bessie "was determined that her children should not be subjected to the same fate."[42] Additional word about the failing health of his mother gave Morison extra incentive to return. In her son's absence, Emily Morison had been overseeing his affairs in America, but the strain of this and taking care of the 44 Brimmer Street home had proven too much for her.[43]

Most important of all, perhaps, Morison was more favorably disposed toward America than he had been when he arrived in England in 1922. "I was in a very disillusioned state" after the peace conference, he later wrote, "but was saved from a cynical attitude toward the U.S. by living in Oxford." Oxford gave him time "to read and think and appreciate the solid worth and essential character of America."[44] In that "cool, sophisticated atmosphere," he explained, "our country seemed more elemental," and the "unity of her history was more easy to comprehend."[45] With the hyperopic vision of an expatriate, Morison was able to arrange the shattered images of the disparate America he had left in 1922 into a patterned mosaic that reaffirmed the unity of American culture. In this sense, he was renewing one of the major aspirations of the founding fathers of the American historical profession—to save history from the skepticism of relativism by affirming a national commitment to the American identity. Ironically, it was a particular relativistic point of view, the expatriate one, that permitted him to do so. By 1925, Morison could justify his request that Oxford University Press market his unfinished textbook in America as well as England with the observation, "My excuse, for offering this book to my fellow countrymen also, is the point of view from which it is written."[46]

With a "firm conviction that his life work lay in America," Morison resigned his Harmsworth chair.[47] In a letter sent from the S. S. *Winifredian* as it steamed toward America, Morison thanked his hosts. "I shall regret" leaving Oxford, he wrote with sincerity, but "[t]he voyage is nearing its end, and America is just below the horizon." Tomorrow "I shall once more taste Walt Whitman's 'joy of being toss'd in the brave turmoil of these times,'" he told his British friends. "My days of wine and roses are over."[48]

Debunking the Debunkers

As if to prove his commitment to a new, more unified vision of America, Morison booked passage on a transcontinental railway tour almost as soon as he returned to the United States. Arranged by Ralph Budd, president of the Great Northern Railroad Company, the trip included speaking engagements and tours purposefully designed to acquaint Morison with parts of the country he had never seen, especially the Northwest. The expedition was both informative and rejuvenating. "My wife and I have just returned from a trip across the continent," Morison wrote Albert Beveridge on his return, "and the whole thing gave one an idea of the Northwest that could be obtained in no other way." The working vacation helped Morison develop a still more unified (and positive) vision of his country and its history. "I wish that there was some provision for forcibly dragging all American historians around the country like this at least once in five years," he told Beveridge. "Nothing like seeing the country to rekindle your faith in its future."[49]

While Morison was in an optimistic mood about the country, his friend was in a pessimistic one. Harding's tenure in office had left Beveridge highly discouraged about the prospects for national unity, and he envisioned American life spiraling ever downward. Discouraged by the inadequacies of his party's leaders in the early twenties, Beveridge ran for the Senate in 1922 but was resoundingly defeated. Only the study of history saved him once again from lapsing into a state of abject pessimism. Within days of his political defeat, Beveridge was back at work on a new historical project, a biography of Lincoln. He envisioned the work as a continuation of "the constitutional interpretation of America, weaving it around the life of Lincoln," as he had tried to do "with the earlier constitutional period around the life of Marshall."[50] He received encouragement from many corners. The *Philadelphia Public Ledger*, for instance, all but applauded Beveridge's defeat because it would allow him time to write his biography. A "tenure of public service would have so sapped his strength and exacted his time that 'Honest Abe' would have been laid on the shelf, probably for eternity, so far as Beveridge was concerned," the paper reported. "Who shall say that the world will not be better off for Beveridge's *Life of Lincoln* than anything this astute Indianan might have said or done these next few years in the United States Senate?" the *Ledger* asked. Indeed, Abraham Lincoln was such a living force in American culture, the paper argued, that an accurate portrayal of his life would have a profound effect on the way Americans thought of themselves.[51]

But Beveridge was disturbed by the implications of some of his initial research. Partisan historians of his party, such as Ida Tarbell, had painted Lincoln as a flawless reformer and had thereby obscured fundamental defects in his character, Beveridge discovered.[52] Tarbell and others had an annoying tendency, he contended, "to insist that our heroes shall be Sunday-school knights, when almost always they are not."[53] Vowing to "de-Tarbell-ize" Lincoln,[54] Beveridge nonetheless worried that "the public does not want the whole truth in the case of heroes."[55] He wrote Morison for advice in the matter and was relieved to find that his friend also believed Lincoln's portrait had been misdrawn. Morison responded by observing that readers who accepted interpretations such as Tarbell's were merely "sentimental sob-sisters" and incapable of distinguishing between accurate history and the highly biased pseudobiographical histories produced first by Lincoln's secretaries John Nicolay and John Hay.[56] "Keep right on the *Life of Lincoln*," he wrote. "I can see that it is going to be a wonderful book, even better than the *Marshall*, and will make Nicolay & Hay look like a couple of ribbon counter clerks."[57]

But Morison was not in complete sympathy with the kind of biography Beveridge had in mind. As chapters of the work arrived for him to proofread, Morison grew increasingly anxious about the image of Lincoln that was emerging. Beveridge's Lincoln was not a profound moralist, for instance, but rather a selfish, amoral politician. He "was not bothered very much about convictions,"[58] Beveridge argued, and "was perfectly willing to risk plunging the country into war on the chance of being elected to the Senate or the Presidency." Recognizing "the possibilities of the slavery issue," this calculating politician, "wholly wanting in scruples," showed a conspicuous "lack of public morality" by taking "the side most likely to advantage him."[59] Morison, however, had a far more sympathetic view of Lincoln. In his lectures at Oxford he told students that the fourteenth president had been hampered by an uncooperative cabinet and by selfish military officers "who distrusted him and one another," yet despite these limitations, Lincoln rose ever "in his moral ascendancy," never losing "his humanity and his humility."[60] Early biographers have missed that "something about Lincoln which made him great," Morison told Beveridge, adding with suggestive hopefulness, "I trust you will find it."[61]

Morison was persistent in his criticisms of Beveridge's manuscript because he feared that his friend was slipping too readily into the debunking mode. He urged Beveridge to consider alternative interpretations of Lincoln and his age, such as those that emphasized the role of geopolitics in the coming of the Civil War. Viewing the Mexican War as an irritant to the controversial issues of territorial expansion and slavery, Morison argued that political leaders in the Civil War era had been too aggressive in their pursuit of new soil, too selfish in the demands they made of the Mexican people, and too unwilling to discuss the use of those lands after they were acquired.[62] Beveridge disagreed. "[H]ow you can form the conclusion that the Mexicans were right and we were wrong in that scrimmage is beyond my poor and sordid mentality," he wrote Morison. Hinting that his friend was revealing too much of his "New England Whig ancestry," Beveridge claimed that his research indicated that slavery was not a concern in the Mexican War or a cause of the Civil War at all. Slavery was an institution tolerated in the North and probably dying in the South, Beveridge wrote. "[M]ost Southern men," he argued, considered slavery "wrong" and "looked forward, in an indefinite way, to its gradual extinction." Slavery was becoming unprofitable, and, if the issue had been left alone, the freeing of the slaves would have probably occurred as a matter of course, "naturally, like the coming of spring."[63]

If slavery was not the cause of the Civil War, Beveridge asked Morison accusingly, then "Who the devil was it who brought the war on, anyway?" Answering his own question, Beveridge suggested that the New England abolitionists were responsible. Beginning in the 1830s, Beveridge argued, the abolitionists began a "crusade against 'the sin' [of slavery], accusing all slave-holders of being robbers, murderers, etc." These accusations, in turn, "arouse[d] the Southern people to a state of mingled terror and frenzy."[64] Everyone knows now, Beveridge added, "that if the abolitionists had kept their mouths shut, slavery would have died, choked to death by economic forces and the spirit of the age."[65] But Morison remained unconvinced by this testimony of abolitionist fanaticism. Slavery was alive and well in the South and would have continued on in its abusive manner had not the abolitionists taken their courageous stand. Concerned that Beveridge was conforming to the debunker's strategy of attacking idealism in any form, he begged his friend to reconsider his portrait of New England abolitionists. "My differences with you regarding the Abolitionists troubles me much more than our dispute about the Mexican War," Morison wrote. The Mexican War issue was "a question of fact largely," but the abolitionist issue was "a matter of judgment and interpretation."[66] William Lloyd Garrison, the Grimke sisters, and Frederick Douglass were heroes to Morison, because like Lincoln they chose to take a stand on an important moral issue despite the consequences. To find selfish motives at the heart of the abolitionist crusade was to indulge too completely in the iconoclastic tendencies of the debunking age.[67]

Worried by the tone and fervency of Morison's criticisms regarding the *Life of Lincoln* manuscript, Beveridge found satisfaction in the comments of other historians who were more sympathetic to his views. Despite his initial impression that Beveridge was "heaping up" too much detail in making his case against the abolitionists, Charles Beard concluded that Beveridge had achieved a remarkable success. After a long walk in Central Park, "when I cleared my mind of 'hunches' and took in the spring air," Beard noted in a letter to Beveridge, "it came to me in a flash that you have consciously or not done a revolutionary piece of historical writing, the kind of masterly analysis by detail which the great novelist attempts."[68] In his own iconoclastic *The Rise of American Civilization*, Beard borrowed liberally from Beveridge's portrait of the Civil War era. Lincoln, in Beard's telling, was more a politician than an idealist, motivated by "circumstances and expediency rather than his own initiative." Bullied by the abolitionists, he inched the nation toward war while naïvely convincing himself that he had been "controlled" by events.[69] "Darn those abolitionists," Beveridge wrote to an agreeable Beard. "The deeper I get into this thing, the clearer it becomes to me that the whole wretched mess would have been straightened out without the white race killing itself off, if the abolitionists had let matters alone."[70]

The collaboration of Beveridge and Beard deeply disturbed Morison, because it not only suggested the continued ascendancy of debunking as a

literary mode, but it also demonstrated the conspicuously regional character of debunking. Many debunkers, he noted, were midwestern historians
who were hypersensitive to the domination of the American historical
profession by the eastern elite. Such a sensitivity had compelled
midwesterner Frederick Jackson Turner to issue his frontier thesis and, in
1926, prompted him to write "The Children of the Pioneers," a lengthy
retort to Henry Cabot Lodge's contention (based on research in the *Apple-
ton's Cyclopedia of American Biography*) that seventy-five percent of the
nation's intellectual achievements had their origin in New England. Turner
argued that the Midwest had produced more than its share of intellectuals,
especially great historians, including Beveridge and Beard. If midwestern
historians were a bit unorthodox and even irreverent in their techniques, it
was because they demonstrated the courage of their frontier ancestors "in
striking out new lines of investigation."[71] But Morison noted that midwestern historians had factionalized the profession by creating a separate and
competing organization for historians in the middle region of the country
known as the Mississippi Valley Historical Association. Dedicated to showing that "the planting of Boonesboro in Kentucky or of Marietta in Ohio is
of equal importance to the landing of the Pilgrim fathers at Plymouth," the
association elected officers and editors only from the Mississippi Valley.
This regional exclusivity undercut the attempts of historians such as
Morison to affirm the nationalizing tendencies of the profession. Because
its unabashed goal was to promote "the historical interests of mid-America"
and to do so by protesting against "the small coterie of Easterners" in
control of the profession, the Mississippi Valley Historical Association was
needlessly contemptuous of the past and vulnerable to the debunking
tendency, according to Morison.[72]

Many of these midwestern historians, most prominently Turner, also
adopted "regionalism" as their central historical theme for explaining
American development, suggesting to Morison how "territoriality" among
twentieth-century historians might have dangerous consequences when
projected backward into the histories they wrote. Noting the importance of
"sections and sectional rivalry" to American history, Turner wrote *Rise of
the New West, 1819–1829* to demonstrate "the transition from a predomi-
nantly nationalist to a predominantely sectionalist outlook in the United
States during that decade." As John Higham has noted, sectionalism appealed to Turner because it "offset a deadening uniformity in national life"
and adequately explained what he viewed as the pervasive divisiveness of
American culture.[73] Beard echoed these sentiments by considering sectional
conflicts along class lines. But no matter what the specific angle of vision
of these regionalists, Morison regretted their insistence on the role of
conflict and diversity in American life. His experience as an expatriate
confirmed what could happen when method recapitulated theme among
debunkers. Obsession with disunity disunified readers; insistence on icon-
oclasm precluded icons.

These considerations gave Morison grist for the mill as he prepared his *Oxford History of the United States*. Concerned with the factionalizing effects of historical relativism, the disunifying implications of debunking, and the divisiveness of sectionalism, Morison sought to write a textbook that would emphasize national unity. He desired to write something that would put "fire in the eye[s]" of young readers, and that would "make a young man want to fight for his country in war or live to make it a better country in peace."[74] Because he contradicted the historiographic tendencies of some midwesterners, his reputation among a few of them slipped considerably. With Beveridge, at least, he was able to converse openly about their differences. While acknowledging their sectional differences, for instance, Beveridge thanked Morison for his comments on the Lincoln manuscript. "I value most highly your critical judgment, your sense of proportion, your insistence on truth, your dramatic taste, and other like qualities," he wrote, adding, "I hope my mss. may, perhaps, be of some little help" in producing the "great *Oxford History*."[75] Indeed it was a help, ironically, since it served as a negative check on the relativistic techniques that Morison had once employed but now so thoroughly repudiated.

Sectionalism Reconsidered

In challenging the midwestern debunkers, Morison was aware that he was placing himself in partial opposition to his Harvard mentor Turner. Turner had never engaged in much iconoclastic activity himself, but his confrontational style had inspired many from his region to do so. Morison recognized that any history of the nation must take some historiographic attitude toward Turner's frontier thesis. "There has not been a major work on United States history written in the last twenty years," Morison realized, "that has not some of the Frontier theory in it." It was "impossible to take a step in American history without stubbing one's toes" on it, he added.[76] Hence Morison was faced with the difficult task of acknowledging the importance of Turner's thesis while challenging its authority. The task was made that much more difficult by his friendship with both the thesis's author and a number of its most ardent supporters, including Beveridge.

Morison reached a compromise of sorts with his former mentor. The opening paragraphs of *The Oxford History of the United States* were an outright acknowledgment of Turner's influence. The first chapter presented a physiographic and geological description of America that established the wilderness as the country's most salient feature. The American seacoast might "soften outlines and play on an Englishman's heart-strings," argued Morison, but inland the wilder character of the landscape presented a truer image of the country. "Inland," he wrote, "the dry air, clear sky, and brilliant sunlight foreshorten distant prospects, and make the landscape sharp and hard." And if America came into focus in the wilderness, then it required but a small leap of the imagination to recognize that the character of the people was also determined by natural surroundings. "The stimulating and exacting climate," Morison continued, made Americans more "nervous, emotional and physically active" than other people. The rain, which fell in certain sections of the country with "business-like intensity," made the inhabitants more controlled. And most of all, the ever changing frontier regulated the movement and temperament of national history. "It was the frontier," Morison announced to his American and British audiences, "moving every year a little nearer the setting sun, which for a century marked the progress of American expansion and largely determined the rhythm of American life."[77]

Morison described the frontier in terms that made even some of Turner's accounts pale by comparison. Game was so plentiful in Morison's America that quail, wild turkeys, and deer practically leaped onto pioneer dinner plates. "At times the flights of wild pigeons darkened the air" so great was their number; cattle and swine grazed at will on "natural herbage"; Indian corn grew without attention during the "hot summer nights"; the American interior was "glutted with nature's bounty"; and "the soft gradation of the seasons" made "the languor in the air" and the fertility of the soil still more impressive. The country was, in short, a veritable Garden of Eden, and the frontiersman was the American Adam.[78]

As much as Morison "loved and admired" Turner, however, by his own admission he "never went the whole road" with him. All historians must acknowledge Turner's thesis, Morison knew, but one could "apply the frontier theory in whole or in part, and to sections or eras of American history, in a variety of different ways; one may emphasize it or minimize it, limit it in space or in time." For his part, Morison believed that the frontier thesis must "of necessity" come to play a lesser role in American histories of the mid–twentieth century.[79] This was in part because Turner's thesis applied most clearly to pre–twentieth century America, when the frontier still existed, and in part because, even in a nineteenth- or eighteenth-century context, Turner's thesis exaggerated the liberating role of the land and the historical significance of the midwestern strain.[80]

To suggest these inadequacies to his readers, Morison inverted Turner's logic, not challenging the frontier's impact but questioning its benefits to the nation. Where Turner had found the frontier the inspiration for much that was good about America, Morison found in it much that was evil. The frontiersman was lazy, rebellious, and insensitive, for instance, to all the splendor that surrounded him. "In a land of such plenty," Morison reasoned, "exertion had no attraction for the unambitious." Because the pioneer "had no immediate incentive to produce much beyond his actual needs," he became "incredibly wasteful and primitive in his habits." Everything he touched seemed tainted. His cabins were usually "unpainted, resembling dingy boxes surrounded by unseemly household litter"; his "fields were full of stumps and acres of dead trees strangled by girdling"; trees were "his enemies, and he neither spared them nor planted them for purposes of shade." It would be decades and largely despite the frontiersman, Morison argued, before Americans would develop the "taste or leisure to appreciate the rugged grandeur of their mountains and forests, and their majestic rivers, swift rapids and mighty waterfalls."[81]

Extrapolating again from physical to spiritual characterization, Morison concluded that the frontiersman was morally and mentally unkempt. Pioneers ignored the importance of community, revelled in self-indulgence, and nearly destroyed the nation in their constant escapes from responsibility. According to Turner, "the most important effect of the frontier has been in the promotion of democracy" and in the escape from corrupting eastern and European aristocracies, but Morison found in this escape a reluctance to help with the important business of constructing a nation. The frontiersman, he argued, left that crucial work to a small portion of the population and undercut political authority whenever possible. Like the Indians, with whom they shared the frontier, "[t]hese children of nature . . . could no more respect a treaty than dogs can be kept from fighting by the friendship of their masters."[82]

The South and the West, because of their frontier constituencies, bore the brunt of Morison's attack. Borrowing heavily from Turner's language but twisting its meaning, Morison demonstrated that the southern colonies were divided along geographic fall lines (tidewater, piedmont, and so on) and sketched the character traits for each section. In Virginia, for instance, the older and more established coastal counties proved a striking contrast to the vibrant but reckless western piedmont. The inhabitants of this latter area, Morison contended, were by and large "illiterate, ferocious and quarrelsome," noted primarily for the animal-like "biting and gouging" they employed while fighting. They were primarily responsible for the series of civil wars that wrecked the South in the eighteenth century, and they rebelled whenever the rules of civilization and culture presented themselves. These "vigorous, lawless, hard drinkers and dirty fighters," who moved from the piedmont across the Appalachians and further west, created a movement comparable in his mind "only with the barbaric invasions of Europe." Morison admitted that some good was associated with the frontiersman, but he confined this to the New England influence. Physiographic features in New England, "a severe climate" and a "grudging soil," had created a stern Yankee personality, which, when transported West, enlightened communities with "education, thrift, ingenuity, and righteousness." Yankees had passed through the "cruder phases of democracy" before they peopled the Ohio Valley and brought to that region a respect for land and a belief in community spirit. The Northwest Ordinance of 1787 was a brilliant piece of legislation, Morison argued, because it maintained the community form of settlement indigenous to New England and saved the upper Ohio

Valley, at least, from the kind of scattered settlement that ruined the South and West.[83]

There were several ironies associated with Morison's effort to adapt Turner's theory to his own uses. In attempting to introduce a corrective to the sectional conceit of the frontier thesis, Morison not only employed his own brand of New England boosterism, but he also engaged in a form of debunking by attacking one of the great heroes of American historical literature—the frontiersman. But Morison justified his actions by reminding himself of the nationalizing intentions that motivated these techniques. Drawing heavily on several dramatic devices employed in the "Great Work" of another Harvard mentor, Edward Channing, Morison reaffirmed his intention to write with a "wholeness of view." Turner's frontier thesis privileged one section of the nation above others and disconnected the Old World from the New, but by fulfilling one of the prescriptions for the "New Parkman," Morison promised to reconnect them. He relied so heavily on Channing that the two joked that *The Oxford History of the United States* was nothing more than an effort to "pot Channing for the British market."[84]

As he had in *The Maritime History of Massachusetts*, Morison used the sea metaphor to shape his narrative and to restore unity to the past. Channing, an avid sailor, had first suggested the potential for nautical imagery in the early volumes of the "Great Work." One reader of *The History of the United States* remarked that Channing placed so much emphasis on maritime themes that "not a demicannon, culverin, or murtherer escaped his notice." This tendency "reflected a typical New Englander's love of the sea," wrote one critic, as well as "certain casual explanations, points of emphasis, and interpretations indicate viewpoints and prejudices traceable to the Atlantic coastline."[85] It came as no surprise to Channing that the American Revolution sprang from the dry docks of Boston; for there colonists had come to expect natural rights of "free trade." In coastal ports merchants had developed the American business ethic and had provided the first structures of business organization. When it came time to form a new federal government, Channing claimed, the nation looked to New England for its model of efficiency and success.[86]

In adopting Channing's maritime metaphor, however, Morison did not slavishly mimic his mentor's New England sectionalism. Stretching Channing's nautical canvas over the frame of Turner's frontier thesis, Morison developed an interpretation that attempted to reconcile the theories of his two irreconcilable mentors. The frontier in Morison's new conception was a vast sea wilderness displaying both terrestrial and maritime characteristics. The language of the sea, for instance, dominated Morison's descriptions of the land. Property in Maryland and Virginia, he wrote in *The Oxford History of the United States*, was but "borrowed from the sea." The "boreal forests of conifers," which "the sharp dry frosts of October" turn into a "tapestry of scarlet and gold," were a gigantic "tidal wave . . . swept up from the coast over the crest of the Appalachians." The mountains, Morison noted, were "arranged in such parallel folds that a view from them suggests immense ocean waves." Prairie schooners "sail westward" across the vast, empty space that was the frontier.[87]

In *The History of the United States* Channing downplayed the role of the West because he thought it antithetical to the East, but Morison treated the West as the potential fulfillment of the East. As the nation moved westward—with the inevitability and expansiveness, Morison noted, of an ocean wave—its most successful experiments were those that were mindful of the maritime commercial lessons of his New England home. Kentucky provided the best example of the use and misuse of maritime commercial lessons in Morison's account. On the one hand, settlers in Kentucky chose "troubled waters in which to fish," according to Morison, because stockaded settlements "erected on western waters" were guaranteed to disturb the Indians. Communities patterned after those in maritime New England were necessary in such a "dark and bloody" land. The wisest migrants planted in communal groups on the "fertile river bottoms of Kentucky" and immediately looked for commercial outlets on the Ohio and Mississippi as their New England forbears had sought commercial connections with England. On the other hand, the "simpler and less ambitious" remained in "coves," or sheltered valleys of the Appalachians. This type of Kentucky pioneer did not learn the rudiments of trade nor (with "the immense ocean waves of the Appalachians" as "a mountain wall behind them") did they find an outlet for their commerce. Hence, these settlers did not grow with America but continued, into the twentieth century, to "wear homespun, shoot game with a muzzle-loading rifle, dance the morris and the running set, and frighten their babes with the name of Claverhouse." In short, the frontiersmen who ignored the lessons of river navigation and trade degenerated into hillbillies; they lived literally and figuratively in a backwater.[88]

Borrowing Turner's notion of the importance of internal improvements to frontier development, Morison noted the maritime lessons therein employed. He argued that in the 1830s, industrialism directly followed the waterways since factories were located "near some waterfall or rapid" and added that technology was often most effectively applied to navigational projects such as the Erie Canal. Improvements in river transportation "made it worthwhile to be industrious" and "hastened the industrialization of the East," he wrote, while making it "easier to reach the cheap western lands." While at times these advances led to "cut-throat competition, in which the big fish swallowed the little fish, and then tried to eat one another," Morison noted, more often than not these advances energized the nation.[89]

The nation might have gone on in this happy mixed metaphoric condition, Morison noted, except for one portentous event—the Civil War. Using the *Oxford History of the United States* as an opportunity to rebut the image of the Civil War that emerged in Beveridge's *Life of Lincoln*, Morison argued that the war was caused not by fanatical abolitionists but by the failure of national politics. The story of the nineteenth century, he wrote, concerned efforts to maintain a sectional balance in light of competition for natural resources. "Churches might split, social differences might deepen, and extremists revile one another," he wrote, "but so long as the Whig and Democratic parties remained national in scope, the Union was safe." As Morison had pointed out to Beveridge, however, the Mexican War ended hopes of unity. Violently opposed in New England, the Mexican War threatened to shift the balance between maritime and frontier interests by altering the epicenter of the nation. Polk's aggressiveness in the conflict and "the conquest of more territory," he concluded, "upset the sectional balance" and revived "the dangerous question of slavery in the Territories." "No sooner were Polk's clutch of eaglets hatched," Morison wrote of the new territories, "than North and South began to quarrel over them." The Mexican War "intensified geographic conflicts, which in turn broke down national politics, and set into motion the series of events which made the war inevitable in 1861."[90]

In presenting the Civil War as the necessary result of a failure to achieve "sectional balance," Morison hoped to demonstrate his belief in the importance of maintaining unified visions in an increasingly disunified world. The Oxford History of the United States represented Morison's attempt to provide unities along several different axes. First, he wished to show that American development was marked by "balances" that provided unstable but sustaining unities—between East and West, North and South, land and sea. Second, he hoped to prove that regional bias was as dangerous to American historical writing as it was to American history. If midwestern historians persisted in their rebellious ways, a "civil war" in the profession would not be far in the future. Third, he desired to unify his British and American audiences, to "stimulate and satisfy the rising interest in American history which is happily noticeable in England,"[91] wrote one reviewer, and to make "the development of the American political system and the intricacies of its workings clear to American readers," added another.[92] Fourth, he attempted to reconcile the disparate theories of his two warring mentors, Channing and Turner, thereby bringing some unity to his contradictory intellectual development.

Most of all, because Morison had rejected historical relativism, he attempted to reverse its tendency to destroy the people's heroes. In presenting a heroic portrait of Lincoln or of the abolitionists in the Oxford History of the United States, Morison hoped to counteract the negative imagery associated with debunking works such as those of Turner, Beveridge, and Beard. He was only partially successful in doing so, at least on an individual basis. Claiming to be "very much interested in seeing your proposed history," Turner declined to read Morison's manuscript on the dubious grounds that he no longer read the manuscripts of his former students.[93] Albert Beveridge never read the published version of the Oxford History of the United States because he died of a heart attack several months before its release, his own biography of Lincoln unfinished.[94] Only Charles Beard remained to be influenced by it, but he was too attached to his own relativistic philosophy to be much altered by Morison's work. Besides, although Morison's history received laudatory reviews on both sides of the ocean, it was overshadowed by the publication of the best-selling textbook of American history ever, released, unfortunately for Morison, in the same year as the *Oxford History of the United States*—none other than Beard's *The Rise of American Civilization*, whose ideas would remain repugnant to Morison for the rest of his career.[95]

In Defense of the Ivory Tower

John Dewey, Charles M. Andrews, Lucien Price
and Progressive Reform in Education

7

History and the Social Studies Movement

The success of Beard's *Rise of American Civilization* indicated that although Morison had abandoned New History and historical relativism, they were still the prevailing modes of historical writing in the late 1920s. In his textbook, Beard revived New History arguments concerning the crass materialism of American life, particularly the philistinism of American higher education. Arguing that postwar education "bent like a reed before new demands as the curricula of colleges underwent changes adapted to an age of industry," he complained that "utility" continued to be the "watchword of the study and lecture room." One of the most insidious aspects of subordinating education to the "machine," Beard wrote, was the standardization of form and theory in textbook writing. Professors who lived "in ivory towers of universities where paychecks came regularly and no questions were asked" had no incentive to write texts that engaged students or familiarized them with contemporary problems. Such a condition was "ruinous to creative intelligence" and prompted some students to call for history books that served a larger social purpose. History texts must be more than descriptive and informational, students urged; they must also be normative, providing standards and methodologies by which all other fields might accomplish their own revolutions for social change.[1]

Promoting his textbook as an alternative to the standardized versions of the past presented by his university contemporaries, Beard endorsed in its pages the ideas of professional educators who wished to promote a " 'progressive' doctrine of education for 'social efficiency.' "[2] Loosely grouped around the "social studies" movement, these educators renewed the presentist arguments of the New Historians for a "usable past" and proposed a reconfiguration of traditional academic disciplines to accomplish it.[3] One of the moving spirits among professional educators in the social studies movement was Beard's friend John Dewey. As former colleagues at Columbia University, Beard and Dewey had frequently lunched together and discussed pedagogical theories. During these conversations, Dewey gave curricular form to Beard's socially motivated philosophy of history. Dewey wrote that history as a "unidirectional process of observation and emulation" must be replaced by history as interactive social science.[4] The educational environment for the study of the past must be broadened outward, literally in some cases, by removing students from the passive and isolated classroom and immersing them in the world at large. Social studies instructors challenged students to experience the "living presence" of historical ideas by introducing courses on current events, encouraging debate formats, approving internships outside the classroom, and giving academic credit for "life experience."[5]

Dewey's ideas about the environmental context for education comported nicely with Beard's philosophy of historical relativism. Ideas, like students, exist in contexts, Beard argued, so social studies teachers should emphasize the changing nature of ideas and develop the critical faculties of their students so that they might make their own choices among them. So persuasive were Dewey and Beard that many states implemented social studies programs for their high schools, and various colleges redesigned curricula to incorporate their educational reforms. The most famous attempt to make over a college according to these "progressive" educational techniques occurred at Amherst College in 1920. Influenced by Dewey, President Alexander Meiklejohn attempted to dispense with traditional classroom education and to substitute a series of seminars, workshops, internships, and independent tutorial projects that stressed the importance of "worldly experience" for Amherst students. Believing that students could be "titillated" to learn not by rote memorization but by exposure to a proper environment for learning, Meiklejohn convinced the board of trustees at Amherst to implement a new curriculum in 1920 based on the social studies concept.[6] For professors of history at the college the new plan had radical implications, since the discipline of history was forced to give up much of its independent status in order to serve as handmaiden to the social sciences. Several of Morison's friends were among the greatest supporters of the change, including journalist Lucien Price, who later made the Amherst experiment the subject of a novel entitled *Prophets Unawares—The Romance of an Idea*.[7]

Morison could not join his friend Price in enthusiasm for "progressive education." Already on the record as an opponent of Beard's debunking and relativistic tendencies, Morison disdained what he later called the "folderols of Dewey-inspired education."[8] The "progressive craze" to teach "trends" not "facts," Morison noted, meant that students were not being trained well enough in the basics.[9] "Somewhere along the assembly-line of their education," he later wrote, "students have had inserted in them a bolt called 'points of view,' secured with a nut called 'trends,' and they imagine that the historian's problem is simply to compare points of view and describe trends. It is not."[10] Morison was especially disturbed by efforts by midwestern universities to make a broad-based social science curricula the core of their students' requirements for graduation. The University of Chicago and the University of Michigan, in particular, rushed too quickly to implement programs with presentist values and violated principles of "intellectual discipline and common sense."[11] He wrote Professor Howard Mumford Jones of Michigan: "The notion that you can by college education, tell graduates just what to do about problems of American life is an idle dream." Rather than prescribing ills in the American system, he added, educators should give students a broader knowledge of their own country and "train their minds so that new problems can be intelligently faced."[12]

Morison was only one of several professional historians in the late 1920s who took a stand against progressive reform in history. Yale professor Charles M. Andrews was the acknowledged leader of this group. In his 1924 presidential address entitled "These Forty Years," to commemorate the fortieth anniversary of the founding of the American Historical Association, Andrews defended traditional approaches to history and warned against progressive educational reforms. Noting that some historians threatened to trivialize the past by denying any sense of objectivity, he took particular issue with Carl Becker's democratic vision. By employing a "vocabulary of the everyday," Becker rightly sought to make history "everybody's affair," Andrews acknowledged, but Becker underestimated the need to follow professional rules and undervalued the higher "processes of historical purification." The irreverence for facts and the "false assumption" that there were no accepted standards for historical writing encouraged untrained amateurs to think they could be counted "as equally scientific and as much deserving of confidence as the most advanced and best trained historians."[13]

To protect against the presentist tendencies of historical relativists, Andrews argued, university scholars needed to band together to uphold standards. "[H]istorical output to-day" should be "largely controlled by our collegiate departments," he asserted, where "historical study is organized, historical needs are known, and historical standards are enforced." The duty of university-trained Ph.D.'s, Andrews continued in imitation of the language of professionalism that was overtaking the fields of medicine and law in this period, was to enforce "discipline" through "higher canons of criticism and interpretation, better balanced judgments, and more rational methods of presentation." Historians should study "history for its own sake" without regard to its practical, public implications and without reference to the latest educational reform. The remarks of critics about obsessive "objectivity, plodding scholarship, and dry-as-dust treatment by the college professor" must "pass unnoticed," Andrews suggested. Scholars should write for "each other," in an atmosphere where "the monographic treatise, and the much abused dissertation of the doctor of philosophy find a welcome and permanent abiding-place." Most of all, Andrews argued, those violating professional standards should be held to task.[14] He concurred with Carl Russell Fish who argued that historians should either be licensed or be held liable to grand jury indictment and prosecution if they misused the past.[15]

Morison was never willing to go so far as to consider prosecuting historians who violated Andrews's standards, but he was willing to endorse them publicly. Not only did he and Andrews work together on a number of professional projects in the years following Andrews's speech, their common resentment of Beard and Dewey encouraged a lasting friendship.[16] On trips to Andrews's summer home in Vermont, Morison doubtless reflected on the vast transformation that had occurred in his own intellectual outlook since the beginning of his career. Just prior to the war, he had regretted his profession's inability to effect any noticeable change in the world or to create a "usable past." Although he rejected the presentist tendencies of New History after the war, he still shared Beard's and Becker's disillusionment with higher education in America. Having fled Harvard to indulge his relativistic impulses, Morison had returned to the United States more convinced of the need for unity and consensus in history and unfavorably disposed toward debunkers. By 1927, some thirteen years after he had begun his teaching career, he had become a detractor of progressive historians, a spokesman for the profession, and a defender of the university. These changes were due in part to votes of confidence he received from the profession and the university, and in part to his own changing attitudes toward the sanctity of the past.

The Place of Tradition

Despite his friendship with Andrews and his sympathy with the professional concerns expressed in "These Forty Years," Morison must have seemed an unlikely crusader in the struggle to maintain educational tradition in America's universities. Having finished *The Oxford History of the United States*, he spent the summer of 1927 once again in idle speculation about retreating from the classroom and living the detached life of a writer in Maine. For the first time since he had been indulging in this dream, however, Morison had the financial wherewithal to do it. His mother had died the winter before, and his inheritance allowed him to build a new bungalow on some family property in Sawyer's Cove, Maine, to refurbish a sailboat, and to buy a new car. He spent his summer days relaxing, far removed from the professional anxieties that controlled his friend Andrews.

"Each day here is such a perfect unity," Morison wrote Lincoln Colcord, "that in the evening after the children are in bed I never write and seldom read, but just sit down and talk it over with Bessie." With him he brought Beard's *The Rise of American Civilization*, but he could not find the time to get to it.[17]

In some ways, Morison hoped his feeling of isolation would never end. "Just now, when the weather has cleared off and the 'rusticators' are gone, in two days I have to go to Boston and move my library and resume (for the last time, I hope), the old grind of teaching 'History 10,' 'History 26', etc.," Morison told Colcord. "I wish I had the courage to say, 'I'll be damned if I will go,' and ask the Stewarts, (your excellent kinsmen), to board me for the winter," he admitted.[18] These thoughts were a reaction to the hurried pace of academic life at Harvard, which he described in an article for the *Harvard Alumni Bulletin*. Taken aback by the "staccato clack of typewriters," the sounds of "hurried steps on the concrete corridors of Widener," and the cries of students and faculty alike to the effect that "we have no time," Morison admitted to occasionally missing "the tune of plashing fountains, [the] gentle clucking of the lawn-mower, [and] the soft footfalls of the Bodleian" at Oxford.[19] Yet he also acknowledged that he could not persist in "a cowardly escape from life" forever.[20] In fact, the bustle of Harvard life was strangely attractive to him, he argued, because it represented not meaningless confusion but "an American overtone to a vital intellectual life."[21] In addition, Morison was more favorably disposed toward it because he had been awarded tenure and promoted to associate professor late in 1925. More secure in his position within the university, in other words, he lost his habitual mistrust of it.[22]

The best indication of Morison's new attitude toward Harvard was his willingness to defend the university against the educational reformers. Deweyan environmentalism had reached Harvard in a number of forms. In its curricular incarnation, it appeared as a proposal by Frederick Merk for a "project method" in history, by which students would be required to study "topics" rather than chronological periods. This proposal was defeated within the department, in part through Morison's opposition.[23] In its social manifestation, Deweyan reform took the shape of a proposal to subdivide Harvard into colleges after the British manner, and this proposal was less easily dismissed. In 1926, Harvard students interested in progressive education issued a "Report on Education" under the auspices of the Harvard Student Council that argued for a radical altering of the university's social geography. The report noted that except for a few local students who commuted, Harvard undergraduates either lived "on campus" in the Harvard Yard or "off campus" in private apartments. Of those who lived off campus, the wealthier occupied lavish apartments in an area south of the campus known as the "Gold Coast," and the poorer students simply found cheap accommodations somewhere in Boston and commuted to school. According to the Student Council report, tensions among "Gold Coasters," the "Yarders," and the "Commuters" damaged the academic atmosphere of the college and suggested the need for a more consistent, "shared" social experience for Harvard students. To accomplish this, the report proposed the construction of numerous "houses" or "colleges" on the outskirts of campus (each with its own dining room, common room, and library), in which upperclassmen would live for three years and participate in social and academic activities. The Student Council also recommended the construction of an experimental "honors house" for the 1926–27 academic year to test the feasibility of the "house" system.[24] Their model was the "live-in" honors colleges at Oxford University, with which Morison had had so much recent contact.

The "house" plan sparked sharp controversy at Harvard. President Lowell supported the proposal because it aspired to the "union of learning and the fine art of living" that he admired in Oxford.[25] "Gold Coasters," however, resented "being herded in with the majority," and the *Harvard Crimson* denounced the plan as a veiled form of "boarding-school discipline" and "Oxford gating." The greatest division of opinion, however, occurred among the alumni. Many graduates opposed the "house system" because it threatened some of the college's most hallowed traditions—its social clubs, fraternities, and eating societies.[26] Others, especially those originally excluded from such traditions, embraced the system as an important step in the democratization of the college. Throughout the 1926–27 school year, concerned alumni and associates filled the pages of the *Harvard Alumni Bulletin* with strong opinions on both sides of the "house" issue.[27] Having recently witnessed firsthand the operation of the "house system," and having had a close association with the college as an undergraduate, graduate student, and professor, Morison's opinions in this matter were highly valued. Characteristically indifferent at first, he eventually came to view the question as linked to the reform efforts of Beard and Dewey, and this conclusion stirred him to action.

In an article entitled "Impressions of Harvard after Oxford," Morison expressed his opposition to the proposal in a manner that underscored his new commitment to historical tradition. Despite his having been excluded from club life as an undergraduate, Morison argued that the presumably more "democratic" Oxford system would "break the present rhythm of student life" by violating long-standing customs and punishing those who did not wish to conform to "house" life.[28] The Student Council plan was too radical, Morison added, and was urged on by students too willing to sell their educational birthrights to reformist pedagogues promising a reduction of academic burdens as a result of more congenial living arrangements. Houses or no houses, college must remain hard work, a reality some Harvard students hoped to ignore by accentuating the social benefits of a house system. To "blow up the foundations" of the college for the sake of imposing a "house" system, Morison argued, would be to overreact to a problem in need of a simpler solution. "[W]hat we really need is a more intellectual set of values among our student body," he wrote, "and this means, on closer analysis, similar values in the community at large."[29]

Morison was still more troubled by the attempt to extend the Oxford model to the classroom experience at Harvard. Odin Roberts suggested in the *Harvard Alumni Bulletin* that the "Oxfordization" of Harvard should be extended to the lecture system, allowing students to attend classes as a matter of choice as students in the honors colleges at Oxford did.[30] "Certainly I should not advocate the adoption of the pure Oxford system, which is not simply a method of teaching, but a method of examination," Morison wrote.[31] In England students were "expected to take care of themselves," he told a group of entering history graduate students in 1927; a candidate for the Ph.D., for instance, was merely required to have a thesis topic approved and to check in occasionally with his advisor. Seminars "were generally few, and not considered necessary." When a graduate student's thesis was due, it was read by a small committee, and the student was given an oral examination. After having invested three or four years' work in the project, a student succeeded or failed solely on the basis of a single examination. "This system at Oxford . . . results in a very high percentage of failures," he warned, "and it is intended to; for very few of the leading teachers in those Universities have the Ph.D. themselves, and they believe that there is no special craft or mystery about writing sound history." They operate under the assumption that "the best men will teach themselves as they go along."[32]

Morison argued that this "hit-or-miss" technique was unsuitable for American scholars, in part because it was too subjective and relativistic. "In this country, and this university," he told the Harvard recruits, "we follow a different system. We are not content to offer facilities for independent study of supermen; we are not such people ourselves. We were helped by the . . . guidance of our system," a system characterized, as Charles Andrews noted, by specific professional standards of operation. The key to success was to have a well-planned regimen, to take the necessary courses, and to apply that knowledge to some worthy scholarship. Achievement in graduate school was not a matter of intuition of "a gift of the Gods" as some Oxford dons seemed to intimate; it was a matter of adherence to rigorous standards and "the first requisite—hard work." Exhorting his students, as Channing had him, to maintain standards, Morison concluded, "We of this generation hope, that before we die, history, the most readable and enduring form of letters, may be restored to the high place and prestige that it enjoyed in the era of Macauley and Motley, Prescott and Parkman, and we wish you of your generation, to do it."[33]

In his opposition to the Report on Education, his comments to Odin Roberts, and his remarks to history graduate students, Morison not only questioned the desirability of adopting British systems at Harvard; he questioned the feasibility. In all three contexts he expressed his distrust of progressive educational reform and affirmed his belief in the durability of traditions. "Oxford is so vital, genial, and beautiful," he wrote, "that few Americans with any sensibility can visit it without feeling 'Why cannot we have this in America?' But the really organic, fundamental things that made Oxford what it is," Morison argued, "are the product of eight centuries of slow ripening, and can be produced in no other way." Fortunately, Harvard students had their own three centuries of tradition to draw on. "Starting in 1636 as a transplanted English college in the wilderness," he noted, "Harvard had worked out a pattern of her own [which] is now too deeply bitten into the metal of [Harvard's] life to be eradicated." To abandon three hundred years of development almost overnight for another system was not only irresponsible; it was futile.[34]

"What, then, can we learn from Oxford?" Morison asked in the *Harvard Alumni Bulletin*. "As I see it, [our purpose is] to aim for quality rather than quantity; to attract undergraduates of widely different types . . . and to impart to our students a sense of value that will give them more zest for study, and a more profitable employment of their leisure. In all these respects we are improving more rapidly than most of our graduates realize," he added. Above all, Harvard did not need a radical alteration according to Deweyian or Oxfordian models. "There is nothing fundamentally the matter with Harvard," he concluded, "and so long as her graduates maintain their traditional attitude of intellectual interest, affectionate criticism, and loyal support, there will be no danger of stagnation or decay."[35]

The Ivory Tower

Many students and members of the faculty agreed with Morison's assessment; they resented the attempt to upset Harvard tradition or to remake the college in the image of another school. Some found social cliques a small price to pay for "traditional social flexibility" and "the liberty to sink or swim" at the college. Others sympathized with the "house plan" but resented the way it was "railroaded through" by the administration. Under pressure from these objectors, the General Education Board turned down an initial request for funds to build an experimental Oxford house at Harvard. But money ironically prevailed to determine the issue. In 1928 Edward Harkness offered Yale University $3 million to build an honors college like that at Oxford. Frustrated by delays at Yale, Harkness made the same offer several months later to President Lowell, who immediately accepted. On November 6, 1928, the *"fait accompli,"* as Morison called it, was announced to the faculty, and by 1930 construction had begun on the first two houses (Dunster and Lowell). By 1931 another five were ready for occupancy.[36]

As Morison's frustrations with reform grew, he identified himself increasingly as a university scholar under attack by radicals. In favor of slow, gradual change, Morison took satisfaction in pointing out the failures of progressive pedagogues who pushed too hard for reform. Not only did he point out the general failure of the social studies movement in midwestern universities such as the University of Chicago, where the social sciences had proven themselves "not yet freed from the influence of emotion, politics, and prejudice," but he also recognized the general failure of its New England variations.[37] Returning to Amherst College in the late 1920s, for instance, Morison was pleased to note that the Meiklejohn influence was gone. "I questioned closely my faculty friends about the Meiklejohn regime," he wrote, and they "agreed that almost the whole trouble with it was the President's conception of higher education." Even Lucien Price was forced to admit that Morison was correct, because one of his friends who had studied at Amherst had gone on to Harvard where he claimed to have "first learned what study and scholarship really were." What he had learned at Amherst, the friend claimed, was "mere froth."[38]

Yet Morison was not so conservative that he denied reformers the right to propose change or to build their castles in the sky. His belief in the fundamental privilege of reformers to consider change was dramatically underscored in the early 1930s when Morison actually joined forces with Beard for a brief time in support of a basic civil liberty. In 1932, newspaper mogul William Randolph Hearst proposed that states implement loyalty oaths for their teachers. Hearst was concerned that radical reformers (he numbered Beard and Dewey among these) had infiltrated American schools with a reform philosophy that threatened basic American principles. Capitalizing on economic fears engendered by the depression, these reformers were introducing subversive ideas to American students, Hearst argued, and should be required to take oaths affirming their commitment to the democratic system.[39] The proposed oath for Massachusetts was representative; it read:

> Every citizen of the United States, entering service, on or after October first, nineteen hundred and thirty-five, as professor, instructor or teacher at any college, university, teacher's college, or public or private school, in the commonwealth shall, before entering upon the discharge of his duties, take and subscribe to, before an officer authorized by law to administer oaths, . . . the following oath or affirmation: 'I do solemnly swear (or affirm) that I will support the Constitution of the United States of the Commonwealth of Massachusetts, and that I will faithfully discharge the duties of the position . . . according to the best of my ability.[40]

As innocuous as this seemed to some educators, it deeply offended others, especially Charles Beard. On behalf of the National Education Board, Beard went on the lecture circuit to condemn Hearst's proposal. Arguing that Hearst "pandered to depraved tastes and has been an enemy of everything that is best in the American tradition," Beard organized a nationwide appeal to educators, urging them to ignore the oaths and to fight for their repeals in state legislatures.[41]

Despite his agreement with Hearst that Beard, Dewey, and others were too radical in their approaches to American education, Morison nonetheless supported the campaign against teachers' oaths, which he viewed as reactionary and repressive. Characteristically, Morison based his objections to the oaths on their implicit threat to established traditions. Describing the oaths as one of the many "temporary fads and fallacies" he despised so much in education, he urged teachers to hold fast to the customs that had served the state well for so long. William Randolph Hearst may think "that this educational system of ours, which ha[s] been leading the country for three centuries [is] going rotten," Morison wrote, but (as in the case of Harvard) all that was really needed was a stricter work ethic. "The teacher is a custodian of tradition, . . . and freedom of expression is an American tradition," Morison quoted Walter Lippmann, adding that to defend freedom in teaching was to come to the support of "not only one of the oldest American traditions" but also the "inner principle of a civilized existence." Both Morison and Lippmann rejected Beard's presentism, but they defended his right to protect against the incursions of "fascism."[42]

In the short run, Hearst prevailed over Beard and Morison, and a mandatory teachers' oath was passed in Massachusetts in the early thirties. Lecturing in Texas when word of the oath arrived, Morison felt embarrassment for his home state and himself. "When the news came through, I had to stand a lot of quips from my Texan friends, such as 'Well, well, so Massachusetts has gone Ku-Klux!' and 'When will the Monkey Trial start?'" he noted. Supposing that teachers' oaths, like slavery, were things "we had passed beyond," Morison felt compelled to break the promise he had made nearly a decade earlier to stay out of public reform work. He not only organized an anti-oath group in Massachusetts, the Society for Freedom in Teaching, but also lead the repeal effort in the Massachusetts State legislature in the fall of 1936. Making comparisons once again between British and American universities, Morison told a special review session of the legislature that the universities of Oxford and Cambridge in the seventeenth century had required all teachers to swear allegiance to "the Solemn League and Covenant" and had routinely excluded teachers and students from college on the basis of religious or other dissent. The practical effect of these British oaths, he noted, was to penalize "all originality and initiative on the part of teachers," thereby excluding Oxford and Cambridge from participation in the "age of enlightenment." Neither university recovered its "ancient standing until the nineteenth century," he added, "when these test oaths were removed, originality was encouraged, and members of any church, or none, could take a degree." Noting that the Massachusetts Teachers' Oath Law "has put this Commonwealth in line with the policy of the kingdom against which our forefathers revolted," Morison urged legislators (as he had Harvard alumni) to ignore British models and to make a "declaration of independence" against hackneyed oaths.[43]

The chair of the legislative committee considering the repeal, Senator Charles G. Miles, appreciated Morison's efforts to provide a historical focus to the discussion and thanked him for the even-tempered professionalism of his comments. Miles did not appreciate the "performances" of several of Morison's Harvard colleagues, however, who had also come to the State legislature to argue against teachers' oaths. According to Miles, a Professor McLaughlin "ridicul[ed] the committee" by speaking primarily to the audience in the gallery and making "incoherent rambling and senseless remarks which seemed to be of a delusional nature." Prancing back and forth at the speaker's podium waving his arms up and down like a "vaudeville . . . clown at a circus," McLaughlin provoked the gallery spectators (mainly Harvard students) to respond alternately by "giggling, laughing, hand clapping, booing and hissing," Miles acknowledged with displeasure. McLaughlin "did more harm to your cause than any who appeared before me at the hearing—vote against the repeal," Miles told Morison.[44] Morison apologized for his colleague, but not for his cause. "Your letter certainly proves that few teachers are politicians or know how to make themselves ingratiating," he wrote. But Morison insisted that Miles must make allowance for McLaughlin's "natural human reaction" to the questions of committee members who were in his estimation "extremely uncivil," especially Representative Pierce, who insisted "[i]t's the perfessors we're after." Pierce's questions were irrelevant to the matter at hand, Morison argued, and were designed to prove that all Harvard professors were Communists. As for the students in the gallery, they were "highly exasperated at seeing their respected teachers and presidents treated like criminals in a dock by politicians who could hardly make themselves intelligible in the English language," Morison added snidely, "and they reacted accordingly."[45]

Despite Morison's best efforts, the Massachusetts teachers' oath was not repealed. The failure of the Society for Freedom in Teaching coupled with the defeat of the only other public project with which Morison had been associated in the last decade (a stay of sentence for Sacco and Vanzetti) soured him once again to reform efforts. Professors had done little to help either cause, Morison reflected later, and in several cases, McLaughlin's in particular, they had done more harm than good. Uncomfortable with working so closely on any project associated with Charles Beard, Morison eventually turned his back on the midwestern historian and his anti-oath campaign. If some of his Harvard colleagues wished to persist in attempts to "reform the body politic," that was their prerogative, but he predicted the college would have "a longer and brighter future if she attempts to fulfill the function she was founded and has been maintained to perform"—advancing learning.[46]

Some of Morison's friends did not quite understand his retreat. Lucien Price wrote an editorial for the *Boston Globe* condemning the way professors had handled the teachers' oath affair, criticizing with special vehemence those scholars like Morison who had come to view "politics as no special concern of theirs" and had returned to the isolation of their "Ivory Towers." Renewing the comparison that had dominated much of the debate over reform at Harvard, Price suggested that European universities such as Oxford encouraged professors to "pour a stream of life-giving thought and action into the blood of their surrounding societies."[47] American universities, he argued, shamefully had not. Morison disagreed with the analogy. "[W]hat reform or revolution has ever been started in a [European] university?" he asked. Arguing that there had been none of the substantial sort of reform Price expected of American educational institutions, he went on to ask how such reform should proceed. Should the president of Harvard "go from one department to another—say from the Astronomical Observatory to the Greek Department, and say, 'Sorry, boys, all this ivory tower stuff has to got to stop?'" Morison asked facetiously. "I'll give you six months to reorganize yourselves and get busy on current problems," he continued in derision. "Everyone has got to bear a hand. No, Mr. Shapley, I don't mean you should use your telescope like Diogenes did his lantern . . . but why can't you f'r instance, find out what they do about unemployment on Mars?"[48]

Nor did Morison appreciate Price's criticisms of the apolitical nature of some professors. "The professors think that 'politics is no special concern of theirs,'" Morison quoted Price. "Well, is it?" he retorted. Why should a professor take any more of an interest in politics than the average citizen does, he asked, especially when, as in the experience of the teachers' oaths, their involvement was only resented and counterproductive? "Doesn't the public really want the professors to stay in the ivory tower?" he asked Price. Furthermore, Morison defended the university's right to indulge in scholarly activities with little ostensible public benefit. To Price's accusation that universities applied funds to "such studies as happen to please themselves" without any consideration for their practical effects, Morison noted that professors were not willing to adopt any "utilitarian standard" for legislating research interests. Universities should not be expected to conform to society's needs, he argued, but society to the needs of universities. Renewing his attack on the "usable past" tradition of New History, Morison noted that whenever scholars sought to be "useful" in the sense that his grandfather Eliot had envisioned, "they attract unfavorable and, I believe, justifiable criticism." Going outside "their proper sphere" by "mingling directly in partisan activities," scholars incur the wrath of a public that "dimly realizes this is not the proper thing for professors to do, and proceeds to throw stink bombs!" he added. Morison argued that he and his colleagues should be "above the partisan passions of the day" and maintain the conservative traditions "that have sustained them for years." If working in their proper sphere required professors to adhere strictly to the professional standards outlined by a scholar such as Charles Andrews or to quarantine themselves in ivory towers, then so be it.[49]

The Tercentenary Celebration

Nothing suggests the degree to which Morison's historical outlook had changed since the postwar period more than his decision to write a multi-volume history of Harvard. Prior to the war he had rebelled against the institutional approaches of his Harvard mentors, had worked to establish a usable past outside the walls of his alma mater, had eschewed "academic" audiences for "he-men," and had considered retirement from teaching altogether. Immediately following the war he remained disillusioned with his departmental colleagues, disgruntled with the materialism of his students, and anxious to escape Harvard for Oxford. Yet by the late 1920s, Morison was at work on an "official" history of Harvard in honor of the three hundredth birthday of the college in 1936.[50] An institutional history in the best tradition of Albert Bushnell Hart, it glorified the Harvard past, celebrated the achievements of his colleagues, upheld detached scholarship against utilitarian educational reform, and reiterated the advantages of Harvard over European universities such as Oxford. Dissatisfaction with debunkers, relativists, sectionalists, progressive reformers, pedagogical idealists, social studies promoters, and "ivory tower" detractors drove him into close identification with beleaguered Harvard. Both man and institution symbolized the obduracy of tradition against the challenges of reform.

Morison had first conceived of the idea for an institutional history of Harvard after experiencing an "epiphany of sorts" while vacationing in Spain during his final term at Oxford. While visiting the Cathedral at Toledo, he happened onto a series of portraits of the archbishops of the city and was struck by their value as a record of the institutional history of Spain. "I wondered where a comparable sequence could be found in North America," Morison later wrote, and "[i]t suddenly dawned on me that my own *alma mater*, Harvard College, was about the oldest institution and certainly the oldest corporation in the United States."[51] This insight awakened him to the importance of "the history of ideas as expressed through academic institutions" and the need to uphold long-standing tradition against transitory educational reform.[52] The tercentenary history became his declaration of allegiance to the stabilizing forces of profession and university.

The tercentenary series began chronologically with *The Founding of Harvard* (1935) and *Harvard College in the Seventeenth Century* (2 vols., 1936). In these volumes, Morison sketched the corporate structure of Harvard, noting with pride that the original Harvard charter of the seventeenth century remained the essential governing authority of the college in the twentieth century. In addition, he noted with pride that the charter had been preserved not by restrictive practices, as James Truslow Adams had averred, but by commitment to broad, liberal arts principles. Adams had argued that Harvard was little more than a training school for Puritan clerics who trained students in the repressive techniques necessary to perpetuate Puritan control of the New England mind. Morison noted, however, that Harvard was not primarily a "divinity school" in the seventeenth century but a college run by dedicated intellectuals interested in the liberal arts. The education of ministers was one of the most important functions of the college, certainly, but the "advancement and perpetuation of learning were the broad and ultimate objects of the foundation." Hence, according to Morison, all Harvard students were trained in the old Liberal Arts tradition—taking courses in grammar, rhetoric, logic, music, arithmetic, geometry, astronomy—while students who wished to enter the ministry had to complete their bachelor's degrees before receiving any specialized training in theology.[53]

Nor was Harvard's liberal arts tradition upheld by self-serving commercial interests as Charles Beard had suggested. The goal of a Harvard education was not to provide the specialized training necessary to take up a trade, Morison noted, and Harvard students did not expect financial payback for their educational outlays. Instead students were trained to enter "a society of scholars" and especially to appreciate the principles of *"veritas,"* or "divine truth," the search for accuracy and fidelity in all things. From its inception, Morison argued in *Three Centuries of Harvard* (1936), Harvard had subordinated all political, economic, and even religious concerns to the pursuit of truth, which had allowed the college to avoid educational constraints of all types, even if narrowly at times. In the seventeenth century, he explained, Harvard had been protected from such wearisome and persistent restrictions as teachers' oaths by a commitment to a "harmonious and balanced" education free "from the devastating control of provincial orthodoxy." In the eighteenth and nineteenth centuries, the pursuit of "a more perfect knowledge" was hindered occasionally by individuals or self-interest groups masquerading as educational reformers, who, like those of the progressive ilk in the 1920s, were only too ready to sacrifice tradition for immediate ends. In the 1830s, for instance, the Massachusetts Board of Overseers attacked Harvard for its "treachery to Calvinism" and its laxity in enforcing evening prayers and daily church worship. Responsible for reviewing the affairs of the college, the Board of Overseers published a report "highly damaging to the University, taunting it with diminished numbers, accusing it of decadence, excessive expense, and sectarianism." President Quincy of Harvard, however, wrote a pungent reply in which he defended the "spirit of religious liberty" at Harvard against those who wanted "not a liberal college" but a "Calvinist" university. Quincy "was none of your mealy-mouthed, apologetic liberals," Morison concluded, but a defender of academic freedom who silenced Harvard detractors by the sheer power of his commitment to divine truth. "The good ship Harvard might lose her freight and the number of her mess," Morison wrote, "but the *Veritas* banner was nailed to the mast."[54]

In the late nineteenth century, the greatest threat to *veritas* came from business. From the Civil War to the early twentieth century, lesser schools had sacrificed academic integrity to "the clank of machinery and the clink of dollars," Morison wrote. Hoping to "save something for the advancement of learning" out of the "great scramble for wealth" in that century, Harvard's President Charles Eliot ushered in an "Olympian Age" at the college, creating graduate schools and providing faculty "the opportunity to train disciples in an atmosphere of professional study and creative scholarship." His elective system, animated by the principle of student liberty, verified the importance of *veritas* to an academic community wherein tradition was the only "safeguard" against material distractions. Yet even so gifted an educator as Eliot was capable of mistakes, Morison warned, particularly overzealous reform. In his enthusiasm for preserving liberty of choice at Harvard, for instance, Eliot had abolished mandatory requirements for incoming freshman, including Latin and Greek. "[T]he pressure . . . of parents wanting 'practical' instruction for their sons . . . had the classics on the run," Morison noted, and Eliot unfortunately encouraged this flight toward "vocational" education. Arguing that "no equivalent to the classics, for mental training, cultural background, or solid satisfaction in afterlife, has yet been discovered," Morison admitted sadly that "Mr. Eliot, more than any other man, is responsible for the greatest educational crime of the century against American youth—depriving him of his classical heritage."[55]

Subsequent Harvard presidents had occasionally acquiesced to reform impulses as well, Morison noted, including President Lowell, whose Oxford house system depended too closely on the excesses of "progressive reformers" who had "mangled and thrown away" traditions in the name of progress.[56] Yet Morison did not dwell on these failures nor on the disruptions of the anti-oath campaign in which he and so many other Harvard faculty had participated. Instead he emphasized the persistence of the Harvard tradition and the noble detachment of her hardworking scholars. In taking this attitude toward the Harvard past, Morison followed both the letter and the spirit of Charles Andrews's suggestions for the writing of history by professionals. *Veritas* was but another name for the commitment to objectivity that Andrews had urged in "These Forty Years." The emphasis in the tercentenary volumes on Harvard's role as preserver of professional standards, for instance, conformed literally to Andrews's dictum that scholarship should be "largely controlled by our collegiate departments" where "historical study is organized, historical needs are known, and historical standards are enforced."[57] Morison even structured the thematic content of the last volume in the series (ordered chronologically), *The Development of Harvard University, 1869–1929*, around the professionalization of academic fields and editorialized against debunkers of the professional ethic. Arguing that the public "is beginning to display an intrusive interest in the 'views' of history teachers, as of old in the doctrines of theologians," Morison claimed that "scholarly standards" rather than public ones must continue to inform the work done by Harvard professors. While "[h]ardly any two members of the Harvard History Department belong in the same camp," Morison concluded, "all consider it unethical to make History the hand-maiden of propaganda."[58]

Readers of the tercentenary history (many of them Harvard graduates) praised Morison for restoring dignity to the traditions of a college that were under constant attack in the 1920s. Harvard graduates, commented one reviewer, could take pride in Morison's demonstration that "there is hardly a controversial sore point in the whole range of higher education which has not been fought over in Cambridge during the last three hundred years."[59] Another announced that the "academic world of America is under a debt of real gratitude to Professor Morison" for providing the "fullest history" yet of America's greatest professional institution of higher education.[60] Morison himself immodestly proclaimed that the tercentenary volumes "have set a high standard for American college and university histories because of their emphasis on the intellectual aspect rather than the brick-and-mortar" and for "descriptions of curricula and of undergraduate life and customs at different periods."[61] Still stronger praise came from Morison's colleagues in history, some of whom had been inclined to doubt his commitment to the college. Albert Bushnell Hart wrote his former student: "As a graduate and an historian of the period in which Harvard was founded, I take this opportunity to express my personal admiration, as a friend, and gratitude as a Harvard man for the service that you are performing, not only for Harvard College but for all American institutions of learning, by your skillful and painstaking and humane treatment of the history of our beloved university." Finding vindication of his own institutional approach in the tercentenary histories, Hart added with collegial spirit, "Now that I am going to 'live happily ever afterward,' I hope to have more frequent opportunities of an exchange of views with the man now connected with Harvard University who seems to me to share most closely my points of view."[62] Even George Santayana, who had left Harvard in disgust for Spain during the great expatriate wave and had never softened in his attitudes toward the college, wrote to thank Morison for the nostalgia that the tercentenary volumes awakened in him.[63]

Morison's defense of Harvard was an expression of the new sense of collegiality he found with his colleagues as well. The final affirmation of Morison's sense of place among them came in June 1936, when Harvard awarded him an honorary degree during the tercentenary celebration. In presenting the award, the dean of the college praised Morison's work on the history of Harvard and thanked him for restoring the reputation of the college to its rightful place among the leading American educational insti-tutions.[64] Morison accepted the highest professional honor his university had to offer by acknowledging the changes that had taken place in the ten years since he had returned from Oxford. "The lot of the professor . . . has become happier," he noted with pleasure.[65] Morison thanked the Harvard faculty for welcoming him to the "community of ideals and of purpose" at Harvard, and he urged them to continue the fight against the "selfish dilettantism" of her debunking critics.[66]

The tercentenary histories, therefore, "integrated" Morison more closely with the Harvard faculty, a group with whom he had admittedly "been hitherto a little aloof."[67] One of the great values of being a Harvard professor, he noted in a fresh burst of enthusiasm for his workplace, "is the opportunity to discuss one's work with colleagues."[68] On receiving tenure in 1925, Morison had been admitted to the inner sanctum of an exclusive yet embattled club with whose members he occasionally took issue; by 1936, he identified so completely with his Harvard colleagues as to suggest a total transformation in his intellectual and personal outlook. A chance meeting shortly after the tercentenary with junior colleague Paul Buck symbolized the change. Passing Buck in the halls of Widener Library, Morison received the usual salutation: "Good morning, Professor Morison." Proceeding several paces down the corridor without responding, Morison paused, reflected, and turned, calling back with a newfound sense of collegiality, "Paul," he said, "[t]he time has come to call me Sam."[69]

The Ragged Edge of Truth

Charles Beard, James Truslow Adams,
Van Wyck Brooks and the
Defense of Profession

8

The Threat of Dialectical Materialism

he issues raised by Morison's defense of tradition in the tercentenary history had wide-ranging professional implications in the 1930s. The role of custom was the focus of several panel discussions in the annual meeting of the American Historical Association in 1934 and the central theme in the keynote address of Eugen Rosenstock-Huessy. Noting that "[h]istory is corrected and purified tradition, enlarged and analyzed memory," Rosenstock-Huessy proclaimed its crucial importance as a stabilizing force in a nation rocked by profoundly disorienting change. Citing the depression as just one of the major causes of this confusion, he argued that professional historians must fight incessantly against those who would use economic crisis to promote radically new historiographies. In particular he disclaimed dialectical materialists, adherents to the Marxian interpretation of history that regarded the past as the story of constant conflict between opposites arising from the internal contradictions in all things. Focusing on the distinctions among classes, dialectical materialists sought to overturn traditional confidence in democratic capitalism and to substitute a new vision of history based on Marxist concepts of class struggle. The attack on tradition was an integral part of this strategy, Rosenstock-Huessey implied.[1]

Not surprisingly, Charles Beard was a major target of Rosenstock-Huessey and others who remonstrated against dialectical materialism. Although not a pure Marxist himself, Beard emphasized class conflict, and his persistent debunking undercut faith in traditional American institutions. Rosenstock-Huessey correctly "warned our profession," Morison later wrote, "that we were losing our hold on the public through wanton and unnecessary flouting of tradition" by historians such as Beard "who embraced dialectical materialism as an easy explanation of past reality," saving themselves "a great deal of painful thought" in the process.[2] Reviewing the first fifty years of the profession's development in another paper presented before the American Historical Association, Theodore Clark Smith singled Beard out for attack, objecting to his abandonment of "objective truth" and his "resort to the economic interpretation of history." Smith believed that the attack on the founders of the Constitution in *An Economic Interpretation of the Constitution* was part of a concerted career-long effort to subordinate fact to ideology by a man who did not "consider it necessary to be impartial or even fair." Believing that "an historian owes respect to tradition and to folk-memory," Smith and others condemned Beard's attempts to capitalize on the fears of economic depression for the purposes of promoting his own "disturbing" brand of Marxist history.[3]

Under increasing attack within the profession, Beard responded to his critics on two levels. First, he defended himself against those who questioned his objectivity, while raising concerns about the feasibility of achieving objectivity in historical writing. In an article for the *American Historical Review* entitled "That Noble Dream," Beard took specific issue with Theodore Clark Smith's contention that dialectical materialists as a group had abandoned objective truth. Simply because he chose to consider the economic interests that lay beneath the surface of politics or because he desired to wrestle with "the quandaries of our life today," Beard noted, did not mean that he was hostile to the search for truth. Instead, Beard distinguished between objectivity as a noble goal and the limitations of human perception that made that goal unattainable in any complete sense. Although competent historians can agree on many particular facts related to a historical period, Beard wrote, it is impossible to "tell the truth of history as it actually was." Smith's "noble dream" of complete objectivity was a "splendid" though unrealizable ambition. Second, Beard argued that dialectical materialism introduced a creative, critical spirit into a profession otherwise committed too readily to maintaining a conservative status quo. Not coincidentally, this defense derived from Beard's feeling that he was the target of a conspiracy on the part of academicians to ostracize historians working outside the university. If dialectical materialism emphasized the struggle between haves and have-nots, then it was an easy transition for Beard, who had resigned his position at Columbia University, to imagine himself as a disempowered outsider struggling for recognition from an established elite. Reaffirming his faith in historical relativism and the principle of choice in education, Beard urged members of the American Historical Association to accept dialectical materialism as a theory of historical explanation with at least as much validity as those theories officially sanctioned by the profession.[4]

The debate over dialectical materialism was particularly intense in 1934 because Beard had been the controversial president of the American Historical Association in 1933. His election to the presidency was itself an indication of how divisive his philosophy could be, since his nomination was finally pushed through despite considerable objections by a diverse group of historians who for one reason or another had grown tired of the "stodginess" and "stagnation" of the profession and looked for Beard to "shake things up."[5] Beard did not disappoint them. His presidential address, entitled "Written History as an Act of Faith," attacked sacred cows and sacrosanct traditions, including the "largely formalistic and old-fashioned" scientific scholarship of the profession's founding fathers and the objective positivism of their conservative descendents.[6] Indignant over these assaults, leaders within the profession hurled retorts at Beard to the effect that his philosophies were antidemocratic and his techniques subversive. In an age when European historians were turning desperately to fascism or nazism for solutions to complicated world problems, the anti-Beard faction within the American Historical Association viewed dialectical materialism as an unwelcome import. Urging American historians to "stop horsing around with strange gods, and to rally to the defense of American traditions," writer Archibald MacLeish spoke for many professional historians when he condemned Beard's historical philosophy as dangerous to the future of the country.[7]

Perhaps no one was as vocal about the threat of Beard's historical principles as Morison. Despite having lost "a good part" of his family's real estate during the depression, Morison never embraced "radical" solutions to America's economic crisis since he feared (as he had in the case of educational reform) that such remedies would be worse than the diseases they sought to cure. On a "motor-tour" of Germany in 1934, Morison and his Bessie were "revolted" by the willingness of Germans to embrace nazism as the "wave of the future," and the ruthless rise of Hitler to power persuaded them that America "had something worth preserving." The couple's only fear was that democracy might prove "too weak or deluded to defend itself," and to avoid that possibility, Morison urged his fellow historians to be gentle with the nation's democratic traditions.[8] Citing Beard's complicity in the "mass murder of historical characters," Morison noted with disdain that in Beard's works "there are no great men or leading characters, only automata whose speeches, ideas, or aspirations are mentioned merely to give the historian an opportunity to sneer or smear." Dialectical materialists "will admit no high-mindedness, no virtue, no nobility of character,"[9] he added. Morison especially resented a book written by Beard in 1936 that outlined the economic motivations for America's entry into World War I. Entitled *The Devil Theory of War*, the book advanced what Morison referred to as the "childish" Marxist theory that "wicked politicians, perhaps shoved along by wicked bankers, marshaled innocent people into war." This interpretation angered Morison not only because it implied that Americans had been compelled to "do things they would never think of doing otherwise," but because it suggested that Americans were about to be duped again into entering a senseless war against an imagined European enemy on behalf of an elusive democractic ideal.[10]

According to Morison, historians needed to counter the disloyalty inherent in Beard's historiography by emphasizing the positive aspects of American democratic traditions. In a 1936 address before the Women's Club of Boston, Morison asserted that America had just survived the greatest depression in its history "with democratic institutions unshaken," and with "no more disorder than the scuffle of the bonus army in Washington." People were satisfied with Roosevelt's leadership, he added, likening F. D. R.'s second term to the "famous Era of Good Feelings" one hundred and twenty years before. Arguing that it was "time to take stock, and consider fundamentals," Morison urged his audience not to panic or to thoughtlessly embrace the radical programs of dialectical materialists such as Beard that promised easy solutions to complicated questions.[11] In so doing, he linked the need to preserve democratic traditions with the desire among historians to maintain professional standards. "Instead of adopting a personal 'frame of reference,'" as Morison referred to Beard's philosophy, "the historian should be very wary of his preconceptions, and be just as critical and skeptical of them as the writings of his predecessor," he wrote. Dialectical materialism is "a danger" to the historian's "professional integrity," Morison claimed, because it "tempts him to deviate from the truth in order to satisfy . . . the emotions of the public to whom he looks for circulation." Arguing that Beard and his followers had not demonstrated "[a]n inherent loyalty to truth," he proclaimed that no person without such a loyalty could be a great or even good historian. "Loyalty to truth," of course, was but another name for *veritas,* the dynamic motive of the university with whose traditions he now identified so closely in opposition to the "radical programs" of progressive reformers.[12]

Morison was not so naïve as not to recognize the difficulty of determining exactly what constitutes truth in any given historical situation. Of course the historian's "own sense of values will enter into the selection and arrangement of facts," he acknowledged, and "[i]t goes without saying that complete 'scientific' objectivity is unattainable by the historian." Yet so much has been written by historians like Beard about the limitations on "'scientific' objectivity," he maintained, "as to obscure the plain, outstanding principle that the historian's basic task is one of presenting a corpus of ascertained fact." In salute to the philosophies of his Harvard mentors, he proclaimed, "For my part, I stand firm on the oft-quoted sentence of Leopold von Ranke, which we American historians remember when we have forgotten all the rest of our German"—that the historian should "simply explain the event exactly as it happened."[13] Beard violated this principle by starting "with the negative, the denial of Ranke's classic dictum" and refusing "to recognize truth as the ultimate goal of history."[14] In addition, Morison also recognized that historians must make concessions to the reading public in order to woo them from the false ideologies of writers such as Beard. He reminded his colleagues that their commitment to traditional institutional approaches must not blind them to the importance of social and cultural history nor cause them to ignore the art of historical writing perfected by many relativists such as Beard. Claiming that Beard had twisted the methodologies of these nascent disciplines and had invented a compelling language to legitimize his own misleading philosophies, Morison urged professional historians to extend scientific rigor to social and cultural history lest they become dominated by "dilletantes, fakirs, and 'historians without fear and without research.' "[15]

According to Morison, the work of his friend Charles M. Andrews had demonstrated the dangers of negligence in this matter. Since the delivery of "These Forty Years" in 1924, Andrews had campaigned tirelessly for the maintenance of professional standards, adhering in his own work to strict principles of objectivity and scientific detachment. His obsession with institutional approaches to the past, however, had caused him to lose readers to a new school of Beardian colonial historians who extended dialectical materialism to social and cultural milieus.[16] In a generally praiseworthy review of the first volume of Andrews's multivolume history *The Colonial Period* (1934–38), Morison warned readers that his friend's institutional approach lacked "freshness." *The Colonial Period* would have had a greater importance, Morison wrote, if it "had appeared in 1904 rather than 1934," because it largely restated what institutional historians such as Osgood, Channing, Beer, "and a host of others" had been saying for thirty years. While granting that "political and institutional aspects of the founding of New England have never been so ably handled in so small a space," Morison nonetheless concluded that "on the social history of these colonies, Professor Andrews is not so happy," since he exhibited "a tendency to make Olympian pronouncements (such as the New Englander's hostility to beauty and exclusive preoccupation with theology), on subjects that he does not (in the preface at least) profess to cover." In the profession at large, Morison warned, "institutional has given way to social history as the aspect toward which young scholars are turning their attention," and elders like Andrews needed to provide examples of proper professional technique in these fields lest Beard and others come to dominate them.[17]

Andrews graciously acknowledged Morison's review and reminded him "that no two people will ever agree on just how history should be written. I have to write in my own way," he concluded, "or not at all."[18] But Morison, believing the matter was more urgent than Andrews understood, portrayed professional historians as engaged in an intellectual battle whose consequences were crucial to the future of the nation. Professionals must fight to recapture readers from the snares of dialectical materialism, he urged, before they became irrecoverably committed to Marxism. Opposed to reactionary measures that would silence Marxist historians altogether (such as teachers' oaths), Morison nonetheless urged historians to provide acceptable alternatives for American readers made vulnerable by the ravages of economic despair. Well-written social histories that reaffirmed basic democratic values and American traditions were indispensable to this effort, Morison concluded.[19]

"Uses of the Puritan Past"

Not surprisingly, the debate over dialectical materialism eventually centered on historical approaches to the Puritan past. In 1926, R. H. Tawney had published an influential work entitled *Religion and the Rise of Capitalism*, which traced the rise of a Puritan work ethic in the western world. Morison, who had "profited" by Tawney's lectures at Oxford, referred to him as "the greatest economic-social historian" of the century, a "man of genius" who "made a great book out of dull facts and refractory material" and thereby demonstrated how social and cultural history could be written profitably.[20] Tawney argued that Puritanism had promoted not only self-restraint, a sense of community values, and a stern morality, but also a commendable work ethic based on "industry, thrift, [and] achievements of wealth." As the cornerstone of American democratic capitalism, Puritanism was credited with influencing the moral values of American institutions, the national faith in civil liberty, the providential belief in American destiny, and the pervasive community spirit of towns throughout the United States.[21]

Tawney's theories were in direct opposition to those of Charles Beard and other dialectical materialists, because his theories legitimized an economic system with which they found fault. In *The Rise of American Civilization*, Beard focused on the injustices of the class structure that resulted from Tawney's capitalistic Puritans. The "niggardly soil, the severe life, and the religious rigor of Massachusetts," Beard argued, encouraged a capitalist system marked by stratification and intolerance.[22] Other historians loosely associated with Beard also made the Puritans their whipping boys. H. L. Mencken and Randolph Bourne had savagely debunked the Puritans in the prewar period, and in 1921 James Truslow Adams had assailed them in *The Founding of New England*. While hardly a dialectical materialist, Adams condemned the strict regulation of Puritan economic life. In promoting practical business activity over intellectual and artistic achievements, he noted, the Puritans had choked off creativity in the name of a Protestant work ethic. The pernicious Puritan ideal "spread throughout the whole land" and was "absorbed into the common national life," Adams argued, until it irrecoverably affected American educational and cultural institutions. Reflecting some of the thinking that had motivated his attack on universities in the early 1920s, Adams criticized Puritanism's elitism, its "sterile moralism," and its strangulation of cultural enterprises in the arts and sciences.[23]

There had been a time when Morison was persuaded by these arguments. In his brief flirtation with New History in the prewar period, Morison had employed the language of anti-Puritanism in the earliest drafts of the *History of Massachusetts*. As late as 1921, he had even endorsed Adams's specific views, announcing in a review that *The Founding of New England* was "the best short history of early New England that has appeared for a generation." Although Adams was at times prone to overstatement, Morison noted, his story of the Puritan travails was told with the "dignity and justice" of a man "[u]ntainted by New England ancestry or residence, uninfluenced by tercentenarian sentimentality, [and] with a broad background and scholarly equipment" who had proven "his capacity as a historian."[24] But by the 1930s, Morison's attitudes had changed. Frustrations with debunking and dialectical materialism accounted for much of the change, as did Morison's firmer commitment to Harvard. Professor Ropes's previous warning that anti-Puritanism might seriously jeopardize his position at Harvard probably affected Morison little, but the tercentenary history had forced him to reevaluate the traditions of the college's Puritan founders. The tercentenary history "gave me an opportunity to study the lives and the ideas of English Puritans who founded New England and Harvard," he wrote, and "the more I learned of the Puritans, the more significant, even dramatic—'romantic,' if you will!—they appeared." What could be more romantic, Morison argued, "than the founding of Harvard, a college of liberal arts in a colony six years old, barely numbering twelve thousand people?" What could be more moving, he added, than "the preservation of high standards in this college through infinite difficulties" with Puritan farmers "contributing their bushels of corn and sixpences to maintain poor scholars?"[25] Unrepentant about the about-face in his attitude toward the founders of Harvard these pronouncements exhibited, he announced with a proud sense of his growth as an historian, "My attitude toward seventeenth-century puritanism has passed through scorn and boredom to a warm interest and respect."[26]

In contrast to Adams, Morison was impressed by the cultural achievements of the Puritans. Despite meager resources and countless external deterrents (including the "levelling influence of the frontier," he noted in deference to Turner), the Puritans "established a tradition of free, popular education, which became the American tradition in the nineteenth century." The "sincerity and beauty" of this effort warranted praise, Morison wrote, acknowledging that although the ways of the Puritans were not his ways and their faith not his faith; nevertheless they appeared to him "a courageous, humane, brave, and significant people."[27] Certainly, he argued, they did not deserve the "various secondary and degenerate meanings" that had come to be associated with them by dialectical materialists. In an article for the *Forum* entitled "Those Misunderstood Puritans," Morison argued that Adams and others had encouraged the average American to regard the fathers of New England "as a set of somber kill-joys whose greatest pleasure was preventing simple folk from enjoying themselves, and whose principal object in life was to repress beauty and inhibit human nature." Such impressions, Morison noted, often derived from "a sour old grandfather, who made the Sabbath hideous with stuffy devotions" and who judged the Puritans solely on the basis of their religious doctrines. It was the duty of professional historians to correct these misunderstandings, Morison concluded, by evaluating the Puritans on the "sincerity of [their] purpose" as well as their doctrine.[28]

Toward these ends, Morison wrote *Builders of the Bay Colony* in 1930, a series of portraits designed to counter the negative stereotypes of Puritan leaders created by debunkers such as Adams. Hoping to demonstrate how colonial history might be written effectively from a social as well as an institutional perspective, he selected biographical subjects who represented the "various aspects" of Puritan life, not merely religious, but "adventurous and artistic, political and economic, literary and scientific, legal [and] educational."[29] He also used the work as an opportunity to renew attacks against the dialectical materialists. Because the debunkers of Puritanism had conspired to rob "the people of their heroes by insulting the folk-memory of great figures,"[30] Morison noted, he was especially interested in dramatizing "the efforts and sacrifices of some hundreds of men and women, most of them unknown to us even by name," who "played an essential part" in the development of American culture.[31]

Hence, in *Builders of the Bay Colony* Morison included portraits of important figures such as Thomas Shepard, whose life demonstrated the hardships that community leaders faced in order to establish the Commonwealth. Morison portrayed Shepard as a tireless servant of the people, sacrificing his family, his friends, and ultimately his health for the community. "There could be little of a material nature in a pioneer colony to compensate" such a man, Morison noted, yet he "accepted hardship and privation without complaint, happy to devote [his] gifts to bringing up [his] people in the way of truth." Likewise John Winthrop was "a superior man of noble character, with a single eye to the Common weal." Winthrop, who acquired considerable skills as a leader by running the family manor and serving as an attorney and local magistrate in England, used his capitalistic expertise and humane generosity to save the colony from internal political and financial destruction. "At all times he was a most devoted public servant," Morison wrote, "neglecting his private affairs to the ruin of his estate" and for many years refusing a salary "when there was no money in the colony treasury."[32]

The capacity of Puritan leaders "to take advice and yield to the majority" was part of their "equipment for leadership," Morison noted, but their most admirable collective trait was their willingness to make hard decisions on behalf of the colony and to take responsibility for their actions. Winthrop's decision to deport Thomas Morton (the fur and firearms trader who set up an irreligious colony at Ma-re mount) was attributed by Adams and other debunkers to Winthrop's "hatred of mirth and jollity." But Morison defended the action, noting that Wintrop's "friendly admonishment" had been ignored by Morton and that all the coast settlements between Maine and Nantasket (none of them Puritan) had supported the deportation. Morton's protests in England probably cost Winthrop his family estate there, Morison noted, but the sacrifice was necessary for the survival of the colony.[33]

In the more celebrated case of Anne Hutchinson, Winthrop demonstrated a similar willingness to take a stand on a controversial public decision despite the personal cost he would have to pay. Hutchinson's "parlor meetings," Morison wrote, fed the belief "dear to religious fanatics in all ages, that God was more likely to reveal his truth to an ignorant than an educated person." This belief "undermined the regular clergy," he noted, and left Winthrop with no choice but to banish her. For this, Winthrop not only sacrificed his position as governor but incurred the endless wrath of historians. But Anne Hutchinson's actions were a legitimate threat to the community, Morison wrote, constituting "an illuminism but one step removed from Fifth Monarchy and Ranters," which placed the "reasoned creed of scholars on perpetual defense against any fanatic who would gain an ignorant following."[34] Adopting a familiar authoritarian attitude, Morison asked that the Hutchinson case be considered from Winthrop's perspective. "It was a period when new sects were beginning to swarm in England," he wrote, "and [e]arnest fanatics everywhere were discovering some little bit of truth in the Bible and organizing a church or a fierce little sect around it." Given this historical setting, it was "at least arguable that the suppression of the gifted lady was necessary to preserve all that the puritans had to give, or bequeath," Morison wrote. "The special circumstances of a new colony yet in the gristle [and] the danger from the very quality and temper of Anne Hutchinson's creed, give strength to the Devil's advocate for intolerance in her case," he concluded.[35]

By championing the sacrifices of Puritan leaders and taking their side against dissenters, Morison was consciously aligning himself with forces of order and conservatism. As with the proposed housing reforms at Harvard or challenges within the American Historical Association, he worked for the preservation of tradition in the face of protest and change. The wisdom of such a policy, he argued, was evident in the Puritan legacy to New England. Because the Puritans believed in tradition and order, Morison wrote, "New England never passed through the gun-toting, frontier-bullying stage of society, so picturesque to read about, but leaving a tradition of lawlessness to the communities so unfortunate as to have been through it." The stern discipline of Puritan leaders may have fallen "heavily on frontier individualists" such as Morton and Hutchinson, he argued, but such rigor "gave to the Yankee race a law-abiding tradition" that endured into the twentieth century.[36]

The persistence Morison demonstrated in his attack on Adams also suggested the degree to which as a historian he empathized with the

Puritans. As a scholar defending the Puritans in an age of anti-Puritanism, Morison himself felt like a member of a beleaguered minority. Promoting objective truth over relativism, he identified with Puritan clergymen who worked tirelessly to defend orthodoxy against the intrusions of false religion and the devil. In dealing with historians like James Truslow Adams, for instance, Morison adopted Winthrop's methods for handling dissenters. First he warned them, then he discredited them, and finally he sought to banish them to a wilderness existence without audience or recourse. Morison even displayed a "puritan sense of self-consciousness" about this by making a public search of his own literary soul for impure motives and biases.[37] In a confessional appendix to *Builders of the Bay Colony*, Morison acknowledged that he had been "gunning" for James Truslow Adams throughout the text and that at times he had been harsh in his criticisms of his colleague. He evoked his advanced degrees as authority and initiated a Puritan policy of expurgation against Adams. Having once praised *The Founding of New England* as the work of a gifted historian, he now warned readers about Adams's deceitful tendency in the volume "to balance inferences upon one another to make a convincing theory for those who are all ready to believe it."[38]

In the appendix to *Builders of the Bay Colony*, Morison took specific issue with Adams's implication that the Puritans were perverts with a "morbid interest in the most indecent sexual matters." Citing Adams's sloppy historical technique, particularly his use of innuendo and inference, Morison reminded readers that it was common practice for seventeenth-century officials to record sexual transgressions in the public record and, in turn, for public leaders such as Winthrop and Bradford to include such transgressions in their histories. "If Winthrop and Bradford had passed over these events, leaving them to be discovered in the court records," Morison noted derisively, "our modern puritan-baiters would have enjoyed accusing them of concealment, hypocrisy, and 'ignoring the facts of life.' " Morison also condemned Adams for his characterization of the Massachusetts Bay Colony as a strict and unpopular theocracy, radically out of sorts with its neighbors' views. In asserting that "four out of five" settlers in Massachusetts were out of sympathy with Puritanism, Adams had irresponsibly misused statistics in Morison's estimation. The "mystic number 'four out of five' " was derived from John Palfrey's nineteenth-century calculations, Morison noted, which were largely guesswork because they were calculated without reference to an accurate census. Furthermore, Adams compounded Palfrey's errors, in Morison's estimation, by restricting the technical meaning of church membership to those who had undergone conversion experiences, thereby including as nonbelievers those dedicated church members who had not yet become "visible saints." Such inaccuracies only confirmed what Morison had been saying all along about historians not committed to objectivity as a goal. Desiring for "presentist" reasons to convey a negative image of the Puritans, Adams had allowed his own "frame of reference" to cloud his historical judgment of the seventeenth century.[39]

In several personal letters to the author of *The Founding of New England*, Morison elaborated his criticisms. Anticipating correctly that Adams would be upset by attacks on *The Founding of New England* from one who had praised it previously, Morison attempted to explain his new attitude. "I have no reason to change the opinion I expressed when it came out," Morison wrote of Adams's book. "There [was]," however, "one fundamental fault with it" that nullified most of its achievements—"that starting from an inherent dislike of the puritans, [Adams] did not take the trouble to know them, much less to understand them." Consequently, Adams had made "a good many off-hand statements about them which [were] not correct."[40] Paraphrasing Ropes's earlier comments, Morison warned that "it is always easier to condemn an alien way of life than to understand it." As in the conflict between Winthrop and Hutchinson, the issue between Morison and Adams was one of authority to preach. Trained as a journalist, Adams claimed to possess the kind of "experienced imagination" that came not from "taking courses" but from "mixing with the world."[41] Morison argued, however, that without appropriate training, worldliness was of no advantage to a historian. Trained in a "calling in which the story's the thing," journalists like Adams sacrificed objectivity for dramatic effect in interpreting world events, Morison wrote. Working outside a community of scholars and independent of professional codes, they produced "pseudo-history" in accordance with a creed that said, "If it accords with the facts, fine; if not, so much the worse for the facts."[42] In the study of Puritanism, Morison added, journalist-historians had developed false theories "as a cover to their ignorance of, or lack of interest in, what went on in the New England mind for a century or more."[43]

As a means of lending professional authority to the study of the New England past, Morison helped create the *New England Quarterly* in 1928 with Harvard colleague Kenneth Murdock and other concerned professionals. "Kenneth Murdock and I were voices crying in the wilderness against the common notions of James Truslow Adams and other popular historians of the day," Morison later wrote of the collaborative defense by Harvard faculty against the incursions by amateurs.[44] Murdock and Morison also inspired Harvard graduate student Perry Miller to rewrite the history of Puritan intellectual thought. By his own admission "an adolescent campaigner in [the] anti-Puritan rebellion," Miller reversed his position after taking Morison's seminar at Harvard and dedicated himself to detailing the "integrity and profundity of the Puritan character."[45] Together the "three M's" (as Morison, Murdock, and Miller were known) made the offices of the *New England Quarterly* the center for Puritan revisionism. The first book review in the initial volume of the *New England Quarterly*, for instance, criticized Adams's "half-truths,"[46] while subsequent reviews in the next few issues referred to his theories as "a series of generalizations," mostly "unsupported, frequently unjustified, and always superficial." He "has left the field just what it was" before he entered it, one critic noted, adding that Adams wrote mainly "pot-boilers which, he feels, American scholars usually produce as soon as they achieve eminence."[47] Perry Miller argued in still another review that the "state of scholarship was so demoralized" by Adams's work that a concerted professional effort must be made to restore it immediately.[48] And while Morison admitted in private that some of Adams's work was "provocative, stimulating and informing," readers of the *New England Quarterly* were informed by him of Adams's tendency to promote a "degenerative and negative type of puritanism."[49]

Defenders of Adams saw in these *New England Quarterly* attacks an elitism so pervasive as to threaten all nonacademics engaged in historical writing. In a letter to the editor of the journal, curator and Morison's former dissertation reader Worthington C. Ford claimed that the journal's reviews were purely "nasty," "too personal," "biased," and "vitriolic" to be countenanced. "Truslow Adams has done more to induce people to read American history than a whole raft of university professors could have accomplished," Ford noted with sensitivity to his own nonacademic place in the historical world.[50] In a private letter to Adams, Ford explained his motivations for writing the *New England Quarterly*: "I had a view of letting Morison know that his magazine ought not to allow personal prejudices to control, as he himself is subject to prejudice which he does not conceal."[51] Concerned that Ford would endorse the fictional distortions of the "gifted amateur" Adams, Morison nonetheless defended his right to warn the public about them.[52]

For his part, Adams admitted to a certain laxity of form and purpose in his historical activities. "I have never taken myself seriously as a historian," he told Morison, and "never think of myself as anything but an amateur and not an important one at that." "It has been a constant source of surprise to me," he noted, "that anyone has taken me more seriously than I have myself."[53] But he denied ever having distorted the truth and reminded Morison, as Beard had before him, that facts were "fuzzy" things. Perhaps "I painted the shadows too dark" in *The Founding of New England*, Adams admitted, but such a tendency did not justify Morison's singling him out unfairly "for attack on a point of view." History was frequently a "matter of opinion," he noted, and all historians have biased opinions, even professionals. Among these is regional bias. Morison "has a brilliant mind and has had wide international experience," Adams wrote in a rebuttal review of *Builders of the Bay Colony*, "but to a greater degree than he realizes, he has remained a Massachusetts man," subject to "localism" and guilty of presenting Puritanism "in a false light for the reader who knows better." Like Beard, Adams noted that all history is relative to the viewer and subject to the historian's predilections and predispositions. Additionally, presentist concerns made it impossible for historians to fairly judge the worth of contemporary works. Arguing about "matters of opinion" was "about as profitable as trying to drown a fish," Adams concluded, and he urged

Morison to "leave the determination of truth among conflicting views to other historians and to the slow passing of time."[54] This Morison refused to do, however, since Adams represented but one of numerous amateurs whose work seemed in his estimation to threaten the stability of the academic profession and (by but a small leap of the imagination) the nation at large.

"The Wine of the Puritans"

Damage done by debunking historians to the intellectual reputation of the Puritans was but one reason why Morison was not willing to wait for the "slow passing of time" to launch his revisionist assault. In addition to complaining about Adams's social and economic history, Morison bristled at the work of former Harvard classmate Van Wyck Brooks, who, only a year after graduation, had published an extended essay on the history of American intellectual development entitled *The Wine of the Puritans* (1908). In his provocative book, Brooks argued that Puritan business conservatism in the seventeenth century had encouraged strict regulation of American intellectual life in the eighteenth, nineteenth, and twentieth centuries. Adopting the symbol of the Puritan to condemn the philistine attitude of Americans toward education, Brooks traced the "sober, unrelaxed industriousness" of his own Harvard undergraduate experience to the strained intellectual life of the seventeenth-century Puritan founders. Brooks argued that "stern economic need" and the Puritan's penchant for the "silent, regular, inexorable grinding of the machinery of rational thought" had been transferred to successive generations of Americans as a wine's bad character is passed on to its successive vintages. Brooks described the attempt to introduce intellectual life to seventeenth-century New England as like trying to "put old wine in new bottles." A wasteful "explosion results," he noted, in which "the aroma passes into the air and the wine spills to the floor." Because Puritan materialism continued to affect the flavor and bouquet of education at Harvard and elsewhere, he maintained, the only alternative was to throw out the bad wine and replace it with good.[55]

Resentful of Brooks's characterization of the Puritan past, and, as a Harvard professor, driven by a sense of loyalty to defend his institution's intellectual contributions, Morison wrote *The Puritan Pronaos* (1936), a work dedicated to correcting misconceptions about intellectual life in colonial New England. According to Morison, historians such as Brooks had incorrectly assumed that Puritanism was incompatible with art and culture or that Puritan life was devoid of intellectual ideas. Inverting Brooks's title metaphor, Morison argued in *The Puritan Pronaos* that the "wine of New England was a series of successive vintages, each distinct from the other" and from which "a certain amount is drawn off every year, and replaced by an equal volume of the new." The "mother-wine" of 1634 "still gives bouquet and flavor to what you draw off in 1934," Morison wrote, with Harvard in particular benefiting from its close association with the harvesting of the original crop.[56]

Brooks's misconception of these vintages derived from his misunderstanding about the structure of leadership in the Bay Colony, Morison noted. Parsons, professors, and artists formed a "pretty close corporation," Morison admitted, and they largely determined what ideas "should be selected, and what rejected." Such control was designed not to be restrictive, however, but to ensure the survival of intellectual life. The "ruling class was trying to enforce an extraordinarily high standard on a poor and hardworking country population, who wanted the labor of their children on the farm or in fishing," Morison wrote, "and could hardly appreciate the social and civic reasons for universal education." Frontier communities outside Puritan control demonstrated how "grueling hardship[s]" could "exhaust and stultify the human spirit unless it have some emotional drive."[57] Ever sensitive to charges of elitism, Morison justified Puritan restrictions by noting the fruits of their careful intellectual pruning, including Harvard College and the best secondary school system in the country. "That is the sort of pioneering—pioneering in things of the spirit—which counts for more in the long run than the clearing of forests, the breaking up of prairie sod, and the building of factories and railroads," Morison proclaimed with sectional pride.[58] Besides, "the alternative to a controlled intellectual life," he argued, as he had in his defense of standards in the historical profession, "was intellectual vacuity."[59]

Morison had the same misgivings about standards for Brooks's later works as he had for *The Wine of the Puritans*. In 1936, Brooks published the first volume of a sweeping literary history of the United States, *The Flowering of New England*, which, according to Morison, propagated Adams's distorted vision of Puritanism and American intellectual traditions. The flowering of art and culture in the "American Renaissance," Brooks wrote, did not occur until the nineteenth century because it took that long for the debilitating effects of Puritanism to be "charmed away." As late as the 1830s, the process of purgation had not been fully completed, he noted, as evidenced by the residue of Puritanism in the works of authors such as Hawthorne. In *The Flowering of New England*, Brooks described Hawthorne as "a man under a spell, bearing the remnants of a race that retained the mental traits of a faraway past." Having come of age in a New England town (Salem) that "had lapsed into quietude and decay," Hawthorne lived in the shadow of the persistent, evil force that had dominated the region since the witchcraft trials. For awhile, a prosperous maritime region, by the nineteenth century Hawthorne's Salem had been reduced to a coastal ghost town. Incapacitated by the memory of his Puritan ancestors, Hawthorne brooded "like a ghost," seated by the "wayside of life."[60]

The use of such consciously fictive sources caught the attention of some scholars, including ex-Harvard professor George Santayana, who noticed the striking contrasts between the methods and interpretations of Morison and Brooks. "Just after your book [*Three Centuries of Harvard*]" arrived, Santayana wrote Morison in 1936, "I received *The Flowering of New England*. If you, by chance, were writing a review of that book, I should be very glad to see it," he added, "because I am tempted to write something of my own, suggested by your book and his." Santayana, the author of his own recent study of American intellectual life entitled *The Last Puritan*, had "doubts" about Brooks's "philosophy of history" and wished to use Morison's work as a corrective to it.[61] Shortly thereafter, Morison received another letter from a disappointed reader of Brooks who described *The Flowering of New England* as a "tissue of inaccuracies, from beginning to end." Identifying Morison as "emphatically the one" to criticize the book, the writer joined Santayana in hoping for a slashing professional review of it.[62]

At first glance, Morison found surprisingly little to criticize in Brooks's book. In fact, there were many things to admire in it, he told Santayana, including Brooks's "treatment of certain figures—notably Hawthorn [sic]" and his "method of writing in his subjects' 'own words,' rather than illustrating with excerpts."[63] Subsequent correspondence with Santayana and further reading, however, completely altered his opinion on both of these points.[64] In an April 1937 article for the *American Historical Review*, Morison criticized Brooks's historical technique. Hoping to make the past more accessible, he argued, the author had integrated quotes into his text without specific mention of source or context. "Having eschewed the use of quotation marks," Morison noted in his review, Brooks "leaves readers perplexed as to whether they are reading Emerson or Brooks, or Emerson slightly misquoted by Brooks." He "tends to jumble facts from different places and eras," Morison added, "as a painter mixes his colors." Noting that "we all make mistakes," Morison nonetheless condemned Brooks's assumption "that he can quote chapter and verse . . . for every phrase that appears in the book." No historian with any professional training and "acquainted with the period can fail to bristle up at this challenge," he concluded.[65]

Morison also reversed his opinion of the portrait of Hawthorne presented in *The Flowering of New England*. To make Salem seem the source of Hawthorne's morbidity, he maintained, Brooks had exaggerated the lingering effects of Puritanism on the town. Salem was not a dilapidated, charred, and haunted village in the early nineteenth century, Morison wrote, but rather "a thriving, bustling seaport." Its residents, including young Hawthorne, were not gloomy and morose; they were as optimistic and as transcendent as their neighbors in nearby Concord. The failure to spread the "sniff of manure" and the fragrance of "blossoms" evenly between Salem and Concord, Morison wrote, discredited both Salem and Puritanism. Furthermore, Morison took umbrage at the lack of attention to schools and colleges in *The Flowering of New England*, "the improvement and extending of which was one of New England's creative achievements."[66] Compounding this error were several misstatements Brooks had made about Harvard, the source of these achievements. Morison testily pointed out in one such instance that Professor Norton's carriage could not have been seen "every Sunday" around 1815 "drawn up beside the president's carriage at the entrance of Holden Chapel," because Holden had not been used for a chapel since 1764, and the Harvard presidents of that day "were sufficiently able-bodied to walk 150 yards to the actual chapel."[67] In explanation of the criticisms raised by his review article, Morison wrote Brooks: "I have had a terrible sweat reviewing the 'Flowering,' [since] I wish to tell historians what a really great book it is, yet point out for your good and still more the good of the imitators, the reckless way in which you throw facts about!"[68]

Brooks, like Adams, referred to himself as a mere "novice in historical writing" who "had to learn how to grow up," and he acknowledged that in describing the lingering effect of Puritanism on Hawthorne's Salem he had "transposed a bit of colour out of its proper setting." In so doing, "I felt I was committing a sin," Brooks confessed to Morison, "and now the murder is out."[69] But also like Adams he would not admit to any deliberate distortions of history, and he was so disturbed by Morison's insinuations to the contrary that he could not be comforted by friends. "More than once have I been reminded of your experience with Sam Morison," wrote Lewis Mumford to a distraught Brooks; "the arrogance of reviewers is almost as amazing as the triviality of their interests, and this holds for the academic world no less than for journalism."[70] Unconsoled, Brooks complained directly to Morison. "I was grieved when you suggested that I put things down 'for effect'," he confessed.[71] "Of course, you are quite aware that when you call me 'reckless,' when you say that I 'throw my facts about,' you are making a serious charge indeed. If one is writing history, this is not playing the game," he argued. "It seems to me much like saying that one cheats at cards." Referring to Morison's *American Historical Review* article, Brooks continued: "I know the sort of review that says, 'It's a good enough book, but you can't trust the man's facts.' I am not disinclined to take some pains with 'pesky facts,' " Brooks noted, adding that any errors in his work were "exceedingly slight, and even on the ragged edge of truth."[72]

It was precisely this "ragged edge of truth," however, to which Morison objected. Brooks had claimed in "Creating a Usable Past" that the past has no objective reality except for that which students of history are able to bring to it, but Morison argued that Brooks's "new mistress Clio" would not tolerate such relativistic thinking. "Now Van Wyck, don't you see the reason why reviewers say things that irritate you?" Morison chided. "You state facts which to this or that reader sound incredible, and lay your breech bare to their kicks because you don't protect it with quotes and footnotes." These errors, "which any competent reviewer can pick up, make him suspicious of the rest, and imagine that you are reckless with facts and 'writing for effect.' " Reaffirming Andrews's commitment to professional standards, Morison added, "I'm not trying to show you up or prove you wrong," but in the writing of history and in the pursuit of factual truth, "it's important to get it right."[73]

High-Class Journalism

Appropriately, Morison's criticisms of Adams and Brooks received an endorsement from members of the profession who shared his sense of disgust with the transgressions of amateur historians. Still disturbed by the inability of the reading public to appreciate the distinctions between amateur and professional technique, Charles Andrews complained to Morison that professional organizations to which he belonged were admitting too many untrained historians to their ranks. "I have been put in the class with James Truslow Adams, where I do not want to be," Andrews noted with reference to his National Institute of Arts affiliation.[74] The institute had been founded in 1898 for the purposes of exercising "custodial jurisdiction over literature and arts," but it continued to admit nonprofessionals like Adams and even to make amateurs like Brooks its officers.[75] Hoping to alter the pattern, Andrews nominated Morison for membership and begged him to consider joining. Morison, however, refused. Arguing in a manner that contributed to his reputation as an elitist, Morison claimed that the nomination was an attempt "to lend respect to an otherwise rather mediocre group." Rather than join himself, Morison urged Andrews to resign. Any organization that "showed such low standards of history as to elect James Truslow Adams," he observed, was no place for serious scholars. "[P]rofessional, academic-trained historians [like ourselves]," he added, "had better leave" the "journalistic historians" to their organizations "to have a good time in and tell each other that they are much better than we are."[76]

Still more disturbing for Morison was the ascendancy of Brooks to the presidency of the institute and the initiatives undertaken during his tenure. Morison objected especially to the decision made by Brooks and other members of the institute's awards committee to honor Charles Beard with a "gold medal" for literary achievement. In some ill-appreciated private correspondence with Brooks, Morison renewed his attack on relativism. "The subject of the following letter you may very likely feel to be none of my business," he wrote Brooks, "but as an historian I feel impelled to write it." In "sundry articles in learned journals," Morison noted, Beard "has expressed the opinion that there is no such thing as accurate history; therefore, everyone who writes history ought to do it for an immediate purpose—influencing public opinion, etc." Unaware of this, the public naïvely assumed Beard's historical technique was accurate, and this impression, Morison added, "Beard takes care to preserve and enhance by a pose of lofty objectivity and a meticulous scholarly apparatus." Morison complained that everything Beard had produced over a thirty-year career, "with the exception of textbooks—in which he is cagey enough not to offend popular sensibility . . . is high-class journalism rather than history, written to promote some -ism or other." Because "I am not a member of the Academy or the Institute, I have no right to protest against the Academy conferring a medal on whom they will," Morison noted with a touch of sentiment, "but as an old friend and classmate of yours, I do protest against your associating yourself personally with an action that is, in my opinion, a disgrace to American scholarship."[77]

Brooks was not moved by Morison's appeal. Refusing to apologize for presenting the medal, Brooks noted that the medal was almost always given to a long-standing member of the institute with a suitable publishing history. "This limited the choice of candidates virtually to Beard, Nevins & Truslow Adams," Brooks wrote, adding, "I don't need to ask you if you would have considered Truslow Adams, which narrows the choice as I see it to Beard & Nevins." Beard was picked over Nevins, Brooks noted, because he was the better scholar. Unwilling to share Morison's "hostile feeling" and "low opinion" of Beard, Brooks argued, "The medal is always given for a man's main life work, & I do not think your estimate of Beard's work is justified or that your statement of his position is fair at all." Sensitive to Morison's accusations about his own supposed relativism, Brooks concluded, "To say that the main body of his history was 'written to promote some ism or other' is to me simply an incomprehensible remark." Beard's work "is on a high plane in *the discussion of human affairs*," Brooks added, and "I respect" him as "one of the significant writers who have stood for something in our time."[78]

The debate over the institute's "gold medal" was but another chapter in Morison's ongoing diatribe against the debunking, relativistic, dialectical materialists of whom Beard was the most visible spokesman. Identifying himself increasingly with professionally trained university professors, Morison began to drive a wedge between himself and those scholars outside academics. Those alienated by Morison found it easy enough to explain his behavior by reference to theories of class struggle and empowerment. Morison was a spokesperson for the established Harvard elite, they argued, who, like his stern New England Puritan ancestors, wished to confer on himself the mark of grace while condemning others to eternal silence. In the struggle between haves and have-nots, Morison represented intransigence, intolerance, and orthodoxy.[79]

But Morison envisioned himself differently. As an upholder of tradition, professional standards, and objectivity, he, like the Puritans, was a crusader for truth and purity in intellectual life. Extolling authority over dissent, Morison argued for the banishment of those like Beard, Adams, and Brooks who failed to understand that historians must "deal gently with people's traditions."[80] In pursuit of this goal, Morison spent the next several decades of his scholarly life attempting to defend professional standards and national traditions against those who would debunk them, by beating such historians at their own game; that is, by using journalistic literary devices to distract readers from the misinformed interpretations of amateur historians and to lead his readers to the more reasoned and balanced views of professional historians.

The Voyage of Discovery

*Charles M. Andrews, William Goodwin
and the New Parkman*

9

Recovering Heroes

I n his defense of the Puritans, as well as in his earlier defenses of Harvard and New England, Morison aligned himself against "amateurs" and those outside academics who showed disdain for the professional "rules" of historical writing. Yet he realized that most readers of history preferred Charles Beard, James Truslow Adams, or Van Wyck Brooks to him. With the exception of *The Maritime History of Massachusetts*, which was written under the influence of these relativistic historians, he had never produced a work of history that was a success in the literary marketplace. A professional dedicated to upholding objective standards could rationalize such failure, but Morison dearly wished to demonstrate that objectivity could be as stimulating as the fictive techniques used by amateurs. "When John Citizen feels the urge to read history, he goes to the novels of Kenneth Roberts or Margaret Mitchell, not the histories of Professor this or Doctor that." Why? Morison wondered. The answer, he reasoned, rested "in [the] eagerness [of American historians] to present facts," for in "their laudable anxiety to tell the truth" they had "neglected the literary aspects of their craft."[1]

Reflecting back over developments in the profession in the thirty years since his graduate training at Harvard, Morison recalled the innocent naïveté of professors such as his mentor Albert Bushnell Hart who "imagined that history would tell itself, provided one were honest, thorough, and painstaking." Regarding history as pure science, Hart had troubled his students little with the "literary" quality of their work. Only Edward Channing had urged his students to consider history as literature, but his works provided few suitable examples of how to accomplish this. Recalling Channing's challenge to graduate students in 1910 to become the New Parkman, Morison informed his students that a "whole generation has passed without producing any really great works on American history." Professional historians had written some valuable books, he admitted, but they had only managed to heap up "pay dirt" for others. "Journalists, novelists, and free-lance writers are the ones that extract the gold," Morison told his seminars, adding that he wished to see "a few more Ph.D.'s in history winning book-of-the-month adoptions and reaping the harvest of dividends." If students would demonstrate the same industry in presenting history as they did in compiling it, they could achieve such popularity, he concluded.[2]

The goal for professionals was to attract readers by employing the literary devices of amateurs without sacrificing objectivity. Morison claimed that the historian could learn much from the novelist with regard to characterization and description, for instance, and he encouraged students in his graduate seminar to read American novelists such as Sherwood Anderson and Margaret Mitchell if they wished to make "people and events seem real." But Morison also warned that a "historian or biographer is under restrictions unknown to the novelist," since "[h]e has no right to override facts by his own imagination." A student writing on a relatively obscure topic might have to use his or her imagination to weave historical facts into a pattern, but the "honest" historian "must make clear what is fact and what is hypothesis."[3] The difficulty of blending both literary art and objectivity accrues from a paradox at the heart of most historical writing, he argued. On the one hand, the historian hopes to "bring the methodological authority of the physical sciences to the study of man's past" by employing scientific language and pursuing objective truth; on the other hand, the historian wishes to give history "philosophical credibility" by privileging "insight and imaginative identification" above "analysis and criticism." These two epistemological points of view are often mutually exclusive, since the need to demonstrate the "aesthetics of sympathy" often causes the historian to employ literary "archetypes" over "carefully authenticated reality" and to blur "the distinction between the created and the discovered."[4]

According to Morison (as well as his mentor Channing), no historian had come closer to reconciling the two sides of this historical paradox than Francis Parkman. Parkman was an indefatigable scholar who spared no expense to get access to the best archival materials in his field. Yet Parkman also had "frequent recourse to the book of life," Morison noted, and obeyed Polybius' dictum "that the historian should be a man of action" who "visited every scene of the actions he describes." Parkman "sojourned in the forest, living only on the fish he could catch and the game that he killed," Morison wrote; "he shot rapids in birch-bark canoes with Indian guides; he even joined a band of Sioux Indians in the Far West, and from that intimacy learned to know the savages as they were, discarding Rousseau's sentimental conception of them." This commitment to a physical involvement with the past allowed Parkman to "re-create the atmosphere in which his characters live and move," suggested Morison, "so that the reader has a sense of participation in the drama" of their lives and a new appreciation for their major and minor acts of heroism.[5]

Happily identified with professionals, Morison nonetheless wished to demonstrate how university scholars could tread Parkman's line between literary art and objective fact. After completing the tercentenary history and the volumes on Puritanism, therefore, Morison turned his attention in the late 1930s to a figure mistreated consistently by amateurs and professionals alike, Christopher Columbus. Twenty years earlier, Morison had begun in early summer to prepare lectures for History 10 for the first day of class on September 25. "By the 24th I was still working on Christopher Columbus!" Morison noted with astonishment. The discoverer's story had so "fascinated" him that he had determined that fall to write a Columbus biography "someday" if possible.[6]

Distracted by public service projects and later by postwar disillusionment, Morison did not begin the biography in the 1920s, and if he had he might have written a substantially different book. By 1937, however, "someday" had arrived along with Morison's recognition that Columbus was a figure ever in need of revision. On the one hand, Morison argued that amateurs like Washington Irving had worked their customary mythmaking on Columbus by perpetuating a series of persistent and absurd rumors about the great discoverer. Irving had used his considerable "seductive" literary charms, for instance, to suggest that Columbus had had to convince the great court mathematicians of the fifteenth century that the world was round. Scenting "an opportunity for a picturesque and moving scene," Morison noted, Irving adapted a fictitious seventeenth-century literary account of the events that portrayed Columbus as outsmarting professors of mathematics, geography, and astronomy. "A gripping drama as Irving tells it," Morison remarked, but "pure moonshine." All fifteenth-century mathematicians of reputation believed that the world was round, he noted; those Columbus petitioned simply doubted (with good reason as it turned out) Columbus's calculations about the distance from western Europe to eastern Asia.[7]

Columbus had suffered as well at the hands of professional historians. The discovery of America was one of the first topics that professional historians had examined after the American Historical Association was founded in the 1880s. By 1889, Harvard librarian Justin Winsor had reproduced all the meaningful Columbian documents available to scholars in the United States in his *Narrative and Critical History of the United States* (1884–1889)[8]; by 1892, European experts had collected and classified every scrap of relevant information in the *Raccolta di Documenti e Studi* for the four hundredth anniversary of Columbus's discovery of America.[9] Over the next fifty years, scholars scoured these sources, producing a myriad of contradictory monographs that did little to alter the public's impression of Irving's mythic Columbus. If professional historians had failed to discover the real Columbus, Morison argued, it was because they had been too obsessed with interpretation and not enough with that fundamental question "What actually happened [to him]?" Employing Parkman's techniques, Morison decided that the only way to solve the problems associated with Columbus's voyages, "really to 'get at' him," was to resail the coasts and islands that Columbus had discovered.[10] Students of Columbus who had actually "tasted the joy of the sea" had an advantage over even Parkman in pursuing such nautical work,[11] Morison argued, since the wilderness of seventeenth-century America was "so changed as to be almost unrecognizable" to Parkman's nineteenth-century world, whereas "the ocean, like the starry firmament that hangs over it, changeth not."[12] In following Columbus, Morison could employ his historical imagination to "view islands and coasts as through his eyes."[13]

In the summer of 1937, therefore, Morison chartered a yawl and began making plans to follow the voyages of Columbus. This reenactment was to be a personal voyage of rediscovery as well, undertaken for the purposes of seeking answers to professional questions that had eluded him since his days as a young professor. Morison felt the mission was urgent, both for himself and for the profession as a whole. "I decided that if I put it off any longer I'd soon be too old to do the research in the way that I wanted to do it," Morison remembered later; so it was "now or never" for implementing Parkman's technique.[14] He wrote to Lincoln Colcord, whom he wished to take along as a shipmate: "I strongly urge & beseech you not to pass this up. I shall be 50 this year and you are older, [and] there are not many years left when we can do this sort of thing except as passengers, and I shan't have another chance to get away in the winter for another seven years."[15]

The first leg of Morison's "hands-on" research was a two-month trip to the Caribbean to search for the cite of Columbus's original settlement in Navidad, Hispaniola. His work was facilitated by his friend Charles Andrews, who allowed Morison to make the Andrews' summer home on Jupiter Island, Florida, his base of operations.[16] Andrews also offered Morison some professional advice. Ever worried about professional integrity, he urged Morison to distinguish himself from the numerous "ocean-going" amateur historians who had attempted similar reenactments before. Andrews was particularly concerned about a millionaire from Hartford, Connecticut, William B. Goodwin, with whom Andrews had had an altercation several years before while still a professor at Yale. Goodwin had invested a good deal of time and money in a "hands-on" search for Norse settlements on the coast of New England and believed he had found one in Saybrook, Connecticut.[17] The recognized authority on the history of early Connecticut, Andrews believed Goodwin's research was insubstantial and took issue with many of his findings and conclusions in a "pretty sharply" worded letter "regarding his manifold errors." Goodwin's response was so "disagree-able" as to suggest that its author was "mentally almost incompetent," Andrews told Morison.[18]

Goodwin and Andrews locked horns again in the late 1930s over a paper Goodwin read before the Florida Historical Society concerning the Celtic voyages to the New World. Goodwin claimed to have found remnants of Irish settlements along the New England coastline, and he reported his early findings to the society.[19] Some members were impressed by his talk, but Andrews, who had retired to Florida in 1931, seriously "doubt[ed] its value." Among other things, Goodwin had based a large part of his claims on several rocks he had discovered in New England that supposedly bore runic inscriptions but that some scholars discredited as the work of modern pranksters. According to Andrews, who doubted both the Norse and the Celtic discoveries, Goodwin was a mere "word gatherer" and "a persistent searcher after mare's nests." He personified the worst in amateur historical efforts, Andrews told Morison, adding, "I have no confidence in him."[20]

Andrews warned Morison about Goodwin because he had heard rumors that the millionaire's next project was to focus on Columbus in the Carib-bean. In the summer of 1937, Morison had no run-ins with Goodwin, but when he made arrangements the following summer with several local residents to assist a Harvard archaeologist from the Peabody Museum in excavating a spot in Haiti, he ran into trouble. Claiming that he had a twenty-year interest in Columbus's islands, Goodwin alleged a four-year prior commitment to the excavation of the same region in Haiti.[21] He claimed that he too had been following Columbus's path as charted in the journals in order to discover "exactly where he went, what he saw and what he determined to do."[22] Aware of the potential duplication of their projects, Morison wrote Goodwin an account of his intentions and early findings as a professional courtesy. This, he confided to Andrews, was unfortunate, since Goodwin returned "a very incoherent and disagreeable letter" that established his "prior rights to all Haitian excavations" and accused Morison of "having double-crossed him." Goodwin "has prepared a regular expedi-tionary force to dig up half of Haiti in search of Columbian relics," Morison complained.[23]

Still worse, Goodwin implicated Morison and Andrews in some sort of scheme designed to sabotage his work. "I have a full report of all that happened at Jupiter Island before you went to Cape Haitien," Goodwin wrote, suspecting that his old nemesis Andrews had enlisted Morison in another attack on his work. Baffled by "this supposed Jupiter Island conspir-acy to thwart the beneficent excavations of William D. Goodwin," Morison asked Andrews, "What do you suppose this deep, dark plot is that you and I are supposed to have cooked up during our peaceful visit there?"[24] Andrews was at a loss to imagine. Goodwin "is . . . in many ways one of the most disagreeable men that it has ever been my misfortune to meet," he replied.[25] Andrews thought that Goodwin represented the very worst in amateur historical technique and restoration efforts. Morison agreed, noting that Goodwin "writes like a crazy man, as I dare say he is."[26] Unfortunately, as Andrews noted, "[Goodwin] is possessed of considerable wealth, which enables him to follow up his program and to carry out certain plans he has fashioned, most of which are of very little value to any one." Furthermore, Andrews remarked, "when once he has made up his mind in regard to what he believes to be his right in any particular case," Goodwin's "bulldog tenacity" is overwhelming.[27]

Goodwin's wealth allowed him not only to continue with his excavation plans but also to spend time spying on Morison's efforts. He began by writing various friends in the Caribbean and asking about Morison's movements. "There is a Professor Samuel Eliot Morison of Harvard University who is also interested in the solution of the site of Navidad," Goodwin wrote a friend, Professor Louis Mercier in Haiti. "I would like to know," he continued, "whether later this past winter . . . a Professor Boggs of the Peabody Museum of Harvard University came up from Venezuela to dig on this site. If he made his headquarters at the Cap, doubtless you would have met him. Can you tell me anything about him?"[28] In addition, Goodwin wrote publishers several letters attacking Morison's project and promoting his own. "I don't know whether you know it or not," he wrote the publisher of a recent three-volume history of Columbus, "but the present Professor of History at Harvard College, Samuel Eliot Morison, is getting up a new history of Columbus" for which "there is no particular need." Morison, "posing as Young Columbus, is very intent on his ideas," Goodwin continued, and these ideas were bogus because Morison had not found the actual site of Navidad. Claiming to have the information himself, Goodwin threatened to withhold it unless he was guaranteed publication rights over Morison: "There is no one in the world today who knows what we [Goodwin and his excavation team] do and we will keep this secret, unless you publish what we suggest."[29]

Morison, however, also had his sources of information. The Episcopal bishop of Haiti, who was one of the amateur historians who had helped Morison in the early stages of his research, reported that "Goodwin's men did nothing but look for buried treasure and drink rum" while in Haiti and were "in bad with the government."[30] The bishop also warned that Goodwin claimed to be "responsible" for Morison's ideas and was bitter about not having been asked to join the expedition.[31] This information corroborated Andrews's claim that Goodwin was disagreeable and dangerous. Morison responded to this allegation in a letter to Andrews: "Of course he had nothing to do with interesting me in Columbus or Haiti. . . . He only sent me a lot of letters about the location of Navidad which were so wild, that I now suspect his intention was to mislead me."[32] Andrews sympathized with his colleague. "Goodwin can believe a great many things that I have no doubt are not true," he wrote Morison, "and I take it in this one particular he has assumed many things that he had no right to assume."[33]

Morison received threatening correspondence from another amateur historian, Grace A. Fendler, who also alleged prior claims to Caribbean findings. In the fall of 1939, Fendler sent out a series of letters to Morison's benefactors, claiming that a copyright of hers was being violated. In April 1934, she explained, she had explored various Caribbean islands known to have been visited by Columbus and had published a digest of her findings. By her account, the most important discoveries included "the suppressed facts" that Columbus had discovered territory "from at least the 40th parallel North down to Brazil" and that Columbus's "Journal of the First Voyage" was "doctored" by Spanish authorities to conceal the extent and value of his findings. Morison's research, she contended, was an infringement on her work, and she added, "I must ask you to consider this letter as legal notice of my rights."[34] Morison was compelled to write back assuring Fendler that there would be no invasion of her rights, and her letter also prompted him to seek further means of protecting himself from amateur historians. Increasingly sensitive to the perception that his work was no different than that of amateurs like Goodwin and Fendler, he sought advice from an old warrior of professional causes. "There is a tendency to regard this Expedition as merely an excuse for a yachting cruise for me," Morison wrote Andrews in July 1939. "[P]erhaps a psychologist would insist it was," he judged, but it would be necessary to "show the contrary" to readers.[35]

Andrews suggested that Morison could legitimize his work by restructuring his research to assure greater professional and institutional support. This Morison did by turning once again to his alma mater for help. Originally, Morison had intended to follow Columbus's voyages in his own private yacht acting out a Parkmanesque vision of independent scholarship. By 1939, however, he decided that the project needed institutional help and solicited as many "official seals of approval as possible" from Harvard.[36] In letters to the president of the college (now James B. Conant), the board of trustees, and members of the alumni association, Morison asked the college to sponsor his research. "Had I been Columbus, I should have asked for the blessing of the Cardinal Archbishop and the Church," he wrote in these appeals, "[but] being a Harvard man, I respectfully beg for approval of the President and Fellows, which will have the same effect of making the enterprise both honorable and eleemosynary."[37] In the spring of 1939, he was granted another year-long leave from classes and the Harvard Columbus Expedition was announced to the world.[38]

"The Golden Age of Sail"

The Harvard connection gave Morison many distinct advantages in his pursuit of Columbus. First, it assured valuable financial support. The Milton Fund at Harvard helped defray the "half-year's salary" Morison expected to lose while continuing his research, and numerous Harvard affiliates across the country sent checks that allowed him to widen the scope of the enterprise.[39] The largest contribution came from a fellow of the corporation and a former overseer who donated money "as a reward for Tercentenary efforts done by her alumnus of 1908."[40] This contribution included the money for a 102-foot steel ketch, *Capitana*, which Morison hoped to use to retrace Columbus's paths from Old World to New. Purchased at a cost of $17,000, the ship allowed him to claim some veracity in his efforts to experience Columbus's life as a mariner on the open sea.[41] The college provided money for the Harvard arms to be painted on the topsail and for a library of nearly three hundred volumes of Columbiana to be provided for the journey.[42] Harvard even helped solicit other academic grants from the Mellon Educational Foundation of Pittsburgh and the Carnegie Corporation of New York.[43]

The inclusion of "Expedition" in the title gave the project a vaguely scientific connotation, an impression Morison worked hard to sustain. The reenactment of Columbus's voyages became a full-scale professional operation, outfitted with the latest oceanographic, astronomical, and navigational equipment, including an astrolabe, which Morison had specially commissioned to meet fifteenth-century standards.[44] The *Capitana* and the *Mary Otis*, a small ketch Morison commissioned to accompany his lead ship, were manned by "officers," all of vast sea experience and each with a specific scientific function to perform in helping Morison to reexperience Columbus's voyages. Some were charged with calculating headings and wind changes and comparing these with the settings recorded in Columbus's journals, and others were studying celestial navigation and lunar tides and evaluating Columbus's understanding of heavenly bodies.[45] Numerous letters were sent to members of the scientific community on behalf of the expedition requesting precise information about maritime activities in the fifteenth century,[46] and applications for scientific grants identified Morison as a "scientist."[47] When one lending institution questioned the scientific nature of the enterprise, Morison insisted that "we are a scientific expedition in the usual sense of the word, since our purpose is to obtain data for the history of Columbus's voyages."[48]

The Harvard name also paved the way for official government sanction of the project. Aggressive in his efforts to get the U.S. government to approve the expedition, Morison even solicited the help of President Franklin D. Roosevelt, a Harvard man several classes removed from Morison. The professor asked the president for a letter of introduction to various ports and dignitaries in foreign countries, and Roosevelt obliged, not only making the appropriate arrangements with the State Department but also sending a "good luck" photograph of himself to "Columbus Jr." and his crew.[49] Subsequently, Morison was given access to official materials, escort on various U.S. Coast Guard vessels, and the use of U.S. Navy reconnaissance planes, none of which were available to his amateur competitors.[50] Furthermore, because the expedition was granted tax-exempt status, additional channels of financial support were opened up.[51] The Atlantic Refining Company provided lubricating oil; the Standard Oil company provided fuel oil; former Senator Henry Hollis of New Hampshire donated wines; Cummins Engine Company loaned a new diesel engine; the American Chain and Cable Company provided wire rope; Olconite Company produced electric wiring; the Plymouth Cordage Company supplied rope; and the Bakelite Corporation donated composition for deck seams. The U.S. Army even provided a surgical kit.[52] Various other companies contributed to the provisions, which included over two thousand cans of fruits and vegetables, six hundred pounds of meat, and three thousand bottles of beverage.[53]

Designated the "Commodore" and purser of the voyage, Morison assembled a crew including several naval experts and fellow Harvard graduates who reflected the scientific, educational, and governmental character of the expedition (see Fig. 1). The leadship *Capitana* was piloted by Paul Hammond (Harvard 1906), who had served in the U.S. Navy during World War I and had been a yachtsman since boyhood. The navigating officer, Jack McElroy (Harvard A.M. 1933), was a lieutenant in the U.S. Navy and a former master in the American merchant marine. The ship's surgeon was a graduate of Harvard Medical School (1934) and an avid sailor. The sailing master was an Estonian, Jarrillo Walters, who had made nautical news by crossing the Atlantic in a twenty-five-foot boat. He was assisted by navigator Dwight Morrow (Harvard A.M. 1935), who had extensive Maine yachting experience. The expedition included ten other experienced seamen (including three who trailed the *Capitana* in the small ketch *Mary Otis*), Mrs. Paul Hammond (a constant companion of her husband "in American and European waters"), and Morison's daughter Elizabeth (Radcliffe 1934), who had cruised extensively with her father. The only inexperienced passenger was Mrs. Dwight Morrow, who had "never been at sea before."[54]

If there was any disadvantage to the Harvard affiliation, it was in the difficulties the name occasionally presented for Morison in his efforts to recapture Parkman's sense of the living presence of the past. From the very beginning of the voyage, for instance, the need to maintain on "official" profile hurt the expedition's ability to complete all the phases of its epic reenactment of Columbus's sail. The original goal was to travel east from Oyster Bay, Long Island, and "to pick up the course of Columbus's return passage of 1493 near the Azores, call at Santa Maria, where the *Nina* put in after a bad storm," and then sail for Lisbon, concluding the admiral's first voyage. From there, Morison and his crew planned to proceed to the Canaries, "the jumping-off place for three out of four of Columbus's voyages." The expedition then expected to sail west back across the Atlantic along the route of Columbus's third voyage to Trinidad, to pick up the trail of the fourth voyage along the Venezuelan coast, and to follow it through the Caribbean to the northern coast of Jamaica and Honduras.[55] This ambitious schedule was soon jeopardized, however, by the need to court the

FIG. 1　*Morison with the crew of the Harvard Columbus Expe-*
dition aboard Capitana, *1939. Morison in jacket and tie,*
kneeling, is second from right in the front row.
Courtesy of the Harvard University Archives.

press at home and abroad. Press releases, photo sessions, and radio interviews became part of the daily routine of the researchers whenever they pulled into ports. Occasionally, these distractions threatened to turn the expedition into a circus affair. Unaccustomed to professors with celebrity status, Harvard undergraduates poked fun at Morison's expedition and the media hype that attended it. The 1940 edition of the *Harvard Lampoon* (see Fig. 2) pictured Morison at the yardarm of his vessel, dressed in Columbian garb and looking out to sea in search of the great discoverer and was accompanied by a spoofing poem.

Morison's desire to demonstrate the high, professional quality of the expedition also interfered at times with the ability of the crew to function. Insisting that members of the expedition conduct themselves with strict formality and professional behavior and in obedience to his authority, Morison put some of the crew to work under nearly military regimen a full month before departure. While the officers tolerated the precise nautical language used on board, the crew did not always appreciate the fact that the decks were scrubbed daily with "holystones" whether they needed it or not. This formality wearied some of Morison's shipmates to such an extent that a few hours after departing Oyster Bay, Long Island, in late August 1939, the *Capitana* was forced to return to shore. The ostensible problem was a reported northeaster against whose power Morison did not wish "to subject our untried ship and green crew."[56] But the real reason for the return seems to have been a near mutiny that developed on board as the expedition got underway. Three of the crew informed Morison that they were "through," already "tired out and sick of it all," and demanded to be put ashore. Morison persuaded them to spend the night on board, but by the morning the discontented had enlisted another crew member in their cause and still insisted on immediate release from their duties. Hoping to prevent the desertion of others, Morison paid the four and attempted to set them ashore in a launch. As the launch embarked, however, it encountered strong winds, and the small vessel eventually ran out of gas attempting to battle the waves. Its crew had to be rescued by the Coast Guard. Hardly an auspicious start to a transatlantic trip, this episode suggested the price Morison would pay for his adherence to professional standards throughout the expedition.[57]

In his private journal, Morison admitted he had "overworked" the crew in an effort to set sail by August, but he thought the four mutineers were "very foolish to leave just as the fun was beginning." He immediately began telegraphing for replacements. Meanwhile, the northeaster broke on the morning of August 29, and the ship's cook became seasick. He remained sick all day, so he was dismissed as well. Morison made some more hasty phone calls and by August 30 managed to secure enough help to continue. By that time, however, the storm had made a mess of the ship's rigging, and another day was lost rerigging and breaking in the new crew. Finally, on September 1 the *Capitana* was ready to sail, and Morison assured his supporters in the first of a series of publicity letters to the *Harvard Alumni*

FIG. 2 *From the* Harvard Lampoon, *no. 119, 21 February 1940, p. 38. Courtesy of the* Harvard Lampoon.

Bulletin that "[d]espite all rumors to the contrary," the Harvard Columbus Expedition was finally under way.[58] Even this assurance was premature, however, as September 3 brought news of war in Europe and raised the possibility that the mission would have to be aborted. The already unsteady crew was instructed to proceed cautiously and to stay posted to the radio for reports of possible submarine activity. The necessary caution put the expedition still further behind schedule and prevented Morison from completing all the research he had planned.[59]

Morison rationalized the delays by emphasizing the similarities between the Harvard Columbus Expedition and the discoverer's first voyage. Both fleets faced a delaying storm just before setting sail, he noted; both experienced a changing of crews; both faced the threat of war in the early weeks of travel. To further re-create the conditions of the fifteenth-century voyages, Morison nailed a silver *albricias* to the foremast of his leadship and promised it to the first crew member to sight land, as Columbus had.[60] Soon Morison could boast that the expedition was verifying many of Columbus's observations at sea. Dropping down to a latitude roughly parallel to Columbus's voyage from Spain to the Caribbean, he sighted the same gulfweed, petrels, and bosun birds that Columbus had observed as he approached the New World for the first time. One crew member presented a long-tailed bird that had stunned itself against the rigging (the bird "remonstrating in typical sea-bird language," Morison noted), as "a triumph in corroborating testimony," since Columbus had sighted just such a long-tail on his return to the Old World in 1493.[61] Still more gratifying was the crew's ability to verify observations from Columbus's journal that experts had doubted for years. According to Morison, historian Ludlow Griscom had suggested that Columbus's sighting of a dove aboard the *Santa Maria* in mid-ocean in 1492 was not credible, since "doves do not fly so far out to sea." Morison, however, reported that on September 7 a mourning dove, "probably migrating from Newfoundland to the West Indies," visited the ship and spent the night on board.[62] "The Admiral's ghost had another laugh on his critics," Morison subsequently noted in his journal.[63]

Morison presented these corroborating bits of evidence as proof that the expedition could reexperience Columbus's original voyage as Parkman had reexperienced the American wilderness. They also demonstrated how scholarship might be combined with practical seamanship to approximate the actual conditions of a past age. At sea, with no one to account to, the expedition settled in to a comfortable routine of "check[ing] on Columbus."[64] While testing the discoverer's celestial observations, Morison expressed his "wonder" and "admiration" for "the nightly dance of the stars," which provided a "fixed" and "immutable" point of convergence between Columbus and himself. "Dynasties rise and die, world empires are aimed at and the aim fails, but still untroubled, the stars shine down on our poor, silly planet," Morison wrote.[65] "I have only to step on deck and take the wheel, or do a bit of deck scraping," he noted, "to sweep the cobwebs from my brain."[66] In the great, empty ocean, "now swept by war, as clean of sail as in Columbus's day," Morison added, "you could recapture the feelings of his men, who had only their Admiral's word, that wealth and glory, not destruction and death, lay over the horizon's rim."[67] Sailing along on the waves, he remarked, "one can easily play discoverer."[68]

The magic of this spiritual communion with Columbus was harder to maintain on shore. As the Harvard Columbus Expedition reached the Azores and later Spain, the need to maintain an official profile required concessions to the local population. In each port of call, Morison was obliged to go to the local newspaper offices, inform the editors of what he was doing, and consent to interviews advertising the ambassadorial nature of the expedition.[69] This publicity often caused annoying delays and confusion, as in Santa Maria, where it attracted a local amateur historian who professed to be an authority on Columbus. He lectured the crew "about Columbus . . . in voluble Portuguese which the interpreter was quite unable to translate," Morison noted, and followed expedition members all over the island, distracting them from their work.[70] Eventually, Morison shook him off through a ruse, but the experience was so annoying that he cut short his research and embarked for Lisbon. There he was bothered by another amateur historian, Dr. Miquel Pestana, Jr., whom Morison described as the "writer of the latest crackpot book on C.C." When a more "sensible historian" finally did present himself, Morison noted in his journal, "I'm so tired of talk I can hardly listen to him."[71]

Franklin Roosevelt's strong endorsement of the expedition encouraged nearly every State Department official in western Europe to make the entrance of the *Capitana* into port the occasion for some elaborate ceremony. The American ambassador in Lisbon, Herbert C. Pell, housed the *Capitana*'s officers in the beautiful home of the U.S. ambassador to Portugal overlooking the Atlantic and attended by fourteen "amiable but inefficient Portuguese servants."[72] The remainder of the visit to Lisbon had the quality of a pageant. On October 16, Morison met various Portuguese dignitaries near the spot where Columbus made his triumphant return to Portugal in 1493 and initiated a ceremonial day "to make some formal tribute to the essential part played by Portuguese seamen, naval architecture, and navigational science in the discovery of America." The U.S. Ambassador Pell delivered a speech, the traditional Harvard oak leaf wreath was presented "amid flashes of news photographers," and the entire party moved on to a lavish dinner thrown by the Portuguese Minister of Public Propaganda, Senhor Antonia Ferro. Ferro served a five-course luncheon with three kinds of Portuguese wines. "When, at the conclusion, Senhor Ferro produced a bottle of 1908 vintage port," Morison wrote, "I was almost ready to agree with my luncheon partner that Columbus was a Portuguese!"[73]

In Spain the distractions continued. Landing in Huelva to research Columbus's travels prior to his first voyage, Morison went immediately to the office of the gobernador civil for help. "He was away," and his "secretary was very stupid," Morison wrote. The president of the local Columbian Society who arrived shortly thereafter offered little additional help. When the gobernador finally appeared, research was replaced by continued lectures on local Columbus myths and more lavish dinners of expensive wine and delicious shrimp.[74] Meanwhile, the hectic social schedule was taking its toll on Morison's fellow passengers. Mrs. Dwight Morrow and Morison's daughter Elizabeth by prearrangement sailed home from the Canary Islands.[75] Unexpectedly, however, Captain Paul Hammond and his wife announced that they, too, were returning home. Hammond needed to return to his business concerns in New York, which were being affected by war developments in Europe, but there is also evidence that Hammond was not getting along with some of the crew. Seaman Kenneth Spear complained to Morison, for instance, that he had "tried [his] best to be a good steward," but "Mr. Hammond" had not given him "a chance."[76] Although Morison remarked that the loss of Hammond "deprived if not crippled" the expedition, he too had felt ill at ease with Hammond's command.[77] In Portugal, Morison transferred briefly to his expedition's sister ship, the *Mary Otis*, and in private letters home to his family he expressed his joy at the switch. The *Mary Otis* is "such a rest from the *Capitana*," he wrote, since there is "no nagging and shouting and everyone does his duty willingly." His dislike for the *Capitana* was "not only a matter of size," Morison noted, "but of atmosphere."[78]

The *Capitana*'s crew may have been restless because they resented being excluded from the social activities enjoyed by the expedition's "officers." In Spain, various acts of defiance by crew members increased. The ship's log, kept by navigator Jarillo Walters, recorded restrictions placed by Hammond on shipmate Bob Cram for having been "ashore all day without permission."[79] A month later, another crew member, Dwight Morrow, announced he was leaving too, and "he did!" Morison told his family indignantly, "No reason given."[80] The distractions in western Europe consumed so much time, in fact, that Morison was forced to leave the mainland before he was able to complete his research there.

Morison's attempt to maintain an imaginative bridge between his world and Columbus's was undercut further by political matters. Along the Venezuelan coast, for instance, the *Capitana* lay at anchor off Yacau Beach and "tried to conjure up that momentous going-ashore on August 5, 1498," when Columbus took his first steps on the American continent during his third voyage.[81] Exploring the coast for Columbus's landing spot "[m]onkeys obliging chattered at us" as they had for Columbus 350 years before, Morison remarked, but the mood was soon broken by "human" monkeys in the form of Venezuelan patrol boats. Patrols had been organized by the Venezuelan government to protect the coasts from privateers, and although these patrols were unsalaried, they received fifty percent of all seizures. Consequently, they were aggressive (and even piratical) in their duties. "Knowing the habits of those near-monkeys," Morison explained, he refused to obey the orders of one such patrol that the crew follow him to the nearest port. The officer in charge insisted that the captain of the port merely wished to entertain the expedition's members at dinner, but Morison suspected that the "local hoosegow was to have been the scene of hospitality." The officer, dressed in what looked to Morison like "dirty pajamas," and his *"hombres,"* a "collection of dirty black-and-tans," then brandished rifles. Morison and his crew, fortunately, had stayed aboard their vessels and outside the three-mile international limit and refused to be bullied into port. After a long standoff, the patrol boat pulled away, but the Harvard Columbus Expedition had to abandon its plans to explore Yacau Beach.[82]

Unable to explore Venezuela, Morison moved on to Panama, where he was again overwhelmed by obligations and official dignitaries. Dr. Mendez Pereira, rector of the University of Panama, welcomed him with lavish ceremony and filled the newspapers with "the most flattering blah about the H[arvard] C[olumbus] E[xpedition] that we have received," Morison wrote. "This was the beginning of a series of festivities," he added, "which wound up a few days later at Panama City, where the expedition was received by President Boyd and entertained by our Ambassador, by the charming Ehrman family, and by my old friend and classmate Henry S. Blair."[83] These contacts proved helpful. Columbus's explorations along the Panamanian coast would have been difficult to chart in the *Capitana* or the *Mary Otis*, Morison noted, "because maps of the region are so inaccurate," and because the coastal areas "are the hardest places to get at I have ever seen on the ocean's rim." President Boyd chartered a diesel-powered market sloop with a native pilot for exploring these regions, and the United Fruit Company placed a launch at his disposal for navigating the treacherous Mosquito Gulf of Panama. These vessels allowed the expedition to make visual confirmations of Columbus's explorations and to feel a closeness to the discoverer that "pleased" Morison "as much as anything on the voyage." The confirmations served, he noted, "to illustrate my thesis that you cannot check up on early voyages by sitting home in a library with charts spread out before you."[84]

Such activities cut deeply into the few weeks remaining for the expedition, however. Morison had planned to circumnavigate Jamaica, but the constant round of social activities in Europe and Central America meant there was "no time" left. "Columbus had no motor," Morison wrote, "but he didn't have to get home to give courses the second half-year!"[85] On January 26, 1940, therefore, the *Capitana* dropped its final anchor off Jamaica (near the spot where Columbus's worm-eaten flagship of the same name was wrecked on the fourth and final voyage), and the Harvard Columbus Expedition was officially terminated.[86] In five months the expedition had made two ocean crossings, covered over seven thousand miles, and compiled an impressive amount of information about Columbus's voyages. Yet parties and receptions, necessary for access to local information, had wasted time; amateur historians had pestered the expedition with pet theories about Columbus; and the crew had often proved uncooperative. All these distractions had broken the special telepathy Morison hoped to establish between himself and Columbus.

Nevertheless, Morison considered the expedition a "grand success," largely because of the occasional moments of spiritual closeness he had felt with the great discoverer. While visiting the La Rabida, for instance, the monastery where Columbus was first received by the King and Queen of Spain, Morison experienced a sense of déjà vu. "I had the weird feeling of having been there before," he said, adding with pleasure that he felt like "Columbus, Jr., coming home!" In Seville he experienced a similar feeling of empathy with his hero. While researching in the Columbian Library of the Moorish court of the Oranges, he read the annotated marginalia in Columbus's nautical and geographical books. "[Y]ou may well imagine how exciting it is for me to read his marginal notes," Morison confessed to his family. He felt close not only to Columbus but to the great American historians of fifteenth-century Spain. "The very smell of these old European libraries arouses memories that seem to go back of my own life; I catch a faint fragrance of that rare alembic of Iberian scholarship, piety and wit, that so inspired Americans like Ticknor, Everett, and my grandfather Eliot."[87] In a letter to the *Harvard Alumni Bulletin*, written shortly after the expedition, Morison noted the ephemeral quality of these mystifying experiences: "Here in our little winter house amid the snowdrifts left by the St. Valentines's Day blizzard, the Harvard Columbus Expedition seems like a beautiful dream; something that one accomplished long ago, in one's youth, in the golden age of sail." Yet he felt confident that he could recapture these experiences in a Columbus biography with the artistry of a Parkman and the accuracy of a Hart. "My maritime researches will now permit me to rewrite the opening chapter of American history," Morison predicted.[88]

Optimistic observers seemed to agree with Morison's assessment. The headlines of the *New York Times* for February 2, 1940, read "Columbus Upheld!" and welcomed home the "lean, wind-burnt man, who appears to be more at home on saltwater than in the erudite halls of history."[89] In March, *Life* magazine featured the expedition in an article and emphasized that the voyage "was more than just high adventure. It was the first empirical effort ever made to check the contemporary accounts of America's discovery."[90] But the *Boston Globe* captured best Morison's twin goals—to provide an account of Columbus's voyages objective enough to be acceptable to professional historians yet amply imaginative and vivid to be suitable for lay readers: "Our historian cultivates a dual personality. One is the austere scholar, the learned and liberal professor who lectures young men in Harvard College, or, it has been, in Oxford University. . . . [whereas] his alter ego gets into a woolen shirt, weighs anchor, takes the wheel, lays a course, knows how to shoot sun and stars, and, at a pinch in a native boat manned by black fellows, can subsist for a few days on biscuit, rum and coffee."[91]

The Dualistic Vision

As Morison shifted from explorer to writer, he entered a second voyage of discovery that recapitulated the struggles of the first in revealing ways. The two audiences for the biography, scholarly and popular, determined the dualistic structure of the work. Published in a two-volume edition, *Admiral of the Ocean Sea* was characterized by alternating chapters for expert and amateur. Volume 1, for instance, began with a very technical chapter on ships and sailing. Offered a bit condescendingly "by a member of the dying race of seaman in sail to the great majority of much cleverer people who know how to run engines," the chapter was designed to demonstrate Morison's authority as a mariner. He described technical terms such as the starboard track, leeway, full and by, off the wind, running free, wearing, beating against the wind and current, clawing off a lee shore, heaving to and lying to, jogging off and on. He also discussed in great detail the latest developments in beam-to-length ratios, the aerodynamics of sail manipulation, and the distinctions between square and lateen rigs.[92]

The next section of the first volume, an abstract prologue characterized by romantic and allegorical imagery, completely reversed the direction. Relying heavily on a biblical vocabulary, Morison began the prologue with a description of the pitiable state of the earth in 1492, which, in accordance with prophecies of the Book of Revelation, seemed to be in its final phase. The Christian world "touched bottom" in that year with the election of the corrupt Rodrigo Borgia to the papacy, he wrote, and people merely waited for the "seventh angel" to "pour out the seventh vial, and the awful Day of Judgment, painted in lurid colors of the Vision of Saint John," to "conclude the history of a wicked world." Columbus arrived literally in the nick of time, however, to put the world back together. His discovery of a virgin New World united the earth geographically and spiritually, giving Europe "another chance" in the experiment with living. What had been essentially lost before Columbus, Morison argued, was a belief in the great principle of "unity" in both its physical and spiritual connotations. Columbus supplied this and was thus essentially a Christ figure who had redeemed the world. Within a few years of Columbus's discoveries, Morison wrote, "we find the mental picture completely changed." After 1492 kings were "stamping out privy conspiracy and rebellion," the Church put "her house in order," "faith in God" revived, and "the human spirit [was] renewed." Christopher Columbus, (whose given name, Morison reminded readers, stood for "Christ-bearer") was a conduit in these processes, uniting the "age that was past" with the "new age of hope, glory and accomplishment."[93]

The alternation in style between the technical chapter on sailing and the literary prologue continued throughout the remaining chapters. At times Morison described the science of sailing in a language so technical as to leave little doubt of the author's qualifications for evaluating Columbus as a mariner. Recounting how a sailor "wear[s] a two-masted lateener," he informed readers in a burst of dense technical jargon that the "enormous yard (equal to overall length on a *baggala* as on a caravel) has to be twisted on its parral (collar) around the mast; and for this reason the sail must hang on strops so the yard can turn without rolling up [Morison's italics]." Without such precautions, he warned, there "is danger of the sail ripping, of the parral jamming, of the mast going by the board when the stays are cast off, of sheet or tack getting away from the men during the run-around, with hell to pay." At other times, however, Morison wrote with the light touch of an artist. Describing the "experience of approaching and passing each island that the Admiral discovered in those brave days of 1493," Morison used a palette ranging "from the most vivid sapphire to a luminous smaragdine." By the time "the sunrise enflames the mountain pinnacles the lower slopes are already shading from gray to green, and from green to a blue that is only a shade lighter than the sea," he composed, and as "the sun rises higher the trade wind blows more briskly; clouds form and pile up on the slopes even if there are none to seaward." By noon the sea "becomes a trembling mirror, broken only by clouds crushed down over its summit," he waxed poetic, reflecting "orange from the declining sun, which as it dips under a clear horizon shoots up in a split second a brilliant emerald flash."[94]

The structural and stylistic dualities of *Admiral of the Ocean Sea* were also reiterated in the biography's alternating narrative voices. At times Morison used the detached voice of the twentieth-century professional historian, condemning the "unprofitable speculation" of amateurs who "were so bright as to 'discover' what had been hidden for centuries, even though they had but a small fraction of the documentary evidence, and none of the oral and visual evidence available to Columbus's contemporaries." Whether authenticating Columbus's journal through linguistic analysis, finding geological confirmation of animal and vegetation records, or demonstrating mathematically the discoverer's inability to use an astrolabe, Morison claimed scientific authority for his assertions. At other times, however, the detached and technical voice of the main narrator in *Admiral of the Ocean Sea* gave way to a second, far less objective voice. On questions not subject to scientific verification, Morison employed his considerable imagination to invent scenes and re-create dialogues. For instance, because little is known of how the crew for Columbus's first voyage was recruited, Morison introduced the theory that Columbus was aided by an ancient mariner who had once sailed west to the Sargasso Sea before turning back. "How vivid it all is," Morison began imaginatively: "The grizzled pilot, who believed he had just missed something big forty years before, becomes greatly excited at Columbus's preparations, confers with him and with Pinzon, and warmly approving their enterprise, undertakes to beat up recruits for them in the plaza of Palos, where the unemployed hung about as they do now. One can imagine the talk," he went on. "Sign on with Master Christopher, you swabs, and he will make you rich for life."[95]

Morison also played with tense to give his readers a sense of participation in the drama of Columbus's discoveries. Speculating dramatically that the night of October 12, 1492, "was one big with destiny for the human race, the most momentous ever experienced aboard any ship in any sea," Morison magically transported his readers on board Columbus's flotilla by slipping into the present tense. "Juan de la Cosa and the Pinzons are pacing the high poops of their respective vessels, frequently calling down to the men at the tiller a testy order—keep her off damn your eyes must I go below and take the stick myself?—pausing at the break to peer below under the main course and sweep the western horizon, then resting their eyes by looking up at the stars," Morison wrote from his imagination. "Lookouts on the forecastles and in the round-tops talking low to each other—Hear anything? Sounds like breakers to me—nothing but the bow wave you fool," his omniscient narrator continued. Interposing his own historical knowledge about the scene, Morison even privileged his ship deck observer with insight others on board did not have, namely, that they were cutting "down the last invisible barrier between the Old World and the New. Only a few moments now," he wrote, "and an era that began in remotest antiquity will end."[96]

Morison's rationale for offering both scientific and imaginative points of view was the same he had offered his students for reconciling the "two separate ways of historical knowing." If facts about a historical episode can be ascertained, he noted, the historian has no right to override them by his imagination; but a historian working on a "remote or obscure subject about which few facts are available" might use his imagination to "legitimately weave them into a pattern" provided he is clear on "what is fact and what is hypothesis."[97] Citing Parkman's gift for balancing the two, Morison argued that his own Parkmanesque retracing of Columbus's voyages made him uniquely qualified to speculate on the discoverer's world. The remarkable similarities between the voyages of Columbus and Morison's Harvard Columbus Expedition caused some readers of *Admiral of the Ocean Sea* to marvel at Morison's powers of imaginative extension, while it caused others to suspect them. The description of Columbus's anxieties about leading a large-scale expedition, for instance, seemed unusually analogous to those expressed by Morison in his private letters concerning the Harvard Columbus Expedition. Columbus desired to have his voyages "pronounced scientifically correct" and "technically feasible" by the experts, Morison noted with self-reflexive implications, and would not undertake his voyages until he had received official sanction from a European government. The discoverer also experienced exasperating problems with his crew, whose members talked endlessly "against their captain behind his back," a habit, Morison revealingly added, not "confined to Latin countries." Columbus was "a Man with a Mission," Morison wrote from a sense of shared experience, "and such men are apt to be unreasonable and even disagreeable to those who cannot see the mission."[98]

At times in *Admiral of the Ocean Sea*, Morison's voice became indistinct from Columbus's. Based on the experiences of the Harvard Columbus Expedition, he moved easily from a description of what Columbus *might* have been thinking to an assertion of what he *must* have been thinking. Morison concluded that on his third voyage to the New World Columbus must have anchored in the harbor of Yacau, for instance, because "the beauty of this little harbor" and "the deep water almost up to the beach, lures one to come in and anchor." Or, again, he discredited the theory that Columbus's rudder was loosened up by foul play off the coast of Portugal, because the Harvard Columbus Expedition experienced a similar rudder problem under innocent circumstances. "I have special reasons for not being favorably impressed by Pinzon's hint of foul play," Morison wrote, "knowing by personal experience that these waters are hard on steering gear." Morison even doubted Columbus's memory when the discoverer's assertions contradicted the findings of the Harvard Columbus Expedition. To explain the discrepancies between Columbus's calculations of sailing speed and his own, for instance, Morison argued that Columbus must have remembered incorrectly. "One forgets these things after a few years," he offered, adding that "one can guess what happened" by reading "between the lines of the sea journal."[99]

Because Morison implied too close a convergence between the voyages of Columbus and the Harvard Columbus Expedition, some critics argued that he allowed himself an interpretive freedom he denied Washington Irving and others. In describing Columbus's triumphant return to the Spanish court after his discoveries at sea, for instance, Morison drew directly from Irving's biography, embellishing on the amateur historian's "eyewitness" account. "[H]is fine stature, an air of authority, his noble countenance and gray hair," Morison wrote of Columbus, "gave him the appearance of a Roman senator, as he advanced with a modest smile to make his obeisance." Still more, Morison presumed to know where Columbus went, what he saw, and who saw him, with a confidence that would have shocked even Irving. Thus, on the return trip from the court, Morison noted that Columbus must have spent one night "in the town of Trujillo, where a thirteen-year-old swinehead's son named Francisco Pizarro would certainly have turned out to see the Indians" he brought with him. Perhaps "then and there," Morison speculated, Pizarro "caught that flame of ambition which led him to the conquest of Peru." Crossing to the town of Medellin, Morison was certain that "a small and delicate boy named Hernán Cortés must have seen [Columbus]." Through a remarkable series of contingencies, in other words, Morison created an enjoyable but unsubstantiated image of the world's future great explorers gathered in a congratulatory procession in honor of the hero Columbus.[100]

Controlled imagination or reckless subjectivity? Whichever tendency one believes Morison demonstrated in *Admiral of the Ocean Sea*, his technical, scientific, and objective vision struggled against an artistic, poetic, and subjective one. Not surprisingly, Morison ascribed this conflict to his hero as well. On the one hand, he argued, Columbus strove throughout his entire career for scientific precision and mathematical verification for his work. In these ambitions, Columbus was hopelessly inadequate, and the royal mathematicians of the courts of Europe who advised their monarchs not to finance Columbus's voyages were absolutely correct in their assessments of his chances. "[W]e all love to hear of professors and experts being confounded by simple common sense," Morison wrote, but the fact remained that Columbus's calculations placed China half as close to Europe as it actually was. On the other hand, Columbus was also a man of faith and imagination who drew his strength not from "superior knowledge" but from "an inward assurance" and "confidence in his destiny." His discovery of an unknown continent did not justify his mathematics, but he "*knew* he could make it," and "the figures had to fit [Morison's italics]." Columbus's "secret communion with forces unseen," Morison wrote, "was a vital element in his achievement," especially in gaining the support of Queen Isabella of Spain, who "had seen a good deal of experts in her reign of eighteen years and realized that half the time they did not know what they were talking about." The Admiral "appealed not only to her reason, but to her instincts," her "feminine intuition," and to her "mysterious knowledge" that he would accomplish something extraordinary. She recognized, Morison concluded, that the "most impressive thing about Columbus's presentation of his case had not been the facts and the arguments but the man."[101]

According to Morison, the rational and imaginative sides of Columbus's "dualistic" personality were reconciled by the discoverer's pragmatism. Columbus's willingness to act, despite his unresolved tensions between scholarship and faith, was the most crucially important aspect of his success. "If Columbus had had a university degree," Morison wrote, "he would never have achieved his goal," because the study of mathematics would have convinced him he was wrong in his mathematical calculations. Likewise, if Columbus had relied wholly on imagination, he would not have completed his voyages either, because imagination is no substitute for nautical experience. The originality of Columbus's sail, therefore, "lay not in its conception, but in proposing to do something about it." Columbus, Morison observed, was a "man of action" who acquired knowledge "the old way, the hard way, and the only way, in the school of experience." His use of "dead-reckoning" as a navigational technique underscored this pragmatism. Equally ill-disposed toward trusting newfangled scientific equipment or phantasmagoric stories about the "deep," Columbus navigated by simply laying down compass courses and estimating distances on a chart. This commonsense, "hands-on" technique, although crude, forced him to rely on his "born navigator's sense of direction" and saved him several times from disasters and natural phenomena that neither fifteenth-century science nor legend was prepared to take on. Columbus was a hero, Morison reasoned, because he was not afraid of following his dream or of taking action when the tides of history dictated action.[102]

Success, of course, was a relative word. Columbus failed in most of his immediate goals. He did not discover a western passage to China; instead he spent the remaining years of his life in a futile attempt to prove that he had done so and to secure the financial and hereditary rights commensurate with such a discovery. Yet in failure, Morison's Columbus also achieved immortal success, and that was the final irony of Morison's pragmatic approach. Focusing by inclination on immediate goals, Columbus was unable to recognize the important consequences "that flowed from his discoveries." On his deathbed, Morison's hero was tortured by doubt and feelings of inadequacy, wondering whether his "racking pains" were the "only return he was to have for all his discoveries and hardships." Once again attributing emotions to his fallen discoverer, Morison continued with self-reflexive implications: "Often and often he must have sought some explanation from the inscrutable divine will that decreed his many sufferings. Was God still angry over the Admiral's pride in those brave days when he had a whole new world at his feet?" But all doubt evaporated when Columbus focused on the practical joy he had experienced in pursuit of his dream. "Waste no pity on the Admiral of the Ocean Sea!" Morison noted. "He enjoyed long stretches of pure delight such as only a seaman may know, and moments of high, proud exultation that only a discoverer can experience."[103]

This pragmatism was not only a device for reconciling the two sides of Columbus's complex personality but also a method for conciliating the dualistic vision of Columbus's biographer. Torn between the obligations of professionalism and the desire to go beyond dull pedantry, Morison undertook the Harvard Columbus Expedition as an experiment in active scholarship. Like Columbus, he wished to verify theory through practical experience by a process of intellectual "dead reckoning," if you will. As with Columbus's voyages, Morison's experiment ended in partial frustration, since time restrictions and managerial problems prevented him from completing his scholarly investigations and gaining a complete sense of spiritual communion with Columbus. Yet the decision to engage history actively, despite these problems, allowed him to discover things that more cautious scholars had missed. Like the great discoverer himself, Morison found unexpected new worlds and experienced the thrill of the search. Back in the classroom at Harvard, Morison urged his graduate students to take more active approaches to their educations: "Above all, start writing. Nothing is more pathetic than the 'gonna' historian, who from graduate school on is always 'gonna' write a magnum opus but never completes his research on the subject, and dies without anything to show for a lifetime's work."[104] Neither Columbus nor Morison had such regrets.

Participatory History

Charles Beard, Admiral Knox and the
Writing of Naval History

———

IO

The Historian as Warrior

The final vindication of Morison's "hands-on" approach came in the critical acclaim for *Admiral of the Ocean Sea*. The two-volume edition was popular among scholars and lay readers; some appreciated it for its scholarly objectivity, and others praised it for its poetic subjectivity.[1] In 1942, Morison was awarded the Pulitzer Prize for distinguished work in biography, and later that year a one-volume edition of *Admiral of the Ocean Sea* was adopted by the Book-of-the-Month Club as a cover selection. The two endorsements gave the biography a wide circulation and netted Morison over $30,000 in the first years of publication.[2] They not only helped secure Morison's reputation as the "Parkman of the Sea"[3] but also helped fulfill his ambition, first voiced in the late 1930s, to share in the "harvest of dividends" that amateurs like Adams and Brooks were reaping. "Did you write *Admiral of the Ocean Sea* with the hope of the big sale that apparently it will have?" one interviewer asked. "Certainly," Morison replied with characteristic pride, and it is a "damn fine thing; naturally I'm delighted."[4]

The biggest payback, however, was the influence the biography had on his scholarship during World War II and beyond. Some of the delays Morison experienced in researching *Admiral of the Ocean Sea* were attributable to the war in Europe, and the publication of the biography coincided precisely with the United States entry into both theaters of the war. For months before the war, Morison had been urging President Franklin D. Roosevelt to abandon traditional American policies of neutrality. "I have had as good an opportunity as anyone (at sea September 1939–February 1940) to think this over calmly," he wrote the president, "and having devoted thirty years to the study of American history, I should have as much background as anyone for a judgment." Arguing that "this country is right now in greater danger of losing her freedom of action and national integrity than at any time before 1861 or since 1864," Morison advised the president that "it will be cheaper in the end to help the Allies now than fight Germany alone, with perhaps Japan on our backs."[5] Morison added that the president's efforts to organize national defense had his approval, but he dissented from Roosevelt's "keep us out of war" motive, arguing that it could be effective only if, by some unlikely miracle, England defeated Germany in six months.[6] "Everything you have done or initiated about national defense has my hearty approval, and I am thankful that you are President," Morison wrote Roosevelt again. "Only I wish that we might move a little faster toward a full partnership in the war, which seems to be necessary if the Axis is not to win." Speculating that Roosevelt was "waiting for Hitler to provide an 'incident' which will fire the American public," Morison warned, "I am afraid he is too smart for that." He concluded with some free advice: "I should think that a strong message to Congress, based on Japanese 'peace terms' and on the abundant evidence in possession of the State Department on Axis designs toward us, would be the way to obtain authorization for an all-out naval and air patrol of the Atlantic, or a declaration of war."[7]

Such a hawkish stand embroiled Morison with many advocates of pacifism, some of whom were Harvard students who were almost overwhelmingly peace-minded, and who branded him a "number #1 warmonger." Morison was puzzled and troubled by the pacifism of students, attributing it to the misperceptions engendered by antiwar novels, plays, and films, left-wing organizations, the Nye Committee, the American Legion, and even the Ku Klux Klan, all of which used "patriotism as a cloak for something else." Not recognizing that war was the only alternative to "a shameful and ultimately disastrous appeasement," he argued, students were among the most surprised when the "awful details" of the attack on Pearl Harbor were announced. Their "incredulity turned to anger and an implacable determination to avenge these unprovoked and dastardly attacks," Morison wrote, and they joined their professor in seeking to bring a speedy military end to the conflict.[8]

Having missed out on the fighting in World War I, Morison was determined to play a role in this one, so he applied for "general duty" with the Navy along with many of his students.[9] Not surprisingly, the Naval Reserves turned Morison down "on account of his age." Undaunted, he developed a plan that would allow him to participate in the war while exercising his gift for historical writing. His idea was to write a history of United States naval operations "from the inside" not only by researching the operational files in Washington, D.C., but by sailing "on naval vessels of all types, in various combat areas" and making historical assessments. In a plan submitted to Secretary of the Navy Frank Knox, Morison noted that his goal would be "to find out how things are done in this war, and to get the 'feel' of modern naval warfare." He requested a commission in the Navy under the direct authority of the secretary of the Navy, so that he might "feel free" to move about the various war theaters. "My historical and practical maritime training, and my ability to present maritime subjects in a readable manner, are my qualifications," Morison wrote Roosevelt, adding that in order to do things the "right way," he must have a "living, intimate connection with the Navy *flagranto bello.*"[10] Citing his recent successful experience with "hands-on" history, he asked the Navy to allow him to do what even Parkman, visiting the scenes of important battles a century after the fact, was unable to do, namely, to witness and record warfare firsthand. In this sense, he would become a modern Thucydides, using his "Columbus technique for naval warfare."[11]

A happy compromise between Morison's desire to participate in the fighting and his wish to use his considerable talents as a historian on behalf of his country, the plan nonetheless encountered resistance. Secretary Knox and others thought a history of the Navy might just as appropriately be written after the war and resented the prospect of a "long-haired professor in uniform."[12] Morison argued that an "armchair job after peace is concluded won't do," because just such a history had been proposed at the close of World War I. A committee had been appointed, plans were made, but the history was never written, Morison noted, adding that the failure to complete the project had had important political and historical implications. "How much better prepared the country would have been for the present crisis," he wrote, "if the story of the Navy in the last war had been rightly told." When this logic failed to convince the secretary, Morison went over his head to the president of the United States, whom he wrote in March 1942. "Dear Mr. President," his letter began, "Since completing my life of Columbus I have been trying to interest the Navy in using me as a sea-going historiographer, without success." Arguing that he was "ready to serve in *any* capacity," he proposed his history of naval operations as "simply the way I can probably serve best." Noting that he had "the right qualifications to do the job for this war," Morison informed Roosevelt that he was fifty-four years old, "in fine physical condition, ready to go to sea at a week's notice, eager to serve," and "a person who gets things done."[13]

This appeal to the president met with far greater enthusiasm than any appeal Morison had previously made to him. Indeed, Roosevelt needed little convincing. As a former assistant secretary of the Navy himself, the president appreciated the need for adequate histories of naval operations. In addition, he had recently finished reading *Admiral of the Ocean Sea*, which Morison had wisely sent him several months before, and was most impressed with it. If the memory of Roosevelt's naval aide, John McCrea, can be trusted, the president had been considering Morison for such a history even before the formal petition crossed his desk. Years after the fact, McCrea

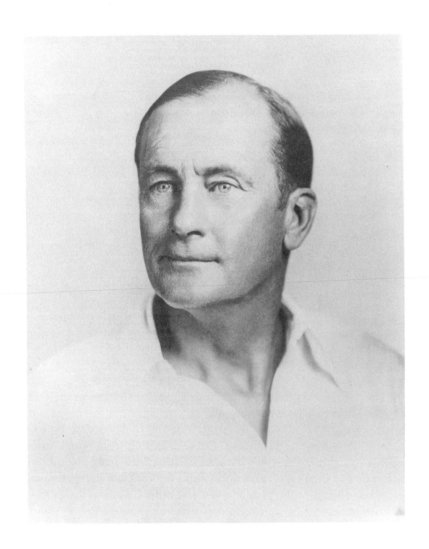

FIG. 3 *Morison in Middle Life, 1942. Describing himself as in "robust" health, Morison requested that President Franklin D. Roosevelt employ him as "sea-going historiographer" during World War II. "I am 54 years old, in fine physical condition, ready to go to sea at a week's notice, and eager to serve," he told the president, who eventually granted his request. Courtesy of the Harvard University Archives.*

recalled a conversation he had with Roosevelt as the pair sat one evening in the offices of the White House.

FDR: John, by any chance have you read the book about Columbus, "Admiral of the Ocean Sea?"

MCCREA: Yes, I have, Mr. President. . . . As a matter of fact, I finished it a couple of nights ago.

FDR: What did you think of it?

MCCREA: I thought it good in every respect. I particularly liked the enterprise and initiative of the author in sailing the routes sailed by Columbus. Doing so gives the work authority.

FDR: I liked it too. I was impressed as you were with his actual sailing the routes. I've been having thoughts the last few days about naval activities in this war and the records that should be kept. . . . It seems to me that the Naval History of this war should be written contemporaneously with the action or as nearly so as practicable. I'm wondering if Sam Morison wouldn't be a good one to do it. Of course, it couldn't be a one-man show. It would require organization and capable helpers in all the theaters of the war. What do you think?

MCCREA: It sounds pretty ambitious, Mr. President, but I would think it well worth a try.

FDR: Maybe Frank Knox could help out.[14]

As a result of this conversation and Morison's subsequent petition, President Roosevelt sent a note to Secretary Knox supporting the project, and all Navy resistance to it vanished.[15] Within a matter of days, Morison received a commission as lieutenant commander and the following note from Secretary Knox: "I think the Navy is very fortunate to have a man of your attainments and high standing to undertake such a task, and I shall be very glad indeed to discuss the matter with you at any time in the near future when it is convenient for you to come to Washington."[16]

Betraying his eagerness, Morison arrived in Washington the next day, discussed matters with Knox, and received his commission. By the provisions of the agreement, Morison was "not to be censored" or prohibited from "free criticism of officers," but he was to respect security regulations regarding secret weapons and coded messages. He was given permission to "rove the seven seas" in U.S. naval vessels and to work at naval bases "as seemed best," and he was granted complete liberty to do his writing wherever he saw fit.[17] Despite these concessions (or perhaps because of them), there was still some resentment toward a commissioned historian with ready access to the president. One of the White House appointments secretaries called the Navy Department to complain about Morison's frequent intrusions: "[D]on't these Naval Officers know they can't come charging over to the White House to see the President, whenever the mood hits them," he yelled. "There is a guy outside right now . . . Samuel Eliot

Morison Lt. Cmdr.-USNR . . . who wants to see the President [and] I think you better have the word passed down there that they just can't do this."[18] But consult the president Morison did, and frequently. In one such meeting in the early summer of 1942, Roosevelt let it be known that the first U.S. naval initiative was about to begin—an antisubmarine sweep of the Atlantic coast to free shipping lanes from German attack.[19] The president hinted that Morison might find it useful to travel "up and down the coast with the shore patrol," so Morison rushed home, packed his bags, and with the blessings of his wife, went off to join the war.[20]

The World at War

Morison's first ship assignment was the U.S.S. *Guineverre*, which was part of the Atlantic patrol team searching for German submarines off the coast of New England. He was a curiosity to her officers. "As my position in the Navy was unprecedented," Morison later wrote, "I had to move warily and gingerly in order to obtain co-operation from those who were doing the fighting." The suspicions of the *Guineverre* crew dissolved, however, when word circulated among its members that the strange guest was the author of *Admiral of the Ocean Sea*, which "told them that I was a sailor before I became a professor," Morison noted, "and thus exorcised the academic curse."[21] He endeared himself in other ways as well. Assigned to a corridor along the coast of Maine, the *Guineverre* patrolled Morison's boyhood sailing haunts around Mount Desert Island, and Morison proved a valuable navigational asset. In addition, the skipper of the patrol ship was convinced to go ashore during one inactive period, where Morison aroused the "locals" who "provided lobsters for all."[22]

Although the work of these patrol boats interested Morison, no submarines were spotted by the *Guineverre*, and he grew impatient for action. When the opportunity presented itself, therefore, he transferred to a destroyer, the U.S.S. *Buck*, which was escorting a transatlantic convoy to England. Convoys were groups of merchant and troop ships guarded by destroyers that travelled in packs on dangerous runs from the United States and Canada to Iceland, England, and Russia. The *Buck* was presided over by Captain John B. Heffernan, who befriended the historian and provided him with much useful information about naval operations during five perilous days in submarine-infested waters off the Scottish coast.[23]

Most useful of all, perhaps, was the cryptic message Heffernan sent Morison after the *Buck* returned to the United States in the fall of 1942. "[I]f you are about to visit Washington," the Captain wrote, "I suggest you go to Admiral R[eeves]—or someone—and say that you would like to take a 'cruise' on an interesting ship very, very soon. But do not mention me." After receiving this "Delphic utterance," Morison wasted no time in presenting himself to the admiral's aide, who agreed that it might be a good idea to report aboard the U.S.S. *Brooklyn*. Taking a night boat from Washington, D.C., to Norfolk, Virginia, he was greeted by Captain Denebrink of the *Brooklyn* and given "the Admiral's palatial suite." Denebrink confirmed "that something very interesting was on foot."[24]

These leads were important because they allowed Morison to take part in what he later described as the "mightiest fleet ever sent forth from America for distant service"—Operation TORCH. From the deck of the *Brooklyn*, he observed rapid movements of troops and supplies and heard rumors to the effect that the vessel would be sailing to western Morocco "to erect a bastion against the submarines" or to "keep the Germans out of West Africa," or "to drive through Algeria to the rear of von Rommel." Rumors crystallized into strategies when he was invited to attend a boardroom meeting between Army and Navy officials in a "sort of sail loft on one of the piers." The room was dominated by a map of the beaches and batteries at Fedhala, about fifteen miles east of Casablanca, which were the operation's objective. Morison was not impressed with the task group commander who presided over the meeting. "[E]lderly, thin, gray and bald, nervous and unpoised," the commander by Morison's account "talks and acts like a Carolinian professor I used to know." He was emboldened, however, by the words of a "tough, sandy-haired Major General Patton" of the 1st Armored Division. "Tell all your friends about this," Patton warned of the mission's confidentiality, "if you want to become shark's meat." Operation TORCH "will give us . . . practice to fight the real sons-of-bitches about 2300 miles inland," he continued, reminding his colleagues with intimidating bravado, "If I find one officer walking to the rear with a wound, it will be the last god-damned walk he makes!" After the strategy session, Morison returned to his cabin and recorded in his notebook: "Well, I am in for something, all right."[25]

Operation TORCH consisted of 101 ships, 5 submarines, 6 armed motor boats and covered approximately 150 square miles of ocean. Nearly 80,000 men were involved in the mission, whose purpose was to occupy French North Africa and "to secure a strategic springboard for invading Italy."[26] In his notebooks, Morison recorded the varying emotional states of the sailors as they steamed toward "the rim of a continent where no major military campaign had been conducted for centuries."[27] At the outset, the sailors were impatient for action and in relatively high spirits. They heartily enjoyed several ballads, composed by Morison under the byline "Sail Easy Mike," that poked fun at the operation's objectives. One of these, entitled "Mohammed Abdullah, Pasha of Fedhala," was printed on ship's press for general distribution. The opening stanza read:

> Mohammed Abdullah, pasha of Fedhala
> At home wore a tarboosh, outdoors a plug hat
> Read latest French novels and Philip Guedalla
> But stood okydoke with the boss at Rabat

FIG. 4 *Morison with U.P. correspondent John Moraso en-*
joying his first meal ashore at the Coq d'Or restaurant,
Casablanca, Morocco, November 16, 1942. Courtesy
of the Harvard University Archives.

From sixty years' diddling and all kinds of fiddling
Mohammed Pasha was completely snafu,
But for social position, eight wives in commission
He kept, and a Tahiti trollop or two.[28]

Although this poem was "soon repressed, because it revealed too much about the mission's intentions," a copy was sent to President Roosevelt who "enjoyed it so much that he kept copies for himself and his staff."[29]

The mood turned more serious as the operation got under way. "Every officer aboard *Brooklyn* is anxious," Morison noted in his diary; "not one thinks we have a pushover."[30] As wartime casualties began to occur, the mood became still more solemn. "Although I did not know your son personally, as a shipmate I was present at his funeral," Morison wrote the parents of one sailor who succumbed to pneumonia while at sea. Inferring from the sailor's name (Lawrence Lowell Weiss) that he had some connection with Harvard or Boston, Morison recorded the scene as the stricken sailor was "committed to the deep." Employing some of the language that had made the maritime scenes in *Admiral of the Ocean Sea* so memorable, Morison wrote: "It was a superb afternoon to say good-bye to our shipmate. Great, high, billowy clouds with deep pockets in them that lashed out rain into the ocean, of rainbow against sun-lighted clouds, golden horizon, blue sea marked on starboard side by 'ships fraught with the ministers and instruments of cruel war,' one more fine young man has given his life for his country and he has had the immemorial privilege of a sailor burial at sea." As if to underscore the danger of the operation, Morison added that "the ship did not check her speed," for just after the body was committed, "a destroyer reported a sound contact and we began zig-zagging violently."[31]

In late October of 1942 the vessels reached their destination, and in their ensuing attack on the French North African coast Morison received his first taste of real combat. The operation began with a "softening up" of the shoreline by the Navy and some antiaircraft blasts. The noise was deafening. "I would really like to go below and slide my head under the bed clothes to muffle the horrible roar of our guns," Morison wrote, "but I'm here to record a battle."[32] This attack was followed by an amphibious assault of the beaches, which Morison witnessed with growing admiration for the Navy tinctured with moments of horror as assault vessels capsized and soldiers loaded down with heavy equipment drowned. When the operation was concluded successfully and the coast was occupied, Morison applauded the work of *Brooklyn*'s officers, who, in turn, applauded him. "By his alert, active, analytical work in recording the events of the action, by his keen fighting spirit which manifested itself throughout, and by his calm manner, he contributed to the general and overall performance of the vessel," wrote Captain Denebrink in a letter of commendation for Morison. "He volunteered for the trip when he learned there might be action," the letter continued, and "[h]is desire to be in the fighting was gratified. He contributed to the success. He was as much a member of the *Brooklyn* crew as any officer or man regularly assigned."[33]

Buoyed by this sign of acceptance by a naval officer, Morison returned to Washington, D.C., to begin recording his observations and to continue his research in the Navy's files. Quartered at the headquarters of Admiral Hewitt, he originally planned to write as much as he could by himself, but he soon discovered that a "two-ocean war" could not be handled by one man, so he enlisted the help of several junior officers already in the Navy. His staff was headed by Henry Saloman, a Harvard graduate from the class of 1939, who was approached by his former professor with the offer while waiting for an assignment from the Navy. "I accepted almost before the words were out of his mouth," Salomon said.[34] In addition, Morison relied heavily on the services of Donald Martin, the only yeoman in the Navy said to be "able to read Morison's handwriting." Martin did most of the typing and clerical work, while Salomon and others went to work researching materials for the lieutenant commander. "Morison would . . . make specific research assignments, and away we'd go," one staff member remembered.[35] In the meantime, Morison returned to the White House to interview Roosevelt about the operations in Africa. Ushered in through an underground passageway (the "Southern Pacific Route"), Morison found the president "most cordial" and talkative. The African mission derived from a meeting between him and "Winston," Roosevelt noted, adding with revealing candor his response to Churchill when arrangements were finalized: "Thank God!"[36]

Over the next several months, Morison turned his attention to "naval bases and theaters of action" in the South Pacific. Stopping first at the headquarters of Admiral Nimitz in Pearl Harbor, he took an immediate liking to the man he regarded as "our greatest naval strategist and leader" after Admiral Ernest J. King.[37] Nimitz made provision for Morison to set up headquarters at "Cincpac-Cincpoa" at Makalapa, Oahu, where he had access to the top commanders of the U.S. Navy for the remainder of the war. At Makalapa, Morison developed an oral history technique that proved so successful that it permanently transformed postbattle naval debriefings. "My history teachers tended to discount [oral testimony] and to put the written document above everything as an historical source," Morison later noted. "In remote periods of history one naturally has to depend on inscriptions, coins, ruins, potsherd, and other artifacts for one's sources, and is lucky to have a papyrus by a contemporary," Morison observed, but he soon discovered that written documents were not "facts in themselves but symbols of facts," and that "everything in a document has passed through a human brain."[38] Conceding to historical relativists the importance of the mind as a filtering agent for facts (but not the mutability of fact), Morison proposed to the head of Cincpac task forces that all commanders returning from missions be required to submit to a brief interview by one of Morison's staffers. Despite considerable grumbling by officers who feared the specter of accountability in such postbattle interviews, the task force commander instituted the procedure, adopting Morison's specific recommendations that officers be given a few days to prepare themselves and to jot down an outline before taping.[39]

Using these techniques, Morison himself interviewed Douglas MacArthur on June 12, 1943. The results suggested how effective oral history could be in capturing the personalities behind important historical events. Noting the "famous hat with the gold leaves around the band, sitting on a console" and the inevitable pipe "with a glass-and-chromium stem and a chromium bowl," Morison asked the general what his impressions of the war were to date. In response, MacArthur launched into what sounded like a "prepared lecture," though it was not. He was "evidently a man much like A. Lawrence Lowell who had acquired the same habit," Morison wrote; "his mind is so full that it just needs a spark to start a lecture going that is, in a sense, prepared because it is already composed in his mind." Recording the details of MacArthur's "monologue" on the terrifying strength of Japan, Morison was later impressed to discover that MacArthur was correct in his assessments about the duration and the ferocity of the fighting in the Pacific. After the general had spoken for thirty minutes or so, Morison noted, he "said he knew I was very busy—which I wasn't—[and] I took this as a hint to leave." After "another gimlet look from his dark eyes and a small, firm handshake, and offering to 'put the Army at my service,'" Morison left.[40]

After recording several other oral histories, Morison moved on to the major battle sites of the Pacific war. Under the supervision of Admiral Halsey's staff, he inspected Guadalcanal when it was still under Japanese air attack, and later, under Rear Admiral W. L. Ainsworth, he participated in several missions "up the Slot" as the body of water between the Solomons was called by the Navy.[41] On July 7, 1943, the night of his fifty-sixth birthday, Morison received another taste of military action. Earlier that day he had strolled around the decks admiring the scenery of the Slot, which reminded him "of the Hudson at Hyde Park, only wider; and there's no Japs in the Hudson, only Republicans." At one o'clock in the morning he was awakened by the deafening sound of the siren announcing "General Quarters." Rushing to the deck, he saw a Japanese task force approaching and heard the report of Navy guns. The sounds of war that had so terrified Morison months before became almost therapeutic to him now. "Saw some pretty fireworks out on the water. One ship seemed to be tossing red balls at another, which caught them and sent up a big blaze," he wrote. He claimed to have had "a wonderful rest" that night, one that "made [him] feel fit to carry on [his] heavy work on the history front."[42] And one sailor remembered his diligence in "gathering facts for his volumes" after such episodes. In the midst of the frenzy on board, with everyone running "around the ship . . . to refresh their memories of her interior compartment arrangements," there sat Morison, he remarked, "calmly jotting down notes on what was transpiring, while more anxious shipmates adjusted life belts and made ready for any eventuality."[43]

In the fall, Morison returned to Washington to help his staff sort out the details of antisubmarine activity in the Atlantic. "One October day in 1943, as we were pouring over reports," Salomon wrote, "Morison received a letter from Admiral Ainsworth, then at San Diego [and] inferred from the contents that it might be a smart thing to pack his duffle bag and shove off for California." Assigned to the heavy cruiser *Baltimore*, Morison "landed . . . right in the middle of the Gilbert Islands operation."[44] At first Morison was not overjoyed with his berth. Admiring the *Liscome Bay*, the *Mississippi*, and other ships in the flotilla of naval vessels steaming toward the South Pacific, he found the *Baltimore* a bit substandard. The ship "is built very badly," he wrote in his diary, and "we've practically had to rebuild her." The welding was shabby, the engines were not properly tuned, the thrust plates were not the same width, and the lubricating system was befouled with filings and dirt. Nor did the human cargo inspire his confidence. The captain "doesn't bother to keep the ship or [its] persons neat and clean," Morison noted, and the men "are as inexperienced as the officers," draftees who were more "urban and more scrubby looking than bluejackets I have seen on other ships." To make matters worse, Rear Admiral Carlton H. Bosco Wright was a passenger, and his cantankerous manner was "very disagreeable to the captain." One message sent by him to the bridge was transcribed by Morison in all its testy sarcasm: "the Admiral's compliments to the officer on the deck, and admires the decoration on the port search light platform, a pair of socks a seaman had triced up to dry in the sun, but wish to know whether it's ship's regulations." It "wasn't," Morison retorted, "but none of his business. There is no sense in having an Admiral on this ship anyway," he added, "Don't know why the Navy does such things."[45]

Soon enough, however, Morison was glad he was aboard the *Baltimore* and not one of her sister ships. In preparing for an invasion of Makin in November 1943, the *Mississippi* reported a fire in its number 2 gun turret. "[S]ome of us saw it flash," Morison recorded from the deck of the *Baltimore*, and "when I looked that way, streams of water were pouring out of it." One of the sixty-inch guns had exploded prematurely, killing over forty men.[46] Then several days later, while sleeping in the chart house of the *Baltimore*, Morison felt "a tremendous explosion, as if we had been torpedoed." As he was snapping on his life belt and noting the time, a young quartermaster rushed in and said the *Mississippi* had been hit. Morison raced to the deck to discover that it was really the *Liscome Bay* that "lighted up the waters as if by starshell." A "black smoking fire was racing along her flight deck and there were frequent explosions which sent bouquets of fire up into the air and great pieces of metal." Morison watched "horrified, as we left her astern; at 05:35 she gave out her last flares and sank." Of the 852 enlisted men aboard only 104 were saved.[47]

As action in the Pacific and the Atlantic increased, Morison was obliged to increase his staff and to expose them to the more dangerous duty he himself faced. While Henry Salomon took part in the remaining Gilbert and Marshalls campaigns and later the Battle of Leyte Gulf, Lieutenant Henry D. Reck (another former Morison student at Harvard) was employed to observe naval operations in the European theater at Anzio, Corsica, Sardinia, and Sicily. Reck also participated in the invasion of southern France, while Lieutenant George M. Elsey covered the invasion of Normandy on D-day.[48] Meanwhile, Morison travelled to the Marianas on U.S.S. *Montpelier*, "witnessed the landings at Saipan and the initial bombardment of Guam" from the deck of U.S.S. *Honolulu*, and then, in the fall of 1944, returned to the Atlantic Ocean to "catch up with anti-submarine warfare" on the USCGC *Campbell*[49] (see Fig. 5). In between assignments, he managed to squeeze in several additional interviews with President Roosevelt, who "looked very well," Morison recorded in 1944.[50]

The final months of the war were the most traumatic for Morison. In the spring of 1945, he returned to the Pacific to observe the island-hopping campaign from the deck of the U.S.S. *Tennessee*. As the vessel lay off the coast of Okinawa, he "narrowly escaped death" at the hands of a Japanese kamikaze pilot. A "suicide plane started to cross our bow and I was watching a gun crew try to shoot it down," Morison recalled. "Just then, somebody hollered 'Duck,' and I did, with no questions asked. That plane crashed onto the deck and killed a gun squad of 40 marines."[51] He was also subjected to the most gruesome aspects of war. A "bluejacket" who had been swept overboard climbed into the life raft of a Japanese pilot who had been shot down, Morison wrote in his diary. This sailor had a "pretty grisly ride" till he was recovered, he added, because "the mortal remains of that Jap pilot were on the raft."[52]

It was with a sense of relief, therefore, that Morison learned in May of 1945 that the Germans had capitulated in Europe and in August that the nuclear explosions over Hiroshima and Nagasaki had compelled the Emperor of Japan to surrender. He admitted later that he had had "a very good time in World War II," feeling "fortunate to be on his favorite element and serving his country in the thing he could do best." He also appreciated the "personal contacts and the friendships" he made in the Navy. But Morison, as much as anyone, felt the effects or the tragedies of war. The fate of two indirect victims of war touched him in particularly personal ways. First, in April of 1945, while travelling toward Okinawa, Morison received word that President Roosevelt had died. "I have lost one whom I had come to regard as a dear personal friend," Morison wrote in his notebook. "The Navy has lost its greatest champion," he added, while "the United States has lost a statesman who restored her economy and her self-confidence, warned and prepared her against the greatest menace to existence, and led her through infinite trials and tribulations to the very eve of victory." Closing his informal eulogy in dramatic style, he concluded, "The world has lost the

FIG. 5 *Aboard the USCGC* Campbell *with Executive Officer and First Lieutenant, October–November 1944. Courtesy of the Harvard University Archives.*

one man since the Emperor Augustus who had a fair chance of giving it another *Pax Romana*."[53]

Second, and the more tragic occurrence for Morison, Bessie died a week after the surrender of Japan. Although she had suffered from heart trouble for a number of years, she had encouraged her husband to go to war. "Although she knew throughout the war that death might come upon her suddenly and alone, as to a soldier at an outpost," Morison wrote in a moving memoir to her, "she made no change in her way of life." Working for the war effort through her various causes, Interceptor Command, Naval Aid Society, France Forever, and Servicemen's Canteens, she continued to do her part while enduring the long absences between her husband's infrequent shore leaves. Mercifully, she had several weeks with him before she died. They spent the first week together in their bungalow in Maine. "I rowed Bessie around the shore at high tide, entering every little cove, each with memories of children bathing, mishaps with boats and picnics long ago," and "marking the familiar times," Morison wrote. Her final week was spent with one of her daughters and her husband in Pleasance, a house built in Canton, Massachusetts, by the Morisons. They "enjoyed an evening of reminiscences, a thing very rare with us," Morison noted, "as there was so much of the present and future to talk about." The next morning he found her silently lying in bed, the victim of a coronary occlusion.[54]

Making Waves

After his wife's death, Morison returned to Washington, determined to "put everything he had into telling [the Navy's] history effectively."[55] The challenge he had faced in writing *Admiral of the Ocean Sea*—to tell a story without getting bogged down in details—was magnified by his current project, which he believed would fill over a dozen volumes. Organizing his staff was an administrative test in its own right. While in the Philippines at the end of the war, Morison had run into his "old shipmate and former pupil, Ensign Albert Harkness, Jr.," who was soon after assigned to the historical staff to handle some of the earliest phases of the naval war in the South Pacific.[56] In Washington, Captain Bern Anderson, Dr. K. Jack Bauer, Lieutenant Richard E. Downs, Ensign Richard Pattee, and "two of the most productive members of the writing staff," Commander James C. Shaw and Dr. Philip K. Lundeberg, were added to the team.[57] Finally, a Japanese language specialist, Roger Pineau, was hired to "run Morison's Washington office, conduct all research concerning official Japanese records and other research as directed."[58]

Morison presided over this small "navy" of men with considerable managerial skill. His normal operating procedure was to prepare each volume in rough outline on yellow legal pads, noting gaps in his information, and then to assign research assistants to fill them in.[59] Roger Pineau, for instance, was asked to prepare a questionnaire about the attack on Pearl Harbor for surrendered Japanese officers to complete.[60] Some workers were encouraged to help draft chapters, which Morison would then proofread and rewrite for his own purposes. When such rewritings were then typed by yeoman Martin, they would be sent to the Naval Command for proofreading and finally to the publishers.[61] A unique contract had been worked out with Little, Brown, and Company by which Morison, who had retired his commission but remained in the reserves, would receive remuneration of roughly $4300 per volume, and profits from the volumes would go to the Navy.[62]

The first volume of the *History of United States Naval Operations in World War II* appeared in 1947. The work was anxiously awaited by those who wished to see how Morison would handle the controversial issues surrounding preparedness and pacificism in the prewar era. The struggle for autonomy between Morison and the Navy that arose during work on volume 1 persisted throughout the writing of the series. By prearrangement the volume contained some introductory remarks by Secretary Knox, with whom Morison had had some disagreements in the earliest stages of his work. Addressing himself to accusations of naval unpreparedness, Knox argued in his introduction that certain elements in American life in the interwar years conspired to make the Navy unready for war, including (1) international treaties limiting naval armaments, (2) propaganda against naval buildup, primarily from college professors, and (3) Army General Billy Mitchell's plan to use air power to the exclusion of naval power as the basis of American military security.[63] Morison disagreed with Knox's tripartite assessment of blame. "[A]part from the want of air power which was due to prewar agreements with the Army," Morison noted, "this unpreparedness was the Navy's own fault." Admitting that in the end, "the Navy met the challenge, applied its energy and intelligence, came through magnificently and won," Morison nonetheless maintained that its victory did not alter the fact "that it had no plans ready for a reasonable protection to shipping when the submarines struck, and was unable to improvise them for several months."[64]

Morison also disagreed with Knox's characterization of professors in the prewar period. Admitting that many students were pacifists, he noted that professors were primarily in favor of intervention and that many universities established naval ROTCs. Using a logic first developed during the teachers' oath issue of the 1930s, Morison also claimed that professors should not have been expected to consider "heavier naval appropriations" part of "their business" until the war broke out. Even university students changed their attitudes after the attack on Pearl Harbor. "Certainly when the time came," Morison wrote, "university students as a whole were rather more forward than other young men in volunteering, and their record in the Naval Reserve has been admirable." As for Billy Mitchell, Morison argued that his actions were an embarrassing reminder of how all the branches of the Armed Forces, including the Navy, shamefully fought for power among themselves. Citing with contempt the "union indoctrinated" attitudes of the merchant marine, for instance, he reminded Knox that because of petty bickering over naval reimbursement for vessels many Americans had lost their lives at the hands of unmolested German submarines. The Navy's failure to warn citizens in coastal resort communities to dim their lights at night made many merchant marine vessels (silhouetted by neon signs) such easy victims of German U-boats that they refused to ship at night. The sinking of merchant marine tankers, Morison observed, "not only fried the water-borne survivors in burning oil, but threatened the success of military operations in Europe and the Pacific."[65]

Despite his objections to Knox's introduction, Morison allowed most of it to stand unedited because he fully agreed with the secretary's thesis—that for whatever reasons, the Navy and the American people were unprepared for war and must never be again. The argument for constant preparedness became a leitmotif in all of the volumes in the *History of United States Naval Operations in World War II*. "Although Americans were loath to discard the concept [of neutrality], deeply rooted in the national tradition and recently buttressed by a legislative structure," Morison wrote, the war "made further persuasion unnecessary" and convinced many that in every phase of a "short of war" policy the Armed Forces must often conduct "operations indistinguishable from war."[66] The moral of the story, as one reviewer of *The Battle of the Atlantic* put it, is that "next time . . . we shall not have the traditional time lag in which to organize ourselves and bring our great military and naval potential to bear. Improvisation paid off in World War II," the reviewer noted, "but even improvisation takes time—time that we shall not have in any war of the future."[67]

Morison dearly wished to drive home his point about preparedness in as artistic a manner as possible and to duplicate his success with *Admiral of the Ocean Sea*. He admitted, however, that naval operations were "exceedingly difficult to relate in an acceptable literary form." Because antisubmarine warfare was a very technical and diverse subject that could not be easily simplified, he devoted a good deal more space than some readers preferred to describing training schools, technical devices, scientific research, patrolling maneuvers, escorting techniques, communication methods, and preparations "for a fight that very rarely took place." Nor were his descriptions of life at sea always stirring, he conceded. "Although personally I have seldom passed a dull moment at sea, whether in peace or war," Morison submitted, "it must be admitted that for most sailors and aviators the Holmesian dictum 'war is an organized bore' has a particular application to this Battle of the Atlantic." It could not be otherwise, he added, since antisubmarine warfare was largely a waiting game in which lookouts "became weary with reporting floating boxes and bottles as periscopes," and "deck officers became exasperated with the vagaries of merchant seamen," while the "monotonous, never-ending 'ping'-ing of the echo-ranging sound gear had the cumulative effect of a jungle tom-tom."[68] These limitations notwithstanding, however, in *The Battle of the Atlantic* Morison did a masterful job of convincing readers that the struggle in the Atlantic "was second to none in its influence on the outcome of the war." In his skilled hands, some of the monotony was relieved by moments of dramatic tension, as when "wolfpacks" of German submarines hunted down vulnerable Allied vessels.[69] Describing the work as a cross between an official action report and a Hornblower novel, one reviewer remarked, *The Battle of the Atlantic* appealed "to those who were in uniform and to the general public as well."[70]

In volume 2 of the series, *Operations in North African Waters*, Morison took up the TORCH campaign, in which he had participated. As in the first volume of the series, he was quick to point out deficiencies in the Navy: its green sailors, some of whom had never been on a ship, its amateurish landings, its inadequate reconnaissance of the African coast, and its failure to notify potential allies on shore of the operation. Morison also highlighted the interservice bickering that undercut the effectiveness of TORCH: "The Army was furious when the Navy set its regimental staffs ashore six or eight miles out of position, and the Navy was furious when ill-trained Army units simply abandoned much of the equipment that had been hauled ashore for them and took off for the interior, . . . [leaving the] African natives [to make off] with all they could find in the general confusion." Morison noted as well that much of the success of the operation was a matter of "luck." The Italians, for instance, had anticipated the expedition, but their plans to defend the African coast were overruled by the Germans, who did not believe the U.S. operation would happen. These problems and lucky occurrences notwithstanding, Morison maintained that the Navy was to be congratulated for its heroic efforts. In less than four months, green troops had been trained for amphibious warfare, and the beginnings of a successful counteroffensive to Axis aggressions had been launched.[71]

Most critics were enthusiastic about the volume, especially military reviewers. Captain Butcher, who "had access to information at the top level of the Allied Command under General of the Army Eisenhower," still found himself "reading every word of the book," because for certain combat operations it supplied details of which even he was unaware.[72] Although the Army's history of the the operation was "thorough, restrained, and almost pedantic," noted military book reviewer for the *New York Times* Hanson Baldwin, the Navy's was more readable because it was more "individualized, bearing on many pages the subjective stamp of Morison." While the Army's historians "serve[d] up great gobs of facts—unseasoned to any great extent by personalities, and with few condiments of evaluation and analysis and none of the criticism," Baldwin wrote, Morison refused to simply let "the reader judge for himself."[73] A reviewer for the Navy noted that the original contempt of officers and enlisted men for Morison and his work would be erased by a perusal of *Operations in North African Waters*: "While the

Navy's plans for recording its work were not, perhaps, fully understood or appreciated at the time by those who had to carry out the department's directives in this respect," he wrote, the finished product justified the project and "laid the foundations for a new kind of naval history, which, while avoiding the specialist approach, does not run to the opposite extreme of a handling so popular that a naval operation seems like an adventure story."[74]

These military reviews delighted Morison, especially because they recognized the dual perspective he had perfected in *Admiral of the Ocean Sea* and hoped to bring to bear on the Naval history. As one reviewer noted, "His is the continuous challenge of pitching his work to the interest of the ordinary reader—the chair bound earthling to whom all warfare is but a confused though exciting yammer of guns and bombs—and yet to be so precise in details as not to call down the apoplectic wrath of live admirals."[75] Morison was still more pleased, however, with the civilian reaction. Many readers congratulated him on his vivid prose, which demonstrated his "real acquaintanceship with the Navy."[76] Only Morison, it seems, could have described the path of a maneuvering convoy as like "the track of a reeling drunk in the snow" or the fighting manner of American destroyers as like "a pack of dogs unleashed: *Wilkes* and *Swanson* with their main batteries yap-yapping, dancing ahead like two fox-terriers, followed by the queenly *Augusta* with a high white wave-curl against her clipper bow, her 8-inch guns booming a deep 'woof-woof'; and finally the stolid, scrappy *Brooklyn*, giving tongue with her six-inchers like ten couples of staghounds and footing so fast that she has to make 300-degree turns to take station astern her senior."[77] If such prose meant that Morison was occasionally prone to a "touch of schmalz," one reviewer commented, he still wrote good history, and the first two volumes of the *History of United States Naval Operations in World War II*, he concluded, were an admirable beginning to what promised to be an outstanding series.[78]

Volume 3 of the history, *Rising Sun in the Pacific*, unloosed a storm flood of reaction, however, and threatened the happy marriage of civilian and military readers. Once again it was Morison's nemesis Charles Beard who tripped the floodgates. Since Roosevelt's death in 1945, criticism had been mounting concerning the entry of the United States into the war in the Pacific. The prevailing assumption among the American people was that unprovoked, Japan had undertaken a dastardly and self-destructive attack on Pearl Harbor that left the American leaders with no choice but to retaliate. In 1947, however, Beard published *President Roosevelt and the Coming of the War*, in which he argued that the president knew of the impending attack but chose to ignore it, because he desired an excuse to push America into war. Beard supported this contention with evidence from the American-Dutch-British (ADB) conference that took place in Singapore in March 1941 for the purposes of determining under what conditions the United States might declare war on Japan. It was decided that Roosevelt might commit the nation to war in the Pacific (1) if Japan directly attacked territories of the United States, Great Britain, or the Netherlands, (2) if Japanese forces moved into Thailand west of the meridian of Bangkok or south of the Kra Isthmus, or (3) if the Japanese attempted to occupy Portuguese Timor or the Loyalty Islands off New Caledonia. According to Beard, these provisions committed the United States to a potential war in the Pacific, yet they were not submitted for any sort of approval to Congress or the American people.[79]

Beard further argued that Roosevelt made no effort to pursue Japanese-American negotiations, although there were indications as early as August 1941 that the Japanese ambassador desperately wanted them. Suspicious of Japanese motives, Roosevelt and Secretary of State Hull placed enormous conditions on a would-be conference, and when the Japanese surprisingly met these conditions, the pair still rejected the proposal for a meeting. Beard admitted that a November 20, 1941, Japanese offer of peace was unrealistic inasmuch as it required that Roosevelt cease helping China financially and that the United States "supply Japan with their required quantity of oil." Yet the proposal should have been a first step toward more realistic discussions, he argued, as high-level military officials had suggested to the president. Roosevelt not only refused to pursue further discussions, however, he compounded his crimes by announcing to the American people in his 1940 election campaign speeches that he was working to keep Americans out of war in Asia. According to Beard, Roosevelt revealed the full hypocrisy of this position when, a few short weeks after he had secured reelection for a third term in office, he informed his cabinet that he had information suggesting that the United States might be attacked soon by Japan. On November 25, 1941, a couple of weeks before the Pearl Harbor attack, Roosevelt asked his cabinet for guidance on how "to maneuver [the Japanese] into firing the first shot without allowing too much danger to the United States." In Beard's mind, this meeting not only implicated Roosevelt in a deliberate attempt to draw Americans into war, but it also raised some disturbing questions about why the president failed to alert naval forces at Pearl Harbor of an impending attack.[80]

Not surprisingly, in *Rising Sun in the Pacific* Morison took issue with Beard's interpretations. Wishing to avoid a protracted battle with Beard over the details of "the surprise at Pearl Harbor," Morison referred his readers to the forty volumes of the Joint Congressional Investigating Committee's report, which he believed explained the matter.[81] He did defend Roosevelt's actions with regard to the ADB conference, however, and applauded the president for his early recognition of the very real threat of the Japanese in the Pacific. Roosevelt had not promised "peace at any price," Morison later reminded Beard, but rather "defense of the freedom and security of the nation."[82] Furthermore, Morison noted that the ADB conference was informal and that the president had made no binding agreements or contractual arrangements. In addition, since the conference proposals were rejected by

Roosevelt's chief military advisors, they were never acted on and were therefore moribund in Morison's view. The August 1941 offer of peace by the Japanese was insincere, he asserted (and the memoirs of Prince Konoye confirmed this point), since it was part of the Japanese master plan to lull Americans into a full sense of security before springing the inevitable attack on Pearl Harbor. Morison also argued that Roosevelt could not have taken the Japanese proposal of November 20 seriously without sacrificing the nation's integrity as a world power. Had he capitulated to Japanese demands he would have had to abandon China while simultaneously fueling the Japanese war machine, and then the United States would have participated in an Asian version of the hated Munich Compromise.[83]

Behind this debate between Morison and Beard raged several ideological issues that had separated the two historians for years. Beard's debunking tendencies, his general suspicions of government leaders, his midwestern isolationism, and his dialectical materialism made it easy for him to view the war as a conspiracy on the part of Roosevelt and others to draw reluctant Americans into a two-ocean conflict. According to Morison, Beard was "endeavoring to inculcate in the rising generation the same self-pity about being tricked into war that bedevilled the generation of the 1920s and 30s." Promoting a "socialized, collectivist state in isolation," he added, Beard was "trying to revive the same masochistic state of public opinion into which he and most of the American people [including Morison] fell at the end of World War I."[84] Such an isolationist attitude had encouraged Beard to wrongfully ridicule military advisors who urged rearmament between the wars.[85] Noting that in his book Beard was "simply indulging in hate against the late Mr. Roosevelt and all he stood for," Morison noted the "disquieting resemblance" of Beard's platform "to the economic autarchy practiced by Hitler."[86]

Supporters of Beard argued that Morison had been for intervention in the European war since 1939 and was a biased reporter on the events that led to U.S. involvement in World War II. Despite Morison's claim that his desire "to persuade the American people not to scrap their navy" was "incidental" to his main purpose of telling "what the navy did in World War II, mistakes and all,"[87] Beard supporters viewed him as the mouthpiece for a hawkish and extravagant administration. "[B]y commissioning a widely known and reputable scholar to write its history," one reviewer noted, "the department was merely buying insurance of a favorable treatment."[88] Another irate Beard disciple expressed his anger at Morison's point of view: "[Y]ou don't know what your [sic] talking about," he wrote. Research like Beard's was "authentic in every detail—and proved beyond a shadow of a doubt that FDR was a traitor to his country. Your account is all whitewash to try and save old nuckel Head FDR."[89] Another wrote after reading *Rising Sun in the Pacific*, "Shame on you. FDR was elected President because he lied to the American people."[90]

The epicenter of the storm against Morison was located at the offices of the *Chicago Tribune*. Long critics of Roosevelt's policies, the *Tribune's* editors were incensed by an accusation Morison made in the pages of *Rising Sun in the Pacific*. The myth that there is a secret to Pearl Harbor "seems to have been hatched in the purlieus of the *Chicago Tribune*," Morison wrote in volume 3 of his series. Several days before the Pearl Harbor attack, the paper had published U.S. strategy plans "as evidence of the 'duplicity' and 'war mongering' of the Roosevelt administration," he submitted, including "vital extracts from the basic strategic plan of the war (ABC-1) and the basic Army-Navy Joint War Plan . . . which, under other circumstances than Pearl Harbor, might have been very useful to Japan, and doubtless were useful to Germany." Impugning the patriotism of the editors, Morison went on to imply that staff writers for the *Tribune* had stolen other materials from the Pentagon and, in subsequent articles, had revealed the basic strategic decision of the war and the basic Army-Navy plans for the war in the Atlantic and against Germany.[91]

Morison's accusation was "a lie, . . . a calculated and malicious lie," *Tribune* editors argued. Noting that the paper had quoted not the basic war plan but a published segment of it called "Rainbow 5," the editors chided, "All Morison had to do was to refer to the story itself to ascertain that it had no connection with the basic plan."[92] Turning to Morison's role in the broad governmental plots envisioned by Beard, the paper attacked *Rising Sun in the Pacific* as the work of a "court" historian taking part in the "official Washington conspiracy to muddle the facts about the Pearl Harbor disaster." Morison was writing "an official navy department fable," the editors suggested, "playing the same old game of cover-up."[93] Taking specific issue with Morison's statements in the third volume to the effect that "Roosevelt failed to take the American people into his complete confidence" because "a climate of opinion" compelled him to "do good by stealth,"[94] a writer for the paper sarcastically defined "good" in Morison's parlance as "a war at a cost of 330,000 dead, a million maimed, and a debt of $252 billion, all to raise up Russia to the status of world menace." Morison was a "fair country historian before he went to work for the politicians," a *Tribune* editorial concluded, but since he had become a "hired liar," who "knows what's expected for his pay."[95]

This controversy confirmed several things for Morison about the writing of Naval history. First, covering such a broad canvas, he could not expect to please everyone. It was enough for him to receive the plaudits of numerous military figures and lay readers, and he could easily discount the politically motivated attacks by the *Tribune*. Second, no matter how earnest he was in pointing out the mistakes made by the Navy in World War II, he would continue to be identified by some as an insider and "court historian." This criticism he could also ignore, since he had satisfied himself from the beginning about the objectivity and detachment of his work. But dismissing the critics' view that the Navy's entry into the war was part of a political scheme was not so easy. This matter cut to the heart of the debunking tendencies against which Morison had acted for decades. Wishing to uphold tradition (as he had with the profession, Harvard, and Columbus) he refused to ignore the *Tribune*'s radical critique of the martyred Roosevelt. In the years that followed, Morison not only worked to buttress Roosevelt's sagging reputation but also engaged in a personal battle with the editors of the *Tribune* over the preservation of the president's historical memory. At stake was the survival of American traditions.

Safeguarding History

*Charles Beard, Howard K. Beale
and the Question of
Access to the Past*

II

The Hyde Park Controversy

More than an attack on volume 3 of the *History of United States Naval Operations in World War II* was behind the *Chicago Tribune* editorials against Morison in the late 1940s. The reputation of President Roosevelt was at issue, as was the important methodological question of how that reputation would be preserved. Roosevelt had stirred up controversy toward the end of his second administration by attempting to effect an answer to that query himself. Recognizing that the papers of all presidents eventually become part of the nation's federal archives, Roosevelt proposed to build a library at his home in Hyde Park, New York, where his correspondence and state papers would be housed for use by researchers. Money to construct the library would come from taxpayers but would be supplemented somewhat by the donation of the Roosevelt mansion at Hyde Park as a national monument. Soliciting the help of historians and other scholars, Roosevelt launched a vigorous campaign on behalf of his library in 1938 in anticipation of a 1940 groundbreaking.[1]

Morison figured prominently in Roosevelt's plans. Late in 1938, he was summoned to the White House and informed of the president's "scheme for an archival building at Hyde Park."[2] At first he was only lukewarm to the idea, since he feared that a library dedicated while Roosevelt was still living might create temptations for the president to interfere in the selection and management of his papers. When Roosevelt convinced him, however, that "he intended to keep everything and [to] do no editing," Morison fell in with the project. The president then presented a list of prominent historians whom he hoped to enlist in the effort and asked Morison to organize a conference for them in Washington, D.C., later that year. After deleting one name from the list (not surprisingly, that of James Truslow Adams), Morison arranged a meeting for December, at which he gave the keynote address. Published later as "The Very Essence of History," the address emphasized that the "mutilation" of presidential papers in the past had prompted the president to preserve his records while still in office. "Some of the Presidents themselves, in the years after they left the White House, threw away material, considering it of little use," Morison noted, and their "families spoiled other papers, children played with them, rats gnawed at them, and so it went, a sad story for the historian."[3] Endorsing House Bill 268, the resolution providing for the establishment of a Roosevelt library, Morison asked the historians gathered at the conference to pledge their time and money to the cause.[4]

Morison's comments attracted national attention, not all in support of the resolution. Many viewed the project as egotistical and politically self-serving on Roosevelt's part. The *Chicago Tribune* lashed out at the president's desire to shape his own historical image. Arguing that "[i]t has been considered fitting, heretofore, that memorials to distinguished public servants should be left to the initiative of a grateful people who, in due time, would know what qualities they wished to admire in their historic characters," the editors complained "[that] Mr. Roosevelt prefers to shape his own memorial to himself and to stipulate how it shall be preserved at the public expense."[5] Others were still more vitriolic in their comments. "The decent citizens of this country are not at all interested in perpetuating your memory to future generations," wrote one infuriated Chicagoan, "in fact, we are only anxious to forget the stench of your egotistical, incompetent, unscrupulous and unspeakably costly administration as quickly as we can get you out of office." This tirade was followed by a pernicious recommendation: "I suggest that you *sell* Hyde Park and give the money to the 'forgotten men' you prate about so much (and then exploit)."[6] Finally, a third midwesterner sent a check to the president for ten cents, which he claimed was the sum total of what he was able to raise for the library. One of Roosevelt's aides passed it on to the Treasury Department along with a curt note: "Collections, probably due to the recession, are pretty slow."[7]

The prospect of a library raised the question of who would oversee the collection, and, again, Morison's name figured prominently. "Someone of stature, with a sense of history, and acceptable to the important men of this day would have to do this job," Eleanor Roosevelt remarked after her husband's death, adding, "I thought perhaps Mr. Morison of Harvard, whom I know was with Franklin from the start in organizing the library, of whom Franklin thought very highly, and who knew a great deal of what Franklin dreamed, might now undertake to work in the library."[8] Although Morison did not take the position, he was instrumental in seeing to the disposition of the papers. Among other things, he had advised the president while he was still alive to place a fifty-year restriction on his personal correspondence and to consider eight separate classifications of materials, each requiring various qualifications for use.[9] Morison's proposed restrictions infuriated some historians, including Charles Beard, who, interestingly enough, had also been considered to head the library.[10] Beard had shown enthusiasm for the library in its early stages of development, but he retracted his support when he discovered Morison's efforts to restrict access to the papers. Urging the president to open his papers to all researchers, Beard had even suggested that Roosevelt annotate and edit them. When these suggestions were ignored after the president's death, Beard became an outspoken critic of the Hyde Park project and of the historians such as Morison who were associated with it.[11]

In an article for the *Saturday Evening Post* entitled "Who's to Write the History of the War?" Beard accused the executors of the president's estate of allowing only the "right kind" of history to be written. The Roosevelt papers were only made available, he argued, to those who promised to toe the "official" line. Apart from the legal questions these restrictions raised, Beard believed that "the cause of truth about the war and the judicious discussion of the great issues that have ensued during the war" had been irreparably damaged by limitations placed on research. Citing his own experience with *President Roosevelt and the Coming of the War*, Beard argued that "[o]fficial archives must be open to all citizens on equal terms, with special privileges for none." With Morison's *Rising Sun in the Pacific* undoubtedly in mind, Beard took specific issue with government-sponsored historians who seemed to be granted free access to all materials and whose works, "prepared to serve a purpose fixed in advance," perpetuate errors more than they eliminate them.[12] Howard K. Beale, a professor of history at the University of Wisconsin, seconded Beard's position, arguing that "there are historians among us apparently delighted to cooperate in the policy of government censorship by accepting commissions to write history under government blessing or even government assignment from archives open to them but closed to others who are therefore unable to check their work." If the history of the war and the Roosevelt administrations was ever "to be adequately written," Beale asserted, the "democratic" right of access to materials must be secured for all researchers.[13]

In his defense, Morison argued that the fear of disclosure was precisely the reason that restrictions were necessary on historical papers. He agreed with the assessment of Herman Kahn, the eventual director of the library, that the surest way to discourage public officials from preserving records was to lead them to believe that "what they put in writing today will be public property in a few months or a few years." Kahn's fears about "unseemly violations" of the late president's "confidentiality" were confirmed for Morison when researchers given access to the Roosevelt-Morison correspondence used it to further implicate the pair in some sort of government cover-up.[14] After having read through Morison's letters to the president, for instance, historian William Neumann wrote to protest the conspiracy he had uncovered in them. "What I cannot understand is the intellectual—or is it emotional—block which you display to the fact that President Roosevelt did believe that it was in the national interests of the United States to enter World War II," Neumann complained to Morison. Claiming that a majority of the voters were opposed to entering the war, Neumann revived Beard's argument that Roosevelt had sought an "incident" to make involvement unavoidable. Neumann implicated Morison in this conspiracy to create an occasion for war. "If you will consult your correspondence with the President, you will find that you wanted to end the 'keep us out of war' hypocrisy in December of 1940," Neumann noted. "And on May 1, 1941, you expressed your fears that Hitler would not provide the 'incident' which the President was awaiting." With an irony intended to injure, Neumann concluded, "On this basis the Revisionists should acclaim you as their progenitor."[15]

Morison did not take kindly to the particular use Neumann had made of his private letters to the president. "Thanks for your appreciation of some of my writings, and also for advising me as to how to write history and conduct myself generally," Morison wrote back derisively, "Your citation of certain letters from me to FDR suggests that you have gone a-fishing in the Roosevelt correspondence for that 'missing link' which will prove FDR responsible for World War II." Morison "cheerfully" pled guilty to being one of those who foresaw the need for the United States to enter the war in Europe, but he refused to admit to any "baiting" on his or the president's part. Advising Neumann to read Matthew, Chapter 23, verse 24 ("Ye blind guides, which strain at a gnat, and swallow a camel"), Morison questioned why Neumann cared at all about Roosevelt's private intentions toward Hitler and Germany. Having shown "the most complete disregard for the scrupulous neutrality" as well as for human life, Morison noted, Hitler was a man who needed to be stopped no matter what the diplomatic rationale.[16]

Morison resented most the attacks that came from those who sought to link the restrictions he advocated on the presidential papers to a campaign against the political leverage of historians such as Beard, Beale, and Neumann. As a means of influencing the 1948 elections, members of the Republican convention circulated copies of Beard's President Roosevelt and the Coming of the War to congressmen in hopes that it might convince them to adopt a more isolationist convention platform.[17] Incensed by the ploy, Morison wrote his representative, Leverett Saltonstall, warning him that the Republicans were about to initiate a campaign against war in general and the supporters of Rooseveltian policies in particular. Ridiculing President Roosevelt and the Coming of the War as "about the most dishonest book calling itself a history that I have ever read," Morison begged Saltonstall not to be swayed by efforts by the Resolutions Committee of the Republican Convention to "try to put some sort of pacificist resolution into the platform, based on Beard's authority as an historian." Vowing to write his own damning review for the Atlantic Monthly, Morison noted that he would be glad to send Saltonstall a copy of the review in advance, if it would help to reduce Beard's influence.[18]

The direct assault against Beard that appeared in the *Atlantic Monthly* angered not only the *Chicago Tribune* but other midwestern papers that concurred with the *Tribune's* anti-Morison editorials. In an article entitled "Harvard's Fuzzy-Minded Teachers," *Tulsa Tribune* editor Richard Lloyd Jones accused Morison of concealing Roosevelt's "political record" in order to obscure its inadequacies and to prevent people from acting to right its wrongs. "Wait until the honest historian gets ahold of him," Jones wrote with reference to Morison. "As custodian of the Roosevelt presidential papers he will not allow people to have access to their own records," a sin that amounts to "pilfering the people of their own property."[19] In a follow-up editorial, Jones accused Morison and other archivists at the Hyde Park library of being "custodians of [Roosevelt's] infamies. You don't *dare* let honest historians see his records," he wrote, and "[t]hat makes a coward out of you."[20] And with still more political and emotional discharge, Jones concluded in yet another private letter, "After we elect Dewey we are going to request Congress to put you on the mat to find out why you *lock up* the people's papers at Hyde Park. You rascal."[21]

Under the influence of threats like these, Morison determined to press ahead with his review of *President Roosevelt and the Coming of the War* as an antidote to Beard's growing influence among Republican isolationists. Although jaded by his peace conference and teachers' oath experiences, he nonetheless felt compelled to make a specific political attack against his fellow historian. Smarting from the insults hurled at him by those who disapproved of his handling of the Roosevelt papers, he sought to enumerate for his audience the rules for the proper handling of historical evidence. Yet ever conscious of the need to knock amateur historians down a peg, as he had once done with James Truslow Adams and Van Wyck Brooks, he refused to sugarcoat his comments or to present them with typical scholarly reserve. Facetiously entitled "History Through a Beard," Morison's review became, by his own admission, "the most controversial thing I ever published."[22]

"History Through a Beard"

In his review of *President Roosevelt and the Coming of the War* for the *Atlantic Monthly*, Morison vented twenty years of frustration against Beard. Acknowledging his appreciation and "admiration" for him as a man, he declared that Beard was "lost as an historian." In a now familiar polemic, Morison argued that Beard's problems as a historian stemmed from his lack of respect for the objectivity of history. *President Roosevelt and the Coming of the War* was filled with "innuendo," suppressed truths, and false suggestions, he noted, adding that Beard's errors of historical judgment in this book alone would take a book "of almost equal length to expose." Selecting a few representative examples, Morison argued that Beard twisted the truth about the Navy's unpreparedness at Pearl Harbor by quoting only the partial text of a Roosevelt communication, which, in its complete version, discredited Beard's point. Of Beard's chapter "Realities as Described by the Pearl Harbor Documents," Morison observed that the designated documents "are 'realities' only in the Beardian sense," that is, they were selected only if they conformed to his thesis about the irresponsibilities of the Roosevelt administration.[23]

Morison also ridiculed Beard for his naïve attitude toward war. Samuel Eliot had disdained descriptions of war one hundred years before his grandson's review, but Morison believed that an adequate understanding of war was crucial to a historian's development. Sensitivity to the difference between preparing for war defensively and seeking war, Morison added, was just one of the subtle insights that eluded Beard. "[O]ne may share Beard's detestation of war as a barbarous survival," Morison wrote, "but one must admit that American liberty, union, and civilization would never have been unless men had been willing to fight for them." To leave essential details of war out of history, he complained, was "an evasion of essential truth." With growing sarcasm, Morison described Beard's role as an isolationist in the 1930s: "[A]loof on his Connecticut hilltop, [Beard] was unofficial high priest for the thousands of churchmen, teachers, and publicists who promoted disarmament in a world where aggressive nations were arming . . . and who prepared the younger generation for everything but the war that they had to fight."[24] Therefore, Beard had cost the United States valuable time in preparing for the war that inevitably, despite his most naïve hopes, had come.

According to Morison, Beard's use of innuendo and his refusal to acknowledge the importance of war to history were all attributable to his "frame of reference" technique. Renewing his attack on historical relativism, Morison charged Beard with trying to divide Americans against themselves with the same critical approach that had created such a profound sense of disillusionment after the war. Stepping up the tone and the intensity of his criticism, Morison referred to *President Roosevelt and the Coming of the War* as "the most dishonest work calling itself a history I ever remember reading, excepting some of the Nazi stuff." Equally poor books "have been written by journalists," he noted in another consistent refrain, but, "as a professional historian," Beard should know "better than to write a book of this sort," and would, too, if "his standards of truth and objectivity" did not "differ from those of any other professional historian." Noting that Beard's thirty-year seclusion on a dairy farm in Connecticut had insulated him too completely from historical scholarship and international affairs, Morison moralized that "isolation breeds isolation." Had Beard stayed at Columbia University, he added, he might have benefitted from "an intellectual rough-

and-tumble that one lacks on a hilltop. You get more back talk even from freshman," he mocked, "than from milch cows."[25]

The tone of these and like remarks was uncharacteristically snide—even for a man of Morison's pungent wit. Referring to "Farmer Beard" as a historian masquerading "in the role of God Almighty delivering the last judgment," Morison urged readers to cast aside his worthless historical pronouncements as the chaff of an unsound mind. In the final paragraph of "History Through a Beard," he unloosed all his repressed anger:

> In concluding, I wish long life and much happiness to Charles the Prophet and to Mary his wife, who have done so much in the past to illuminate American history. May they rise above the bitterness that has come from brooding over their lost horizon of a happy, peaceful, collectivist democracy insulated from a bad world"; and "[m]ay Dr. Beard recast his frame of reference once again, raise his sights a little higher than the Connecticut hills, and apply his erudition, wit, and craftsmanship to writing history without innuendo, history tolerant of mistakes that men make under great stress.

Most of all, Morison concluded with a philosophy he first used himself in studying the Puritans, "may he try to understand rather than to blame and to sneer, and even discover before he dies 'that highmindedness is not impossible to man.' "[26]

Many readers of "History Through a Beard" applauded these attacks, which they felt were long overdue. Chief Justice Felix Frankfurter wrote to say that *President Roosevelt and the Coming of the War* needed "the gunfire of critical exposure," adding that Beard was "so entangled, largely unconsciously, in the natural egotistic desire for self-justification that he fails to observe those criteria for arriving at truth and understanding."[27] Bernard De Voto called Morison's piece "one of the best reviews written in our time."[28] William Langer, by his own admission "one of Beard's particular *betes noires*," called "History Through a Beard" a "graceful . . . deflating job," and Morison's acquaintance Storer Lunt wrote, "I have been hoping and waiting for someone of your stature to meet Mr. Beard in the ring; . . . your . . . having him up against the ropes most of the time gave me both relief and enormous pleasure."[29]

But Beard's supporters were furious with the review and questioned Morison's ethics in having written it. Howard K. Beale viewed the entire disagreement as a function of Morison's Harvard and New England elitisms. "Somehow the profession must break the monopoly that a little group of reviewers centering in the northeast enjoys in the media that give or deny national reputations to books," he wrote in a rebuttal. He was particularly disturbed because Morison's reviewing in the *Atlantic Monthly* a title competing with *History of the United States Naval Operations in World War II* (which was under contract to the Atlantic Monthly Press and Little,

Brown) represented a conflict of interest. Because Morison was on the payroll of the publishing house doing the reviewing, Beale argued that readers should discount his remarks on Beard by the same logic that disqualified biographies done in the pay of a subject's family or that prohibited conflicts of interest for public figures. Still more, Beale objected to the intimate nature of Morison's attack on Beard. Arguing that reviews should not be used as opportunities to "vent personal grudges," Beale noted that Morison had lost his "sense of proportion" and had derived too much pleasure "out of devastatingly piling inaccurate detail upon detail" and giving "an unbalanced and incomplete picture of the book." Beale was astonished to find that Beard's book had been assigned to reviewers who so thoroughly disagreed with Beard's point of view, "some of them so violently that instead of considering the book on its historical merits they launched into violent personal attacks." Morison's "History Through a Beard" was particularly obnoxious, he implied, because its author "stooped to a cheap pun in his title."[30]

Even Morison's friends in the Navy believed Morison had gone a bit too far on their behalf. "Of course the Beards' basic history is poisonous from our point of view," wrote Rear Admiral M.L. Deyo to Morison, "but it seems to me that there have got to be all kinds of histories presented to our ignorant citizens, for the Lord knows we are ignorant about such matters." Arguing that all histories must inevitably have a point of view, Deyo added that *President Roosevelt and the Coming of the War* was at least consistent with the Beards's general isolationist convictions, which they shared in common with a great many sincere people. Even Morison's retort that Beard's later works resembled the propagandist efforts of Hitler's *Mein Kampf* did not convince military leaders like Deyo (who detested Hitler) that the *Atlantic Monthly* review was fair.[31]

Most interesting of all, however, was Beard's reaction to the review and the unfortunate timing of its arrival. "Many thanks for your essay," Beard wrote magnanimously from a hospital bed in Connecticut. Having read it (over the objections of his wife) with "much pleasure and with some improvement of my intellectual parts," Beard claimed, he admitted that he had grown "too old for turmoil." Beard died several weeks later in that same hospital bed, and the *Chicago Tribune* did not miss the opportunity to infer that Morison's article had somehow contributed to his rapid decline.[32] The title "History Through a Beard" "probably seemed quite funny to Capt. Morison," the *Tribune* noted, but to those who were aware that "Mr. Beard was declining toward death, it seemed not in the best taste."[33] Infuriated by this insinuation, Morison consulted with his Harvard colleagues about how best to respond. Their advice, he summarized later, was not to get "into a pissing contest with a skunk." As the years passed, Morison was mildly apologetic about the timing of "History Through a Beard," but he stood by everything in it.[34] In September 1948, he responded to a letter from Dixon Wecter that complimented him on his article and said that his attack "was written just in time." Morison went on to explain that several years before Beard's death a symposium of pro- and mostly anti-Beard reviewers was about to publish a number of articles on the historian in the *New Republic*, but Beard became very ill. Arguing that it would be in bad taste if the symposium articles were published at the time of his death, the editors cancelled the pieces. But Beard "fooled them," Morison wrote a bit callously, "by surviving to write worse and worse books."[35]

Morison's insensitivity in the matter of the Beard review can best be explained by reference to the times in which it was written. Convinced that *President Roosevelt and the Coming of the War* was about to be used to launch an isolationist Republican campaign, Morison believed that the future of the Navy was at stake. If a pacifist movement got under way with anywhere near the momentum it did after World War I under Beard's inducement, then the Navy would be disbanded, the spoils of victory squandered, and the return of war assured. Of lesser importance, but nonetheless on Morison's mind, was the effect any cutback in naval appropriations might have on his *History of the United States Naval Operations in World War II*. The rise to power of Republican isolationists might even have a pernicious effect on projects associated with the previous administration. If so, then even the Hyde Park experiment might fall victim to the excesses of Republican historians without "consciences or portfolios."

Presidential Privileges

The best indication that professional historians sided with Morison in his debate with Beard was their electing him president of the American Historical Association in 1950. Introduced to the audience of his peers and admirers in the Grand Ballroom of the Steven Hotel in downtown Chicago by toastmaster and longtime friend Ralph Budd, Morison accepted the nomination because, as he added later with modesty, "[m]ost American historians who live long enough are elected to the presidency" and "the only thing the president does is deliver an address."[36] In preparing his presidential address, Morison was inspired by the text of an address given at Oxford by Cyril Falls about the place of military history in general history. Remarking that historians in the United States "treated military history with a reprehensible neglect," he told Falls that Americans were "mentally and spiritually unprepared for the tough struggle that was forced upon them."[37] Not surprisingly, in his speech he focused his complaints against Beard, who, even in death, seemed to challenge him. Punning on Beard's earlier presidential address "Written History as an Act of Faith," Morison entitled his address "Faith of an Historian" and, by his own admission, paid his "disrespects" to the man who had done more to hurt the nation than any other historian.[38]

Morison argued that Beard had done a grave disservice to the nation because he had not prepared students of history for war. Because Beard always detested war, Morison noted, he inspired "a procession of historians who, caught in the disillusion that followed World War I, ignored wars, belittled wars, taught that no war was necessary and no war did any good, even to the victor." These antiwar historians "did nothing to preserve peace," he told his audience, and bore the blame for not having alerted the American people to the fact that "war does accomplish something, that war is better than servitude, that war has been an inescapable aspect of the human story." In addition, by ignoring war, Beard upset the balance of history and disturbed the subtle equilibrium among social, cultural, institutional, and military aspects of the past. "This principle of balance or proportion—what the French mean by *mesure*—is, I believe, the most valuable quality for a historian, after intellectual honesty," Morison explained to his audience. Reviving some of the synchronic philosophy of the sociocultural historians at Harvard, Morison noted that *mesure* required historians to consider social forces when constructing political history or cultural causes when sketching institutional developments. Predicting that "no unbalanced history can live long," he concluded his presidential address by arguing that histories such as those produced by Charles Beard would in due time become curiosity pieces "like those nasty antipapist and anti-Protestant tracts of the seventeenth century, which serve only to illustrate the partisan passions of the times."[39]

These presidential pronouncements by Morison provoked much criticism, as expected, from Howard K. Beale and other supporters of the late Charles Beard. Beale claimed that in "Faith of an Historian" Morison had knocked down a "straw" Beard that had no resemblance to the actual historian. "I have looked up all the references for the statement[s] that you make that I could find in Beard myself and certainly Beard does not say in any of the places cited what you in your presidential address said he did," Beale complained to Morison.[40] Taking specific issue with Morison's assertions about Beard's supposed avoidance of war, Beale delivered his own address, entitled "The Professional Historian: His Theory and His Practice," at a subsequent session of the American Historical Association. Calling "Faith of an Historian" the "most recent example of confusion" regarding standards in the profession, he chided Morison for his inaccuracies in his portrait of Beard and for his double standard in condemning Beard's "frame of reference." In "an amazing page of distortion, innuendo, and misrepresentation," Beale wrote, "Morison classes Beard first with Debs, then with Hearst, and then with dictatorships, and accuses Beard of saying what he never said, namely, that the historian *ought* to 'adopt a conscious frame of reference' and then 'so select and arrange the facts of history as to influence the present or future in the direction that *he* considers socially desirable.' " If Beard had chosen to influence the future in ways that Morison believed socially desirable, Beale reminded his audience, Beard would then have been writing with what Morison would designate as "a sense of balance" and an "urge to get at the truth." Morison "considers Beard's interpretation deliberate bias but regards his own counter interpretation based on opposite values as 'balanced' history and 'truth,' " he chided.[41]

Intending to publish his remarks, Beale asked Morison for permission to quote his comments in their personal correspondence on the matter.[42] The suggestion angered Morison, and he consulted his lawyers for advice. "Howard Beale, who is generally regarded by his colleagues as a psychopathic case," Morison wrote, "is preparing a sort of posthumous *Festschrift* on Beard . . . in which he lit into me and other historians, claiming we were all biassed [sic]," and "asks my permission (after insulting me) to quote my letter to him." Hoping to avoid publication of the remarks, Morison suggested that his lawyer send a letter to Beale stating that the sentence beginning "In an amazing page of distortion," and so on, is "slanderous, libellous (or what you will) and, if published, will be the occasion of a libel suit." If Beale wished to escape the consequences of such a suit, Morison added, he should replace the lines by the statement "I believe Morison misrepresented Beard's attitude in this address." Make it understood that "I don't expect him to agree with me," Morison added, "but I don't propose to lie down under such statements as this."[43] Morison's lawyers drafted a letter conveying these sentiments, although they advised their client that Beale's remarks were "on the borderline" and did not constitute "an open and shut case of defamation."[44]

The inability of Morison's lawyers to establish a clear legal authority for his position suggested the considerable cloudiness of these matters. Many in the profession believed Beale was within his rights to say what he had, particularly in light of Morison's remarks about Beard in his *Atlantic Monthly* review. University of Wisconsin historian Merle Curti supported his colleague, arguing that Morison had discredited the presidency of the American Historical Association with his vicious attacks.[45] Former Wisconsin professor Curtis Nettels, however, upheld Morison and discredited Beale. In a letter to Morison, he wrote: "If I had had my way, you would have been chosen many years ago [as president of the AHA], when I was on the nominating committee in 1939. You would have given the presidential address in the early 1940s, and all of this would not have occurred." Nettels went on to report that a former student of his at Wisconsin, Robert Brown, had written an attack on Beard's *Economic Interpretation of the Constitution* for his doctoral dissertation. "He has told me that he had a dreadful time completing the work on his degree," Nettels confided, "by reason of Curti's opposition to his anti-Beardian findings."[46]

The Beale-Morison debate was so actively discussed within the profession because it evoked issues of vast importance to historians. Beale's defense of Beard was connected to his ongoing campaign against elitism in the profession. Not only did he resent the parochialism of eastern professors, but he also took exception to the special status conferred on some of them by the government. Renewing his attack on the *History of United States Naval Operations in World War II*, Beale cited Morison's presidential address as evidence of the increasing intrusion of "official" agencies into the historical process. "The huge amounts of government money available make it particularly tempting to sell one's freedom and to rationalize the resulting control of what is written," Beale wrote, especially on the part of "the government historian paid by the government to write its history, and the semiofficial historian screened and given special facilities by the government." Apart from the question of cost, Beale asserted, there were disturbing political aspects to the question of government patronage. If Morison charged Beard with baiting Republican isolationists, then Beale felt justified in accusing Morison of promoting the specific agenda of Democratic President Harry Truman. The *History of United States Naval Operations in World War II* was nothing more than a thinly veiled endorsement of Truman's war in Korea, Beale implied; like World War II, it was a war that had been pursued by Democrats against the will of the American people.[47]

Beale's suspicions about the Democratic nature of Morison's historiography seemed to be confirmed by the announcement late in 1950 that President Truman would attend Morison's presidential address. Hoping to enlist the aid of historians in his effort to hold back communism in East Asia, Truman asked to be included on the program just prior to Morison's address. The president never gave the remarks, as things turned out, since a North Korean offensive made it impossible for him to attend the conference, but he asked Morison to read the following letter, which served as an introduction to Morison's remarks about military preparedness in "Faith of an Historian":

Dear Mr. Morison:

As the American Historical Association assembles for its sixty-fifth annual meeting, I wish to extend to its members my best wishes for another year of constructive work. I regret that I am not able to extend these greetings in person, as I had hoped to do. You are aware of the circumstances which prevent my being at your meeting.

In the critical effort which the free nations of the world are now making to preserve peace, the work of American historians is of the utmost importance. Communist countries are distorting history and spreading untruths about our achievements, our traditions, and our policies. We must keep the record clear, so that all the world may know the truth about what we have done and what we are continuing to do to build a peaceful and prosperous family of nations.

Since the Federal Government's activities are of central importance in our national defense effort, and since historians of the future will wish to probe deeply into the Government's activities, I am directing that a Federal historical program be instituted, with a primary purpose of recording the activities which the Federal Government is undertaking to meet the menace of communist aggression. Such a program will need the advice and assistance of the

American Historical Association. The Government will need your help in defining the objectives of the program, obtaining qualified historians, and insuring that its work meets the high standards of the historical profession. I shall be pleased to receive the views and advice of the American Historical Association on these matters.

Communist imperialism has made falsehood a dangerous weapon; but truth can be a far more potent weapon. American historians can contribute to the cause of the free nations by helping the Government to record and interpret the policies our Nation is following to secure peace and freedom in the world.

Very sincerely yours,
Harry S. Truman[48]

For those such as Beale who were already concerned with government intrusions into the historical profession, the proposed federal historical program confirmed nightmarish fears. With such government-sponsored history, Beale noted, readers of history would not know whether restrictions had been imposed by the government or whether historians would be conscious of things they could not write because of imagined restrictions. Additionally, if the government were to determine what constituted "truth" in history, or how "truth" might be used as a "potent weapon" to use Truman's phrasing, there could be little defense for those who dissented from the government's established views. The federal historical program would leave its participants "open to suspicion," Beale wrote, adding his fervent hope "that this sort of official and semiofficial history of which we have had so much will decline and go out of fashion."[49]

As usual, it was the *Chicago Tribune* that had the final and most direct word on this matter. Implying that Morison was as subservient to the wishes of Truman as he had been to Roosevelt before him, the editors characterized him as a stooge of the State, no less guilty of partisan history than the Communists he and Truman ridiculed. In an article entitled "When History Serves the State," the *Tribune* argued that "[t]he difference between the sort of historiografy [sic] of [Stalin] and the kind advocated by Prof. Morison eludes us," since historians in Russia "are expected to distort the record in order to preserve the party line," and Morison, too, "conceives it to be the duty of historians to uphold the existing regime in all its undertakings." In his presidential address, the editors claimed, Morison established the " 'party line' for historical orthodoxy in the United States," and despite subtle attempts at concealment, he could not obscure his "real mission"—to involve Americans in "the brawl promoted by Mr. Truman in Korea."[50]

Naval History and Korean Conflict

The impression that Morison was a spokesman for the Truman administration was enhanced by his lectures, writings, and statements in the press.

First, Morison was outspoken in his defense of Truman's nuclear policy. The decision to drop atomic bombs on Hiroshima and Nagasaki was "not only justified," Morison argued, but necessary, since "it is difficult to see how the Pacific war could otherwise have been concluded, except by a long and bitter invasion of Japan." Furthermore, Morison backed Truman's plan to create a large nuclear arsenal capable of neutralizing the aggressive postwar movements of the Soviet Union. The United States "must build up the largest stockpile of atomic-built bombs to maintain peace," he urged, going on record with President Truman and Secretary of State Dean Acheson as agreeing "that there is no excuse for preventative war, moral or strategic," and "that only superiority in atomic warfare and the unified military strength of the Army, Navy, and Air Force would deter Russia from her aggressive course." World War II should have convinced all Americans, Morison argued, that "preparedness" was the only responsible course of action for a world power.[51]

In his pitch for preparedness Morison put particular stress once again on the need to provide a balanced approach to war. Hoping to "get a bigger bang for a buck" as Morison put it, some strategists called for the buildup of a long-range "strategic" air force, with a stockpile of atomic bombs that could provide a massive retaliatory strike capability. This method of prioritizing meant that the Navy would be "put in moth balls" again, a condition that would run contrary to the whole thrust of recent military history, according to Morison. Hence, Morison actively campaigned to reinstate the Navy as an equal partner in the services triumvirate. "The services are a three-legged stool," he wrote. "Without each leg, the trustworthiness is always questioned."[52]

Volumes 4–8 of the *History of the United States Naval Operations in World War II* provided vivid historical examples of the need for such a balance. Covering naval operations across hundreds of thousands of square miles and in climates ranging from ice-cold to tropical, these volumes shared a common theme: when the branches of the armed services cooperated and were given equal weight by the Joint Chiefs of Staff, the United States military machine was formidable; when imbalances occurred, disaster was inevitable. In volume 4, *Coral Sea, Midway, and Submarine Action* (1949), for instance, Morison noted that the Battle of Coral Sea was "the first purely carrier-against-carrier naval battle in which all losses were inflicted by air action and no ship on either side sighted a surface enemy." On the basis of this victory, Morison maintained, many "air power enthusiasts" predicted "that it had set a pattern which would always be followed" and conferred special status on the Army Air Force. Generals Hap Arnold and George Kenney encouraged this thinking by making outrageous claims about the successes of the Army Air Force, Morison argued. At Midway, for instance, six new Avenger torpedo planes and four Army B-26's were sent to attack the Japanese fleet. They did not make a single hit, "not even a near miss," Morison noted, yet one pilot managed to stretch the long bow in telling of his success at torpedoing a Japanese carrier. After examining the Japanese records after the war, Morison's staff was convinced that no damage and only a few casualties were inflicted on enemy ships by land-based planes of the Army Air Force.[53]

This false reporting to bolster the reputation of one arm of the service over others might have been harmless had not a grave importance been attached to accurate reporting in the matter of hits. Army Air Force exaggerations, Morison claimed, often convinced naval and army commanders that they were attacking smaller forces than they actually were, and several military engagements and lives were lost when miscalculations occurred in these matters. Furthermore, Morison noted, the Army Air Force compounded the errors by refusing to admit its own mistakes. At one point in the struggle for Coral Sea, U.S.S. *Farragut* was attacked by three bombers, which proved to be B-26's belonging to the U.S. Army Air Force. Even though photographs confirmed the identity of the planes, Army Air Force commanders insisted no mistake was made and "prohibited further discussion of the matter."[54]

Fortunately, the Japanese were still more prone to these interservice squabbles and imbalances than the United States military. Admiral Yamamoto, for instance, was certain that the Japanese Air Force could defeat the U.S. Navy off the island of Midway without relying on naval bombardment or troop engagements. The Japanese strategy seemed destined for success, since visibility on the day scheduled for attack was up to forty miles, conditions "much too good for the . . . health" of U.S. carriers, Morison noted. But relying exclusively on air power forced Commander Nagumo to coordinate his fleet movements with the refueling needs of his pilots, leaving his Navy vulnerable if the air strikes failed to repulse the enemy. Admiral Spruance of the U.S. Navy made the fortunate military decision to send his planes out during one of these refueling intervals, Morison noted, and he caught the enemy with his "pants down." The subsequent defeat of the Japanese at Midway, the "turning point of the war" as far as Morison was concerned, was not the result of some ancient code of naval deployment that made the Japanese fleet reluctant to "come out and fight," as some armchair strategists averred according to Morison. Imperial Headquaters "had always been advocates of the one big, decisive naval battle," he wrote, and the Japanese continued to think along those lines after Midway. But only too late did they realize that "no battle could be won without carrier planes" (and, conversely, that no "air arm" could single-handedly subdue an enemy's navy), and after Midway the Japanese command had few planes at its disposal.[55]

The ability to appreciate balance as a military strategy was fundamentally a democratic trait, Morison noted, analogous to a recognition of the importance of checks and balances to efficient government. "Military and absolutist regimes are undoubtedly well fitted to get the jump on an unsuspecting or unprepared enemy," he wrote in *Coral Sea, Midway, and Submarine*

Action, "but the history of modern warfare proves that they cannot win over representative governments in the long run." Because Imperial Headquarters in Japan was rigidly divided into an Army Branch and a Navy branch with the Navy completely subservient to the Army, Army Minister General Tojo dictated most military policy to Admiral Yamamoto. As Tojo underestimated the strength and determination of America and was more concerned with the possible entry of Russia into the war, Morison noted, he refused to listen to Yamamoto's frequent demands for more planes and better joint planning after Midway. This interaction presented a stark contrast to the "democratic" operations of the U.S. Joint Chiefs of Staff. "Occasional deadlocks in our J.C.S. between Army and Navy points of view were indeed embarrassing, and made one of the strongest arguments for unification of the armed forces," Morison observed, "but these disagreements were nothing to what went on in Imperial Headquarters." On the American side, once plans were voted on and agreed to, the branches were unified behind them. U.S. strategy meetings demonstrated democracy in action and vindicated, through successful planning, the very principles for which the war was being fought.[56]

In Volume 5 of his naval series, *The Struggle for Guadalcanal* (1949), Morison reiterated his theme, this time with reference to disagreements between the Navy and the Marines. Marines placed on Guadalcanal in August of 1942 were not provisioned adequately by Navy transports before they disembarked to fend off a surprise attack at Salvo Island, Morison argued. This left them trapped on Guadalcanal among enemy ground troops without food and shelter in a jungle "hell-hole" where many were slaughtered or died from disease. The Navy defended itself by arguing that it was preoccupied with the Japanese fleet, which, in the "first day of a long series of outrageous, desperately costly blunders," sank four cruisers. Resembling a "vicious prehistoric monster, . . . with two heads, hydra-like" and "deadly at both ends," Morison wrote, the Japanese fleet "put the bite on the Northern Force" in one of the "worst defeats ever inflicted on the United States Navy." Resentful of the implication that the Navy had abandoned the Marines out of cowardice, naval officers pointed to the "ocean graveyard" between Guadalcanal, Savo and Florida Islands as proof of sacrifices made. Yet this argument did not even satisfy other naval personnel, who condemned several deadly mistakes that officers had made. Such backbiting represented a nadir in American military fortunes in the Pacific war, Morison stated, and might have proved more costly if the Japanese had not failed (because of dissension within their own ranks) to capitalize on it. The eventual mending of these tears in the American military fabric (and the ongoing shredding of the Japanese) was what ensured the ultimate success of American forces.[57]

The "divided-we-fall" theme was reiterated in Morison's volume 6, *Breaking the Bismarcks Barrier* (1950) and in volume 7, *Aleutians, Gilberts and Marshalls* (1951). In the Papuan campaign on New Guinea, Morison explained, enormous casualties were incurred (nearly 3000 American and 5600 Australian), because of the "want of Allied sea power in the Solomon Sea." The Allied forces had as many troops as the Japanese and more air power in this campaign, he wrote, but they failed to deploy them in a balanced attack strategy. Employing the metaphor he had used in the press relative to the Korean struggle, he moralized, "modern military strength is like a tripod, one leg being the ground forces, another the Navy, the third air power; with struts representing amphibious forces, carrier planes, and the like connecting and strengthening all three."[58] In the case of the Solomon Sea campaign, "the naval leg was so much shorter than the other two that the whole structure tottered." If the southwest Pacific command had had at its disposal an amphibious force of beaching craft supported by carriers, cruisers, and destroyers, he argued, "the Japanese could have been overtaken in a week." Likewise, in the Allied attack on Attu, in the Aleutians, the American troops on shore begged the *Pennsylvania* for more gun support. This request made the sailors indignant: "What! wear out our big guns, waste our AP, when the soldiers are supposed to be doing the fighting ashore!" they cried.[59] The coveting of weapons for sea warfare was repeated in the invasion of the Gilberts, where, according to Morison, the Navy failed to bomb the beaches of Tarawa sufficiently, leaving enemy outposts virtually unscathed. This carelessness made the subsequent beach landing a blood bath and caused Marines to legitimately claim that their "buddies would now be alive" if the Navy had given adequate support.[60]

The Marines and the Army fared no better at times. In the Makin Island campaign, General Holland M. Smith ("Howlin' Mad Smith") of the Marines claimed that the Army, under General Ralph Smith, turned in "a miserable, dilatory performance," moving so sluggishly as to give "the enemy ample time to reorganize and dispute every step." Howlin' Smith claimed that General Ralph Smith's 27th Battalion was "too old, [and] the morale of the men had declined from too long a stretch of garrison duty." When the same division moved slowly on Saipan, Howlin' Smith erupted and relieved Ralph Smith of his command. Morison argued that the Smith versus Smith controversy stemmed from a fundamental misunderstanding between the two branches regarding tactics. The Marines believed that troops should dig in at night and fire only when absolutely necessary, "because night shooting seldom hits anyone but a friend and serves mainly to give one's position away." Allowing the enemy "to infiltrate, keeping good watch to prevent his accomplishing anything," Marines "liquidate the infiltrators" at daylight, a technique that requires the "fire discipline of seasoned troops who have plenty of élan but keep their nerves under control." The Army, Morison observed, preferred to shoot enemy infiltrators on sight. These two differing strategies unfortunately clashed on the first night of the Saipan campaign, when trigger-happy GI's shot at anything that moved, including Marines. Such disagreements were only reconciled by the gradual reintroduction of democratic checks and balances in operational prerogatives, and not, tragically, until scores of U.S. soldiers had been killed in the process.[61]

And finally, in volume 8, *New Guinea and the Marianas* (1953), Morison highlighted the tragedy of General MacArthur's attempt to make the Navy a mere appendage to the Army. In the early volumes of the *History of United States Naval Operations in World War II*, MacArthur was described as a "fatherly but resolute figure," who, "[w]hile dodging bullets" in one skirmish, "cheered the weary, rewarded the brave, and tossed out the incompetents."[62] When the general knew he had ordered an operation that would put the Navy in jeopardy, Morison wrote of MacArthur's early command, he "gallantly determined to share the risk and see it through."[63] But in later volumes of the series, Morison's attitude toward MacArthur changed. In volume 8 Morison hinted that the general had become too obsessed in his insistence on a single path to Tokyo in the "mopping up" operations of 1945. Believing himself "honor bound to liberate the Philippines," MacArthur acknowledged only "one road to Tokyo, his own," Morison wrote, even when it was apparent to officers in other branches of the service that that road was not the most advantageous from a military point of view. "Why should Admiral Nimitz and the Pacific Fleet necessarily tail along with him [MacArthur]," Morison noted, or confine themselves "to narrow seas commanded by enemy land-based aircraft" when to do so would be "idiotic?" he argued. When Nimitz and other Navy officers suggested a secondary road to Japan through the Marianas and the Philippine Sea, General MacArthur "reacted vigorously against their proposal," displaying a monomania revealing of an unbalanced military mind. He was "an international and in some respects a supra-national figure" whose tragic flaw was his insistence on consolidating power under himself alone, Morison wrote. No one in the southwest Pacific command "doubted who was boss," Morison argued, adding that "his dynamic personality and dramatic qualities presented to the world a picture somewhat different from the one seen by subordinates who translated his decisions and orders into action."[64]

It was not coincidental that Morison's more negative portrait of MacArthur appeared in the middle volumes in the series, since the writing of these volumes coincided exactly with the downturn in MacArthur's military fortunes. In 1951, Truman had fired the World War II hero for insubordination because of his actions in Korea. As had been the case in the South Pacific, MacArthur's "egotism" continued to compel "him to regard any operation that he commanded as crucial" and to lose his sound military judgment.[65] After reading Francis Parkman's description of Wolfe's assault on Quebec in 1759, of all things, the general decided to attack North Korea for the purposes of driving the Communists back into China, thus abandoning the U.N. war aim, which was to stabilize the 38th parallel. "His own staff didn't like it; the navy didn't like it; but he insisted," Morison noted, hence Korea became a "Costly Renewal of U.S. Lesson in Japan War," as one newspaper article by Morison put it.[66] MacArthur regarded "the Korean War as the center of the world-wide struggle against communism" and was presumptious enough to appeal over the president's head to the Republican party and public opinion when Truman objected, according to Morison. MacArthur's "overweening ego" prevented him from seeing that an invasion of China would make an " 'unconditional surrender' kind of war" into a "war of mutual annihilation." Truman had no choice but to retire the leader whose hubris had been apparent to keen observers such as Morison since the end of World War II.[67]

If the war in the Pacific was a tribute to cooperative action, then the Korean conflict could only be won through similar cooperation. Therefore MacArthur had to be relieved and joint planning reestablished, and Morison went on record with Truman in suggesting that "MacArthur must go." The "actual orders were unnecessarily abrupt," Morison later wrote, and that was unfortunate, but the announcement had to be made at half-past midnight "to forestall a morning-paper scoop" by none other than the *Chicago Tribune.* There could be little doubt that Truman was right "in relieving a general whose attitude to his civilian commander in chief had become insufferable," Morison concluded.[68] In his early war interview with Morison, MacArthur had said "that a theater commander should be allowed to act independently, with no orders from President, United Nations, or anyone."[69] Such an attitude was "incompatible with representative and responsible government," Morison wrote, and incompatible with the kind of democratic balance he advocated for all military operations.[70]

Some critics of Morison's *History of the United States Naval Operations in World War II* claimed that in his attack on MacArthur Morison was once again acting as a mouthpiece for the Truman administration. They explained his behavior by reference to the special privileges that had been conferred on him first by Roosevelt and the curators at Hyde Park and then by Truman. Civilian historians were not privy to battle reports, classified statements, Japanese war testimonials, or communiqués of the Joint Chiefs, C. Vann Woodward noted, adding that the legitimacy of Morison's judgments simply could not be challenged until the public had access to the records he used. "Captain Morison concludes that 'Midway was a victory of intelligence,' " Woodward argued, yet "the sum total of what he tells us about Naval intelligence in this battle—admittedly the key to the victory— is that it was deduced from a variety of sources!" From such a "meticulous historian" as Morison, he added, this kind of vagueness could "mean only one thing: Navy security is still up to its old tricks."[71] And military journalist Ira Wolfert argued that "Mr. Morison, in the end, for his conclusions, adopts the Annapolis way of looking at things." Citing him as "a Harvard professor, trained and talented," Wolfert nonetheless remarked that "out of some misguided admiration, perhaps, [Morison] parrots the words and attitudes of men who do not regard words as an historian should—as verses of truth—but who use them as wind to further the progress of their private vessels."[72]

Morison's response to these reviewers was the same he had offered years earlier to critics of the Hyde Park library or debunkers of Roosevelt. It was necessary to restrict access to materials, he argued, so that responsible historians (those professionally trained and knowledgeable about military affairs) could provide balanced approaches to war. In the hands of sensationalist papers like the *Chicago Tribune*, or debunkers like Beard, or psychopaths like Beale, Morison argued, such materials would be used in the service of "innuendo," suppressed truths, and false suggestion. While distortions of this kind might be tolerable in certain ages, Morison concurred with President Truman's argument that in cold war America such distortions carried tremendous risks. The decisions made by historians "will not, as a statesman's may, throw his country into a bloody war or a shameful capitulation; they will not, like the soldier's, win or lose a campaign," Morison noted in "Faith of an Historian," "but they may well enter into the stream of history and vitally affect the future." The Greeks failed to listen to Isocrates when he warned them of alien domination, Morison remarked; with a similar sense of urgency he noted that in a cold war environment, "a mad or obstinate people" must not fail to "hear the voice of an historian."[73]

Consensus History

*Dwight D. Eisenhower, Winston Churchill
and the Politics of* Mesure

I2

A Balanced Approach

orison's emphasis in the middle volumes of the *History of United States Naval Operations in World War II* on the need for balance and unity in military operations echoed the principle of *mesure* he had first articulated in "Faith of an Historian." In that presidential address before the American Historical Association, he gave voice to a new mode of historical writing, dubbed by its critics "consensus history," which sought to dissolve dualisms in favor of unified and holistic interpretations of the past. If Beard and other prewar historians had emphasized the role of conflict in American culture (section versus section, class versus class, ideology versus ideology), then consensus historians concentrated on "the continuity of American history, the stability of basic institutions, the toughness of the social fabric."[1] Consensus historian Richard Hofstadter called for a reinterpretation of American political traditions according to the common climate of opinion that overshadowed political differences. Emphasizing the "staple tenets" of political agreement among Americans ("the sanctity of private property, the right of the individual to dispose of and invest it, the value of opportunity, and the natural evolution of self-interest and self-assertion, within broad legal limits, into a beneficient social order"), Hofstadter argued that even personalities as diverse as Jefferson, Lincoln, and Wilson shared a faith more similar than dissimilar.[2]

Consensus history had deep roots in the nationalism of the postwar period. Echoing the "end of ideology" philosophy of the 1950s, consensus history appealed to "homogeneity, continuity, and national character," and it developed from the patriotic desire of Americans to present a unified image of themselves to a world split by ideological disputes.[3] To many, this new form of history had definite political ends, as well. It emphasized the status quo or what Arthur Schlesinger, Jr., son of Morison's Harvard colleague, called "the vital center"—an American middle ground between the forces of reaction and the forces of revolution.[4] Daniel Bell concurred, calling for an "end to ideology" in America or national recognition of the necessity for an ideology that, with conscious irony, rejected all ideology.[5] Critics of the consensus school complained that the end of ideology philosophy was "strikingly conservative," because it implied "a massive grading operation to smooth over America's social convulsions" and created "a paralyzing incapacity to deal with the elements of spontaneity, effervescence, and violence in American history."[6] But Morison and other consensus historians argued that the conservative point of view had been undervalued by American historians. If a historian chooses to record the role of conflict and liberal change in the past, Morison wrote, he or she must "appease them as well by showing how the 'pointers with pride' were too complacent, and the 'viewers with alarm' were too nervous, how every winning cause had elements of evil, and every losing cause had some kernel of good." Although his own approach to the past had followed the "Jefferson-Jackson-Franklin D. Roosevelt line" of liberalism, Morison noted, he believed there had been "altogether too much of it" within the profession. "[T]he present situation is unbalanced and unhealthy," he argued, "tending to create a sort of neoliberal stereotype." There is "no excuse for the historian going off balance," he added, especially in a cold war environment when the United States so desperately needed a history "written from a sanely conservative point of view."[7]

Consensus history seemed to mirror conservative political realities in the United States as well. The "end of ideology" philosophy was central to Dwight Eisenhower's conservative Republican campaign for the presidency in 1952, to which Morison contributed political endorsements in the Boston papers. Many of Morison's Harvard colleagues supported Adlai Stevenson, whose "intellectual" approaches they favored, but as a military historian, Morison had an appreciation for the considerable leadership skills of Eisenhower. "There has been so much talk about 'Professors for Stevenson,' " he wrote in the Boston Post, "that I wish to place myself on record as a warm supporter of General Eisenhower." Although he had a great personal respect for Stevenson, he announced that the Democratic party had been "in power too long for their health, and ours." Noting that General Eisenhower was a "man of character, of integrity, of achievement and of vision," Morison claimed his candidate would bring "a fresh new breeze into our political life." Most of all, "he has the soldier's virtue of getting the best out of different kinds of people," Morison concluded. "His assignments since 1941 have called for statesmanship of a high order, and he has proved that he has it."[8]

That Morison could support a Republican candidate was itself an indication of his commitment to balance, since he had been so closely aligned with the Roosevelt and Truman administrations. In his *Boston Post* article Morison quoted Goethe to the effect that every soul struggles with two opposing spirits—the one that creates and the one that denies. He believed that the nation had persisted too long in the false belief that one party alone could reconcile these spirits by demeaning and excluding the other. American political stability depended on a balance of power in a two-party system and a resolution of the conflicting ideologies that prohibited consensus. A loyal Democrat, Morison nonetheless believed that the Republicans had a better candidate for the job in 1952, and he refused to allow partisan sentiments to obscure that fact. "Since first voting forty years ago," Morison noted, "I have consistently supported the Democratic party because it seemed to be the creative, hopeful, forward-looking party at a time when most Republicans in this part of the world were bogged down in reaction." He said he had come to see the merits of a new Republican image, representing the "can-do" spirit, and he hoped Democrats in his state would be levelheaded enough to support the change.[9]

Shortly after Eisenhower's victory, Morison wrote the president-elect and exhorted him to keep consensus at the heart of his political agenda. "Now, will you allow me as one of your ardent supporters to emphasize the need for an understanding and agreement among Republican leaders as to politics and measures?" he wrote. Making an analogy between Eisenhower's current situation and that of his nineteenth-century predecessors, Morison noted that Harrison Gray Otis had written Whig leaders after their 1840 victory asking that a "broad foundation . . . be laid for a great 'Country Party' on primary principles and mutual concession, extending in every direction and embracing all the great interests of the Country." Although such a party "has not yet existed among us," Otis noted, "events seem to indicate the practicability of forming it," and without such a consensus "the Cossacks will be upon you in one or two years." The moral of the the story was that this broad agreement within the Whig party was never achieved, largely, Morison believed, because in 1840 there were "too many prima-donnas in the party to agree on anything." The tragic result was the Civil War. "History never repeats itself exactly the same," Morison informed Eisenhower, "but there is enough similarity between the situations of 1840 and 1952, so it seems to me, to make old Otis's warning valid."[10]

The primadonnas in the Republican party included Senator Joseph McCarthy and others who were creating divisions rather than a broad consensus in national politics. In addition, Eisenhower faced budgetary challenges, with some advisors advocating deficit spending and others seeking a balanced budget. Morison, of course, urged a "balanced" economy, as long as appropriations for defense were not cut. Morison also had advice for Eisenhower on how to reach a consensus on the proper balance of power between government and the business world. Applying the tripodal analogy of the Armed Forces in *History of the United States Naval Operations in World*

War II to the relationship between government, industry, and labor, he wrote: "The present division of power . . . may be compared with the medieval division between church and state. We all seek a balanced society, as the Middle Ages did, and so far have been rather less successful than the Middle Ages." The current situation "is overbalanced in favor of organized labor," he noted, "but let us be patient and remember the century and a half that elapsed after the industrial revolution began, before labor got anything out of it, and the progressive fall in real wages between 1893 and 1916." Urging Eisenhower to have faith that the American people could reach an equilibrium of opinion on these matters, he concluded, "For God hath not given us the spirit of fear, but of strength, and of love, and of a balanced mind."[11]

Morison predicted that Eisenhower's "balanced mind" would make him one of America's greatest presidents. "Eisenhower more than once during the war showed that he could do what others said was impossible," Morison noted, "that he had power of decision equal to Washington's or Lincoln's and that he had the humanity to get on with all sorts and conditions of men." The president's election eve speech buoyed Morison's hopes still further. "[D]eeply moved by its Lincolnian character," Morison predicted the speech would be "treasured as one of the greatest American orations for its form, content, and sincerity."[12] He maintained with increasing hyperbole that "no President since George Washington entered office with a greater bank of goodwill in which to draw, at home and from abroad." Everyone "liked Ike," even those who did not vote for him. The "British and European soldiers and statesmen who had met him during the war or as head of NATO, felt that he understood their problems," Morison observed, and "even the Soviets seemed to thaw a little" when he succeeded Truman.[13]

The "mood of affirmation and consensus" created by the election of war hero Eisenhower encouraged many historians to follow Morison in his optimistic predictions for the future. As a group, American historians came to believe "that 'everything would be all right,'" Morison wrote, that the disillusionment that had hung over the profession like a pall for so many years would now give way to a burst of sanguine light. With the "Korean War concluded, budget balanced, no more starry-eyed visionaries in the top ranks of government, or crypto-communists in the lower echelons, [and] no dubious characters from city wards slinking in and out of the White House to 'fix' things," he noted, the stage was set for the revitalization of historical writing in America. A president "tested by battle, intellectual enough to head a great university, strong enough to bang the heads of service chiefs together and work out a defense policy that the country could afford" could inspire by his very example a new commitment among historians to the study of national character rather than national dissent. If Eisenhower's "historic role" was to be a "restorer of peace and order after an age of violence and faction," then according to Morison, his "role as historian" involved restoring comity and consensus to a profession racked by political conflict and divergence.[14]

Eisenhower and National Character

Part of Morison's consensus historiography consisted of offering readers examples of American heroes whose lives exemplified the imposing dignity of national character and simultaneously refuted the antiheroism of debunking dissenters. Not surprisingly, after 1953 Morison replaced the fallen MacArthur with Eisenhower as the major heroic protagonist in the *History of the United States Naval Operations in World War II*. In volumes 9, 10, and 11 of the Naval series, he described Eisenhower as a supreme leader who could make decisive military decisions and who stressed unity and balance of command. Noting that the general was committed to "real unity of command and centralization of administrative responsibility," Morison applauded Eisenhower's efforts to overcome the "national prejudices" that made consensus in joint, international military operations so difficult to achieve.[15]

In volume 9, *Sicily-Salerno-Anzio* (1954), for instance, Morison elaborated the special difficulties faced by a supreme commander in Europe. In contrast to MacArthur's command in the Pacific, where the United States "called the tunes to which a single enemy had to dance," in Europe, America "had a very important ally, and two major enemies" to consider. Needing to reach compromises with the British on all major initiatives on diverse battle-fronts, Eisenhower was required to generate a level of international cooperation that even under peace conditions would have been unprecedented. His task was made still more difficult because the Americans and British disagreed on the most basic features of war planning. Both agreed only that the Allies needed to take the offensive in 1943 to relieve the eastern front for the Soviets, but they could not come to a consensus on where that front should be. The British wished to attack the Axis in its "soft-underbelly," through the Mediterranean and up the boot of Italy, in Greece, and in the Balkans. But American strategists believed that a frontal attack from England was the only way to defeat the German armies and resisted almost every proposal to divert forces to the Mediterranean. It was mainly Eisenhower's responsibility to devise and implement a war plan that could reconcile these alternative visions, and, according to Morison, it was to his great credit that he was able to do so. "The two teams were like two steeplechasers," Morison wrote, "the one [British] concentrating on leaping the next obstacle, the other [American] thinking mainly of the last stretch and taking each fence in his stride." The British viewed Americans "as impatient amateurs in the art of war, who happened to have the 'arsenal of democracy' at their disposal and so must be humored," whereas Americans

FIG. 6 *Harvard's historian taking notes on the installation of Nathan Pusey as Harvard's twenty-fourth president, October 24, 1953. Courtesy of Emily Morison Beck.*

viewed the British as "reluctant to assume great risks." Despite "an almost complete cleavage of opinion," Morison noted, Eisenhower convinced both sides to display a "comradeship in arms" that "was remarkable." Under his urging, Roosevelt agreed to attack Italy from Tunisia at Sicily and the British acquiesced in a fall 1943 target date for Operation OVERLORD—a cross-channel attack on the European mainland.[16]

As Supreme Allied Commander, Eisenhower encountered many of the same problems MacArthur faced in the Pacific, not the least of which was how to balance and unify the disparate branches of the American Armed Forces. In the Pacific naval gunfire support had proven crucial to amphibious landings. In the Italian campaign, however, Army officers still resisted the use of naval gun power for land bombardment and wished to relegate the Navy to transport duty. Because Army officers hoped to surprise the enemy with its amphibious landings, they argued that prelanding bombardment would be counterproductive, but having witnessed the effectiveness of the naval barrage off the African coast during Operation TORCH, Eisenhower convinced the Army to give up its "ancient prejudices" against this form of warfare. Eisenhower also showed strong leadership in dealing with the bickering between sailors and soldiers that often occurred in joint military operations. In Operation HUSKY, for instance, GI's attacking the island of Sicily by amphibious landing came under enemy fire and therefore left the unloading of equipment to Navy personnel who followed in subsequent assault waves. Navy officers, however, believed it was their primary duty to maintain their ships at a safe distance from the shore, not to unload Army equipment. "Officers of the naval beach party and the Army Engineers shore party rode up and down in jeeps bellowing orders which made slight impression amid the uproar," Morison noted, and supplies moved too "slowly" for those fighting on the beachhead to make use of them. In some cases the "rabble" took over as "untrained and insubordinate . . . rejects from combat units . . . devoted their energies to rifling soldiers' barracks bags and the personal baggage of officers." Much to his credit, Morison wrote, Eisenhower disciplined these errant troops (some received court-martials) and once again maintained order and unity by sheer force of character where division and disagreement had reigned.[17]

Eisenhower also had to deal with the Army Air Force, which had proven very rebellious in the Pacific. According to Morison, the Army Air Force was "trying to prove that air power, alone and uncoordinated, could win the war." From this isolated position, he added, the Air Force "almost managed to prove the opposite." When Navy admirals asked for planes to protect shipping, for instance, often the requests were refused because Army Air Force officers did not believe it was their duty to support ground or naval forces at a beachhead. Meanwhile, when this reluctant branch of the services did choose to fight, its efforts were tragically inadequate. "The Army Air Forces, as usual at this period in the war, were not always discriminating in target selection," Morison wrote of the HUSKY campaign.

In one instance, sacred "[c]hurches were damaged or destroyed, many noble buildings gutted, and civilians buried under the ruins of their dwellings" by inaccurate bombing raids. In another instance, the Air Force ill-advisedly attempted a parachute troop landing in a region undergoing Allied bombardment, and sixty pilots and crew were killed. When the Air Force failed to contend adequately with the German *Luftwaffe* at Salerno, Eisenhower took charge of the Air Force and "saw to it that they provided close support to ships and ground troops." Making "prompt and resolute" decisions in the face of confusing disputes among the branches and the Allied strategists, the general managed to save what might otherwise have been a disastrous Italian campaign.

In volume 10, *The Atlantic Battle Won* (1956), Morison shifted his attention to submarine warfare but continued to emphasize the need for a coordination of service branches. At the beginning of the war, antisubmarine warfare was "decentralized" and ineffective, Morison noted, as the Navy bickered with the Army Air Force about who should have priority in attacking U-boats and British convoys fought with American ones for right of passage. Eventually Allied leaders settled on a policy of carving up territories and responsibilities and protecting these with a balanced defense system that drew on the strengths of all Allied forces. The key was a balanced approach to warfare. "Carrier-borne aircraft" must depend on "a ship as a roving base," surface "hunters" needed to be "led to their quarries by air reconnaissance," and Navy vessels were required to act "as U-boat bait for land-based aircraft as well as warships," Morison argued. Meanwhile, the Germans demonstrated the consequences of failing to unify. Goering (head of the *Luftwaffe*) and Doenitz (head of the Navy) feuded constantly to the detriment of the German war cause. "The portly Reichsmarschall did not care to build up the Grossadmiral's prestige at his own expense," Morison noted, and failed to provide air support to fend off American planes attacking German U-boats. Furthermore, the German Navy failed to keep the Army informed of the status of the war in the Atlantic, so that German prisoners captured in North Africa and sailing to America acted on false rumors "that U-boats were sinking practically every Allied ship in the Atlantic." What the German military machine lacked, in short, was a figure like Eisenhower to serve as a reconciler of interservice disagreements and to coordinate the various aspects of the international Allied assault.[18]

According to Morison, the defeat of the U-boat in Atlantic waters was crucial to the final phase of European operations; without it Operation OVERLORD could never have succeeded. Therefore, Morison wrote volume 11, *The Invasion of France and Germany* (1957), as a final tribute to Eisenhower's commitment to unified military strategy. The volume centered on the general's leadership abilities as demonstrated in the famous D-Day invasion of June 1944. In the spring of that year, Eisenhower called a conference of all Allied commanders at St. Paul's School in London to discuss Operation OVERLORD. Admiral Deyo described the meeting to

Morison: "As we took those uncompromisingly hard and narrow seats, the room was hushed and the tension palpable. It seemed to most of us that the proper meshing of so many gears would need nothing less than divine guidance," since a failure "could throw the momentum out of balance and result in chaos." Not surprisingly, the first to speak was Eisenhower, and his balanced assessments and "quiet confidence," according to Deyo, "dissolved . . . the mists of doubt." When Eisenhower finished, Deyo remarked, "the tension was gone. Not often has one man been called upon to accept so great a burden of responsibility," he added, "but here was one at peace with his soul."[19]

In masterminding OVERLORD, Eisenhower faced great challenges in not only balancing the disparate parts of the American military machine but also reconciling British and American concerns. A considerable amount of backbiting took place in the organizational stages of the operation. The British accused the Americans of failing to supply adequate landing and beach craft for OVERLORD, "or, as it was sometimes put, starving NEPTUNE [the British name for OVERLORD] to fatten the Pacific Fleet," Morison noted. There were further disagreements about the number of troops each would supply. But most of all there was a dispute about the starting date. The Americans insisted on the late spring of 1944, while the British hoped to put the inevitable off still longer. Target dates were selected for June, but uncooperative weather and contrary tides on the first target date forced Eisenhower to delay the operation. The general recognized that another delay meant not only that security might be breached, but that OVERLORD would have to be abandoned altogether, since the Germans would have had time to prepare the coast of Normandy for invasion. Yet pushing ahead in bad weather could be disastrous. On June 5, 1944, Eisenhower met with his forecasters, listened to arguments on both sides, "paused a moment, and at 0415 June 5 made the great decision—'O.K. We'll go,' he announced."[20]

This was the most strategic decision Eisenhower ever made, Morison argued. Had he delayed two weeks for the next possible June landing (given the tides), the weather would have been so violent that any attempt to land would have been in vain. Employing his considerable talents as a dramatic writer, Morison attempted in volume 11 of his series to convey the emotions of the soldiers and sailors under Eisenhower's command as they approached Normandy on D-Day. As he had done in his description of Columbus's first sighting of the New World in *Admiral of the Ocean Sea*, Morison slipped into the present tense to increase his reader's sense of participation in the drama of the event. "The sky is still overcast and the wind a fresh NW, but the sea is moderating," Morison wrote. "As far as the eye can reach, the Channel is covered with ships and craft 'fraught with the ministers and instruments of cruel war,' the small ones tossing and heaving, the great ones steadily advancing, all destined for a part on the great D-day." Placing the readers on board ships "that have already reached the Far Shore, awaiting eight bells to usher in D-day," he recorded the "instinctively hushed" voices of the Allied troops. "Every bridge is dead quiet, but the atmosphere is alive with emotion," he added. "Men feel a quiet exaltation, something more than confidence, as though the Admiral of Heaven were directing and reassuring them." Citing Deyo's description of Eisenhower's inspirational leadership, Morison concluded, "There were indeed things so remarkable in this crossing as to suggest divine guidance."[21]

Eisenhower continued to shine throughout the remainder of the Allied operations. Morison noted with admiration that after the D-Day invasion, the general successfully advanced his troops under strong resistance to the interior of Germany and compelled the nazis to surrender. On July 13, 1945, two months after negotiating the important armistice treaty, Eisenhower officially disbanded his staff with an emotional farewell speech. "[W]ith an aspiration that he is still endeavoring to fulfill as President of the United States, as I write these words eleven years later," Morison concluded, Eisenhower remarked, "It is my fervent hope and prayer that the unparalleled unity which has been achieved among the Allied Nations in war will be a source of inspiration for, and point the way to, a permanent and lasting peace."[22] It was this hope and prayer for unity that had compelled Morison to support Eisenhower in the election of 1952 and to project him as the embodiment of the ideal national character in the *History of the United States Naval Operations in World War II*.

Imbalances

Despite Morison's enthusiastic response to Eisenhower's career as a soldier, Ike never developed into the president he had hoped for. In fact, Morison eventually concluded that despite his "genial character and transparent honesty," Eisenhower "failed in the historic role cast for him." Peace and order were not restored abroad during his administrations, nor were violence and faction quenched at home, primarily because Eisenhower "disliked politics and politicians and attempted to leave sordid questions of patronage to others." Organizing his administration "somewhat like a military staff," the former general expected men below him "to work out in detail what needed to be done." Although Eisenhower recognized that the president had to make the ultimate decision in both political and military matters, "he disliked doing any preliminary thinking about it himself," according to Morison. In the military this worked well, since someone had to be the strategist and theoretician, but in politics this form of organization was disastrous. "Contradictory recommendations would come to him on defense and other matters from two or three different departments, each already watered down while passing up from lower echelons," Morison explained. The president would simply return the differing recommendations and ask for a consensus on which to base his decision. Therefore a decision was almost always a compromise, "and often a wishy-washy one," he concluded.[23]

Eisenhower's failure to maintain consensus within the nation was demonstrated further by his inability to secure a consensus on either domestic or foreign policy. In addition, the president made some unfortunate cabinet choices that hindered his leadership abilities. Eisenhower's selection for Secretary of the Treasury, George M. Humphrey, was not, in Morison's estimation, a "good team player" and even attacked Eisenhower's "balanced budget" proposals publicly. Humphrey was unable to work with other branches of the government as well, and, according to Morison, could bring no consensus, even within the government, to the issues of the economy. Despite these failures, Eisenhower showed an uncharacteristic unwillingness to dismiss this insubordinate subordinate or to rescue his balanced budget proposal, and consequently he helped precipitate several recessions during his eight years as president. In foreign policy, Eisenhower was still more irresolute. New nuclear imperatives rendered much of his considerable military knowledge obsolete, and Eisenhower was forced to choose among a bewildering range of foreign policy options. Morison and others had assumed that the president would follow the "symmetrical" approach to foreign affairs he had employed so effectively during the war, maintaining a mobile military striking force large enough and balanced enough to respond wherever foreign crises arose with implications for Americans. But this strategy was opposed by proponents of "asymmetrical response," who wished to impede enemy aggressions throughout the world by threatening "massive retaliation in spots chosen strategically by the United States." Hoping to cut the armed forces budget by $5 billion, Secretary of the Treasury Humphrey lobbied political leaders to support a defense strategy based on "the deterrent of massive retaliatory power." While Eisenhower "veered between the two points of view, seldom taking a strong stand," he tended to favor the Humphrey plan. This obligated him to a role as "world policeman with no big stick," Morison wrote, with "only the big bang of the A and H bombs" at his disposal, "which he dared not use, well knowing that he would spark off mutual destruction."[24]

By implementing this asymmetrical approach with inconsistency, Eisenhower's Secretary of State, John Foster Dulles, compounded its errors. Dulles reasoned that a reduced military establishment could not support the French in Dien Bien Phu in 1954, and thus the United States would be abandoning Vietnam to the Communists, unforgivably Morison argued. When Arab nations denied Israel access to the Suez Canal despite a protest from the United Nations in 1956, Morison added, Dulles acted with "incredible gaucherie and stupidity." Morison considered Nasser of Egypt "an Arab Mussolini" with "the same rolling eyes, calculated rages, lust for power, and contemptuous disregard for treaty obligations or international law." Americans should have joined UN forces in seizing the canal from Nasser, but afraid to make the Suez crisis the test case for his theory of "brinksmanship," Dulles capitulated. Eisenhower, the man who had made his reputation as a fighter, was equally passive and claimed that America was "committed to a peaceful settlement of this dispute, nothing else." This capitulation encouraged the Russians, who "hinted at dropping atomic bombs on England and France" if they supported a UN initiative against Egypt. "The Eisenhower administration piously proclaimed that it had prevented the outbreak of a world war," Morison noted, "but Russia's threat to start a war on this issue was a mere bluff that nobody dared call on the eve of a presidential election." The politics of the Humphrey-Dulles-Eisenhower team "were far short of heroic," he concluded.[25]

The U.S. leadership reacted similarly in 1956 when Hungary revolted from Soviet rule. "Here again was opportunity for resolute action to support freedom and justice," Morison noted. But, again, Eisenhower "muffed it," doing no more than declaring that the "heart of America goes out to the people of Hungary." The heart of America "was not enough," Morison wrote, with growing contempt for Eisenhower's passivity. Ironically, the man who had endeared himself to Americans through his willingness to take intelligent risks in war now found it impossible to "act boldly." The Eisenhower administration "did nothing about Castro, refused to enlarge the Korean War, . . . dropped Indochina into the Lake of Geneva, let our allies down and flinched from Russian threats over Suez, ran away from Hungary, and apologized for the U-2," Morison noted with chagrin. "President Eisenhower called the personal story of his first administration *Mandate for Change*," he wrote, but "the historian is entitled to ask, 'What change, except in men?'" "There was little change in domestic affairs," Morison pointed out, because "basic New Deal measures were continued and even enlarged upon," while in foreign affairs "there was the same cold war challenge. . . . Russia, China, and Egypt called the tunes to which [the Eisenhower-Dulles] team responded as best they could."[26]

Morison's research for the *History of United States Naval Operations in World War II* might have provided him with some advanced indication that Eisenhower was a better general than a politician. In the fall of 1953, Morison visited President Eisenhower in the White House to get information for his volumes on the European theater of the war and was privy to an exchange that suggested the former general's inability to deal with politicians such as British Prime Minister Winston Churchill. Churchill had been politically motivated in his resistance to an early cross-channel attack, Eisenhower argued, since he wished to draw the fighting away from England and make the eastern front the center of combat. "Churchill sought always to impress the military with the need for political considerations," Morison quoted the president as saying at the meeting, whereas Eisenhower felt the Army's job "was to fight and win, and not always be encumbered by politics in doing so." Many British generals such as General Alexander "sided with us," Eisenhower told Morison, "but wouldn't stand up to Churchill." Once

Churchill's mind was set on an operation, it was nearly impossible to dissuade him, he added, even with sound military advice. Whenever Eisenhower himself tried to intervene in this politicking, he was, by his own account, soundly rebuffed by Churchill. At the Casablanca conference, for instance, Ike asked Churchill what he thought the overall Allied strategy was, and (according to Morison's notes) he "was as much told it wasn't his business," to which he supposedly replied, "so, you just want to fight, eh. Well, we can find plenty of places to do that!" Eisenhower's inability to control the political machinations of Churchill in World War II, in short, foreshadowed his political ineffectiveness as president.[27]

Despite Eisenhower's failures, however, Morison hoped history would be kind to the two-term president. He later wrote: "[L]et us not be too critical of President Eisenhower. At a relatively advanced age, devoid of political experience, he was elected largely as a symbol of what Americans admired, and he retained their confidence to the end." When he took over the presidency in 1953, the nation was characterized by "malaise and hysteria; he left it with the country's morale restored and prosperity assured," Morison wrote. "These intangibles, apart from any positive accomplishments, make Eisenhower's eight years in the presidency memorable," he concluded.[28]

Morison was generous in his final assessment of Eisenhower because he could sympathize with the president's difficulties in dealing with politicians, particularly Winston Churchill. In fact, in writing the *History of the United States Naval Operations in World War II*, Morison had also had direct run-ins with the British prime minister. In the late 1940s Churchill began his own multivolume history of World War II, *The Second World War*, which became a formidable competitor to Morison's series. Although he recognized that Churchill's history was different in scope and purpose, Morison nonetheless feared that the prime minister's work might duplicate and eclipse his own. These fears were confirmed in the worst possible manner when the first installments of *The Hinge of Fate* (volume 3 of Churchill's series) began to appear in the *New York Times* in 1950.[29] Reading Churchill's description of the attack on Pearl Harbor, Morison became suspicious that the British leader had used volumes 3 and 4 of the *History of the United States Naval Operations in World War II* as his primary source of information without acknowledgment. A second installment in the *New York Times* on the Battle of the Coral Sea confirmed his suspicions.[30] In his descriptions of the events of the Pacific war from 1942 to 1943, Churchill borrowed heavily and almost exclusively from the *History of the United States Naval Operations in World War II*, with "no acknowledgment or hint that he might have obtained this from me," Morison complained. Outraged at what he viewed as a violation of his copyright, he penned a letter to his lawyers inquiring about possible recourse: "It is transparently clear to me that he obtained all his information from my volume IV, of which he made a very accurate and intelligent digest," Morison protested. Of course, "anything I write is free to all subsequent historians to quote from or use, and I don't wish any claim against Winston Churchill," Morison informed his lawyers, "but ordinary courtesy dictates some sort of acknowledgment."[31]

Morison's indignation grew when Churchill's volumes not only topped the nonfiction best-seller's list but were also awarded the Nobel Prize in literature. His lawyers had written Churchill's American publisher, Houghton Mifflin, requesting recognition of the prime minister's debt to the *History of United States Naval Operations in World War II*, but they received only a promise of a small acknowledgment in the preface to any subsequent editions.[32] Without making reference to any specific obligations or sharing credit for his Nobel achievements, Churchill merely noted in the preface to the volume: "I wish to acknowledge my debt to Captain Samuel Eliot Morison, U.S.N.R., whose books on naval operations give a clear presentation of the actions of the United States Fleet."[33] In turn, Morison congratulated Churchill with ironic praise in a piece for the *Saturday Review Gallery*, noting with obvious reference to the prime minister's borrowings that the "entire historical profession is honored in the honor to Sir Winston." He went on to compliment Churchill as a "great historian" who wrote with "verve, style, honesty [and] imagination," but he did not fail to remind readers of Churchill's considerable debt to other historians, especially himself. "Turn to *The Hinge of Fate* [Volume IV], on the Battles of the Coral Sea and Midway," Morison noted, and one will find numerous examples of his "superb craftsmanship." Churchill "boiled it all down from one of my own volumes—and handsomely acknowledged his debt in the Preface," Morison wrote with tongue in cheek, adding with false modesty, "I could never have done it so well myself."[34]

Morison understood that Churchill's volumes were likely to remain more popular than his own, since they were written for the lay person by an important participant in the events and were soaked through with Churchill's forceful personality and powerful political visions. No professional historian could deny their worth. "[I]f any historian, British or American, won't join in the cheer," Morison wrote, "let him be condemned to sit forever in a college library, reading Ph.D. dissertations." Yet Morison believed that Churchill's volumes suffered from some of the excesses of amateurs such as James Truslow Adams and Van Wyck Brooks. For one thing, Churchill was not "impartial" or even "objective" in his volumes, because he "was too close to events, too much a part of them" to render unbalanced historical judgment. An advocate of participatory history, Morison nonetheless argued that an eyewitness observer of history must maintain his or her neutrality, which Churchill had failed to do. In addition, Churchill "had neither the time nor the staff to sift everything to the bottom," as Morison had done for the *History of United States Naval Operations in World War II*. Consequently, "some assumptions of the time are accepted as facts, when the facts turn out to be different," he noted.[35] Hence, Morison implied, Churchill's *The Second World War* would inevitably be surpassed by other histories with a greater sense of balance and judgment (like his own series), books less likely to win the Nobel Prize for literature but perhaps more valuable as scholarly contributions in the long run.

Given this attitude toward Churchill's *The Second World War*, Morison had every incentive to distinguish his interpretation of events from that of the British politician turned historian. Comparing important issues related to the prime minister's activities in the European theater as treated in both histories suggests that Morison did just that. While Churchill portrayed himself as a compromiser in Allied strategy sessions, the Churchill who emerged in the pages of the *History of the United States Naval Operations in World War II* was a pushy statesman who aggressively pursued his own positions at the risk of the entire war effort. Churchill demonstrated his considerable skill as a politician, since he frequently got what he wanted, Morison noted, but he also betrayed his lack of understanding of military strategy and war policy. The picture of Churchill that emerged was, in short, a complete contrast to the Eisenhower who appeared in vivid portraiture in Morison's naval histories. Ike was a brilliant military figure but only a fair politician who found it difficult to stand up to the likes of Churchill. What was needed in war as well as peace, of course, was a balance of the two, a broad consensus on political and military strategies. To function in a cold war world, public leaders needed to dissolve the dualisms that contributed to misunderstanding and conflict in themselves and among other nations. Consensus required not only recognizing "convergent cultures," "national characters," and a "comity of nations," Morison noted, but it also demanded a leadership corps broad-minded enough to appreciate their amplitude.[36] In their single-minded visions Eisenhower and Churchill were historical holdovers from a period in which exclusivity of thought and egocentricity of vision embroiled the world in a devastating international war.

Balance was what Morison believed the *History of the United States Naval Operations in World War II* had over *The Second World War. Mesure* did not necessarily win Nobel Prizes, but for Morison his rewards came in providing objective history for a generation of Americans born during the war years. "There is no royal road for a young historian to acquire a sense of balance," Morison told students who would one day have to decide between Churchill's and his own methods, although "a becoming humility toward his fellow workers, and skepticism toward himself as toward them will be of assistance," he noted. These were the qualities Churchill lacked. In failing to acknowledge his debts and in attacking those who opposed his interpretations, the former prime minister had violated the principles of balance that required the "national historian to give credit to other nations for forces and ideas that have influenced his own" and impelled "him to do justice to movements and personalities that he instinctively dislikes."

Honest criticism was necessary, Morison noted, "but the bad taste and worse temper" of Churchill and other "contemporary English historians" was "deplorable," he concluded, since it violated the consensus on which so much of the past and future depended.[37]

Administering History

*Richard Bates, William Halsey and
the Conspirational Aspects
of Consensus History*

13

Anticommunism and the Conspiracy Theory

Because of his strong stand on behalf of a deeply conservative historical tradition, his belief in a symmetrical approach to foreign policy, and his aggressive attitude toward the Soviets, many assumed that Morison subscribed to the conspirational theory of history at the heart of much consensus historiography. Put simply, the conspirational theory suggested that the Soviets, who had been aggressively acquiring satellites in Eastern Europe, would not rest until a world revolution had been achieved at the expense of democratic institutions; that Communists were penetrating to the highest levels of government in the United States and infiltrating labor unions; and that a conspiracy was afoot to begin a sweeping revolution in America by tearing down the apparatus of capitalism. The answer to this threat of revolution, many consensus historians argued, was to reaffirm the unanimity of democratic values and to pursue a vigorous anticommunist crusade against those who would challenge the hegemony of those values in their histories.[1]

The anticommunist crusade took many forms within the profession. A lively debate ensued in the early fifties about whether membership in the Communist party ought to disqualify a historian from college teaching. One of Morison's former students, Samuel Flagg Bemis, removed his name from the membership rolls of the American Association of University Professors when the organization refused to endorse a policy of automatic dismissal for professors who were members of the Communist party. Richard Hofstadter refused to criticize the University of Washington for dismissing avowed Communist professors. "I dislike these Stalinists so," he argued, "and I wonder what they would do for us or to us if they had control of things." Other members of the profession complied with special congressional committees when asked to "name names" of historians engaged in promoting communist ideas. Daniel Boorstin, for instance, testified at length about his activities as a member of the Communist party from 1938 to 1939 and implicated various of his associates in Party ventures. He testified that his conversion away from communism had been completed by the postwar period, and that he now used every opportunity as a writer and classroom teacher at the University of Chicago to profess his faith in consensus historiography. "I have . . . attempt[ed] to discover and explain to students, in my teaching and in my writing, the unique virtues of American democracy," Boorstin avouched. "I have done this partly in my Jefferson book [The Lost World Of Thomas Jefferson], which, by the way, was bitterly attacked in the Daily Worker as something defending the ruling classes in America," he added, "and in a forthcoming book called The Genius of American Politics." At Harvard, a proposed appointment for Sigmund Diamond was blocked by the dean of the faculty on the grounds that, unlike Boorstin, Diamond had refused to "name names" or affirm his commitment to the American consensus.[2]

Hofstadter, Boorstin, and other anticommunists within the profession presumed Morison was a kindred spirit. He had certainly used the language of anticommunism to good advantage in his attacks on Beard in the late 1940s. In "History Through a Beard," for instance, he condemned Beard's commitment to a "worker's republic [where] labor requited and carried on in conditions conducive to virtue." Referring to Beard's "Fabian" vision, Morison suggested that his nemesis was inspired, in part, by "the Communist propaganda against an 'imperialist war.' " In addition, he noted that while Beard himself was not a Communist, his dialectical materialism "repelled men of good will from written history and turned other men, including many not of good will, to Communism." Those of Beard's friends who "did not go Communist are now rather lonely," he concluded. Furthermore, Morison argued that Beard's "frame of reference" was vaguely subversive, since it "is the only kind [of history] that historians are allowed to write under a dictatorship." George Orwell's Nineteen Eighty-Four "gives us a glance" into the future projected by Charles Beard's historiography, Morison noted in "Faith of an Historian." In the "totalitarian England" of Orwell's "imagination, so horribly like Russia of today that it makes one shudder," he maintained, "the government keeps a corps of writers constantly at work writing new histories to replace the old, at every turn of its policy." In Beard's future historical world, Morison argued by analogy, "[n]ational figures associated with liberalism or democracy are either smeared or, like Trotsky under the present Red regime, ignored as though they had never been."[3]

In addition, Morison, like Boorstin, appeared to cooperate with congressional investigations into the un-American activities of former members of the Communist party. Morison testified by affidavit, for instance, in the famous Alger Hiss case of 1949, a trial that fed the conspirational fears of Americans who worried that communist agents had penetrated the inner sanctuaries of American policymaking agencies. Morison was asked to present evidence because Whitaker Chambers claimed to have met Hiss several times at a Peterborough, New Hampshire, home that had once belonged to the Morisons. Chambers gave the FBI a description of the premises, including a depiction of the driveway leading up to the house from the main road, which he had used for his rendevous with Hiss. From the account, Morison presumed Chambers was lying, since the Morisons had closed up the driveway from the main road years before and built a second one leading from a side street. Reasoning that Chambers probably had given the FBI a description of the house from some old photograph or postcard sold in the village, Morison concluded that "naturally a man [Chambers] who has been a Communist a good part of his life does not drop the habit of lying for a good cause."[4]

Morison was outspoken in his belief that Communists had "infiltrated" the government. In a series of lectures delivered to Canadian audiences in 1955 and entitled "Freedom in Contemporary Society," Morison talked at length about the negative influence of a group of Communists who had penetrated key departments of the government, including the Treasury, State, and Defense departments. Communists in Russia and China had subjected thousands of people to hard labor, imprisonment, and execution, he remarked, and "we know perfectly well that they would do the same . . . in the United States, if they could." To those who wished to offer Communists "the safeguards of liberty when their object is to kill liberty," Morison issued a rhetorical rejoinder based on recent events in Eastern Europe: Should we give the Communists the opportunity to attain power by legal means when Communists do not extend the same freedoms to their constituencies? The "celebrations of V-E Day were not over" before the "iron curtain fell, and Czechoslovakia, the democratic republic formed in our own image, . . . was subverted by communists who had been accorded full civil rights," he stated. Unwilling to simply allow the Czech example to repeat itself in the United States, Morison argued that something must be done to protect democracy against communism, and that historians must take the lead. He could not agree with the old relativistic warrior Carl Becker, who had written that communism was bred of paranoias and inconsistencies within democracy itself. "It seems to me that this is a flabby fallacy, of the same class as that one which says that society is the guilty party to an individual's crime," Morison argued, "or that the Treaty of Versailles was responsible for Adolf Hitler."[5]

"Nor am I one of those who call the anticommunist crusade of the decade 1945–55 a 'witch hunt,' hysterical though much of it has been," Morison claimed. "There were no witches in 1691 or any other time, but there are real communists in 1956." Morison agreed with his former student Samuel

Bemis that the anticommunist crusade should extend to the classroom. Communists were not entitled to civil rights, so long as they denied them to others, he argued, especially "communists on college faculties." Although his colleagues raised a collective eyebrow over such pronouncements by the man who had once led the fight against teachers' oaths, Morison continued to maintain that a university should not protect "an enemy to freedom of learning, if one be found in its midst." He was willing to make some concessions to prior members who had reneged their affiliations to the Party, but he maintained that no academic position should be granted to any current or ex-Communist unless "reconversion" was complete, since membership in the Communist party indicated a "defect in character or feebleness of intellect." Morison even approved of the self-scrutiny anticommunism had produced on college campuses. "[T]here has been too much screaming about [McCarthyism] in academic circles of the United States," Morison argued, and "too little examination of conditions within the university."[6]

These and like statements convinced many of his colleagues that Morison had acquiesced in the common anticommunism of the day. Howard Beale claimed that Morison's conservative and elitist historiography caused him to fear the unconventional, to stifle dissent and radical politics, and to prohibit freedom of academic expression. In an address before the American Historical Association, Beale claimed that Morison and other consensus historians had encouraged the efforts of McCarran and McCarthy and had made history a mechanism for "social control." To illustrate his point, Beale cited the 1952 presidential address of the American Historical Association of Conyers Read, the inspiration for which he attributed to Morison's 1950 address. According to Beale, Read had learned from Morison to spout the administration's gospel that historians must use history to serve democratic and national ends. Where "the facts will not serve such ends," Read "insists we should suppress the facts," Beale summarized, adding with disgust that "social control over what historians write is justified since the value we believe in must be defended even against historical assault." According to Beale, this kind of logic encouraged the historian to reject "the very values he should seek to protect," for in arguing so, Read and Morison were "advocating what on a large scale . . . the USSR has done to the destruction of all freedoms." Following the consensus path down the road to anticommunism, he concluded, would destroy the historian's usefulness as a seeker "after truth."[7]

Despite his concerns for the "palpable threat" of communism, however, Morison disagreed with critics who characterized him as a rabid anticommunist or a simple mouthpiece for the administration. In fact, he was quick to point out that where necessary he had condemned the government's handling of the matter or deferred from the "consensus." While painting a threatening portrait of communism in America in *Freedom in Contemporary Society*, for instance, Morison sketched a still more sinister image of an America darkened by prejudice, repression, and intolerance. Despite the dangers of a "red menace," he argued, a still greater hazard resulted from the reactionary methods used to deal with communism. "We need constantly to . . . ask ourselves whether the proposed remedies are not worse than the disease," Morison wrote, noting that attempts by the Truman and Eisenhower administrations to meet the crisis within the framework of democratic government had succeeded only in menacing political freedoms in the United States. Governments of, by, and for the people "are not free from the danger that the people themselves, in times of insecurity, will forget their basic principles and override all historic rights and immunities," he argued. Such an occurrence would jeopardize the worth of democracy as a political system and would constitute an ironic abandonment of the nation's historical mission. "What use to defend our liberties by such means as will destroy them?" he asked.[8]

Morison was particularly disturbed by the growing size and power of government agencies established to control the spread of communism. Concerned about the "mushrooming growth" of "administrative bodies" necessitated by the McCarran Act and Truman's Federal Loyalty Program, Morison feared the "menace of a bloated and irresponsible administrative arm" more than he feared communism itself, and he remonstrated particularly against Eisenhower's antidemocratic measures. Ike's security checks and purges, which resulted in the firing of 6900 "security risks" in seventeen months, represented an unconscionable and "pusillanimous catering" to McCarthy, he claimed, and required assigning functions that might have been exercised locally in the hands of the state. Morison was concerned personally with the extended reach of administrative arms into the teaching profession. Noting sarcastically that communism was rare among college professors since "many of them are not bright enough to know what it is," he argued that campuses should be self-policed by school officials who operated without the scrutiny of authorities outside the university. Some states had passed laws forbidding the discussion of communism in the curriculum or preventing libraries from purchasing books by Communists, but Morison argued that such legislation deprived professors of "one of their best means of curing undergraduate 'pinkos,'—making them read a few hundred pages of Karl Marx and discuss them!" These were hardly the sentiments of a liberal-minded educator; nonetheless Morison reasoned by a kind of inverse and ironic logic that government needed to allow a college community the freedom to restrict the freedoms of its own members.[9]

Morison was especially disappointed that Eisenhower, a former college president, had not taken a stronger stand in defense of the autonomy of universities. Except for a half-hearted indictment of "book burners" in an address at Dartmouth College, which "was about as effective as a speech against witch-hangers in Salem might have been," Morison argued, the president had done virtually nothing to safeguard institutions of higher learning from the "menstruations" of demagogues like Joseph McCarthy.

Since most Americans disliked intellectuals, they did not mind seeing professors "insulted and browbeaten by some lowbrow jack-in-the-office," he wrote, which made it the president's responsibility to combat the "ugly anti-intellectualism" of McCarthy.[10] This was especially the case with regard to the efforts of federal "heresy-hunters" who viewed rooting out Communists from academic institutions as their prerogative. In January of 1955, for instance, a "subcommittee of a subcommittee of a subcommittee of Congress" investigated a supposed "communist cell" at Harvard. One of Morison's colleagues, Dr. Kamin, refused to acknowledge the authority of the committee to inquire into university affairs and was cited subsequently for contempt of Congress. Although Morison did not question Congress's rights in the matter, he was appalled by the histrionics and the anti-intellectualism of the government's "star witness," Joseph McCarthy, who "prepared to enjoy another Roman holiday with the modern setting of flash bulb photographs and an applauding mob." Although the judge ruled in favor of Kamin, Morison feared similar investigations of Harvard faculty members would lead to further encroachments by federal authorities into the university's internal affairs.[11]

Morison soon discovered, with frighteningly personal implications, that his fears of authoritarian excess were justified. Beginning in the early 1950s, the attorney general's office produced a list of subversives and sent congressionally approved inquisitorial teams "trotting about the country, allegedly to gain information on subversive activities" but really to initiate "a series of 'star chamber' proceedings, in which all legal safeguards to a defendant are ignored." Morison was "astonished" to find that his name had been included in a privately compiled list of "Harvard Red-ucators" for the "crime" of having made a donation to a society headed by Dr. Cannon of Harvard for the relief of Spanish war orphans. Remembering his experiences at Fort Devens in World War I, Morison protested vehemently against the vicious practice of "publicity-made inquisitors . . . blacken[ing] the good names of good citizens almost at will." Arguing that the attorney general's list had become "a touchstone for disloyalty and sedition and a means of 'making hay' for professional red-baiters," he complained that if a professor so much as "attended cocktail parties where communists were present, or had a communist friend, or belonged to a communist club twenty years ago when he was in college," he was presumed to be a threat to national security. Although in the end, Harvard and Morison withstood the efforts of McCarthy sympathizers to intrude on university affairs, Morison warned that the university must vigilantly "guard against fighting fire with fire, as that mischievous old saw recommends, which in this era means fighting communism with the weapons of communism, so that in the end neither they nor we will retain the armor of liberty."[12]

Morison's qualifying statements regarding the anticommunist crusade caused some to view him not as a rabid anticommunist, but, interestingly, as a subversive and communist sympathizer. An editor at the *Chicago*

Tribune, for instance, included Morison with Alger Hiss in the category of "Egotistical, Arrogant, Eggheads of Harvard and New Deal Fame" who gave him "a Pain in You Know Where."[13] It was ironic that the *Tribune* would describe Morison as antiauthoritarian, since the paper had so vehemently condemned his affiliation with the government during the war years. The transition in editorial approaches reflected not only the emergence of a Republican era after twenty years of Democratic dominance but also the *Tribune* readers' growing faith that postwar government was committed to protecting rather than threatening American liberties, a faith they could not muster during the Roosevelt and Truman administrations. For his part, Morison explained his shift in attitude toward government by a parallel but reverse logic. Whereas once the federal system had been dedicated to preserving traditional freedoms and had existed in proper balance with local and private concerns, he maintained, it had now insinuated itself on all manner of private and public institutions and had produced imbalances in the national mind.[14]

That Morison found himself at odds with the "consensus" view revealed an important aspect of its historiography. Consensus was an ephemeral concept, capable of assuming multiple personalities and as whimsical and transient as the American people themselves. If one were willing to adhere slavishly to administrative authority, of no matter what stripe, then consensus could prove a lasting and persuasive psychology. But if conditions changed so as to disaffect one from the majority, or if the majority itself came to question the agencies and processes responsible for the control of consensus, then it must have only a limited appeal as a historical tool. Indeed, the potential for a "consensus" historiography to alienate its former supporters was immense, as witnessed by Morison's disaffection with the Eisenhower administration in the mid-1950s. His gradual retreat from activities that had formerly contributed in significant ways to his professional identity also suggested his disillusionment with institutional authority. After 1953, he never again participated in any vital way in the activities of the American Historical Association,[15] and, in 1955, he decided to retire from Harvard even though he was permitted, by university rule, to continue teaching for at least two more years.[16] After forty years of college teaching, Morison ostensibly withdrew from his classroom duties to allow himself more time for scholarship, and his last lecture was received by colleagues, friends, and students with an appreciation moving enough to suggest that both he and they would regret the severing of bonds. But his Harvard retirement was also part of a general withdrawal from the "leading institutions in society and those who were their spokesmen." Universities, like governments, preferred "official versions" of events, and Morison had grown weary of the intrusions on time and thought that his university affiliation required.[17]

No better example exists of Morison's desire to distance himself from traditional agencies of authority, however, than his effort to alter his relationship with the Navy in writing the final volumes of the *History of United States Naval Operations in World War II*. Once a commissioned officer literally on the government payroll, he became, after 1955, a potential litigant against the U.S. Navy, seeking to modify his contract, to gain greater control of his staff, to safeguard his literary rights, and to assert his opinions independent of Navy brass.[18] In reconfiguring his affiliation with the Navy, he sought not only to address practical matters that had grown increasingly irksome to him after more than a decade of work on the *History of United States Naval Operations in World War II* but also to liberate himself from the institutional associations that had made him, in the eyes of many readers, little more than a fawning spokesman for an increasingly fragile consensus.

The Enemy Within

If conspirational theories of history implied doubts about the stability of consensus, then increasing problems with the production of the *History of United States Naval Operations in World War II* induced paranoic feelings in Morison that a broad-based scheme was afoot to discredit his series. A number of reviewers had conspired from the beginning to disparage the work as the prosaic offering of a "court historian," of course, but since the mid-1950s, a more insidious form of criticism had emerged. Its source was within Morison's naval staff, and the criticism ensued from mild complaints by project contributors that they were not getting due credit for their work on the series. Within the first few years of the enterprise, for instance, Morison lost the services of two aides who were dissatisfied with their yeoman's chores and irritated by the minimal recognition they received for their literary outputs. "[T]wo of the young officers attached to me left in rather a huff," he noted, because they believed "they were being deprived of expressing their own creative powers." Disturbing as these rumblings of discontent were, however, Morison dismissed them as the annoying whines of inappropriately ambitious officers. "I have observed," he added spitefully, "that they have not been able to publish anything since they left."[19]

Other complaints had a more telling effect on Morison and the progress of his series. He was particularly vulnerable to the charge that he was not giving due credit to researchers for the considerable work they had done. Students in History 68, Morison's Harvard course on the history of the Navy, were frequently assigned research projects from his file of unfinished work for the *History of United States Naval Operations in World War II*. Although the course was theoretically open to all Harvard students and papers could be written on topics from the eighteenth century to the twentieth, it frequently became a seminar comprising just a few ex-Navy officers who wrote papers on topics including "Putting up DEs in Mothballs," "Tactical Use of Picket DDs in Fast Carrier Groups," and "Training in Anti-Submarine Warfare during the Concluding Months of the War," which later appeared in chapters of the naval history.[20] The adaptation of the work of several Ph.D. candidates created still more controversy. Philip Lundeberg's Harvard dissertation written for Morison was adopted almost wholesale for use in volume 9 of his series.[21] Bern Anderson also earned his Ph.D. under Morison, who relied heavily on his student for a wide range of materials that later found their way into the naval history. A memo to Anderson from the operational files of Morison's staff suggests the level of Anderson's involvement in every phrase of volume 11.

> I have just completed reading your "Dragoon Buildup & Planning" and am very pleased with it. I intend to drive down to Newport someday the week of the 30th to talk to you about it. In the meantime, could you explore a couple of questions with available material:
>
> 1) Why did Churchill [insist] on his Balkans project . . . It seems which ??? Brittany ??? It seems to make no sense at all—indicates some deepset prejudice against Southern France landing.
>
> 2) In order to show how impractical his Balkans project [was], can you assemble some material on the Ljubljana gap as to width of the valley, highest altitude one or two track railroad, two or three or four lane road, how many miles to Budapest, how many miles to get over mountains and debouch into the plains. Have you any evidence that the British had a definite plan for that operation. If so we might get a look at it in London.
>
> . . . Also how did the deployment of the troops landing in southern France fit in with Ike's overall plans for penetrating Germany. He did consider them indispensable, did he not? And what did Monty think about it?[22]

Although neither Lundeberg nor Anderson voiced any complaint about these tasks or challenged Morison's liberal borrowings from their written reports, others questioned the ethicality of relying heavily on student assistants who received only minimal credit for their work.

Commander Jim Shaw, for instance, asked the question that Lundeberg and Anderson could not in light of their doctoral obligations to Morison: "What credit do I receive and in what volumes?" Disappointed to learn that his work would be acknowledged only briefly in the preface to any volume, he worried that employment on Morison's staff would bring no "advance in writing reputation." His fears were confirmed by the Navy's response to his application for a professorship at the Naval War College. Given "rough treatment" by the "line officers" at the War College because of his lack of scholarship, Shaw could not convince them that the *History of United States Naval Operations in World War II* was in part his own work. "[R]egardless of how valuable the history is to the Navy," he complained to

Morison, it amounted to a form of "professional retrogression" for him. Shaw's proposed plan to make his work on the naval history more professionally serviceable to him failed because of Morison's intervention. Shaw asked if Little, Brown would permit him to write a one-volume compendium of the naval series once the fourteen volumes were finished.[23] Morison presumed that they might but acknowledged his prior claim to such a volume. It was Morison rather than Shaw who eventually produced the one-volume synopsis of the series entitled *Two-Ocean War*.[24]

Roger Pineau's contributions to several volumes were so substantial that he was told in private by Morison that if he had been resident at Cambridge during their production, he would have been recommended for a doctorate.[25] In researching the tank battle of Gelsa in Italy, for instance, Pineau plotted the resting place of nearly every spent shell on a gridded chart of the region, interviewed numerous participants in the battle, contacted historians and researchers also working on the Gelsa campaign, and spent time on weekends driving far into the country on a Sunday to take an oral history from a veteran of the engagement. Pineau had done the kind of work that at least one assistant before him "had left up in the air" because "it was beyond his abilities," Morison noted.[26] Yet Pineau received only passing credit for these contributions, and he was eventually forced to resign from work on the series because he could not live on his salary as a civilian assistant.[27]

Henry Salomon, a member of the staff since the middle of the war, had similar complaints about Morison. In 1947 he left the project to help produce "Victory at Sea"—a massive BBC production designed to provide a visual account of naval operations in two oceans in World War II. With a musical score provided by Richard Rogers and a text derived extensively from Salomon's work on the *History of United States Naval Operations in World War II*, "Victory at Sea" received international recognition.[28] Its success, however, instantly embroiled Salomon in controversy with his old boss. In the first place, Morison believed he was entitled to an honorarium because the film used material acquired on behalf of the naval history. Salomon objected to such payment at first, but a threatening letter from Morison's lawyers convinced him that a $5,000 honorarium was in order.[29] Second, Morison objected to the wording of the film's introductory frames, which announced the script's author as "Henry Salomon, collaborator in the fourteen-volume Bancroft-prize winning *History of U.S. Naval Operations*." In an indignant letter to Salomon, Morison argued that "By S. E. Morison" should be added to the announcement, or "Morison's" inserted before the title. "Already I have heard a lot of ribbing about 'Salomon's naval history,'" he informed his old employee, "and while that sort of thing won't hurt my reputation, it will certainly not help you."[30]

When the unaltered attribution persisted in a prospectus of the BBC documentary, Morison became more agitated. His anger boiled over when this prospectus encouraged a reviewer for the *MacFadden Magazine* to assume that Salomon "wrote fourteen volumes of the *History of U.S. Naval*

Operation, received the Bancroft Prize, and was decorated by the Secretary of the Navy for it."[31] Referring to Salomon and others as mere "research assistants," Morison announced that he had been "over-generous" in describing them as collaborators in his prefaces and that, in turn, they had grown "a little too big for their boots." To those unfamiliar with the *History of United States Naval Operations in World War II*, Morison argued, the BBC prospectus made it appear as if "Victory at Sea" was coauthored by Salomon, an impression that "simply creates ridicule and contempt for a pretentious young man," he noted. Claiming that the BBC was "either too dense or something else to admit that they are misrepresenting both Salomon and myself," Morison petitioned the General Counsel of the Navy Department to prepare a formal letter of protest against the broadcasting company.[32] Meanwhile, Morison's personal lawyers in Boston renewed his objections to the prospectus, announcing that when Salomon "describes himself as collaborator in the whole series of the Naval History volumes, without even mentioning Professor Morison as the author or even suggesting that there was a principal author, you can be sure that Mr. Morison is very bitterly upset."[33]

Finally, Morison's fears of a broad-based conspiracy were fed by the efforts of individuals loosely affiliated with the series who sought to sabotage it in one way or another. These included various members of equivalent historical staffs in other service branches who were compiling their own histories of the war. The Marines, the Air Force, and most prominently, the Army, were preparing multivolume histories of their own, and they had frequent recourse to each other's research. Morison was perceived as uncooperative by these other service historians, in large part because he refused to participate in various cross-service symposia on military history organized by the American Historical Association.[34] One of these historians, G. W. Prange of the Army Historical Staff, was particularly resentful of Morison. Because he had served under MacArthur's direct command, Prange was enraged by the portrait of the General that appeared in the *History of United States Naval Operations in World War II*, and "not only set up roadblocks to our research efforts in Japan," according to Roger Pineau, "but in some instances literally lied to Morison." Prange confided to his colleagues in related service branches that if the Navy's historian was not interested in cooperating with the Army, then he "wasn't going to write Morison's history for him."[35]

In light of these and other staff difficulties, the Secretary of the Navy appointed an outside committee of historians to report on the department's "Historical Organization and Programs." Authored primarily by chairman Allan Nevins, the committee report claimed that there were noteworthy "deficiencies in the program." Referring to the *History of United States Naval Operations in World War II*, Nevins noted that "Morison has published the best, single record of operations in a modern war in the English language, and other useful books have been issued. But quantitatively the amount of publication has fallen below that of the Army." Nevins concluded that the Navy had "not given the operational services all the stimulus and instruction for which they can legitimately ask nor has historical work as a command function in the fleets been kept at the level desired." Nevins expressed the committee's hope that the Navy would use all its resources to facilitate Morison's work by increasing not only the size of his staff but also the administrative support for it. Greater attention from high-ranking naval authorities would go a long way toward putting out the various brushfires that had been started by various disgruntled officers in Morison's employ, the report implied.[36]

Ironically, the Navy had earlier tried to exercise greater authority over the *History of United States Naval Operations in World War II*, but Morison had blocked such efforts. As in the case of the anticommunist crusade, he felt that using the authority of the Navy too aggressively would be like prescribing the proverbial remedy that was worse than the disease. For all the inconveniences of having to deal with students, low-ranking officers, and civilians, Morison could avoid being too closely associated with the strong administrative arm of the Navy by maintaining a calculated space between himself and the "Navy Brass." Hence, when Secretary Knox originally proposed that the naval series be given a staff of dozens of men on a scale commensurate with Army efforts and that the Navy's historical department be intimately involved in the project, Morison objected. "Instead of building up a large staff, as I was invited to do by Secretary Knox," he wrote, "I have kept my staff to a minimum," thus avoiding the historical equivalent of the "bloated and irresponsible administrative arm" that had so hampered national politics in the 1950s.[37]

Throughout the writing of his series, Morison made a special point of emphasizing the gap between himself and "official" Naval authority. When Captain Mundroff, head of the Military Requirements and Development Bureau, wrote to complain about the opinionated nature of the *History of United States Naval Operations in World War II*, it was cause for Morison to celebrate his independence as a scholar. Unconcerned that the captain's "philosophy of history differs diametrically from mine," Morison proclaimed in an unusually blithely manner that "historians have a duty to voice opinions." History "is not uncontrovertible . . . [it] is not a mere narrative of events," he proclaimed, adding that "the value of judgment influence[s] the selection of facts" and that "the more dryly factful a history is, the fewer readers it has." Eschewing the strict "objectivist" position with which he had been identified for years, he noted that President Roosevelt chose him to write the history of the U.S. Naval operations because he knew that Morison "would insist on raising opinions and making judgments after due consideration of the evidence and deference to people" who knew more about the subject than he did. "That I have done," he concluded. No relativist, he insisted that none of his historical evaluations were "glib or offhand," since they were "all based on careful consideration of the evidence and usually on extended conversations with officers who were involved." But he also wished to make it clear that he was no mere mouthpiece or spokesman for an official Naval point of view.[38] When a Japanese translator who had been hired by the Navy described Morison in an essay as a "pro-Roosevelt" historian, Morison was "so disturbed" by the comment he considered firing the man. Morison was a historian "with a capital H," Roger Pineau wrote the translator on behalf of his commander, "interested only in the truth" and disdainful of "the partisan viewpoint."[39]

Whenever the high-ranking Navy officers attempted to interfere too much in the operations of his small staff, Morison reacted with predictable fury. Director of naval history Edward Kalbfus was a particular source of irritation in the beginning. Although busy preparing reports for Congress on the Navy's role in the Pearl Harbor affair, Kalbfus insisted on overseeing many of the administrative details of the Morison history as well. One staffer complained to Morison while Kalbfus was at sea that Kalbfus was "extremely opinionated," "[a] very tough man to deal with," adding with apprehension, "I am keeping my fingers crossed, and hope the Admiral maintains his distance and does not meddle into work."[40] This hope proved ill-fated. When other members of Morison's staff attempted to acquire the services of a cartographer without passing the paperwork over Kalbfus's desk, the director erupted. "We were summoned before the August presence," one of Morison's personnel wrote, "and he amplified his remarks to me about keeping my nose out of administrative business which was not my concern." The conference with Kalbfus was "as you would expect a monologue punctuated by our 'yes sirs,'" and "a copy of sound military decisions was found on the desk and spread out for our edification." It was a demeaning example of the "great and good father lecturing the little boys in the ways they should go and reminding them not to repeat their errors," he complained.[41]

Morison refused to tolerate these intrusions for long. "Old K is so damn unpredictable," Morison wrote by way of apology to his employee. "I know too how unenthusiastically disturbing these outbursts are having experienced them myself both in academic life and (more often than you would suspect) in my brief naval career," he noted, acknowledging that from "the number of naval officers who have used me as a whipping post I have reached the doubtful consolation that everyone in the Navy has his Kalbfus to bear."[42] After struggling with Kalbfus for several years, Morison eventually achieved his autonomy by influencing a decision to replace Kalbfus with an old friend, John Heffernan. Morison presumed that a Heffernan-Morison partnership would allow him the freedom he desired, but unfortunately Heffernan's tenure was cut short by an imbroglio. Heffernan was reprimanded because he had discharged a civilian historian who was making little progress on a project for the Navy and "transferred elsewhere some military members of his office staff who were conniving with the said historian in these practices." Subordinates claimed that Heffernan was hard to work for and that his "house-cleaning" had been motivated by personal animosities. A Navy investigation presumably confirmed these assertions because shortly after being appointed director of the history division, Heffernan was relieved of his command.[43]

While Morison was unable to save his friend's job, he was able to exert considerable influence on the replacement selection. Morison informed authorities, for instance, that if Heffernan were relieved of duty, he would "try to carry on the history of naval operations under almost any other director whom the Navy might appoint, except Captain Karig." Karig, who was the coordinator of the Navy's *Battle Report* publications—strategic command analyses for World War II—had always resented Morison's work for the Navy and had actively campaigned against it. "Captain Karig's attitude and actions, against me and my work have been such that I could not, consistent with self-respect, continue the history of naval operations under him as a director," Morison wrote the search committee for Heffernan's replacement. "I should have to relinquish [the project] after the present volume," and "the Navy's contract with Little, Brown & Company, who pay all costs of publication and pay the Navy a royalty, would then be voided" if Karig were appointed.[44] This threat was never carried out since Karig was not given the position, but in having made it, Morison declared his willingness to abandon his connection to the Navy if his history could not be pursued in accordance with his terms of operation.

Nothing suggested the degree to which Morison wished to distance himself from the authoritarian aspects of naval history more than his relationship with Admiral Richard Bates, author of a tactical equivalent to Karig's reports entitled *Evaluation Battle Plan, 1942–1945*.[45] Bates had a reputation for being an exhaustive researcher as well as an expert on tactical affairs. During World War II he had been the "energetic" head of staff for Admiral Oldendorf in the Philippines, and, according to Morison, Bates's tactical genius was a major factor in the Allied victory in the South Pacific.[46] In his presidential address before the American Historical Association, "Faith of an Historian," Morison paid tribute to Bates's "awesome scholarship," noting that the admiral had spent two years producing a four-hundred-page monograph on a naval engagement that had lasted only forty-two minutes.[47] Yet Morison also recognized that Bates's compulsive thoroughness made young officers under his command feel that their work was "esoteric and irrelevant" and ultimately prevented Bates from completing his assignments. "Skilled, honest, and laborious," Morison noted, the admiral never quite appreciated the futility of trying to provide an exact "blow-by-blow study" of even one battle in the war in the Pacific.[48] "[F]or want of records sunk or lost, for lack of knowledge of what individual sailors, Japanese and American, out of the some ten thousand engaged, thought, felt, and did," even the meticulous Bates "could produce only an approximation of what happened on that tragic night."[49] Although the early volumes of the *History of United States Naval Operations in World War II* benefitted from Bates's research, therefore, Morison could not postpone the history of the latter years of the war while waiting for Bates to complete his *Evaluation Battle Plan* volumes.[50] In a review of volume 8 of the *History of United States Naval Operations in World War II*, Admiral Robert Carney castigated Morison for not adopting Bates's painstaking methods or checking his conclusions with the knowledgeable tacticians working on projects like the *Evaluation Battle Plan*.[51] Noting that if "we waited for Rafe Bates we might have to wait for years," Morison reminded Carney that while "the Bates method is fine for professional use," it "would tire and disgust general readers for whom my work is written."[52]

Although Bates and Morison were good friends and in general had a tremendous respect for each other's work, Bates occasionally revealed his disgust with what he perceived as Morison's willingness to compromise thoroughness for the sake of producing books quickly. Referring to Morison's work as the "Official-Unofficial History of Naval Operations in World War II," Bates's staff was under strict instructions not to accept Morison's interpretations as fact. Occasionally Bates would display what one of his staff described as an "incredible wrath" at Morison's "too-ready acceptance of the validity of documents provided by Japanese commanders in the War in the Pacific." In one instance he cleared the desk of an assistant in anger when he discovered that the officer had used Morison's facts without testing their accuracy. Bates especially disliked that much of Morison's research was adapted from oral histories and testimonies taken from witnesses sometimes years after events. On his office wall was a sign that said "the smallest note on a scrap of paper is more reliable than the finest memory," and as a staff member recalled, Bates' own "compliance with the dictum was sometimes awesome." If naval officers embellished accounts of their own actions in military engagements years before and the facts suggested otherwise, "the wrath of Bates could be frightening."[53]

Numerous altercations with the authoritarian arm of the Navy confirmed Morison's belief that he needed to maintain a tactical distance from those in higher echelons of command. As in the case of anticommunism, he recognized that failure to address the major and minor conspiracies at work in the offices of the *History of United States Naval Operations in World War II* might threaten the completion of the enterprise. Yet he remained committed to handling these problems without evoking the higher authority of the Navy or obligating himself to accept its priorities for his work. Fundamentally, both communism and the writing of the naval history boiled down to a matter of freedom. Just as he believed that Communists who recklessly attacked democratic institutions should be silenced, Morison believed that irresponsible historians should receive the same treatment. But, like the Communists, historians had the right to "exercise the freedom of speech, writing, and association that all citizens enjoy, without being molested or discharged" from their positions. And the right of free speech included "the right to be heard," Morison noted with antiauthoritarian voice. "[I]t is not much use, if you have something unpopular on your mind, to be told to go into the woods and tell it to the birds and the squirrels."[54] Freedom of expression must be encouraged even if at times it violated the prerogatives of the ruling consensus. The greatest threat to the principle of freedom, he argued, were not the objections of individuals in the dissenting minority but the excesses of administrative agents acting for the prevailing majority.

"A Son-of-a-Bitch Named Morison"

Morison's antiauthoritarian position had a marked effect on the *History of United States Naval Operations in World War II*. In the remaining volumes on the war in the Pacific he was far more outspoken about the inadequacies of the Navy, far more forthcoming about the personal agendas of naval officers, and far more willing to indict administrations (both military and political) for exacerbating the problems of war. "The temptation is strong to devote final comments on the battle of Leyte Gulf to a eulogy of the superb skill, heroism, and aggressiveness displayed by both sides, by all forces and groups, and by the individual seamen," he wrote in volume 12, *Battle of Leyte Gulf*. "Yet we should not cater to complacency; nor would it be honest to brush off errors on the ground that they were canceled out by what was done superbly well." According to Morison, the largest error in the Battle of Leyte Gulf occurred when Admiral Halsey of the Third Fleet was decoyed away from a strong Japanese surface force attacking the Seventh Fleet. Inferring from his pilots' reports that the major part of the Japanese fleet was coming from the North, and wishing "to deal the Northern force a really crushing blow," Halsey pursued without even leaving a patrolling destroyer in the area. "One might have been in the age of Drake," Morison noted derisively, adding that even "Lord Nelson would have left a frigate."[55]

Halsey's error was compounded because he had ignored the sound advice of three task force commanders who expressed their objections to his plans. The admiral's stubbornness in this regard was attributable to his old-fashioned thinking. According to Morison, Halsey believed in the need to destroy the enemy's fleet completely and considered that his peers in the Navy were exhibiting "undue caution and a lack of spirit" at Leyte. "[B]eing Halsey," Morison wrote, "he hoped very much" that the Japanese fleet "would come out to fight," and such naïve thinking caused him to be fooled by a diversionary tactic. In describing Halsey's "football coach" mentality, Morison said, "[he] hated the enemy with unholy wrath and turned that feeling into a grim determination by all hands to hit hard, again and again, and win."[56] "But for the bravery of the Navy flattop aviators and the gumption of Ziggy Sprague [Commander of the Seventh Fleet]," he concluded, "there would have been a Roman holiday in Leyte Gulf that day."

Halsey's "fumble" almost cost the Navy a major part of its fleet and months of progress in the war in the Pacific.[57]

Morison did not tone down his attacks in later volumes. In volume 13, *The Liberation of the Philippines*, Morison accused Halsey of making grave mistakes on matters of routine nautical procedure that cost lives and jeopardized strategy. Like the Japanese at Midway, Halsey's fleet was caught refueling at an inauspicious moment—in this case, during a typhoon. Refueling required ships to remain parallel to one another at dangerously close intervals, and thus they were vulnerable to enemy attack and bad weather. Photographs on the radar screens of Halsey's fleet should have indicated that a major storm was on the way. With the "appearance of an Edgar Allan Poe thriller," the photographs revealed "those confused pyramidal shapes characteristic of hurricanes," with wind velocities "reported over 100 knots in the gusts" and the seas "worse than the foulest epitaph can describe." When Halsey realized his mistake, he ordered a stop to the fueling, but he then committed an additional blunder by taking his task force directly into the eye of the storm. "They were in a worse state than Phoenician galleys blown off shore," Morison wrote, for unlike those ancient galleys, whose masters "had long since learned" to "heave-to, lie dead in the water, and let the ship find her way in the midst of the sea," Halsey tried to "argue with a hurricane" by steering into its center. Eight hundred sailors were drowned in the ensuing storm, and Halsey's hubris in the matter greatly angered Morison. "For some reason that goes deep into the soul of a sailor, he mourns over shipmates lost through the dangers of the sea even more than for those killed by the violence of the enemy," Morison wrote. The least he could do "for those brave young men who went down doing their duty on 18 December 1944," Morison maintained, was "to set forth at length the cause and details of the catastrophe, in the hope that it may never recur."[58]

In volume 14 of the series, *Victory in the Pacific*, Morison noted that Halsey again misread weather signs, steering his task force into a second typhoon. An official board of inquiry issued a strict reprimand after concluding that in the first instance Halsey had made an "error of judgment"; in the second instance, the Secretary of the Navy called for removing Halsey as task commander. High-ranking Navy officials discussed the matter at length, however, and dissuaded the secretary from issuing the removal on the grounds that Halsey "was a popular hero, and that such action would boost enemy morale." The Navy's reluctance to make an example of Halsey was contemptible, Morison asserted, because it sent a message to other commanders that reckless behavior would be tolerated as long as it was undertaken in pursuit of the dastardly enemy. It revealed not only naval administrators' unwillingness to control their own but also their lack of courage to challenge popular but imprudent heroes in the midst of an international crisis. Similar to the U.S. government's attitude toward Senator McCarthy and the anticommunist crusade, the Navy was reluctant to make a strong stand against a figure whose tireless struggles against "the enemy" remained popular with the people, no matter how brash, ill-considered, and ultimately tragic those struggles proved to be. The Navy's refusal to adequately discipline Halsey, Morison argued, was another example of an administration defending the indefensible behavior of an individual in order to obscure its own failings and inadequacies.[59]

When Morison's assessments were published in the late 1950s, they invoked a predictable reaction from Halsey and his various defenders in the Navy. Infuriated by Morison's portrait of him in the *History of United States Naval Operations in World War II*, Halsey met with high-ranking naval officials to complain about the work of their historian. "Ham Dow came in to see me last Friday," Halsey wrote in a letter to Admiral Carney, "and we discussed a son-of-a-bitch named Morison."[60] Halsey protested that the "so-called Naval Historian" condemned the strategic decisions of fleet commanders, while he, "in his high understanding and knowledge of the rather difficult subject of strategy, pontificates on what the decision should have been and spreads it for all to see." He particularly resented Morison's "attempts to prove the correctness of his strategical statements by the agreements he secured from [the] Japs" in interviews with enemy commanders years after the end of the war. The U.S. government "wasted much money on the education of many Naval officers throughout the years," Halsey quipped scornfully, since "Samuel Eliot Morison could have stepped in and done . . . better than the Americans trained as naval officers did."[61]

These complaints did not fall on deaf ears. As was expected, Admiral Carney defended Halsey in a review of volume 12 of the series. Arguing that the "complete elimination of the Japanese fleet" was a distinct possibility in the Battle of Leyte Gulf, Carney maintained that Halsey's actions might "have spelled 'finis' to the Nip fleet for the remainder of the war" if he had been successful. Furthermore, he renewed his complaint that the "source material for some" of Morison's "conclusions was obtained from junior personnel not familiar with command level appraisals and decisions."[62] Other officers and former members of Halsey's staff attending a lecture given by Morison at the Naval Historical Foundation also complained about the "very pointed manner" in which Morison referred to their admiral's "blunders." Asking for a transcript of the lecture, Halsey accused Morison of deceit and misrepresentation of facts in the matter. "I was told you stated that you have talked to me and discussed the Battle of Leyte with all the senior commanders who participated," he wrote. "I have no recollection of having talked to you in regard to this battle. If I am wrong, will you kindly refresh my memory and tell me the circumstances on when and where we talked?"[63]

Although Morison claimed that the transcript of his lecture was not readily available, he defended himself by reminding Halsey that they had spoken at service headquarters at Makalpa, Hawaii, in early 1945. Reiterating that Halsey himself had betrayed his eagerness to engage the entire

Japanese fleet in an old-fashioned slugfest, he paraphrased the admiral's feelings after the battle at having to give up this goal to support the Seventh Fleet in Leyte Gulf. "[You] afterwards told the writer," he noted, "that it was the only move in the battle for Leyte Gulf that [you] regretted."[64] Nor was Morison averse to confronting Halsey directly with blunt candor about his assessment of the battle. "As regards 'Halsey's blunder,' " he wrote, "I admit that I did use that phrase in summing up at the end, and that it was unfortunate," he noted with half-hearted apology; " 'error of judgment' would have been preferable, and I shall use that phrase in the future."[65]

Morison's refusal to back down to Halsey or his Navy defenders provided a further example of his antiauthoritarian point of view. Still the defender of national traditions and a forthright supporter of the Roosevelt and Truman presidencies, Morison nonetheless departed from the consensus view of the war on matters of administrative control. Where he found examples of abuse and excess on the part of civil and military authorities, he spoke out with increasing voice. In volume 15 of his naval series, *Supplement and General Index*, he questioned the military wisdom of the Navy's fast withdrawal from the Pacific after the war. With the example of Korea fresh in his mind, Morison noted that the "sudden cessation of hostilities created the urgent problem of 'getting the boys home,' and so much political and private pressure was brought to bear as to weaken very seriously the armed forces left in the area." Citing his postwar interview with General George C. Marshall, Morison noted that "it was not a demobilization; it was a rout." If the Navy had been more resistant to such pressures and more in control of its "misplaced sentimentality," subsequent military reinvolvement in the Pacific might have been avoided.[66]

But the best example of Morison's general suspicion of administrations came in his reassessment of the nuclear resolution of the war. In *Victory in the Pacific*, Morison continued to argue as he had in 1945 that the dropping of the atomic bombs was necessary for ending the war. Revealing some of his lingering cold war anxieties, he added that there was a need to end the campaign quickly since Russia would have insisted that Japan be "divided like Germany or Korea, if not delivered completely to the mercy of the Communists." Whether the Japanese could have been convinced to surrender quickly without the explosions over Hiroshima and Nagasaki "nobody knows or probably ever will know," he wrote. But he was now prepared to argue that America "overreacted" in its enthusiasm for nuclear devices. "Apart from the humanitarian arguments, which must be taken into account, against using the bomb," Morison noted, "was it not the possession of atomic weapons that contributed to the international tensions following the war? Can it be imagined," he added, "that Russia would have worked feverishly on nuclear development if we had simply tested the bomb and not used it?" This was a distinct retreat from his earlier defense of Truman's nuclear program and confirmed his theory about remedies and cures. The well-intentioned buildup of nuclear arms to prevent a Soviet presence in the

Pacific had backfired with the same predictability as had the stockpiling of administrative bodies for the purposes of limiting the threat of communism.[67]

Hence, after twenty years of work on what Morison later described as his "greatest challenge" as a historian, the *History of United States Naval Operations in World War II* came to its dramatic conclusion. Begun in the early forties under the watchful eye of President Roosevelt and as an alternative to the debunking relativism of historians such as Beard, the series was identified with a status-affirming culture of consensus. It was an open celebration of America's Navy, whose officers were "highly competent . . . in making decisions in a fluid tactical situation, the test of a great commander by land or by sea."[68] By the end of the 1950s, however, Morison was more inclined to note that mistakes had been made, mainly "due to excess of zeal in coming to grips with the enemy." While this was the most "pardonable kind of error," it was also the most dangerous, since it often led to what Morison described as a "my country right or wrong" attitude.[69] When authoritarian bodies such as the government or the military sought to rationalize such mistakes through an elaborate series of false justifications, they only complicated matters further, as had been the case in the efforts to curtail communism in the United States. By the late 1950s, Morison had moved from a strict consensus point of view to a mildly critical one, debunking heroes like Halsey where necessary, disassociating himself from the military historiography of professional bodies such as Harvard or the American Historical Association, and questioning the centrist interpretations of "official" naval historians such as Karig and Bates. Such criticism, halting though it may have been, indicated a new independent direction for Morison's work in the remaining decades of his life.

The Breakdown of Consensus

Henry Steele Commager, Alfred Knopf,
Daniel Boorstin and the "Personalized
Interpretation" of History

14

Vita Nuova

M orison and other historians attributed administrative abuses in the late 1950s to the efforts of authoritarian agencies to maintain order and control in a world characterized by rapid change. While it was possible in the decade after the war for these agencies to claim that a national consensus existed about the kind of world Americans desired, no such easy agreement emerged in the years in which Morison completed the final chapters of the naval history. Developments in his private life increased Morison's experience of the breakdown of consensus. In 1949, Morison had been "knocked off balance" by his reintroduction to a distant cousin, Priscilla Shackerford, "whom he had always admired, long loved, and finally won" through marriage. Twenty years his junior, this singer and Baltimore socialite radically altered his disposition by bringing him passion, variety, and "a light-hearted gaiety that he had never known." She introduced "music as well as laughter" into the 44 Brimmer Street house, he noted; and her "charm and social graces" expanded his "social sense of freedom." Most of all, she dramatically influenced his attitude toward his work. She not only encouraged him to write new and different works of history but also critically analyzed draft chapters and "greatly contributed" to Morison's "happiness and well-being while the work was going on." Without her he would be "just a retired gaffer . . . with no ambition to write, or do anything but ride and sail," Morison wrote in a third-person account some years later. With her, he became an inspired and transfigured writer who felt as if he had entered a new phase of his life. After marrying Priscilla, he felt "so fundamentally different in feeling and spirit" that he believed he had entered his "vita nuova," a "new life."[1]

If Priscilla's presence awakened Morison to an appreciation of imbalance, passion, and change, then it also burdened him for the first time with real financial troubles. Wishing to lavish on her the kind of material expressions of his love that he had not been able to provide his first wife, his savings dwindled rapidly. Not only did he pay Priscilla's way to Europe and Asia so that she might accompany him on all his research trips, he bought her expensive dresses for her singing engagements and contracted to have a comfortable summer home built for her at Northeast Harbor, Maine, called "Good Hope." Assuming that his fixed income (a $4000 pension from Harvard and $15,000 per volume for the Naval history) would be substantial enough for the couple to live well, Morison discovered to his chagrin that the high inflation of the 1950s drastically reduced his buying power and forced him to adopt financing procedures with which he was uncomfortable.[2] "I am glad to be able to enclose my check for $800 to complete payment on Mrs. Morison's seal-skin coat," Morison wrote a New York City furrier. "Never having indulged in installment buying before," he added with nervous humor, "this has weighed heavily on my conscience although I haven't actually stayed awake nights fearing that you would have to sleep on a Central Park bench in view of my financial delinquency."[3] In addition, Morison sold off some of his personal library to friends,[4] published an edition of his collected essays—"to cash in on" the numerous articles he had written for historical journals "and never got a cent for"—and even went on the lecture circuit for a brief stretch at the end of the 1950s in order to supplement his income.[5] "[T]he reason I rushed about and gave so many lectures at this time was mainly financial," he noted later, adding that although "many people assumed that [they] were rolling in wealth" because of their lavish life-style, these were actually "thin years financially" for the couple.[6]

A memorandum dated January 1, 1957, suggests the degree to which the financial needs of his "vita nuova" influenced his historical writing. In his New Year's resolutions, Morison developed a five-year plan of future historical projects designed in large part to alleviate his financial pressures. "Plans and schedules alike were dictated by certain very mundane considerations," he wrote; "to produce books that would provide us with income, to use my already acquired craft for maritime history, and to write on subjects that could be worked on at Northeast Harbor, and also require interesting travel." He first proposed to revive several pieces of unfinished work, which he hoped could be completed from old notes with but slight additional attention. One of these was a history of Harvard in the eighteenth century, a part of the tercentenary history that he had been forced to abandon under the pressure of deadline in 1936. He hoped, he wrote Priscilla, that Harvard would consent to rehire him for two years at his previous salary (about $16,000 per year) so that he might bring a sense of closure to the series.

FIG. 7   *Morison at the Podium. During a scholarly career that spanned nearly seven decades, Morison delivered literally thousands of lectures, not only to students, but in the years after his retirement from Harvard, to paying audiences. "The reason I rushed about and gave so many lectures at this time was mainly financial," he later admitted. Courtesy of the Harvard University Archives.*

Another proposed volume would be entitled *Journals and Other Documents on Voyages of Columbus*, which could be done expediently: "nine-tenths of the work was done before World War II," he wrote, "so with one-tenth more it can be finished." In addition, Morison contemplated an "easy and profitable" one-volume condensation of his naval series, entitled "The Two-Ocean War," which had first been suggested by Commander Jim Shaw several years earlier.[7]

Aside from these revisions and amendments of earlier works, Morison also sketched plans for several new works. He hoped to get permission to use the papers of John Adams so that he might write a biography of the former president that would be "the crown" of his "scholarly career and fairly profitable." He also planned to produce a one-volume history of the American people, which "we will depend on for future royalties," he told Priscilla. "I must start on it and make substantial progress this winter." And finally, he proposed a life of John Paul Jones, which would be "an anticipated best seller."[8] Such an ambitious schedule caused Priscilla to worry about her husband's health, with some justification, since later that year Morison would turn seventy. But he rationalized his plans by reference to their financial needs: "You must try to understand that I am not writing these books for conceit or fame, but for you," he explained. "*The Oxford History of the American People* we decided on after long discussion as the best means to assure you a steady royalty income in the future. John Paul Jones, ditto. These are contracted for and I could not back out now even if you wished me to and thought you would no longer need the money." Because of inflation, the decline in other sources of income, and their mutual desire to keep the Good Hope summer, she probably would "need" the money, he urged, and he, in turn, could benefit from the "continuity" such projects would bring to his writing. "I have arranged my work more intelligently than any other writer I know, so that we can spend summers at Good Hope and produce there under top conditions. There writing can be combined with healthy recreation." In closing, he reiterated to his wife that he had "*not* taken on more than I can do in the next five years, given good health and your love and understanding."[9]

Some of Morison's numerous projects were never undertaken. The Harvard Corporation refused to grant Morison a salary to complete the tercentenary history,[10] and the executors of the Adams papers would not allow him access to the materials he needed to write an adequate biography.[11] In the summer of 1957, he did begin work on the biography of John Paul Jones, however, and turned to it with the flurry of a man anxious to realize a quick and tidy profit from it. In between work on volumes for the naval history, Morison travelled to Paris to research some of Jones's letters in the Archives Nationales.[12] Later that year his diary revealed that he was doing "Heavy work" on Jones's part in the battle off Flamborough Head (the engagement in the North Sea during the American Revolution in which the naval hero supposedly uttered the famous lines: "I Have Not Yet Begun To Fight"), by "improvising a sort of war game board" on the floor of his living room to plot maneuvers. Ever mindful of his idol Parkman's techniques, Morison even followed the route of Jones's funeral procession through Paris to the cemetery where he was first buried in order to "convey a sense of it to the reader."[13] In little less than a year and a half of work, during time borrowed from other projects, Morison completed *John Paul Jones: A Sailor's Biography* and waited anxiously for the expected financial windfall.

According to the criteria by which he formerly measured success, *John Paul Jones* should have pleased Morison a good deal. Scholarly reviewers commented on the valuable service he had performed in describing with objectivity the man whose life had been the subject "of more romance and controversy" than that of any other American naval hero. Paying his "disrepects" to "chapbook historians," Morison had made a special effort to dispel the "fabrications" of pseudohistorians who had used countless "mythical sources" to write hundreds of "fictitious books" about Jones.[14] He confessed in his preface that he was slightly nervous about the reception of a book that sought to straighten out Jones's historical record. "It is much easier to write a novel about a complex character like Paul Jones than to write a biography," Morison wrote. After studying Jones for years, he still felt as though there were problems in his life that he had never cleared up. "It would have been so easy to set up an imaginary Jones whom I could 'know all about,'" Morison continued, but "I am an historian, not a novelist, and I feel I owe it to [John] Paul Jones's memory to write a true biography." In exorcising the "romantic" Jones from his story, he depicted a more dispassionate hero, one to whom even Emerson's dictum "Every hero becomes a bore at last" could be applied.[15] But when *John Paul Jones* received the 1959 Pulitzer Prize in biography, Morison felt vindicated in his technique from a scholarly point of view at least.[16]

Yet much to Morison's disappointment, *John Paul Jones* was never a financial success. The biography sold well in its first weeks and went into a second printing as quickly as most of Morison's other volumes.[17] But readers grew disinterested in the work when its deflating tone was widely discovered. Unlike reviewers for scholarly journals, critics in popular magazines despaired of its "emasculating" qualities. "In his closing chapter Mr. Morison writes: 'As Emerson well observed, 'Every hero becomes a bore at last,' '" noted one reviewer. "I think one can go further: a biography of a hero who becomes a bore at last is itself in danger of fetching up on boredom." In addition, the reviewer noted that although the book represented an exhaustive "feat of research," it was "a bit exhausting, too," tiresome reading for the average landlubber anxious to spice up his routine day with a bit of exciting naval heroism. Morison assembled "no end of data"—inventories of the provisions for Jones's ships, distribution lists of his prize money, and so on—but "is it literary art?" the critics asked. "I think not," answered one, who argued that the "aim of biography is not merely to record but to reveal." Noting that "[p]roportion is more illuminating than masses of detail," the reviewer asked, "What powered Paul Jones?" In Morison's biography "you read what he did but you don't know what he was."[18]

The insipid reaction of popular readers to the Jones biography was in part a function of its inability to capture the imagination. Unlike Morison's other Pulitzer Prize–winning biography *Admiral of the Ocean Sea*, this volume conveyed no intuitive sense that the author had identified with the subject. Having sailed in the wake of Columbus's voyages, Morison felt an empathy for the discoverer and used Parkmanesque techniques of tense manipulation and literary allusion to intensify these feelings. Although he visited many of the sites of Jones's major battles, Morison never achieved a "flesh and blood" portrait of his protagonist. The failings of *John Paul Jones* were owing as much to lack of time, perhaps, as anything else. Unable to spend the years necessary to clear up all the mysteries of Jones's complex life or to write in a more creative fashion, Morison had conceived of the project as a money-making proposition and had delivered the work to his publishers prematurely. He eventually regarded it as a literary stillbirth of sorts as well as a financial disappointment. "For all my work," he noted the year of its publication, "I am still many thousands in the red at the year's end."[19]

Editorializing the Past

Morison's financial anxieties had wide implications for his standing in the profession at large. He quickly developed a reputation for being a parsimonious negotiator of contracts, and he frequently antagonized publishers and editors by complaining too loudly of their stinginess in dealing with him. For instance, Morison offended the publishers of *American Heritage* by referring to their publication as a "leech magazine" when he discovered that he would be paid only $300 for a reprint of a selection from his naval series.[20] The *Encyclopedia Americana* took still greater umbrage at his refusal to write a five-thousand-word article on "Exploration and Discovery" for $200. Morison's comment that he would not even advise one of his assistants to do so comprehensive an article for that sum provoked the editors of *Americana* to note that many of its most respected contributors in the past—such men as Judge Joseph Story, Lord Rutherford, Hilaire Belloc, Admiral A. T. Mahan, Simon Newcombe—undertook to write encyclopedia articles as a form of public service.[21] Morison was unimpressed with the suggestion and wrote back testily: "About the year 1869 my grandfather wrote the general article on the U.S.A. for the 9th edition of the *Encyclopedia Britannica* for $100. But times have changed, and even invoking the great names of Justice Story and Admiral Mahan cannot persuade me to look upon your offer of $200 for a 5000-word article . . . as a 'Princely stipend.' "[22]

Morison also offended more recognized editors like Alfred Knopf, who contracted with him to produce a new edition of William Bradford's *Of Plymouth Plantation*. Difficulties between the two began when a bill for $300 for author's alterations made in the proofs was far greater than Morison had expected given the agreement he had signed. "Sam thought that to live up to that clause in the contract would be unfair to him," Knopf later wrote, since the Bradford "was a very special case" due to its size and complexity.[23] When Knopf balked, Morison lashed out, claiming that he would lose money on the first edition if such costs were subtracted from royalties. "Here he was in grave error," the editor wrote later, "for we had printed five thousand copies of the book, which bore a retail price of six dollars, and if we sold out that edition his royalties would amount to a great deal more than that nominal advance." Not wanting "to take an intransigent attitude toward an old friend" and his "favorite living historian," Knopf proposed to split the cost of the alterations.[24] Morison accepted the compromise, but he was hardly mollified. "All right; I accept your generous offer," he wrote, "but will you please arrange to have them taken out of royalties, as I am scraping the barrel at this time of year."[25]

This compromise did not end the disputes between the two. According to Knopf, Morison attempted to play too intrusive a role in the marketing and advertising of *Of Plymouth Plantation*. One November morning the head of Knopf's advertising department received a letter from Morison pointing out the "great opportunity" he was missing "for pushing the Bradford by failing to cash in on" some "free publicity the Pilgrim Fathers" were receiving during the Thanksgiving season. Not only was the movie *Plymouth Adventure* currently being shown at Radio City, Morison noted, but the Thanksgiving season provided a perfect seasonal "opportunity to sell a lot more copies," an opportunity that "should not be neglected."[26] Still smarting from his losses for corrections in proof, Knopf was resistant to the idea of pouring more money into the project. "There is no possibility of any publisher's being able to do for a book like the Bradford the things that you suggest," he wrote Morison. Not only was Knopf dubious about any tie-in between the book and the film *Plymouth Adventure,* which was based "on an altogether different book," but Knopf also added astringently that "nobody in his wildest dreams" could translate the "free advertising the Pilgrims received at Thanksgiving" into "sales of a $6.00 book of rather special kind."[27] Morison accepted Knopf's judgment but complained privately that "Knopf hasn't pushed the book at all vigorously."[28]

Morison's most acerbic language, however, was reserved for his collaborator on another important financial project, Henry Steele Commager. In 1928, Morison had taken Commager, "then a young and unknown scholar," into partnership to extend the coverage of his *Oxford History of the United States.*[29] The first edition of this collaborative project, entitled *The Growth of the American Republic,* came out in 1930. At first the work did not sell well, but in 1942 its sales jumped dramatically because it was "the only textbook that was not isolationist or pacifist." During the war, the "GAR," as they called it, "jumped to the head of the advanced United States history textbook field."[30] Morison received ten percent royalties on volume 1, covering material up to and including the Civil War, and Commager got a similar rate on volume 2. Such a royalty schedule meant that during the war, Morison and Commager each collected between $10,000 to $13,000 annually.[31] Morison greatly appreciated that income in the 1940s, but he came to view it as an absolute necessity in the 1950s.

Unfortunately for Morison, there was an inverse relationship between his need for royalties from *The Growth of the American Republic* and their availability. By the late 1940s, readers of survey textbooks had changed perceptively in their preferences for materials and philosophies. In the first place, Americans in the cold war era had lost their enthusiasm for "hawkish" interpretations. In his influential 1947 article, "To Take the Poison Out of Textbooks," Allan Nevins called for "a sharp reduction in the space given to war" in American textbooks and in "the emphasis, placed on war heroes." With Morison and Commager clearly in mind, he urged jingoistic text writers to give "peace development" a "correspondingly fuller treatment."[32] In the second place, *The Growth of the American Republic* seemed outdated, offensively so, to readers with a new postwar sensitivity to race relations in America. Students at City College of New York protested against the use of the Morison and Commager text because of its racist characterizations of blacks. "Sambo . . . suffered less than any other class in the South from 'its peculiar institution,' " Morison had written, adding that "[t]here was much to be said for slavery as a transitional status between barbarism and civilization." In defending himself to CCNY students, Morison compounded the problem by asking what was wrong with the "Sambo" stereotype. "[T]he Negroes were the most successful slave race; that is, as slaves, in modern history," he argued; "much more satisfactory, as slaves, I mean, than the Greeks, the American Indians, or any Oriental population. There must be some essential docility in their character that made it so." Statements such as this one convinced CCNY and other institutions to drop *The Growth of the American Republic* from required reading lists, triggering a noticeable decline in the royalty earnings of Morison and Commager.[33]

Morison was content to allow the sales of *The Growth of the American Republic* to drop off slightly while he had other sources of income, but with his retirement from Harvard and his increased expenditures with Priscilla in the mid-1950s, recapturing the textbook market became a high priority for him. He urged Commager to consider a revision of *The Growth of the American Republic*. "The GAR has become so profitable, (and I assume you find the 10–12 grand a year as helpful as I do) that we can't afford to let it peter out," Morison wrote his collaborator. "[M]erely because it's successful," he added, "some smart-aleck publisher will probably bring out an imitation that will be just different enough so there will be no infringement of copyright." In order to attract readers, Morison suggested that Commager "modernize" his second volume by covering the Truman administration "in some fashion," since "one of the great talking points of salesmen is 'right up to date.' " For his part, Morison offered to write new sections on pre–World War II diplomacy and to contribute sundry other chapters on both world wars. With hard work, he concluded, a new edition could be ready for the fall 1960 academic market.[34]

Commager was equivocal from the start. Evasive at first, he cited the many distractions, including travel and lecturing obligations, that would make undertaking the revision difficult.[35] When Commager finally did begin work on the volume late in 1959, his slow progress infuriated Morison and the editors at Oxford University Press. "Over a year ago you assured either me or the press that you were 'almost done' and would certainly be finished in 1960, and you produced chapters on Civil War for Volume I," Morison wrote angrily in the fall of 1960. Having declined many opportunities for speaking engagements and articles (including a $1000 article on Harvard Presidents for *Life* magazine) in order to fulfill his part of the contract, Morison was outraged by reports that Commager had taken a long vacation in Europe, written articles and reviews for the *New York Times*, and lectured from Maine to Minnesota, instead of concentrating on the revision. "Haven't you any sense of obligation to me, not to speak of the Press?" Morison complained. "Your casual attitude toward the GAR now dooms it to be ready no earlier than the fall of 1962, and if you continue to put pleasure ahead of duty, not until 1963." Complaining that they were "losing adoptions rapidly, owing to the supposed obsolescence of GAR," Morison contended with a deep sense of regret that their rivals were "digging in and getting the big royalties that ought to be fattening the coffers of the Oxford University Press and Morison & Commager." "This letter may make you angry," Morison concluded, and "I hope it does, as I am angry with myself for having trusted your promises instead of saying 'To hell with GAR, let it die, as Felix [Commager's nickname] won't pull his weight.' "[36]

Commager responded to Morison's complaints with heartfelt contrition but without a completed volume. His defense was a literary one, based on the contention that good writing required time and that publishers' schedules should be designed to accommodate writers, and writers should not have to accommodate publishing schedules.[37] But Morison was interested in royalties and began to scheme to produce a revised volume on his own. Noting that Commager was "an awfully nice fellow and we are good friends," Morison nonetheless complained that his coauthor had become "increasingly difficult" to work with, and he began to lobby for a divorce in the relationship.[38] Commager refused to relinquish any part of his claim to *The Growth of the American Republic*, however, asserting that "from the beginning," both men had "contributed equal amounts to the book."[39] Morison disagreed and continued to lobby for a divorce in the relationship. "What I want, and what I believe the Oxford University Press of New York people want, is an entirely new one-volume text written *by me alone*," he insisted. "I would like to do this as an almost sure money-maker for my old age," he added, "but Commager stands in the way." Asserting that Commager wanted a share in this writing and in the profits, Morison concluded, "I don't want him to, as I know by experience that that would mean my doing at least three-quarters of the work, and getting only half the profits."[40] But Morison's plans never came to fruition, and eventually the two authors were forced to add a third collaborator, William E. Leuchtenberg, in order to complete the revision of the second volume.[41]

In light of these developments, both Morison's financial anxieties and his penurious reputation grew. Oxford University Press published the first volume of the 1962 edition of GAR independent of Commager's uncompleted second volume, but Morison was still anxious to have an entire new edition. "Volume I is out, printed, in circulation; but it will be feeble support for our old age without its twin, Volume II," he wrote the beleaguered Commager. "This is a real cry of distress," he added, "Our competitors advance a pace" and the "faith of our adopters is almost shattered. Please do something at once."[42] Commager's defense that "it is more important that the book be as the authors want it than that it be a week or so ahead of some time or other," no longer carried weight with Morison.[43] With the GAR "growing less profitable every year," Morison even turned in desperation to the foreign market, authorizing his lawyers to secure whatever monies they could from threatened suits against copyright violations by foreign publishers.[44] *Das Werden der Amerikanischen Republik* appeared in Germany several years ago, Morison noted, yet "I am not aware of having received a cent in royalties." In addition, a "Spanish edition, engineered by the Nelson Rockefeller wing of the State Department during the war, has never appeared," he informed his lawyers. "And the other day an Italian named Morra told me he had made an Italian translation for a Florentine publisher, of which I had never heard anything. All these translations should be looked into, in my interests," he instructed.[45]

By 1962, therefore, Morison had acquired a reputation among publishers as a somewhat intimidating and irascible writer of history. Since the mid-1950s, his financial concerns had caused him to quibble with editors of encyclopedias, representatives of prominent trade houses such as Knopf, and friends such as Commager. Unwilling to suffer fools gladly, Morison could be especially brutal to young, inexperienced employees of publishing companies, such as copyreaders, whose "corrections," he claimed, gave him "more trouble than they are worth." One such young woman, just graduated from Smith, "demanded that I include Mark Twain in my account of the Emerson-Thoreau group," he noted with incredulity; others "bother me with pedantic mistakes such as putting accents on French words that have been anglicized." As he explained to Alfred Knopf concerning their tussle over the cost of alterations, "I am losing money correcting in galleys the copy-readers' errors."[46] Most of all, however, his obsession with pecuniary returns raised suspicions within the profession about his scholarly motives and his personality. Despite his contention that he never produced "potboilers" for rapid sale on the open market, some of his colleagues noted that his style had become "breezier and breezier."[47] They also remarked that the need to "produce in order to insure long-term financial security" had turned him into a "brusque" and "crusty" old man.[48] "It was the pressure to work, to get things done, paired with the need to have his way," wrote one more sympathetic contemporary, "which sometimes turned away the admiration of lesser mortals."[49]

The "Little Book" and the "Big Prize"

Despite his increasing reputation as a somewhat crotchety and avaricious historian, Morison remained to his closest friends a man with "a soft heart and a strong, almost childlike desire to be appreciated."[50] This need was demonstrated in 1961 when a convalescing Morison (he had contracted a virus in February) penned a short memoir of his boyhood for his friends and fellow Bostonians. Entitled One Boy's Boston, the "little book" was somewhat playfully submitted to Houghton Mifflin for publication, and the press accepted it with alacrity. Disclaiming any larger historical purpose for writing the memoir, Morison informed readers in the preface that he was "merely jotting down memories and impressions of childhood and boyhood in Boston, sixty-odd years ago" and recording "some of the people who passed through, or influenced" his young life.[51] Friends who read the slim volume delighted in the anecdotes Morison recounted and marveled at how expressive and forthcoming this presumably irascible and "taciturn" man could be. A highly personalized book, One Boy's Boston documented with candor the failings as well as the successes of Morison's extended family. Whether noting the infidelity of his Cousin Willy Otis, the social snobbery of his grandmother Eliot, or the political biases of his Republican relatives, Morison demonstrated his willingness to discuss the "shady episodes of family history," and he did not avoid the "personal quirks" in his own development. He not only recounted the horrors of his Little Lord Fauntleroy outfit, but he also included a photograph of himself in "love locks" and lace collars and laughed at his sensitivity to "pimples"—"the great cross" of his young life. One Boy's Boston evoked such nostalgia and hearty appreciation among his living friends, in fact, that several collaborated on a "20th Century Fox" parody of the work. With frolicsome sentimentality these friends suggested Joan Crawford for the role of Sammy's nurse, Lizzie Turner; Bette Davis as his mother; and Mary Pickford, who "volunteered to come out of her quarter-century of retirement to play the role of Sammy as Little Lord Fauntleroy."[52]

Despite Morison's assurances that there was no historical purpose to the memoir, One Boy's Boston reveals a good deal about his historical temperament in the early 1960s. Employing the "realist" methods of his favorite writer, Henry James, Morison described life as a boy in late nineteenth-century Boston with references to a wide range of sensory impressions. He recalled the "equine" flavor of his old Beacon Hill neighborhood, "the vast sweep of apple blossom in the late spring" at Beverly Farms, and the "old gas pipes in the Morison home" that occasionally leaked, leaving "always a faint odor" in the house. He remembered marking the night hours by sounds rising from Brimmer Street—until 10:00 P.M. "the street was filled with young people learning to ride the bicycle"; at 11:00 P.M. "the dog-walkers emerged," and then "the cats began their nocturnal concert." He also had acute visual memories of the "gaiety" created by the "varied colors" of the streetcar trolleys with their "fascinating advertisements." These visual recollections often triggered associated memories of taste. Riding in the trolley cars and reading the advertisements with his friends, Morison recalled, "our mouths watered at Deerfoot Farm's assurance, built around a picture of an attractive piglet, that its sausages were 'Made of Little Pigs and Choice Spices.' " Finally, Morison's boyhood evoked memories of touch and feeling. He recalled riding the "herdic," a miniature omnibus on two wheels, which seemed "to have been designed as a vehicular hair shirt." A ride on one of these contraptions "over cobblestones of downtown Boston," he recollected, "jolted the very teeth out of you."[53]

These sensory descriptions suggest how highly personalized Morison's historical vision could be. Even a consensus history of late nineteenth-century Boston would have required at least some discussion of certain divisive trends and influences that threatened the stability of urban life. In *The Growth of the American Republic*, for instance, Morison reported that the 1890s was plagued by "[p]roblems of housing, of sanitation and health, and of education," and he characterized Boston as one of several "breeding places for vice, crime, and epidemics."[54] Because *One Boy's Boston* is a subjective account of the Boston experienced by *one* boy, and because that experience is filtered through the mind of a boy narrator, there is little treatment of these matters in the memoir. The reader does not discover Boston through a complex matrix of sophisticated political and social analyses or deeply patterned psychological influences but rather through rose-colored and sometimes myopic glasses. A succession of people move in and out of the narrative, for instance, famous and not famous alike; but they are all treated as equal subjects of curiosity for a boy. Hence the indomitable Oliver Wendell Holmes is mentioned in nearly the same breath with another Harvard graduate, "a seedy character" who picked through the trash cans on the Common and reproved Morison once for saying "Yeah!" instead of "Yes." Morality in *One Boy's Boston* is predicated not on the church, but on the aphorisms of Morison's nanny, Lizzie Turner. Such a vision of Boston life, assembled from bits and pieces of dinner conversation, scattered photographs, and old family stories, was egocentric to be sure, but it also gave the past a highly personalized meaning.[55]

FIG. 8 *Samuel Eliot Morison with grandson Cameron*
Winslow Beck at the helm of yawl **Emily Marshall,**
taken in August 1951. Morison is wearing a
Portuguese fisherman's hat. Courtesy
of Emily Morison Beck.

Individualized expressions are often discouraged in a culture of consensus, since all history is expected to conform to an agreed upon body of facts. But in the increasingly fragmented, pluralistic world of the early sixties, personalized reminiscences such as Morison's attracted audiences. *One Boy's Boston* "proved to be my most successful and appreciated small book," he wrote, and it went a long way toward softening his colleagues' impressions of him as a hard-boiled, choleric old man.[56] Late in 1961, a dinner was held in his honor by friends who remarked with appreciation on the growing simplicity and idiosyncrasy of his style. "There is a special quality to Morison's simplifications," historian Edmund Morgan noted in a letter to the dinner guests. "They are not mechanical reductions of complexity, achieved by omission"; they are "rather in the nature of insights, sometimes compressed into a single metaphor, and almost always they single out the human elements of a situation, relating it to the everyday experiences of everyday men." That is why his particular brand of history cannot be imitated, Morgan concluded; "[i]t is an expression of his own vision."[57]

One Boy's Boston undoubtedly helped Morison's personal and financial reputation, but only modestly when compared to the enormous boost he received in these areas from another unexpected surprise—the 1963 Balzan Award. The Balzan Prize was established by Signor Eugenio Balzan, an editor who fled Mussolini's Italy and bequeathed a large fortune to his daughter with the request that she "establish a foundation to provide a prize for peace and awards for achievement in the arts and sciences."[58] Because of his prodigious work on the Naval history and his five decades of commitment to historical scholarship, Morison was selected for the award in February, and by early May he and Priscilla were in Rome touring the illuminated Capitoline at night with old family friends the Mason Hammonds, meeting Italian naval historians, and awaiting an audience with the Pope. It would be hard to underestimate the impact this reward made on Morison's outlook in the remaining years of his career. It provided him with the kind of international recognition that relieved his feelings of being unappreciated by the Navy, various editors such as Knopf, and collaborators such as Commager. Escorted by Swiss Guards to the "imposing Sala Regia," he was seated among cardinals, bishops, and monsignori and presented to the Pope, who made the award recipients feel like "very important people indeed." Pope John XXIII reminded Morison of his "beloved grandfather Eliot, the idol of [his] boyhood," and he "hoped and felt that Priscilla's ancestors" as well as his own "knew about this high honor which had come to their descendants at the very center of Western Civilization, under the benediction of the most beloved Holy Father of our century."[59]

The award also carried a cash stipend of 225,000 Swiss francs (about $52,500) and a "massy gold medal," which considerably reduced Morison's anxieties about his financial future.[60] Furthermore, as part of his Balzan duties he was asked to give a testimonial of his experiences as a historian, which he published together with several scattered essays in another modestly remunerative book, *Vistas of History*. His Balzan essay, "The Experiences and Principles of an Historian," gave him an opportunity to elaborate his new, more personalized vision of history. "An historian should yield himself to his subject," he wrote of his realist technique, should "become immersed in the place and period of his choice, standing apart from it now and then for a fresh view; as a navigator, after taking soundings off a strange coast, retires to peruse his charts and then emerges to give the necessary orders to continue the voyage safely." Referring in *Vistas of History* to his "cubist" methods, Morison added that he often strove to study not exclusively political, social, economic, or cultural history, and he tried to "coordinate all four aspects during a definite period in a specified area." Above all, he noted, historians must be unwilling to abandon their own realistic sense of an era for the fashionable conventions of the contemporary consensus. "If [historians] should try to rewrite history in the light of Freud, nuclear fission, and an assumed collapse of democracy, I wish [them] well," Morison told his Balzan audience. "But if [they are] bent on explaining past ages to modern youth, [they] must attempt to describe the economic and social order which in those ages flourished, and eventually faded into something else."[61]

Morison closed his Balzan address with a personal profession of faith, doubtless motivated in part by the pious surroundings, but also by his new spirit of expression and disclosure. "Faith in the Christian religion is one thing that 'makes me tick,' " he wrote. "It may be conceit, but not (I hope) hubris, which makes me feel that in a small and humble way I am doing what God appointed me to do." Reviving some of the sentiment of his father confessor Smith O. Dexter, Morison added, "As I look back over the years and observe the state of the world today, my last word to my fellow historians is to remind them that they are responsible both to man and to God." They "must avoid exacerbating the angry passions of race and nation which destroy the world"; at the same time "they may help to prove that hate, greed, and pride have been destructive forces in human history." With a special appeal to the next generation, he concluded that younger historians must prove to be instruments by which "the brooding dread of our time may be dispelled, and a new and radiant era opened in human history."[62] Never before had Morison come so close to a rejection of detached, dispassionate, and consensual history in favor of personalized, subjective, and nearly relativistic imperatives.

"Damn the Libidos"

Toward the end of his Balzan speech Morison noted that he would "dearly love" to cap his career with a textbook on American history written especially for high school students; "one which would lead them to love their country's past instead of considering it a bore—the result of lame teaching and foot-dragging texts."[63] He had been working on just such a volume, *The Oxford History of the American People,* since his New Year's resolution of 1957. His initial progress, however, had been poor. His diary for 1958 recorded his frustration with trying to encompass all of American history in a single volume: "I'm appalled at what I've taken on. . . . If God will only spare me to finish the Oxford History and the Naval History [completed in 1961], I'll ask no more of Him, or of life. Priscilla will be taken care of, and I can sing *Nunc Dimittis.*" But the prospect of completion seemed hopelessly distant, especially since there was too much new scholarship to absorb in preparation for an all-inclusive text. Again, in February of 1959 Morison complained to himself in a note in his personal journal: "I resumed work on *The Oxford History of the American People* but found head winds through Andrew Jackson." Although he had acquired the research assistance of a student of the Jacksonian period, Sydney James, he still moaned, "Why did I undertake this? God help me!"[64]

In the years after writing *One Boy's Boston* and winning the Balzan Prize, however, Morison found the work much easier to accomplish. This ease of composition was in part a result of reduced financial pressures and an increase in time for writing, but it was also a function of his new subjective approach to the past. About midway through the writing of *The Oxford History of the American People,* Morison abandoned his goal of comprehensive coverage and adopted a more idiosyncratic approach. Dropping footnotes from his text, he began to work from memory, presenting a highly individualized portrait of American history. "I work" in the same manner "as a Maine housewife rolls out pie crust—dubbing in a pat of butter here and there, and rolling it again," he noted. "After the second or third rolling, but before the literary pie goes into the oven, I read it aloud to my wife, who is a very acute critic."[65] Priscilla Morison told reporters, "He is writing feverishly, brilliantly, his last part of the great U.S. History and is using as many snippets and sources as a mouse lines his nest with; nothing escapes his notice," she said. "He is a human blender, grinding it all, distilling it all, eliminating, counter-checking it all against a hundred arguments, to be finally his own resolution and conviction." Her biased belief was that "it will be a good book, *sans doute,* and a 'must' for all educated or would-be educated Americans."[66]

Morison shared his wife's optimism. Not since the publication of *The Maritime History of Massachusetts* forty years earlier had he been able to write in "one fell swoop" as he was currently doing. Adopting the motto "A chapter a day keeps the doctor away," he promised readers a more personalized and readable history than *The Growth of the American Republic,* with which it would now compete.[67] In 1964, he finally finished writing the book, which he described as "my legacy to my country," and which he hoped would "help support Priscilla and me for many years."[68] It was far and away the most "subjective" survey of American history he had ever written. Producing a textbook like the GAR had required that he consider space divisions, Morison told a National Book Award audience, since teachers insist that authors devote as much time to the period 1750 to 1800 as to 1800 to 1850. And the authors of textbooks adopted for use in high school or college are also subject to the whims of school boards, Morison noted. *The Growth of the American Republic* was unexpectedly dropped as a text by a public high school, he told one reporter, because the students were reading beyond their daily assignments and thus interfering with their study of other subjects. "Can you imagine that?" he asked. Publishers of textbooks, he added, "require a good deal of writing about aspects of American history, of which I am grossly ignorant" and "about which I have no great desire to know more." Unable to understand the history of banking, Morison decided "to hell with banking" in *The Oxford History of the American People*, but an author of a textbook could not make those kinds of decisions, he contended.[69]

Eliminating topics such as banking from his narrative gave Morison space to discuss popular culture and American leisure activities about which he took a greater interest. Referring to his volume as a "social history," he sought to inform readers about how people lived and amused themselves, what sports they followed, and what arts they pursued. Indulging his own personal preferences, he also included a good deal about horses and sailing ships. Where else but in a Morison history could one discover "that Columbus' first voyage cost his sovereign less than a court ball" or that "Cabot's [voyage], which left half the New World to England, cost Henry VII just fifty pounds?" asked one reader.[70] While the digressions of this "matchless anedoctalist" might not be appreciated in a balanced, academic world in which "history seems to be written by computers or committees," *Newsweek* noted, "it is good to hear again the sound of a civilized man talking in a personal, idiosyncratic, crotchety, opinionated, even dogmatic voice." Most writers of textbooks "steer a balanced course, play it safe, hope not to give offense," *Newsweek* added, succeeding only "in writing the bland concoction of orthodoxies known as 'standard' history." Morison's work succeeded, the magazine concluded, because the author was not afraid to use the personal pronoun "I" or to introduce the stamp of his "distinctive personality."[71]

A handful of reviewers even appreciated Morison's efforts to make concessions to new social sensitivities of concern to American readers in the 1960s. *The Oxford History of the American People* contained little of the racial indifference that had alienated readers of *The Growth of the American Republic* at City College of New York in the early 1950s. Morison not only removed objectionable stereotypical descriptions such as "Sambo," but also he paid tribute to the long-suffering Indian race, who, in his opinion, had received "a poor deal from most American historians and a raw deal from the American people."[72] Yet Morison wished it to be understood that his recognition of new trends in social history was not motivated by any historical "frame of reference." While more than "a mere chain of amusing anecdotes," he argued, *The Oxford History of the American People* was not characterized by any "thematic unity" or social agenda.[73] There is no thesis, no "significant hypothesis," and "no new revision of truth to fit the times," Morison stressed in an interview, because "I am skeptical about there being any *pattern* in modern history, except man's never-ending quest for liberty and security." Claiming that human history is "as unpredictable and unreasonable as *homo sapiens* himself," Morison disavowed that his work had any formal purpose. "David Donald in the Washington *Post* was kind enough to say that I have made an 'original interpretation' in that I emphasize the continuity of American habits, ways and institutions," he wrote, "but I disclaim that, as continuity is just another word for history."[74]

Some reviewers, however, did not find such unpatterned history worthy, especially those with long-standing suspicions about Morison's regional and class preferences. Not surprisingly, the *Chicago Tribune* led the way in this line of attack, calling *The Oxford History of the American People* "disappointing" because of its lack of purpose and intellectual "rigor."[75] In a comment intended as criticism (but doubtless it had the opposite effect), another reviewer concluded that "Mr. Morison seldom provokes a thought or raises an issue, as his contemporary historian, Charles Beard, did in his own retrospective swan song, 'The Republic.' "[76] Other dissenting critics of *The Oxford History of the American People* did not agree that it was value-free or devoid of pattern. They argued, instead, that the book was patterned on the unique (and distorted) vision of Morison himself. "The opinions, being Morison's, are definite, and they have been remarkably consistent throughout his life," wrote one reviewer, adding that the accent of the book was "still New England," and "for one half of the 1122 pages Western America appears only in the problems it produced for the East."[77] Another reader puzzled over the absence of Morison's "vaunted sense of *mesure* when it comes to things nautical," commenting that "even our wars have not all been fought at sea alone, though through this volume—when not necessarily counting words or pages, but vivid impressions instead—one wonders!"[78] The most vitriolic and humorous of these attacks on Morison's "biases" came from a professor of pugilism in the Midwest who vented some long-standing anger at eastern elitism by commenting on Morison's false assertion that Gene Tunney knocked out Jack Dempsey—Tunney won on points. "How such childish literary blunders can be overlooked by so-called knowledgeable editors puzzles us no end," the professor wrote. "We laughed at the bigotry which saturates your book, but the unforgiveable error re the K.O. can only be attributed to senility," he commented nastily, adding that Morison was in need of a "good long rest" or "[e]ven better, another honorary degree from Podunk College."[79]

The most important negative criticisms of *The Oxford History of the American People*, however, came from old warriors of the consensus school who viewed Morison's idiosyncratic style as a defection from traditional, objective historiography. In an article facetiously entitled "Damn the libidos, full speed ahead!" Daniel Boorstin criticized Morison's "Personal Interpretation of History." In its attempt "to escape from the slavery of dogmas" and from "the dangerous quest for single explanations," Boorstin noted, Morison's book plunged "without direction into the dark and muddied well of personal feelings, hobbies, and prejudices." The dominant principle of Morison's brand of personal history, "if it should be so dignified," Boorstin commented, "is that their author Knows What He Likes." By abandoning the established canon in favor of highly idiosyncratic approaches, Morison may have freed himself from the excesses of rigid dogma, Boorstin acknowledged, but he had not liberated himself from his own prejudices, and during his long life, Morison had had the "opportunity to collect over several decades a good many prejudices which make it especially difficult for him to catch the spirit of the most recent past." In fact, while many historians used personal interpretation to introduce radically new ideas, Morison employed it to resurrect obsolete and anachronistic ones. Betraying a "hostility to Modern Times," Boorstin maintained, Morison was curiously blind to some of the most pervasive movements in twentieth-century American life, including Deweyian progressivism and Freudian psychology. Although his scholarship was up-to-date, his "grandfatherly" tone ("itself not inappropriate in a historian of Professor Morison's eminence and ripe years," Boorstin remarked somewhat callously), "often makes it hard to believe that this is our contemporary speaking to us."[80]

Dubbing personal interpretation "whimsical history," Boorstin urged a return to traditional, patterned interpretations of the past. The lack of any structure or reference to an agreed upon body of facts in *The Oxford History of the American People* made an eccentric such as Morison less palatable to a consensus historian such as Boorstin than even the relativist Charles Beard. "Beard, who tried an emphasis and an interpretation which many of us would not share," wrote Boorstin, "nevertheless stated clearly the stakes for which bolder historians play." Beard understood that in writing history he was experimenting not only with personal style but with interpretation.[81] Other critics invoked the negative example of Beard to condemn Morison's subjectivity as well. When in 1948 Professor Morison wrote a review of Charles A. Beard's "distastefully biased and distorted *President Roosevelt and the Coming of the War, 1941*," wrote Richard Heffner of the *Saturday Review*, "he used the occasion not only to destroy Beard's incredible isolationist fantasy" but also "to discredit Beard's devotion to historical relativism." While justified in his attack on Beard's naïve assumptions, Heffner argued, Morison hypocritically employed his own brand of subjective relativism, and therefore readers of *The Oxford History of the American People* were "merely seeing history through still another Beard."[82] Max Lerner also noted the irony of the Beard connection. In trying to write "the book the Beards didn't write but might have," he contended, Morison had failed far more noticeably than the Beards to reveal the "grand and irreversible forces" at work in American culture. Although a historian has the right to choose his own "master ideas" for use in his histories, Lerner concluded, "he must have some master ideas to give him direction."[83]

Morison made several attempts to defend himself against these attacks by reminding his critics of his calculated retreat from institutional authority. *The Oxford History of the American People* had not been written to reaffirm any school of historical thought or to please professionals, he noted. Eschewing the "scholarly apparatus" of footnotes and bibliography, Morison assured readers that "a certain amount of eruditon" could be taken for granted in the work.[84] His goal, a conscious imitation of his motivations for writing his other highly subjective work, *The Maritime History of Massachusetts*, was to write for his wife and "John Q. Citizen," who had helped him to "understand the moving forces in the history of our nation."[85] He wished to escape both the relativistic dilemma of Charles Beard and the consensual reductionism of Daniel Boorstin by simply writing with passion and style about the things that moved him. If this mode of writing brought down upon his shoulders the wrath of historians who viewed it as rudderless, ideologically neutral history, then so be it. At least he was free from the voices of authority—public service administrators, faculty relations, professional colleagues, school committee members, Naval officers, and reviewers—that in the past had demanded so many concessions from his history. This was *his* book, written for "fun" and dedicated to presenting *his* uncensored views about the past.[86] Much to Morison's delight and surprise, it was also his most profitable book, confirming Albert Beveridge's prediction that people would read history if it was written without ulterior motive or hidden agenda.

The only question left unanswered by the reception of *The Oxford History of the American People* was a methodological one—how far would Morison be willing to go in the direction of subjectivism to continue his rebellion from authority? Although he was disgusted by their comparing him and Beard, critics such as Boorstin, Heffner, and Lerner had all noted a faint relativism creeping into his work. To Morison's way of thinking, personalized history and "frame of reference" history were completely incompatible, since the former rejected the ideological determinism of the latter. Morison shared little in common with the New Left historians who seemed to be the new spokespersons for a relativistic revival in American historiography. But in an age when consensus historians complained that history had become dangerously fragmented and pluralistic, Morison's idiosyncratic style had rebellious overtones. As members of the American historical profession struggled to form new coalitions and consensus in light of sweeping societal changes, Morison's nonconformity set him further and further apart from his peers.

The "Reusable Past"

Samuel Eliot Morison and the Narrative
Tradition Revisited

15

The Vietnam Crisis

Despite some negative criticisms of his work, Morison was a relatively optimistic, self-satisfied historian in 1965. *The Oxford History of the American People*, produced at a time "when many historians were writing gloomy things about America," enjoyed continued success and helped secure his financial future.[1] Nearly all other of the many scholarly projects he projected in his 1957 New Year's Day resolution had also been completed, and he could now look forward to a comfortable retirement with summers at Good Hope and winters at 44 Brimmer Street. As he approached the age of eighty, he was still married to a wife he adored, remained in good health, and continued to receive awards and praise for his writings. In 1964, he was invited to the White House to receive the Medal of Freedom, awarded by President Johnson to thirty "humanists"—including Walt Disney, Aaron Copland, T. S. Eliot, Helen Keller, Carl Sandburg, John Steinbeck, and Dean Acheson—who were collectively congratulated for having "made man's world safe, his physical body more durable, his mind broader, his leisure more delightful, his standard of living higher, and his dignity important." Although many of the things Morison valued in the world "had been slipping since 1963," he concluded on behalf of Priscilla, "God has been very merciful to us personally."[2]

Some of Morison's associates were in a far more pessimistic mood. Many were disgruntled with the increasing U.S. presence in Vietnam and found in that war a disturbing affirmation of America's least admirable tendencies. Although *Growth of the American Republic* had sold in 1942 because of its hawkish attitude, for instance, Henry Steele Commager was openly critical of the president's war policy and his misuse of history in promoting it. "[S]urely you don't expect LBJ to know any history, or even pay attention to it, except as suits his purposes," he wrote Morison in an effort to enlist his friend's help in the antiwar movement.[3] If another edition of the GAR were ever published, Commager remarked, perhaps sarcastically, the assessment of the Johnson administration would be none too flattering: "I would simply say that I feel that this is the worst administration in the whole of our history; that LBJ is more deeply distrusted and more fiercely disliked tham [sic] any President in our history; and that he richly deserves the distrust and the dislike." Commager regarded the Vietnam conflict as the most disgraceful war in American history and bristled at Johnson's refusal to acknowledge the many objections responsible citizens were raising to it.[4]

Commager assumed that his collaborator was "on the other side" in the matter of the Vietnam War,[5] but Morison had some definite reservations about the American presence in Southeast Asia. Perhaps nothing suggests the degree to which Morison had drifted from consensus, in fact, than this former court historian's refusal to support U.S. Navy operations off Vietnam. In 1964, Morison expressed his hope that President Johnson would be able "to protect the United States from being torn apart by factions" over the Vietnamese issue, but he soon relinquished this conservative dream.[6] By 1967, he had lost all confidence in "the military-industrial complex" and expressed his fears about the long-range effects of a protracted presence in Southeast Asia. "A Democrat, and warm supporter of you personally and of your domestic policies, I followed your lead on Vietnam until a few months ago," he wrote the president in August of 1967. "Since that time, reading and reflection have persuaded me that the course of events points to the necessity of a change of higher strategy on our part." Morison pointed out that the increased bombing of Hanoi had not ended the resistance of the North Vietnamese; that reinforcement of American troops had been countered effectively by Russia's sending more weapons and supplies; and that to liberate South Vietnam from Vietcong rebels was not feasible except by a long war involving a drain on man power that the United States could not afford. He concluded that the "consequences of continuing our present strategy are so predictably disastrous that admission of failure and loss of prestige are preferable to going on with it."[7]

By the election of 1968, Morison had come to view U.S. involvement in Vietnam as an enormous mistake. Citing British military analyst Liddell-Hart, Morison called the American presence in Vietnam an example of "strategic overstretch"—an attempt to extend power too far from a home base. History suggested that such overextension could not be maintained for long, technological and military advantages notwithstanding. "It was proved in the strategic bombing survey after World War II that the saturation bombing of Germany didn't bring the war near an end. It just killed a lot of civilians," Morison asserted. "It seems to me that is just what our bombing of Vietnam is doing today." Claiming that the American people had grown "sick" of the Vietnam War, "whether they believed in it originally or not," he hoped that the president would soon recognize that they only wanted "to get out as cheaply as possible."[8] Morison urged a negotiated settlement that would involve a heavy withdrawal of troops, adding that "a bold and skillful peace offensive" on Johnson's part, even if it failed, would be preferable to protracted war. "In conclusion, Mr. President, I am not a peace demonstrator, signer of petitions, writer of angry letters to newspapers," Morison granted, "but as a senior citizen who loves his country . . . I beg you freshly to ponder the situation."[9]

These questions were of more than just passing concern to Morison, since he was engaged in writing a biography of Matthew Calbraith Perry, a figure of enormous importance in the history of American–East Asian relations. Unwilling to simply "rest on his oars" after completing the *Oxford History of the American People*, Morison decided to write a history of Perry's life and of his primary accomplishment as a naval officer—opening up diplomatic relations with the Japanese in the 1850s. Unlike his wide-ranging, breezy *Oxford History of the American People*, the Perry biography was a more conventional bit of history, developed through primary research in the Perry letters and journals scattered throughout the country and presented as a contribution to professional scholarship. As in his other naval histories, particularly his biography *John Paul Jones*, Morison cited his long experience with the sea and the Navy as his credentials. Entitled *Old Bruin* (the nickname Perry acquired for bellowing out commands on ship like a big mountain grizzly), the work traced Perry's early career as a naval officer, his part in the settling of Liberia, his important role in the naval victories of the Mexican War, and his reputation as the "Father of the Steam Navy." According to Morison, Perry was not "the dashing, hotblooded, impulsive type of naval officer" that John Paul Jones was; instead he was "methodical, serious, conscientious, bent on becoming a good officer, getting on with his fellow reefers, winning the respect of the ratings and the esteem of his superiors." On the surface, at least, there seemed nothing particularly contemporary or even compelling about Perry or his biography. To some, *Old Bruin* was merely a throwback to Morison's earlier professional commitment to maritime topics and his more traditional style of writing.[10]

Yet a good deal of the "personalized" style of *The Oxford History of the American People* reappeared in *Old Bruin*. In a continued effort to achieve empathy with the historical figures he described, Morison traveled to the scenes of Perry's greatest actions—to Mexico, to trace the Commodore's coastal movements during the Mexican War, and to Japan, to document his experiences in the "open door" mission.[11] Although these trips did not clear up mysteries about landings and sightings (as Morison's similar "firsthand" technique was designed to do in *Admiral of the Ocean Sea*), they nonetheless gave him an opportunity to understand Perry's point of view and even to make some historical discoveries. "We found treasures in a musty old Victorian building at the University of Tokyo and in a private collection of an American," wrote Priscilla, who accompanied him on these research trips. "Sam soaked up impressions Perry must have had," she added, recounting their re-creation of the first Japanese sighting of Perry's "Black Fleet" in Japanese waters.[12] Morison also helped collapse the distinctions of place and time by projecting his nineteenth-century subject forward into the twentieth century. Hence, wherever possible, he reminded his readers of the presentist implications of Perry's actions. The commodore's defense of the hanging of sailors aboard the USS *Somers* evoked, in Morison's telling, "[a]rguments and innuendoes of the sort which have become familiar in discussions of Pearl Harbor and the assassination of President Kennedy." When Perry relieved Commodore David Connor of command in the Mexican War, American sailors cheered the change in favor of "firm and vigorous action" with the same fervor, Morison recalled with some irony, that "animated the South Pacific Force in 1942 when Halsey took over that command." And in recounting the impression Perry's arrival must have made on a culture closed for centuries to westerners, Morison developed a twentieth-century aeronautical analogy: "A parallel situation would be an announcement by astronauts that weird-looking aircraft from outer space were on their way to earth; nobody would know how to receive them."[13]

Morison did not pass up the opportunity to acknowledge the contemporary ramifications of Perry's East Asian foreign policy. The commodore, whose farsighted predictions for the strategic importance of the western Pacific were "remarkably accurate," according to Morison, understood the "national necessity" of acquiring coaling stations and naval bases near Japan for which the American government cared nothing in his day. In addition, Perry perceived the need to develop peaceful relationships with the nations of Indochina, especially the coastal country of Vietnam. "In view of later difficulties in that part of the world," Morison wrote, "it is interesting that Perry wrote to Secretary Dobbin about the Vietnams (then Cochin China)" concerning the need "to secure the friendship of these singular people." The alternative, Perry concluded, would be an eventual war of rebellion against the U.S. presence in these regions, backed by that other dominant "growth" nation, Russia. The "Saxon and the Cossack will meet once more, in strife or in friendship, or another field. Will it be friendship?" Perry asked; "I fear not! The antagonistic exponents of freedom and absolutism must meet at last, and then will be fought that mighty battle on which the world will look with breathless interest; for on its issue will depend the freedom or the slavery of the world—despotism or rational liberty must be the fate of civilized man." With remarkable clairvoyance, Perry added, "I think I see in the distance the giants that are growing up for that fierce and final encounter; in the progress of events that battle must sooner or later inevitably be fought."[14]

Perry's diplomatic successes in Japan suggested important lessons for American policy in Indochina in the 1960s as well. Without firing a shot, Perry had managed to liberate a land and a people from the bonds of feudalism. One false step in those first crucial days of his visit, Morison noted, and "there would have been no treaty, no opening, but a big fight in which the Americans, despite their superior fire power, might have been overwhelmed by sheer numbers."[15] Much of Perry's success was achieved by his astute sensitivity to human character and his appreciation for diplomatic process. Reviewing the unsuccessful efforts of European powers to come to terms with Japan, Perry concluded that the Japanese were "too sagacious to be influenced by specious arguments or propositions of friendship, unless those professions are accompanied by corresponding acts . . . of national probity." Accordingly, he "acted imperiously, which the Japanese understood" rather than "arrogantly, which would have offended them," while remaining steadfastly devoted to the American mission. Perry understood that America could not escape the responsibilities created by her growing wealth and power but that the nation must also prevent wars that could easily be "avoided by less aggressiveness on one side and more realism on the other." Morison argued that if Perry was an imperialist, as he was frequently characterized, he was "an imperialist with a difference," because he refused to annex territories forcibly or to compel people to accept religious or economic ideologies. With conscious reference to the failure of American diplomatic efforts in Vietnam during the 1960s, Morison concluded, "If this be imperialism, let us have more of it!"[16]

For some readers of *Old Bruin*, such presentist analogies smacked of ideology and historical relativism. But, as in most of his later works, Morison sought to distinguish his subjective brand of history from the kind of writing in which Beard had engaged. In a letter to a former Oxford student, historian Denis Brogan, Morison explained the differences. "I happened to look up what Beard had to say in *Rise of American Civilization* about Japan Mission Commodore Matthew C. Perry, on which I am now working," he wrote, and "[Beard's account] is typical of how [he] forces everything into his preconceived mold." Desiring to prove that Perry's mission was the work of "capitalist-imperialist Whigs," Beard distorted certain facts about Perry's mercantile and naval backgrounds. In *Rise of American Civilization*, we are told that "Perry is from Providence, a center of the China Trade," Morison noted, yet he was actually "from Newport, which had no China trade," and "none of his family had anything to do with it." Perry was a strong Jacksonian Democrat, Morison added, and although the Japan Mission "was set on foot by the Filmore administration, it did not get under way until Pierce's, which sent it off with éclat" and "accepted the treaty with Japan with enthusiasm." Beard also included "a lot of nonsense about the 'professionals in the navy department' conceiving a 'philosophy of action' " for Perry's life's work, Morison wrote to Brogan. "The only actions Perry conceived were 'manifest destiny' in Mexico, which Fred Merk has brought out in his excellent recent book on the subject, and the need of coaling stations to enable the new steam navy and merchant marine to operate across the Pacific in competition with the British." Such misconceptions were deliberate, Morison concluded, introduced to enlist history in the service of Beard's dialectical materialism. By contrast, subjective interpretation (of which there was some in *Old Bruin*, he admitted) was never employed on behalf of ideology or to the detriment of the factual record of Perry's career.[17]

Reviewers disagreed, as usual, in their assessments of Morison's technique. Some, for instance, complained that he could be every bit as partial as Beard. "Contemporary allusions and an air of informality will be regarded by some as strong points," one critic noted, but "[i]t is more difficult to make a case for the author's open partisanship. With few exceptions he dismisses all criticisms of the United States, stands solidly with the Navy whenever it is under attack from other Americans, and supports Perry against all comers, even those from within the Navy itself."[18] Another disliked the subjectivity and "realist" components of the Perry portrait. "Ever since *Admiral of the Ocean Sea*, Morison's life of Columbus, some people have harbored the outrageous suspicion that this eminent historian is fundamentally a frustrated novelist," he wrote. "In the earlier book he transformed Christopher Columbus from a steel engraving into a creditable personality; in this one he does as much for Matthew C. Perry," knowing full well that "to make a living human being emerge from the printed page is usually accounted part of the art of the novelist."[19] Others applauded the personalized quality of the work. One reader noted that "in this large and handsome volume, Morison perhaps comes to life more than his subject."[20] Another critic noted that while "lesser historians might be chided for getting themselves into the act, Morison's charming firsthand descriptions of places where Perry called as well as of the sea itself makes the commodore's activities seem so much more real and meaningful."[21]

Despite judgments both good and bad, *Old Bruin* was not a financial or popular success. Morison was inclined to view its failure as once again the fault of editors. "Ted Weeks mistakenly persuaded me to entitle [the biography] 'Old Bruin,' " Morison wrote a friend. "That was Perry's nickname in the Navy, but the public seemed to think that I had written the story of a pet bear or something."[22] He also complained about his editor's principles of inclusion and selectivity. "The book, incidentally, has not been much of a success," he wrote Denis Brogan. "The reason, I think, is that I let myself be persuaded by Ted Weeks to pad out the earlier chapters with accounts of Perry's father and brother instead of confining myself to him."[23] And, of course, Morison was disappointed by President Johnson's inability to emulate the important example of Perry's diplomatic savvy in East Asia. Although he never presumed that *Old Bruin* would have a presidential audience in the way that a biography such as *Admiral of the Ocean Sea* had, Morison did hope, naïvely as it turned out, that his work might influence some readers in high office to reconsider policy in the Orient.

Most revealing of all, however, was Morison's sense that *Old Bruin* had fallen victim to the distractions of the time. Having treated "change as erosion rather than explosion," he lost the interest of readers who desired more action and controversy in their histories.[24] In particular, readers were suspicious of Perry's lifelong dedication to a military arm of the government that was increasingly under scrutiny in the 1960s. Hawkish in general outlook and an avid promoter of manifest destiny, Perry embodied too many of the values currently under attack in Vietnam protests throughout the country, and therefore many readers would not regard him highly. Morison sympathized with some of these concerns, but he begged readers to understand that Perry stood for a strong Navy, indispensable at all times, even in an unpopular foreign war. Those "wedded to the Marxian dialectic" will inevitably "denigrate" American presence in the region as the work of "imperalist[s] harboring territorial designs," he noted, but Morison believed that responsible politicians (and historians) must find some way to safeguard American interests without rejecting completely the idea of military presence.[25] The fundamental question for the electorate in 1968, Morison argued, was what candidate would provide Americans with the best strategy for ending the war in Vietnam while reestablishing the integrity of American diplomacy and military strength in the Pacific.

The Crisis of Professional Authority

Despite his Democratic preferences, Morison eventually took some comfort in the 1968 election of Richard Nixon, since the Republican president promised to gradually return the war in Southeast Asia to the Vietnamese (it was called Vietnamization), and because, as Perry had in Japan, Nixon successfully opened up diplomatic relations with China in 1972. But Morison's store of good will for Nixon was limited and quickly depleted by the president's mismanagement of both domestic and international affairs. Nixon's inappropriate tactics for dealing with student antiwar protest and his manipulation of history disillusioned Morison and many of his colleagues. "Personally I think much of the unrest among the young is due to the lack of veracity in all countries, some more some less, not only in government and other official declarations & publications," wrote one friend to Morison, "but in the way history is constantly being taught differently, according to political circumstances, after each war, or even each election or the coming of a new ruler."[26] No ardent supporter of student protesters at Harvard, Morison was inclined to criticize the excesses of groups such as SDS (Students for a Democratic Society), whose "bad manners" he blamed on "modern 'permissive' upbringing" and Deweyian education.[27] He reminded Harvard alumni who sympathized with the student takeover of University Hall in the spring of 1968 that the student demand for a "restructuring" of the faculty was a "remedy worse than the disease," since (as in the case of the anticommunist crusade) it would ultimately result in more rather than less administrative supervision. His advice to graduates of Harvard was "to support the Administration and the University as you have in the past."[28] And the Morisons certainly had little understanding of the broader countercultural currents running through the protest movements on college campuses. While attending a dedication ceremony of the "Morison House" at the University of California, Santa Cruz (a student residence named after him owing to the efforts of former student and Santa Cruz faculty member, Page Smith), he and his wife were approached by a "Pan-like student" with "beard and long hair," who, "upon being introduced to Priscilla Morison, extracted a flower from his beard and presented it to her with a courtly air." Her reply, Page Smith recorded, was "something in between an exclamation and a plea, 'Mercy'!"[29]

Yet Morison did sympathize with the theoretical goals of the student movement and defended those goals against the attacks of Nixon. Recalling the efforts of students during World War I to get the United States into the League of Nations and to search for ways of obtaining peace in the world, Morison reflected to reporters, "I was right in the midst of that at Harvard. I don't think that the movement nowadays is essentially different." The accusations of antipatriotism used by administrations then as well as now, he added, were essentially unfair. "It would seem, superficially, that [patriotism] was at a very low ebb," he noted, "[b]ut it seemed like that in the period between the two world wars, and the American people responded nobly to the challenge of World War II." Applying the lessons of history to the present, he added, "I don't doubt that they would respond equally well if they had an equally great or greater challenge now." The war in Vietnam, he implied, was not a fair test of their loyalty.[30]

Morison also became disgusted with the political intrigues that eventually embroiled Nixon in the Watergate cover-up and ended his political career. "We voted for Lyndon Johnson but, until Nixon came on the scene, we came to regard him as one of our worst presidents," Morison wrote. Citing Nixon's record of corruption and deceit, he told a friend abroad that the "events in Washington have indeed turned the stomachs of many patriotic Americans." Some pride could be taken in the manner in which the nation exorcised itself of its corrupt leaders, but this was small consolation for the damage done to the office of the president.[31] The resulting crisis of authority, he predicted, would have potentially devastating residual effects on numerous American institutions. Morison was keenly aware, for instance, of the effect that Nixon's resignation would have on the university and the historical profession. Even before Watergate, the American Historical Association had shown the strains of continuing challenges to its authority. As the American identity shattered under the force of racial, gender, and class revolutions in the sixties, professional historians found it impossible to maintain faith in a stable national character and difficult to accept the implications of a growing historical pluralism. A crisis of confidence ensued, and the frustrated professional historian in "search of stability" became a leitmotif of American historiographic literature. Peter Novick has recently written that the "brazen mendacity" of Nixon's staffers in the Watergate crisis produced a "concomitant increase in skepticism about 'official truth,' and for some, about truth of any kind—not the least academic."[32]

As such comments suggest, the historical crisis of the late sixties and early seventies was unlike any that had preceded it in nearly a full century of professional activity. Disputes there had been plenty. From the inception of the American Historical Association in the late nineteenth century, institutional historians had quibbled with sociocultural historians, as Morison had discovered in the Harvard history department while an undergraduate and graduate student. New Historians had challenged the objective "detachment" of historical positivists and had established the concept of a "usable past" to render history a public service, as Morison had prior to World War I. Cynicism about the war and about the ability of historians to affect change had encouraged historical relativists and debunkers in the 1920s and 1930s, who in turn were challenged by defenders of national traditions such as Morison. Such antidebunkers helped establish a consensus historiography in the 1940s and 1950s that was itself attacked by New Left, subjective, and pluralistic historians in the early 1960s. But these disputes had largely arisen among professional historians (or ex-professionals such as Beard) who argued the fine points of historical methodology without questioning the integrity of the professional enterprise. "When the American historical profession was founded, unquestioned assumptions" about the nature of historical investigation "had played a central role in rendering unproblematic the profession's constituent beliefs," Novick has written. "One hundred years later the radical questioning of these assumptions was to play just as central a role in rendering those beliefs deeply problematic."[33]

By the mid-1970s some historians spoke openly of deserting or even disbanding the established agencies of the American historical profession. Believing that "the historical profession was fragmented beyond any hope of unification," some historians began to argue that the problems of the American Historical Association were endemic to its organizational structure. Initiated in the 1880s as a defector from Samuel Eliot's public service–minded American Social Science Association, the AHA had never been able to escape the stigma of elitism and exclusivity. Professional historians had come to insist on certain "rules" of historical procedure and, as the organization grew in size and power, it became necessary for writers of history to justify their existence by demonstrating the value of their work to the profession itself. Young historians were encouraged to fill a need in the profession by writing on topics previously unexplored by professionals or by taking up historiographic controversies generated by professional journals and organizational meetings. Such imperatives, buttressed by tightly controlled procedures for admission to graduate school, academic employment, and archival collections, preconditioned the kind of history produced by American historians. In an age justifiably suspicious of organizations and administrative power, some historians argued that nothing short of a total purging of all historians from institutional affiliations could break down such preconditions and save history from the abuses of professionalism.[34]

The effect of this line of thinking was to create a nostalgia for a preprofessional era, when historians were free to operate outside the established procedures of the profession. Joan Hoff-Wilson reminisced about an early, untainted American Historical Association of the 1880s, dominated by figures such as Herbert Baxter Adams who kept a balance between "amateur or independent historians" and "professional or academic historians."[35] Others drew inspiration from "romantic historians" of the mid–nineteenth century, arguing the merits of Parkman, Prescott, and Motley against those of their professional descendants. An unfortunate epistemological change (referred to as a paradigm revolution in the parlance of the 1970s) had occurred in the "professional age," some argued, in which the "Great Person" in history so cherished by the romantics had been subordinated to amorphous institutional or sociocultural forces; chance had been replaced by scientific laws; and, most of all, narration had been demoted on the list of the historian's priorities in favor of historical argument and proof. Calling for a reversal of these tendencies, historian Lawrence Stone looked forward to a "revival of narrative" in the 1970s. In an article subtitled "Reflections on a New Old History," Stone called for historians to rally around an earlier conception of historical scholarship, one that allowed historians to recover their autonomy as "story-tellers."[36] And recognizing that lay readers of history read primarily amateurs only, C. Vann Woodward endorsed Stone's plan, hoping that privileging narrative form would help historians recover some of their "lost prestige."[37]

Despite its sentimental attachment to the "golden age" of historical writing, the "revival of narrative" tradition was not simply whimsical or nostalgic. It was based instead on some rather sophisticated philosophical and literary principles, especially a form of "structuralism" that recognized the mimetic quality of historical writing. As Jack Hexter explained, the goal of narrative history was "to reproduce a story lived in the past, whose structure and appropriate mode of representation were latent in the events themselves."[38] As Peter Novick paraphrased the technique, the historian "first discovered in the historical record the meaning of past reality, then accurately and artfully represented what he or she had found."[39] Employing such methods, historians could avoid the relativism of much of twentieth-century historical writing by creating narratives in which subject matter and structure were intertwined. Rather than pursuing a usable past—one written in presentist terms with special meaning only to contemporary readers—revivalists of the narrative tradition campaigned for a "reusable past"—one equally accessible (or inaccessible) to every age and every reader because it would be written in a literary form concerned with intrinsic rather than extrinsic descriptions. Since structure recapitulated theme in this narrative mode, contemporary distractions, like those created by professionalism, could be easily guarded against.

Whenever proponents of the "revival of narrative" argued their case, Morison was mentioned as a prime example of the technique. There was a double irony in this endorsement. In the first place, this counterprofessional argument was advanced primarily in professional journals. In the second place, Morison seldom read such journals after the 1950s nor participated in the association's activities. Indeed, Morison's gradual retreat from involvement with professional organizations after the 1950s caused some to view him, again ironically, as a rather forward-looking retrospective historian. Despite his aloofness, however, Morison was unquestionably the most suitable spokesman for the narrative revival. No living historian had done more to safeguard the memory of the nineteenth-century romantics. In a 1957 article on William Prescott, subtitled "The American Thucydides," Morison had preserved the memory of those literary historians who valued "vivid and spirited narrative style" above all else. Prescott was a master of *narrative*, "which history essentially is," Morison wrote, and this fact "too many modern historians have forgotten." Prescott's accomplishments were all the more heroic because they were attended by "thirty-five years of courageous struggle to overcome a grave physical disability." Fighting an incurable eye ailment, Prescott was forced to write by means of a noctgraph, "a sort of slate crossed by a grid of stout brass wires between which, with an ivory-pointed stylus, one could write on carbon paper, which made an indelible impression on another sheet of paper placed underneath." Such tedious labor was not a necessity, Morison noted, since his family was financially stable enough to allow him to forgo a career. "But in Boston every young man was supposed to 'make an effort' as the phrase went," Morison noted in recognition of his grandfather Eliot's efforts at a career as a historian. Prescott himself observed "that an American who neither made money nor cultivated letters might 'as well go hang himself; for as to a class of idle gentlemen, there is no such thing here.' "[40]

While Morison admired Prescott, Francis Parkman remained his favorite. Parkman, too, labored under a severe injury to his eyes, which prevented him from working more than two or three hours a day. "It is a curious coincidence that the only other American historian, Francis Parkman, to be mentioned in the same breath with Prescott, had to undergo a similar experience," Morison wrote.[41] While Prescott's infirmity prevented him from visiting the scenes of South American history he described, Parkman made a habit of examining "every spot where events of any importance in connection" with his themes took place and observing "with attention such scenes and persons as might help to illustrate those [he] meant to describe." In short, Parkman's subjects were, in his own words, "studied as much from life and in the open air as at any table."[42] Morison had followed this technique himself throughout his career, in the Harvard Columbus Expedition, then in his research for the *History of United States Naval Operations in World War II*, and finally in his research on Perry in Japan. The procedure was so successful for him, in fact, that Parkman became his unequivocal idol. On Morison's desk in his study, next to autographed photos of Franklin D. Roosevelt and Harry S. Truman, was a treasured photo of Parkman, given to him by the historian's granddaughter; in the bookcase behind the same desk was his set of Parkman, inscribed with the endearing words of tribute: "my favorite historian."[43]

Morison's dedication to Parkman was evidenced in two written tributes to the historian's work—an edited edition of his writings, *The Parkman Reader* (1955), and a small biographical book, *Francis Parkman* (1973). In these works, Morison outlined the components of Parkman's narrative style that made his works so immortal. In a tripartite division of praise, he noted that the nineteenth-century historian "combined depth and accuracy of research, literary skill, and sensitivity, both to natural beauty and to the human heart, as few historians of any age or country have done." Noting that Parkman was the equal of any of the professionally trained historians of the twentieth century in searching out and interpreting new materials, Morison also reminded readers that Parkman had what most of them lacked—literary style. His incredible talents "in the three qualities that make good historical literature, research, evaluation and literary presentation," Morison wrote, "have caused the works of Parkman to endure longer than those of any other American historian of his era."[44] In an interview with a journalist reporting on the revival of the narrative tradition in the 1970s, Morison concluded that Parkman "is the historian whom I most admire as he has a combination of impeccable scholarship, outdoor experience and a remarkable narrative style. Nobody has ever combined those three factors in such a harmonious degree."[45]

These three features of narrative style were precisely the ingredients that proponents of the revival of narrative tradition wished to reintroduce into the profession in the 1970s. Some believed that such a procedure could be accomplished simply by urging historians to pay more particular attention to the narrative details of their works. The most extreme of these revisionists, however, argued that the narrative mode was incompatible with professional prerogatives and that the narrative revival could not be achieved without a complete severing of all professional connections by historians. Hayden White, whose historical consciousness in *Metahistory* (1973) was described as "pre-professional," made "invidious comparisons between what he saw as the current debased state of historiography, and earlier centuries when it was truly a 'moral science.' " Seconding Morison's call for a reestablishment of links to the "classic practitioners and theorists of [the] golden age in the nineteenth century," White encouraged historians to consciously employ narrative tropes in their work, and thereby to achieve "transcendence" over the antinarrativity of "modern academic historiography."[46] Perhaps no work of the 1970s conformed more to his model than Morison's last historical production—*The European Discovery of America: Northern and Southern Voyages.*

The New Parkman

Appropriately, Morison was inspired to write *The European Discovery of America* by the need to fill a scholarly hole created by professionals. Not since amateur historian John Fiske wrote his two-volume *Discovery of America* in 1892 had a scholar attempted a broad, synthetic reevaluation of the age of exploration.[47] To be sure, professionals had spent much time squabbling over pre-Columbian voyages to the New World and the authenticity of Phoenician and Celtic artifacts. But no new narrative retelling of the entire history of European ventures to the New World in both the northern and southern hemispheres had been accomplished, in large part, as Stone, C. Vann Woodward, and White had argued, because such epic undertakings rarely appealed to specialized professionals. Metahistory of the kind that nineteenth-century historians pursued seemed impossible in an age characterized by impatient tenure committees, highly focused professional meetings, and anxious publishers. "The older I get, the more I envy the great historians of the past, like Gibbon, Macaulay, Parkman, and Ranke," Morison wrote historian Bernadotte Schmitt. "The sources that they were required to read by a proper sense of their professional duty were tiny in number or extent compared with ours." In addition, they "had the time to ponder and synthesize; we are hurried on by publishers' deadlines and the moving finger of time." To produce the kind of inclusive history they wrote, Morison concluded, a historian must have nearly superhuman powers of organization, selectivity, and independence.[48]

If Morison seemed superhuman enough to write an old-fashioned synthetic history of the age of exploration, he still could not escape completely the distractions of a professional world. From the first he was embroiled in various small controversies of the sort that had limited the ambitions of potential metahistorians throughout the twentieth century. "All honest efforts to throw light on historical darkness, such as this era, have my enthusiastic support," he wrote in the preface to *The European Discovery of America.* "But it has fallen to my lot, working on this subject, to have read some of the most tiresome historical literature in existence." He was weary of young men seeking academic promotion and old men seeking publicity, "neither one nor the other knowing the subject in depth," only some "particular voyage or a particular map." Such pseudohistorians, he noted, did not have the breadth of knowledge necessary to write meaningfully on the age of discovery. Yet they continued to produce "worthless articles" and "effusions" to which the "so-called learned journals" were "altogether too hospitable."[49] F. J. Pohl's book on Norse discoveries, Morison wrote, "will be nothing but a crackpot work. He thinks every hole in a ledge along the New England Coast was excavated by the Vikings."[50] Norwegian historian-explorer Thor Heyerdahl's sail across the Atlantic in a papyrus craft, designed to prove that South America was populated by Phoenicians, was, in Morison's estimation, "a great fake." Heyerdahl's voyage "doesn't prove anything," he wrote, "but that Heyerdahl had a great time and made a lot of money."[51]

By far the most persistent and annoying professional debate in which Morison felt obligated to participate before issuing his *European Discovery of America* was the Vinland map controversy. In 1965, Yale University Press published a 1440 map that represented Vinland as a distinct place, presumably confirming a Norse discovery of the New World before Columbus's in 1492.[52] Morison was unhappy with the publication for two reasons. First, and most important, he thought the map a fake, since it corresponded too perfectly to a modern Mercator projector to be an example of fifteenth-century cartography.[53] Second, Morison was dissatisfied with the manner in which Yale University Press packaged the supposed discovery. In a piece in the the *New York Times*, he condemned the "scholarly sleuths of Yale" who "fluffed up" the discovery into a quarto of 259 pages, plus index and "cannily" issued it at the approach of Columbus Day. The Yale University Press was aware, Morison argued, that "journalists avid for something new and topical to write" would "snap up" the story of the Vinland map and "gravely" distort its importance.[54]

Morison's remarks triggered a tidal wave of reaction. Edmund Morgan of the Yale history department wrote Morison to say that his *New York Times* review had been greeted "with howls of pain from the Yale Press and chuckles of delight from everybody else—or nearly everybody." Noting that he and his colleagues in the history department had been "disgusted by the way in which the whole business was handled," he added that they "were pleased to see the appropriate knuckles rapped."[55] But others dismissed the review as an example of petty academic rivalry. "The conservatism and scholarship of the authors themselves is certainly beyond reproach," one critic noted of the Vinland map, adding that "Harvard men can afford to be more generous towards this great discovery by Yale scholars."[56] And still others viewed the review as a defense of Columbus's claim to the discovery of the New World. Morison argued, however, that he was not defending Columbus; in fact, he observed that it had been generally known since 1837 that Norsemen reached some part of America around the year 1000. Yet these discoveries were insignificant, he concluded, since the Norsemen did not establish any permanent colonies in the New World.[57] When carbon dating later revealed the map was a forgery, produced with post-1920 ink, it was comedian Jimmy Durante who provided Morison with his touché against the editors at Yale Press: "These guys is nuts. Of course, I never met this Columbus poisonally. But I know dat when he got here, he played for nobody but Indians. There wasn't no Norwegians around in the audience.''[58]

In addition to these pesky professional battles, Morison faced pressures from publishers, both financial and editorial. He sent a preliminary manuscript of *European Discovery of America: Southern Voyages* to several publishing companies and received an enthusiastic first response from Ted Weeks of the Atlantic Monthly Press. Concluding that the two-volume work was likely to be Morison's ''magnum opus,'' Weeks praised the historian's ''sapience, his mellowness, and his unmatched experience as a navigator.'' Morison ''knows firsthand the hazards which the early mariners encountered, the fogs, the icebergs, the head winds, the tricky tides and rocky coasts,'' he wrote a colleague, ''and this knowledge not only informs his scholarship, it gives his imagination the authority to cut through the myths, to interpret the sagas and to laugh away the humbugs.'' Weeks advised Atlantic's business office to offer royalties of 15 percent on all copies sold through the trade, 50 percent of all book club income, and 50 percent of paperback reprint income up to $25,000, at which point all paperback income would be shared at 60 percent to the author and 40 percent to the publisher. In addition, the Atlantic offered a total advance of $212,000 as follows: $42,400 on the signature of the contract, $42,400 on delivery of the first volume, $42,400 on notification that the second volume was underway, and $84,000 on delivery of the second volume. ''We dearly want these books,'' Weeks wrote Morison, ''and will do them proud.''[59]

Despite this generous offer, one which Morison would have leapt at in the financially troubled 1950s, he accepted a matching offer from Oxford University Press. His decision was based on Oxford's promise to match the Atlantic's offer and his sense that Oxford ''does a better job'' on ''big'' works, which the narrative history was projected to be.[60] Oxford was excited as well by the prospect of publishing Morison's volumes. ''The material itself is superb,'' wrote one of Oxford's editors to Morison. ''We would pay our top trade royalty of fifteen percent of the list price.''[61] But this figure did not satisfy Morison, who rejected the first draft contract that Oxford sent him, on the grounds that it did not meet the Atlantic's terms plus 17½ percent royalty. ''If you suspect O.U.P. is trying to 'weasel,' '' Morison wrote his lawyers, then ''I suggest you telephone Weeks, ask if he is still willing to abide by terms he offered in letter of 17 April, drop O.U.P. and contract with Atlantic.''[62] This threat never had to be carried out, but ongoing disputes over photographs and presentation of the volumes, as well as money for expenses incurred, soured a bit the relationship between author and press and distracted Morison from his larger narrative purpose.

These professional intrusions notwithstanding, Morison attempted to write a narrative history in the nineteenth-century style of Parkman. His first goal was to emulate Parkman's eyewitness technique as he had done profitably so many times before. He had contemplated writing the history of American discovery by resailing the coastal routes of the great explorers, but because he had reached his mid-eighties, such a reenactment was out of the question. So Morison arranged for two friends and amateur pilots, Mauricio Obregón and Jim Nields, to fly the routes. Accompanied by their wives, one of Obregón's sons, and a *Life* magazine photographer, they flew over the Caribbean in search of the landings of Columbus, Vespucci, and others; they "buzzed" the eastern and western coasts of South America and the islands of the Pacific in pursuit of the circumnavigation of Magellan; and they were escorted through the Straits of Magellan by the Chilean Air Force. In addition, they were transported along the California coast in quest of Drake's landing sites by the U.S. Coast Guard. Throughout the expedition, Morison conversed with local authorities and attempted "to apply his background knowledge, his common sense, and . . . his personal knowledge of sailing to make sense of the sources."[63]

There was some risk involved for Morison in following Parkman's methods at his advanced age. Before leaving for South America, for instance, he left his secretary, Antha Card, instructions for the completion of his volumes in the event of his death.[64] In following the paths of the explorers, he planned to travel forty thousand miles by air and sea in three months, which raised concerns about the effect of the rapid pace of his work on his health. There were stretches through the trip when Morison tired, especially in South America, where authorities wished to make it a "People to People" project in order to improve international relations. Morison submitted to literally dozens of interviews about his research, his impressions of the coastline, and his upcoming book, and complained about them privately to Priscilla.[65] Both knew, however, that public relations were important to the book, and Priscilla added that her husband must learn, "painfully for him," that "all success demands payment."[66] Morison encountered some further difficulties en route to Thailand to investigate the landings of Magellan's expedition. Forced to refuel their plane in the "shoddy airport in Saigon," he came face-to-face with the war in Vietnam. The airport was filled with South Vietnamese soldiers who were guarding hundreds of small camouflaged planes to be used in "defense raids" up north, Morison wrote. After being thoroughly searched and then interminably delayed, they were finally able to proceed, but not before Morison had developed a considerable resentment for the South Vietnamese Army.[67]

Morison rationalized these inconveniences as the necessary cost of pursuing Parkman's "on-the-spot" techniques. By using such methods, he hoped *The European Discovery of America* would bear the marks of Parkman's unique narrative style. Morison's two volumes certainly conformed to Parkman's tripartite division of skill. In the first place, Morison demonstrated Parkman's sense of scholarly accuracy and balance by providing exhaustive information on the professional debates surrounding the age of discovery but relegating that information to a set of footnotes and bibliographies at the end of chapters. Those patient enough to work through this subtextual story line were often treated to Morison's devastating and sometimes witty critiques. Citing "Occam's Razor," William of Occam's principle that "in explaining obscure matters, imaginary things should never be postulated as existing," Morison noted that the principle had been so frequently violated that "mythical coasts and islands have become almost as substantial as New York." As a corollary to Occam's Razor, Morison offered two principles ("Morison's Musings," he called them). The first was the axiom that "the invention or publication of some new method of navigation does not prove that it was promptly used at sea."[68] This principle had been violated by historian Eva G. R. Taylor, among others, who tried to revive the "phony voyages" of the Zeno brothers to the New World in 1476 on the assumption that they had been exposed to new nautical theories allowing such a trip. "As for the late Eva Taylor, she is really a pain in the neck, as she writes with such assurance from a regrettable ignorance," Morison wrote a friend.[69] The second axiom stated that "No theory is valid that makes nonsense of what follows." British geographers had argued, for instance, that sailors from Bristol had discovered Newfoundland as early as 1480. If there were any truth to that rumor, Morison argued, "the prudent and economical Henry VII would never have called it the 'New Isle,' much less rewarded John Cabot for discovering it." After reading the "foolish fancies" of such "moonstruck historians," Morison wrote, readers of *The European Discovery of America* would find it "a relief to return to the cold facts."[70]

In the second place, Morison emulated Parkman's sense of empathy. Invoking distant cousin T. S. Eliot's injunction in "East Coker" that "Old men ought to be explorers," Morison referred repeatedly in the pages of his two-volume history to his own perceptions as a reexplorer of great discoverers such as Columbus and Magellan.[71] Admitting that he would have liked "to have been the first to burst [the] silent sea," Morison added, "Well, I know if I ever get to heaven and find Columbus and Magellan, they're the first people I want to interview. I feel very friendly with them."[72] Based on his own vast experience with the sea and sailors, he felt sufficently knowledgeable to concur with the discoverers' preferences for "young fellows" who "make better seamen and obey orders more briskly than old shellbacks who grumble and growl"; to excuse Columbus for a mathematical error, since "any sailor will condone a mistake of that nature"; and, "[a]s one who has 'lived' with him vicariously for several years," to speculate on the looks and personality of explorer John Davis. "There is nothing like a personal visit to newly discovered lands to bring home to one the pioneers' dangers and difficulties," Morison added with reference to his Parkmanesque style. Noting that his "admiration for them increases with time," he concluded that his years of "living with the records of heroic navigators and with the ordinary grousing, grumbling, believing but blaspheming mariner," made him uniquely qualified to appreciate their actions. "God bless 'em all," he wrote with a sense of personal nostalgia. "The world will never see their like again."[73]

Like Parkman, Morison relied on his empathetic understanding of the explorers to fill in gaps in the historical record. Although he complained of Eva Taylor's refusal to stick to "cold facts" when available, he felt justified himself on occasion in "supply[ing] a little imagination to bridge the known facts," because unlike Taylor, he claimed to know the sea. He imagined Leif Eriksson and his "cronnies lounging . . . at night and exchanging tales about their former adventures"; he visualized Cabot's men telling "unbelievable fish stories in Bristol"; and he presumed to know the humiliation Cartier must have felt when subjected to a rare display of Indian insolence at the departure of one of his ships. "One can well picture this scene," he noted— "glowering Frenchmen in the boat, braves exhibiting bare buttocks, little boys urinating, and men, women, and children raising just such an unholy clamor of whoops, laughs, shouts, and yells as only Indians could make." Noting that such imaginative re-creations of events associated with the age of sail and oar should fortify us "against a mechanized culture which reduces man to a moron," Morison warned that only those who had experienced the Americas as part of "a completely new and strange world" (as he had by sea and air) could pass suitable judgment on the performances of the earliest explorers.[74]

In the third (and most important) place, Morison sought to emulate the rich historical style of Parkman's generation. Not only did he cite Parkman and Prescott extensively in *The European Discovery of America*, he also adapted many of their literary tropes and conventions. Reviving the "Great Man" in history theory, for instance, Morison emphasized that exploration was the work of a few dedicated individualists who frequently struggled against institutions (the Church, monarchs, universities) to achieve their great successes. Columbus's formidable "character" provided the ego necessary to defy court mathematicians (who knew their math but had no imagination) to discover a new world. Amerigo Vespucci, "liar" though he was in Morison's mind for exaggerating his own discoveries, had the individual initiative to make three long transatlantic voyages and to convince skeptical geographers of his findings. It was the "sheer audacity, wit, and ability" of Magellan that allowed him to undertake the circumnavigation of the globe, in Morison's opinion "the greatest and most wonderful voyage in recorded history." Morison reserved special appreciation for those individuals who had lost their lives in pursuit of heroic dreams. "In closing let us not forget the gallant ships and brave mariners who lost their lives pursuing these voyages," he wrote in the conclusion to *The Northern Voyages*. Men like Raleigh, Cabot, the Corte Reals, Gilbert, Frobisher, John Davis, and Verrazzano, as well as the "thousands of mariners whose remains lie under the seamless shroud of the sea," Morison wrote with adulation, were heroes who "deserve to be perpetually remembered as precursors of two great empires in North America."[75]

Morison also appropriated Parkman's use of "chance" as a thematic principle for *The European Discovery of America*. Twentieth-century historians had come to view history as the careful working out of scientific laws, he noted, but the history of the fifteenth and sixteenth centuries could only be appreciated by those who understood, as nineteenth-century romantics did, that exploration was a fortuitous activity. The history of America, Morison reminded readers, was based on an accidental discovery by explorers operating by "the greatest serendipity of history." Highly sensitive to "the danger of their calling," sailors crossed the Atlantic "by guess and by God," particularly the latter. "In the great days of sail, before man's inventions and gadgets had given him a false confidence in his power to conquer the ocean," he noted, "seamen were the most religious of all workers on land and sea." Rarely doubting "the efficacy of prayer, or that he owed his life to the compassionate help of His Divine Majesty," the discoverer had a healthy appreciation for miraculous, mysterious, and unexplained occurrences. Some of the inability of professional historians in the twentieth century to understand the great explorers of the past, Morison averred, came from their inability to recognize the metaphysical commitment of all sailors, cabin boys, and explorers alike, to "the hands of the Almighty."[76]

Morison emphasized the role of nature in his history as well, attempting to approximate Parkman's genius in describing natural settings. Not only did he revive the image of the ocean as a "watery wilderness" (which Morison had first used in tribute to Turner in *The Oxford History of the United States*), he also painted its powerful beauty with elaborate brushstrokes. Anyone who has "spoomed" before the Pacific trade winds knows what Magellan's western voyage must have been like, he noted. "Bluest of blue seas, white fleecy clouds flying to leeward, frequent bursts of flying fish pursued by dorados . . . velvet nights with the old familiar stars returning . . . the zodiacal light in the east," and the memory of it must "wring the heart of every old salt," Morison argued. Morison came still closer in his approximation of Parkman when he portrayed in highly stylized terms the Canadian wilderness made famous by the latter. "There is nothing more superb in nature than this autumnal pageant in Canada," Morison wrote of Cartier's first fall in the New World. "Yellow birch leaves, brilliant scarlet, gold, and crimson maple, bronze ash and walnut, flash their colors against a background of green conifers, of which alone the larch, or hackmatack, turns its needles to gold before snow falls." "During the halcyon days of autumn, the colors are reflected in the river," he added in phrases eclipsing even Parkman's; "then a line gale strips the leaves from the branches and, when the wind drops, they float on the calm water like a stippled painting."[77]

Most of all, Morison adopted the didacticism of nineteenth-century historians, especially that of his grandfather Eliot. Ever ready to discover in the past important lessons for living in the present, Eliot had failed in his effort to inspire readers of the Civil War era with the historical insight that collapsed civilizations could repair themselves. Ironically, Eliot's grandson, using nineteenth-century techniques a century later, attempted to convince

Americans torn by the violence of the 1960s that a better world awaited them. "I am highly conscious of writing amid 'the tumult of the times disconsolate,' as Longfellow wrote of the 1860s," Morison wrote in the introduction to *The European Discovery of America*. "And to those now whimpering about the state of the world, and especially Americans predicting the collapse of society, I will say, 'Have faith! Hang on! Do something yourself to improve things!'" Citing the historical record of exploration, Morison asked: "What if England and France had given up trying to establish colonies? . . . What if they had written off North America as worthless, for want of precious metals? Where, then, would you be?" Hoping to reduce the despondency of his own age, he reminded readers of the "skeptical generation" that "thinking men" in the sixteenth century also "seriously believed that the world would crash; . . . yet a new era of hope and glory and enlargement of the human spirit was about to begin." If the Elizabethans, "constantly on the verge of disaster," could produce the likes of Shakespeare, Morison asked, then "Why not in our era?"[78]

The key to surviving an age of crisis, Morison argued, was to remain open to new discoveries. "In human affairs there is no snug harbor, no rest short of the grave," he moralized. "We are forever setting forth across new and stormy seas, or into outer space." Comparing the explorations of Columbus, Cabot, and Magellan to the moon landings of Armstrong and Aldrin, Morison argued that their lack of immediate purpose should not obscure their larger psychological impact. "Futile" and "unsuccessful in immediate results" as the voyages of Frobisher were, "we would not erase those three voyages from the roll of maritime history," he noted. "If nothing else, they taught England to 'go through with it' to glory, dominion, and empire." Aware that no amount of "hero-worship" could conceal the "plain fact" that the voyages were "failures, if we compare their objectives with the results," Morison argued that "[f]ailure and success are not absolutes, and the historian should attempt to understand the one as well as the other." The "gallantry, persistence, and enthusiasm" of the early explorers, he concluded, should be an example "to sailors and space explorers for all time to come" who hoped to liberate their ages from oppression and stagnation.[79]

The point of this "do something" philosophy was not lost on his professional readers. Unable to resolve debates that threatened to rip the profession apart, historians had reached a crisis point similar to that faced by Europeans in the age of discovery. Because everyone in the fifteenth century believed Ptolemy was right about the circumference of the Earth, no one dared even imagine that one could sail west to discover new lands until Columbus did it by using centuries old techniques. By the same logic, Morison urged historians not to become paralyzed by the limitations of theory but to simply "do history"—to write engaging prose and to rediscover in the age-old narrative technique a style suitable for producing lasting works of history.[80] Having found such liberation in *The European Discovery of America*, Morison proclaimed it his "most intellectually satisfying" work. Not only had the volumes allowed him to rediscover the scholarship of his grandfather and other historians in the "golden age" of nineteenth-century historical writing, but also they had taken him back to the beginning of American history—to the great age whose discoveries had shaped the destiny of the nation to whose history he had devoted his scholarly career. *The European Discovery of America* provided a sense of closure and fulfillment to a professional life that had begun six decades ago, when Morison first began preparing lectures on the discoverers for Channing's History 10. By the mid-1970s, it had become his alpha and omega.

Some professional historians, still troubled by the growing divisions within the American Historical Association, dismissed the offerings of Morison and the narrative revivalists as nostalgic and antimethodological. In a rather nasty book about the inability of historians to agree on a "logic of historical thought," *Historians' Fallacies*, David Hackett Fischer denounced Morison and the revivalists for their insinuation that the historian "is supposed to go a-wandering in the dark forest of the past, gathering facts like nuts and berries, until he has enough to make a general truth."[81] But most readers applauded the refreshing narrative quality of the book. Referring to Morison as the "Francis Parkman of the Ocean trails," one reviewer noted the "bright, informal, easy-to-read narrative style" of *The European Discovery of America: Southern Voyages*.[82] Another marveled at Morison's ability to make "a second-person" account seem like a "first-person report." "One has the curious sensation that it wasn't just Magellan who sailed through the straits, or Drake, or La Maire and Schouten who sailed round the Horn," the admirer wrote. One gets the impression "that somehow or other, defying time and the elements, Sam Morison was there, perhaps in a previous incarnation, jogging the elbow of the Admiral of the Ocean Seas, tut-tutting Magellan for his ill-advised amphibious landing that led to the navigator's death, frowning at the inhumanity of Cavendish, scorning the cupidity of ship chadlers, [or] quarreling with Charles V for his neglect of his seaman."[83] Such realistic writing, one reviewer hoped, would convince the troubled historical profession that hope, like Columbus's landfall at San Salvador on October 12, 1492, was just over the horizon.[84]

Whether Morison had such lofty professional intentions for *The European Discovery of America* or not, he certainly derived a good deal of personal satisfaction from its completion. "All my life I have wanted to write the full history of the discovery of America, and now I've done it," he told reporters. Grateful that he had retained his "faculties to finish it" and that reviewers did not have to say, "Poor old Morison—he's a bit past it," Morison asked his friend Reverend C. Harris Collingwood to make a public statement of his "thankfulness for God's mercy."[85] Collingwood made the acknowledgment the next day, in his Good Friday sermon for 1974, noting that it was a remarkable achievement for any man to persevere for fifty years with a dream and to thank "Almighty God for the strength to complete the task." If Morison was flattered by these words, which suggested a comparison

FIG. 9 *Morison at the Helm. In publicity photos like this one for* The European Discovery of America: Northern and South-ern Voyages, *Morison called attention to his own lifelong devotion to sailing. "My feeling for the sea, is such that writing about it is almost as embarrassing as making a confession of religious faith," he told reporters. Courtesy of the Harvard University Archives.*

between him and the God-fearing mariners about whom he wrote, he was still more humbled by Collingwood's analogy between *The European Discovery of America* and the Crucifixion. For both, the Reverend implied, the simple message of the Sixth Word was sufficent to convey the significance of the event: "It is finished."[86]

Great Circle Sailing

With the completion of *The European Discovery of America*, Morison's writing career came to an end. In a series of interviews in 1975 and 1976, he cited numerous reasons for his decision to stop producing histories, age being a major factor. "I'm too old and tired now," he remarked at the age of eighty-seven, "and I've finished everything I promised myself I would do 50 years ago." With the image of Beard perhaps in mind, he asked, "Why should I jeopardize my reputation by going on, like one of those ancient historians who fall into decline and finally receive only pitying reviews?"[87] Reporters who visited Morison at home, which was still the 44 Brimmer Street residence in which he had been born, agreed that he had reached a grand and noble age. They found it difficult, in fact, to imagine him as anything but a dignified elder statesman. "I am trying to picture him . . . a little boy with blond curls and a Fauntleroy suit 'running tiddly' on the ice of the frozen Public Garden duck pond," wrote one reporter. "The Admiral is the last person one would ever suspect—to apply to himself one of his own comments on George Washington—of having been a young man. He is far too—well Roman."[88]

Morison had also lost some of the combativeness that had made him so lively and controversial. Too tired to "enjoy a good set-to" with other historians anymore, Morison declined opportunities to rebut critics of *The European Discovery of America*. He had even mellowed toward those students, colleagues, and publishers with whom he had worked closely and whom he had somewhat domineered in the past. On the occasion of his eighty-eighth birthday on July 9, 1975, a friend captured this change of temperament in a playful poem:

> Fourscore and eight! The numbered years unfold—
> Our Admiral takes 'em, witty, wise and bold.
> He launches tomes as other men launch ships,
> Gets rave reviews, and gathers in the Chips.
> Nothing withheld in age that youth can give—
> Not hearty Appetite nor courage to live;
> Nothing abated of his zest to learn,
> He still can roast a Critic to a turn.
> Yet something's added—warm, and fair to see.
> 'Tis sheer Benevolence, ardent Courtesy.

Is this the Teacher that in Harvard days
Peered at the student through an icy haze?
Is this the Captain who for virtue's sake
Would make the bravest of the crew to shake?
Me thinks he shifts the order of the vine—
Turns youthful vinegar to noblest Wine.[89]

The once "uncompromising" man who had been intolerant of "the academic milch cows" and the "swivel-chair tacticians," had become a beneficent "grand old man."[90]

Part of Morison's decision to stop writing history was also based on the loss of his second wife. Having struggled for years with cancer, Priscilla Morison succumbed to the disease several months before the publication of *The Southern Voyages*. Morison never really emerged from beneath "the shadow" of "great grief" occasioned by her death. In a moving tribute to her—a privately printed memoir entitled *Vita Nuova*—Morison recounted their last days together as he raced against time to complete his manuscript for her. Approaching "the end of a long literary voyage," he noted, "I read [chapters] aloud to her before grievous pain made it impossible for her to pay attention."[91] After Priscilla's hospitalization, the end came swiftly, and regrettably there was not a proper sense of closure. "I did not react as I should have to what I now believe to have been a hint from Heaven," Morison admitted. A few minutes after midnight on February 22, 1974, Morison was awakened by the front doorbell ringing. When he opened the front door, he found a taxi driver who said a cab had been ordered for 44 Brimmer Street, but he did not know by whom. Having been told by the doctors that his wife was improving, Morison concluded that there must have been some mistake and sent the taxi away. "Although it seems odd to confer an angelic mission on a Boston 'hackie,'" Morison later wrote, "I really believe that this one was a divine messenger; and if I had been sensitive enough to heed him, I might have been with my darling during her last hours on earth. Blindness of heart, my besetting sin, lost me this final boon." Robbed of the chance to spend these last precious moments with his wife, he simply wished to follow her to the grave. "Now as a tottering old man thrusts out his hand to steady himself on a tree or post, so I throw out my heart to the light of my life, . . . praying 'Oh, God, bring my soul to hers, and that right soon; and grant us the supreme boon of eternal life together.'"[92]

If fate intervened to deny Morison a sense of closure in his marital life, it was more generous to him in his historical life. As a young boy he had sensed (if he had not quite understood) the disappointments of a grandfather whose historical vision was shaped by the romantic writers of the nineteenth century and by the patrician desire to create a usable past. Hoping to retain history's vast readership while making it a public service industry,

Samuel Eliot founded the American Social Science Association to facilitate both dreams. But the ASSA quickly splintered into numerous subunits, including the American Historical Association, which pursued specific disciplinary and professional ends and abandoned at times both the narrative and the utilitarian aspects of Eliot's vision. In the final years of his grandson's career, however, those goals were reunited, although perhaps in a form that Eliot would not have recognized. Morison had never ignored the profession as some amateur writers had done throughout the twentieth century; indeed, he had been president of the American Historical Association and had lashed out continually at journalists, debunkers, and fiction writers who presumed to write history without the proper credentials. If history was to be usable, Morison argued throughout his career, it must be reliable. But as the formal, institutional structure of the profession began to weaken under the pressure of radicalizing events in the 1960s and as professional historians began to lose readers, Morison turned increasingly to the subjective, idiosyncratic, even romantic vision of his nineteenth-century predecessors. In posing the narrative tradition as an alternative to the objective, scientific, and professional ambitions of AHA members, Morison recognized that history could also not be usable unless it was read. In adopting such a posture in his final works, Morison brought his career full circle back to the preprofessional world of his grandfather Eliot. His popular narrative works such as *The Maritime History of Massachusetts*, *Admiral of the Ocean Sea*, and *The Oxford History of the American People* defined the perimeter of this figurative circle and his professional and academic ones such as *Harrison Gray Otis*, *The Oxford History of the United States*, *The Harvard Tercentenary History*, and *The History of United States Naval Operations in World War II* served as the circle's center.

Morison also lived long enough to appreciate the many accolades he received on the completion of his great scholarly circuit. "Samuel Eliot Morison looms over other American historians like an intimidating patriarch," wrote one admirer;[93] "Rear Admiral Morison is probably the most widely read historian in the world," claimed another.[94] Numerous other reviewers of his career heralded him as "America's greatest living historian" and the "dean of American historians."[95] One friend remarked on the many prizes and plaudits bestowed on Morison in the last years of his life: "you seem to be collecting awards as if you were out gathering flowers."[96] Perhaps the most meaningful of these was also the most appropriate. In 1970, the Society of American Historians granted Morison a special silver Francis Parkman medal in recognition of his "many distinguished contributions to the objectives our organization seeks to advance."[97] Created as a means of reacting to the stale, scientific monographs dominating the profession, the bronze Parkman medal was awarded by the society each year "to the historical work [that] . . . best typifies the kind of history Francis Parkman stood for, combining sound research and literary distinction." But only once previously had the organization granted a special silver Parkman medal, and that was to the founder of the Society, Allan Nevins. No one in the twentieth century had done more to "encourage literary distinction in the writing of American history and biography," the award commendation stated, than Samuel Eliot Morison.[98]

In his last years, Morison identified more with Francis Parkman than even the award's committee of the Society of American Historians could have suspected. With the 1892 publication of Parkman's *Half-Century of Conflict*, Morison had once noted, the final volume of that historian's epic series on the French and British in North America was completed and "the last *voussoir* fell into place in the great arch of his career. Shortly thereafter, suffering from a variety of physical ailments, Parkman announced the end of his writing career over the objections of friends and relatives."[99] Morison's friends reacted in a similar manner to his announced retirement from writing. "I would feel sad to hear you say you would not write another book, if I believed you," wrote one acquaintance. "You will take a rest, I hope, after this strenuous period of work, and then the pen will begin to move, and you could write with your eyes closed—and you will when the spirit moves you."[100] Similarly, an interviewer refused to believe that Morison's sixty-year career was over. "I don't know about this, at all," he warned his readers. "No, I would not be even remotely surprised to hear that some brisk Saturday morning . . . he has cast off the mooring rode, stacked the backstays, hoisted the mainsail and jib, and sailed out on a last graceful curvet at the turn of a spring tide to investigate . . . the exact routes of Noah's Ark." Having sailed once again, "he will sit down at the convenient time, take up his pen, and, updating the facts and correcting the figments of the Ibn Abbas, proceed to write out the history of the voyage in detail."[101]

Some thought that retirement would kill the historian. "I could not conceive of Morison not writing history," Wilcomb Washburn wrote, and "I feared he would die when he stopped writing."[102] Perhaps this writer's fears were not ill founded. In early May 1976, Morison suffered a massive stroke from which, his doctors concluded, no recovery could be made. When death finally stilled his pen on the fifteenth of May, many of those closest to him still could not believe his career and life had ended. "Some things—like the writings of Admiral Morison—seem as though they should go on and on without end," wrote one admirer. "The end comes as a bit of a shock, as with the cutting down of a tree that has been a neighborhood landmark."[103] Another observed that Morison had "filled the shoes of Francis Parkman for so many years," and that he had "covered so much territory in them" that readers naturally expected him to walk in them forever.[104] Still another imagined the impact Morison would have on his new celestial audience. "St. Peter, greeting him, will feel embarrassed that he himself hadn't taught as long or had as much patience," he wrote; whereas St. Paul will regret "that in his own lifetime he hadn't sailed as far or written as much." Only God, this playful admirer admitted, "will feel perfectly at ease."[105]

Of all the tributes to Morison, perhaps the most appropriate was that of longtime friend Walter Whitehill. "Ovid would have enjoyed describing the metamorphoses of Samuel Eliot Morison," he wrote in appreciation of the historian's long and versatile career. "What other man ever has been, or is likely to be, a professor both at Oxford and Harvard, a private of infantry and a rear admiral?" Whitehill asked. Equally comfortable in "academic costume or blue naval uniform," in "oilskins" or "opera hat and cape," Morison was at home "presiding over the meetings of the American Antiquarian Society" or "striding purposefully into Widener Library in well-cut riding costume, carrying green baize bags full of books." And he could write with equal adaptability, at times "mingling the periods of an Edward Gibbon or a Winston Churchill with the pithy homeliness of a New England general storekeeper." In everything he did, Whitehill concluded, there was "the underlying basis of style and quality, whether in the wine, food, company, conversation, or the writing of history." And, "certainly in my friendship with him," Morison's companion concluded, there was "a great deal of human kindness."[106]

In the meantime, the "profession" of history, which was born with Morison in the late nineteenth century, threatened to die with him in the nation's bicentennial year. Struggling to create new syntheses for the two hundredth anniversary of the nation, many historians found themselves unable to find meaningful unities or purposes. "As a broad community of discourse, as a community of scholars united by common aims, common standards, and common purposes, the discipline of history had ceased to exist," wrote Peter Novick of the period.[107] The 1960s and Watergate had done much to erode American faith in a culture of consensus or a national character. Under such circumstances, many turned to Morison for relief and direction. His narrative mode and idiosyncratic style seemed to promise a return to an age when history was essentially a matter of "telling stories." If some objected "to the inherent political conservatism of narrative histories, in which structures were implicitly accepted as a given background against which individual actors shaped events, treating those structures as unproblematic," at least readers took pleasure in reading his works and profited from them.[108] In a letter to Morison's family dated three days after the historian's death, Arthur Schlesinger, Jr., paid tribute to Morison's most lasting virtue:

> Your father was a most important man in my life. It was from him that I first understood the importance of style in history. He knew that the essence of history is the reconstruction of the past, and he used his enormous literary gifts to fuse narrative and analysis into a single texture. But I mean style in a larger sense too—his whole attitude toward life and society.
>
> One feels that his death breaks a last link to the classic past. He was in the apostalic succession, the last heir of the great New England tradition—Bancroft, Parkman, Prescott, Motley, Henry Adams—and there is no one to come after.[109]

Morison could have asked for no finer epitaph than this. Yet perhaps he would have prayed for the addition of an optimistic line or two holding out the possibility that new Parkmans would arise from the ashes of a smoldering profession as one had in fulfillment of Edward Channing's prophecy uttered nearly sixty years earlier at the start of a new career and a new age.

EPILOGUE

When I began my investigation of Morison just several years after his death, the fate of the American historical profession seemed somewhat in question. The pessimistic tone of historians has eased some since the 1970s, and it seems clear that the profession will survive in one form or another. Whether the optimism about solving the problems of historical knowledge expressed by the founders of the American Historical Association will ever return remains to be seen. In the meantime, Morison's reputation continues to grow in inverse relation to the fortunes of the profession. As professional historians isolate themselves from popular audiences, these readers turn appreciably back to the works of Morison. Whether describing the capriciousness of Columbus, the frailty of the elder John Paul Jones, or the uncertainty of life at sea during war, Morsion acted on the belief that success would come to the historian who was responsible to both God and man. Perhaps history in the narrative style as he wrote it, with its emphasis on the foibles of human actors strutting and fretting on historical stages, will be rejuvenated in the decades ahead. If so, the American Historical Association will need to reevaluate its position relative to Morison, determining whether to embrace or reject his narrative revivalism and his unique conception of a "usable past."

In the meantime, monuments to Morison's genius continue to emerge. In 1977, *American Heritage* magazine announced the establishment of the Samuel Eliot Morison Award for "the best book on American history by an American author that sustains the tradition that good history is literature as well as high scholarship."[1] In announcing the $5000 award, editor Bruce Catton noted that "[a]nyone privileged to work in the field of history must feel bound to pay a tribute" to Morison as a "great master of a great craft."[2] In 1979 the Navy commissioned a guided missile frigate in his honor, the U.S.S. *Samuel Eliot Morison*. In a ceremony held at the Bath Iron Works, principal speaker Elliott Richardson noted that the name Morison was synonymous with integrity. Likening the historian to George Washington and Abraham Lincoln in this regard, Richardson hailed Morison as "the most distinguished American historian of this century." Bumper stickers were produced to commemorate the occasion with the ship's logo "Making History for Others to Record."[3] A coat of arms was even commissioned, picturing a gold quill dipping into "the inky waters of the deep" and red and white bars signifying "the famed multivolume history of the *U.S. Naval Operations in World War II*." An early mariner's astrolabe represented "Morison's retracing of the pathway taken by Columbus," and a sword and cutlass symbolized his "vigilance and readiness."[4]

Most prominent of all, however, remains the Morison statue on the

Commonwealth Mall Plaza. As I write these final lines, I am once again before the indomitable Sphinx. The contrasts I noted at the statue's unveiling still remain, but now I find in them a reassuring tribute to Morison's longevity and versatility. If Morison was never both sailor and historian at the same time, as the sculpture implies, he was certainly both at different intervals, and many other things as well. The complexities in Jencks's sculpture convey adequately the intimidating diversity of the historian's interests and knowledge; they remind us that in the search for "truth" and "passion" Morison went beyond mere storytelling or antiquarianism. He inspired readers of all ages to understand not only their nation's past but its literary tradition and to take that tradition seriously. His was a monumental intellectual achievement, and he himself appreciated the need to memorialize such achievements. Citing the "vivid and spirited narrative style" of Prescott, whose "scrupulous care and integrity" throughout each of his nearly two dozen volumes attracted thousands of Americans to the study of history, Morison complained nearly a century after Prescott's death that in Boston there was not "a statue, a tablet, or even an inscription to tell the visitor that here lived and worked the greatest of American historians."[5] Thankfully the same cannot now be said of an equally great and perhaps more cryptic historian, Samuel Eliot Morison.

NOTES

The following abbreviations for archive collections will be used in the notes following the first mention of the collection.

ABH   Albert Bushnell Hart, Pusey Library, Harvard University
CMAP   Charles M. Andrews Papers, Yale University Library
FDR HP   Franklin Delano Roosevelt File, Hyde Park, New York
HUA   Harvard University Archives
MSEM   Manuscripts of Samuel Eliot Morison, Pusey Library, Harvard University
NOA   Naval Operational Archives, Washington Naval Yard, Washington, D.C.
NWC   The Papers of Admiral Richard Bates, Naval War College, Newport, Rhode Island
PAJB   Papers of Albert J. Beveridge, General Correspondence, 1890–1927, Library of Congress.
SEMC   The Samuel Eliot Morison Collection, Harvard University Archives, Pusey Library
SEP BA   The Samuel Eliot Papers, Boston Athenaeum
WBGP   William B. Goodwin Papers, Connecticut State Library, Hartford, Connecticut
WP   Wendell Papers, Houghton Library, Harvard University

PREFACE: THE GREAT SPHINX

1. The George B. Henderson Foundation was established by George B. Henderson who died in 1972. Monies from the foundation are to be "devoted to the enhancement of the physical appearance of the City of Boston for the benefit of its citizens." For more on the dedication ceremony and its participants, see Program, Dedication Ceremonies for the Samuel Eliot Morison Memorial, 15 October 1982.

2. Thomas Boylston Adams, "Samuel Eliot Morison: Passionate Historian," included in correspondence from Mary O. Shannon, Executive Secretary, Boston Art Commission, to Gregory M. Pfitzer, 3 November 1982; in possession of author.

3. Penelope Jencks received her B.F.A. in painting from Boston University in 1958 where she studied with Hans Hoffman. She has received several rewards for her work, including the Massachusetts Artists Foundation Award and the Macdowell Colony Fellowship.

4. Thomas Boylston Adams, "Passion and Truth Are the Life of Memorials," *Yankee*, January 1983, 94–103.

5. Samuel Eliot Morison to Charles Page Smith, 29 December 1964, "General Correspondence," SEMC HUG(FP)—33.15 box 12. The Samuel Eliot Morison Collection, Harvard University Archives; hereafter all references to this collection will be cited SEMC; Samuel Eliot Morison will be abbreviated SEM.

CHAPTER 1: HISTORICAL ROOTS

1. Morison, *The Class Lives of Samuel Eliot and Nathaniel Holmes Morison, Harvard 1839* (Privately printed, 1926). See also, "The Diaries of Mrs. Emily Marshall (Otis) Eliot,"

6 vols., (30 June 1859–31 December 1864), M59 Reel 969, Schlesinger Library, Harvard University.

2. Morison, "Genealogy: Morison-Greene," SEMC HUG(FP)—33.1 box 2. On the deaths of Eliot's sons, see Samuel Eliot, *William Samuel Eliot, 1854–1874* (Cambridge, Mass.: Riverside Press, 1875).

3. Morison, *One Boy's Boston* (Boston: Houghton Mifflin, 1962), 13.

4. "The Diaries of Emily Marshal (Eliot) Morison," 17 vols. (1 January 1868–December 1922), MS 79-1923, Schlesinger Library, Harvard University. For more on Morison's mother, see Morison, *One Boy's Boston*, 14–15.

5. Samuel Eliot to His Executrix, 20 October 1894, "Personal and Family Correspondence and Letters," SEMC HUG(FP)—33.6 box 1.

6. Morison, *One Boy's Boston*, 31, 41–42.

7. Ibid., 18.

8. Morison, *The Class Lives of Samuel Eliot and Nathaniel Holmes Morison*, 18. See also SEM to Miss Henning, 13 January 1942, "Letters on Samuel Eliot's Last Illness and Death, 1898," SEMC HUG(FP)—33.6 box 1.

9. Morison, *One Boy's Boston*, 31.

10. Ibid., 50–51.

11. Morison, *The Class Lives of Samuel Eliot and Nathaniel Holmes Morison*, 19–20.

12. Morison, *One Boy's Boston*, 76.

13. Morison, "Autobiographical Sketch," Biographical Papers, SEMC HUG(FP)—33.1 box 1. For assessments of Eliot's career, see "Famous Persons at Home," *Time and the Hour* 65 (Boston) 21 May 1895. George Harvey Genzmer, "Samuel Eliot," *The Dictionary of American Biography* vol. 4, ed. Dumas Malone (New York: Charles Scribner's Sons, 1936), 84; "The Samuel Eliot Memorial Fund," from the *Alumnae-Girl's School Newsletter*, December 1898, Cambridge, Mass.

14. Morison, *One Boy's Boston*, 2.

15. Eliot, Preface to *History of Liberty: Part 1: Ancient Romans*, 4 vols., (Boston: Little, Brown, 1853), vol. 1: i. For more on Eliot's post-Harvard travel and education, see "Journal of a Tour to the South," 21 January 1839, and Logbook No. 5: "Europe, 6 August 1842 through 22 September 1842," The Samuel Eliot Papers, Boston Athenaeum; hereafter this collection will be referred to as SEP BA. I wish to express my thanks to Stephen Nonack of the Boston Athenaeum for permission to read his unpublished paper, " 'This Office of Usefulness': Samuel Eliot as an Educator."

16. "Samuel Eliot," *Horae Scholasticae* (22 October 1898).

17. Alden Bradford, *History of Massachusetts* (Boston: Richardson and Lord, 1822–29). For more on Bradford, see Morison, "Memoir of Alden Bradford," Proceedings of the Massachusetts Historical Society 55 (1921–22): 153–65.

18. Prescott, quoted in George H. Callcott, "Historians in Early Nineteenth-Century America," *New England Quarterly* 32 (1959): 518.

19. Charles Haight Farnham, *A Life of Francis Parkman* (Boston: Little, Brown, 1901), 106.

20. Mason Wade, *Francis Parkman* (New York: Viking, 1942).

21. For more on the use of these literary devices by nineteenth-century historians, see David Levin, *History as Romantic Art* (Stanford, Calif.: Stanford University Press, 1959).

22. Francis Parkman to Samuel Eliot, 8 November 1856, SEP BA. See also George Bancroft to Samuel Eliot, 23 July 1849, ibid., and William Prescott to Samuel Eliot, n.d., ibid.

23. Eliot, Preface to vol. 1, *The Liberty of Rome, a History with Historical Account of the Liberty of Ancient Nations*, 2 vols. (New York: G. P. Putnam, 1849).

24. Ibid.

25. Callcott, "Historians in Early Nineteenth-Century America," 501.

26. Barrett Wendell, "Samuel Eliot," Proceedings of the American Academy of Arts and Sciences, 34 (Cambridge, Mass.: American Academy of Arts and Sciences, 1899): 646. See also Review of Liberty of Rome: A History, by Samuel Eliot, North American Review 70 (January 1850): 136–53.

27. Eliot, 19 April 1851, "Diary: 19 April 1851–22 December 1852," SEP BA.

28. Eliot primarily participated in educational "experiments" of various sorts—private tutoring, lecturing at the Warren Street Chapel School, a professorship at Trinity College, and the presidency of Trinity. For more on this phase of Eliot's career, see Eliot, 19 April 1851, "Diary: 19 April 1851–22 December 1862," SEP BA; Samuel Eliot, "The Scholar of the Past and the Scholar of the Present," Inaugural Address, Trinity College (Hartford, Conn.: Press of Case, Tiffany and Company, 1856), 6–7; Glenn Weaver, The History of Trinity College, 2 vols. (Hartford, Conn.: Trinity College Press, 1967), vol. 1: 101, 118; and "Trustees Minutes, Trinity College, 20 June 1861," (Hartford: Case, Tiffany & Co., 1861).

29. See, for instance, his complaints while traveling in Europe as a young man in "Logbook No. 5: Europe, 6 August 1842–22 September 1842," SEP BA.

30. Eliot, [1864], "Journal: 20 January 1863–15 November 1875," ibid.

31. Eliot, Introductory Note, Journal of Social Science 1 (1869): 2.

32. Thomas Haskell, The Emergence of Professional Social Science: The American Social Science Association and the Nineteenth-Century Crisis of Authority (Urbana: University of Illinois Press, 1977).

33. L. L. Bernard, Origins of American Sociology: The Social Science Movement in America (New York: Thomas Y. Crowell, 1943), 564, 573. See also, Eliot, "Civil Service Reform," Journal of Social Science 1 (1869): 119; Eliot, "American Church Review," Journal of Social Science 5 (1872): 98; and Eliot, "The Relief of Labor," Journal of Social Science 4 (1871), 15–24.

34. J. Franklin Jameson, "Early Days of the American Historical Association, 1884–1895," American Historical Review 40 (1934): 1–5. See also John Higham, History: Professional Scholarship in America (Baltimore: Johns Hopkins University Press, 1965), 6–13. Note that the prominent historians and public figures among those listed as members of the American Social Science Association include Charles Francis Adams, Jr., John Lothrop Motley, Henry R. Torrey, Justin Winsor, and F. W. Palfrey ("Officers and Members of the Association," Journal of Social Science 1 (1869): 195–200).

35. "A New Historical Movement," Nation (18 September 1884): i–iii.

36. Ibid.

37. Boston Herald, 7 September 1884, as cited in "Secretary's Report," Annual report of the American Historical Association 1 (1885): 9.

38. "Secretary's Report," Papers of the American Historical Association, vol. 1, no. 2, first series (1885), 12–13. See also Andrew D. White, "Studies in General History and the History of Civilization," ibid., 16–17.

39. Higham, History: Professional Scholarship in America, 106–7.

40. Bernard, Origins of American Sociology, 4.

41. Peter Novick, That Noble Dream: The "Objectivity Question" and the American Historical Profession (New York: Cambridge University Press, 1988), 47–60.

42. Eliot, "Diary, 2 September 1897–29 May 1898," SEP BA.

43. Eliot, Epiphany 1877, "Diary: December 1876–7 June 1897," SEP BA.

44. Wendell, "Samuel Eliot," 649.

45. SEM to Martha Mitchell, 28 October 1944, SEMC HUG(FP)—33.1 box 1.

46. Morison, Vistas of History (New York: Alfred A. Knopf, 1964), 55.

47. Morison, One Boy's Boston, 3–4, 15.

48. Morison, "Autobiographical Sketch," SEMC HUG(FP)—33.1 box 1.

49. SEM to Mrs. Samuel Eliot, 8 November 1898, "Samuel Eliot Morison's Letters to and from his grandparents," ibid., 33.6 box 3.

50. SEM to Grandma, 1 May 1900, ibid. See also Morison, "Autobiographical Sketch," ibid., 33.1 box 1.

51. Morison, *One Boy's Boston*, 67, 37, 36.

52. Morison, "Autobiographical Sketch," SEMC HUG(FP)—33.1 box 1.

53. Morison, *One Boy's Boston*, 45.

54. "Letters from 'Pu,'" 16 June 1900, 20 July [1898], and undated, Eliot Family Letters: Chronological File, 1877–1910, SEMC HUG(FP)—33.6 box 3.

55. Morison, *One Boy's Boston*, 77.

56. Sam Vaughan to SEM, undated; SEM to Mr. and Mrs. Samuel Eliot, 12 August 1898, "Samuel Eliot Morison's Letters to and from his grandparents," SEMC HUG(FP)—33.6 box 3.

57. Morison, *One Boy's Boston*, 78, 80. See also Morison, "Autobiographical Sketch," SEMC HUG(FP)—33.1 box 1.

CHAPTER 2: THE MAKING OF A HISTORIAN

1. Rollo Walter Brown, *Harvard Yard in the Golden Age* (New York: Current Books, 1948), 13, 37. For Morison's perspective on Charles Eliot, see Morison, *Three Centuries of Harvard* (Cambridge, Mass.: Harvard University Press, 1936), 331, 334–36, 342–44. President Eliot was Morison's grandfather's cousin.

2. Kermit Vanderbilt, *Charles Eliot Norton: Apostle of Culture in a Democracy* (Cambridge, Mass.: Belknap Press, 1959).

3. Brown, *Harvard Yard in the Golden Age*, 14.

4. For more on the social standing of the Morison family in Boston, see Morison, *One Boy's Boston*, (Boston: Houghton Mifflin, 1962), 47–58.

5. Morison, *Three Centuries of Harvard*, 416.

6. Ibid., 423, 422, 424.

7. Morison, "Autobiographical Sketch," SEMC HUG(FP)—33.1 box 1.

8. SEM to Edward D. Bennett, 15 March 1966, ibid., 33.15 box 2.

9. Morison, "Autobiographical Sketch," ibid., 33.1 box 1.

10. Ibid.

11. Morison, *Three Centuries of Harvard*, 370–71.

12. "Transcript of Grades, Samuel Eliot Morison, 1904–07" Holyoke Center, Harvard University.

13. Morison, "Autobiographical Sketch," SEMC HUG (FP)—33.1 box 1.

14. For more on the evolution of the elective system, see Morison, *Three Centuries of Harvard*, 234–37, 341–46, 384–90.

15. Morison, "Autobiographical Sketch," SEMC HUG(FP)—33.1 box 1.

16. Ephraim Emerton, "History," in Morison, ed., *The Development of Harvard University, 1869–1929* (Cambridge, Mass.: Harvard University Press, 1930), 152. Morison was responsible for certain sections of this article; when referring to these sections, I will make special mention of Morison's authorship. For more on the early history of the department, see Morison, *Three Centuries of Harvard*, 344–49, 375–76.

17. John Higham, *History: Professional Scholarship in America*, (Baltimore: Johns Hopkins University Press, 1965), 92–103.

18. "Division of History, Government, and Economics, Records, 1896–1951," Records of the History Department, Divisional Records, Harvard University Archives (hereafter cited as HUA), UAV 453.5; Emerton, "History," 153.

19. Emerton, "History," 154–56. For more on Adams's assessment of his own work at

Harvard, see Henry Adams, *The Education of Henry Adams* (Boston: Houghton Mifflin, 1918), 302–3.

20. Emerton, "History," 158–59, 160, 161, 166–76.

21. "Minutes," Records of the Department of History and Government, 1891–1910," Records of the History Department, Divisional Records, HUA UAV 454.1.5.2.

22. Emerton, "History," 159. For more on Sir Henry Maine (historical jurisprudence) and William Bishop Stubbs (British institutional history), see Higham, *History: Professional Scholarship in America*, 159–60. For more on George Waitz (German constitutional historian) and Fustel de Coulanges (French institutional historian), see Harry Elmer Barnes, *A History of Historical Writing* (Norman: University of Oklahoma Press, 1937).

23. Including the Constitutional History of England since George I, Principles of Constitutional Law, English Constitutional History from 1845 to George I, Early Mediaeval History with special reference to Institutions, French History to Louis XIV with special reference to Institutions, the Constitutional Development of the United States, the Federal Government of the United States, and Early American Institutions. These courses are referenced with brief descriptions in"Courses of Instruction," *Harvard College Catalogue* (Cambridge, Mass.: University Press, published yearly, 1890–91); see also Emerton, "History," 159.

24. Emerton, "History," 162.

25. [Silas Macvane] to A. Lawrence Lowell, 24 January 1903, "History 1: 1902–1919," History Department, Correspondence and Papers, c. 1900–1955, HUA UAV 454.22.8.

26. On Coolidge, see Harold Jefferson Coolidge, *Archibald Cary Coolidge, Life and Letters* (Boston: Houghton Mifflin, 1932).

27. "History Department Statistics," Correspondence and Papers, c. 1900–55, HUA UAV 454.22.8; "Conspectus of Courses in History and Government—Remarks on the Table of Statistics," Records of the History Department, HUA, ibid.

28. Morison, *Three Centuries of Harvard*, 376; Morison "Section 3," in "History," 172.

29. Morison, *Vistas of History* (New York: Alfred A. Knopf, 1964), 55.

30. Emerton, "History," 159; Higham, *History: Professional Scholarship in America*, 159–65; see also Albert Bushnell Hart, "How to Study History," in *How to Study History, Literature, the Fine Arts* (Meadville, Pa.: The Chautauqua-Century Press, 1895).

31. Albert Bushnell Hart, *National Ideals Historically Traced, 1607–1907*, vol. 26 of A. B. Hart, ed., *The American Nation: A History*, 26 vols. (New York: Harper & Brothers, 1907), xiv.

32. Higham, *History: Professional Scholarship in America*, 77–78.

33. Ibid.

34. Charles Homer Haskins to A. Lawrence Lowell, 13 January 1903.

35. "History 1: 1902–1919," Records of the History Department, Correspondence and Papers, 1900–1955, HUA UAV 454. 22:8; Charles Homer Haskins, "The Historical Curriculum in Colleges." Reprinted from the Minutes of the Association of History Teachers of the Middle States and Maryland for 1904 (New York: Knickerbocker Press, 1904), 2, 6, 8. See also Morison, "History," 170.

36. "Minutes, History Department Meeting, 16 January 1903," Records of the Department of History and Government, HUA UAV 453.5. The committee included Haskins and Channing, and their majority report suggested "the establishment of two new general courses, one on Medieval History and another on English history."

37. Charles Haskins to President Lowell, 13 January 1903, "History 1: 1902–1919," Records of the History Department, HUA UAV 454.22.8.

38. [Macvane] to Lowell, 24 January 1903, ibid. See also, Haskins to Lowell, 2 February 1903, ibid.

39. "Remarks of the Chairman," 20 April 1910, Conspectus of Courses in History and Government, ibid.

40. Morison, "History," 171.

41. "Courses of Instruction," *Harvard College Catalogue, 1904–05.*

42. Haskins, "The Historical Curriculum in Colleges," 14, 11.

43. "History Department Statistics," Correspondence and Papers, c. 1900–10, HUA UAV 454.22.8.

44. Minutes, Meeting of the Harvard History Club, 12 November 1907, Records of the Department of History and Government, 1891–1910, HUA UAV 454.1. 5.2.

45. Morison, "History," 176.

46. "History Department Statistics," Correspondence and Papers, c. 1900–55, HUA UAV 454.22.8.

47. Edward Channing, "The Present State of Historical Writing in America," Reprinted from the Proceedings of the American Antiquarian Society for October 1910 (Worcester, Mass.: Davis Press, 1910).

48. Morison, "A Memoir and Estimate of Albert Bushnell Hart," Proceedings of the Massachusetts Historical Society 77 (March 1965): 44 n.25. Morison writes, "In the new history reading room at the top of Widener, one may see in the late Julius Klein's 'Bayeux Tapestry' of the history department a rather malicious caricature of Hart scuttling across the Yard with the bulging green bags of notes. This represents the Coolidge point of view; Klein was one of his disciples."

49. "Reading List for History 1(a)," HUA HUC 8904.338.1.56. The complete reading list also included Thomas Hodgkin, *Dynasty of Theodosius* (London: Oxford University Press, 1889); Charles Bemont and Gabriel Monod, *Medieval Europe from 395 to 1270* (New York: Henry Holt, 1902); and Ephraim Emerton, *Introduction to the Middle Ages* (Boston: Ginn, 1888).

50. Morison, "Student Notebook for History 1(a)," ibid.

51. Morison, "Autobiographical Sketch," SEMC HUG(FP)—33.1 box 1.

52. Morison, "The Expedition against Cadiz, 1596," Thesis for History 27, HUC 8905.338.27.56, 15–16, 19–20.

53. Morison, "History," 160.

54. Morison, "The Suppression of the Paris Commune: May 20–27, 1871," Thesis for History 16b, HUC 8905.338.16.56, 1, 15, 34, 54.

55. Morison, "History," 173–75.

56. Barrett Wendell to SEM, 3 June 1906, General Correspondence, SEMC HUG(FP)—33.15 box 13.

57. Ibid.

58. Morison, "History," 174.

59. Morison eventually took the following courses in the fields of literature, philosophy, and history: Bliss Perry's English 7b, "The Age of Johnson, 1748–98" (see Morison, "Notes and Reports for English 7b, HUC 8906.324.7.56); William James's Philosophy D (see HUC 8906.370.56); Charles Gross's History 9, "Medieval History" (see "The Influence of Dunstan on Church and State, 924–988," Thesis for History 9, HUC 8907.338.9.56); Professor Nielson's English 28, "English Literature, from the Publication of the Literary Ballads to the Death of Scott, 1798–1832" (see Morison's student papers: "Shelley's Politics," "Byron's Political Opinions," and "The Personality of Charles Lamb," HUC 8906.324.8.56).

60. The full title of Santayana's course was "Philosophy 10: Ideals of Society, Religion, Art, and Science, in Their Historical Development." Morison's notebooks for this course contain many endearing tributes to Santayana, including a cartoon picture of him with the caption "our gentle-eyed professor" HUA HUC 8904.338.1.56.

61. "Midyear Exam for Philosophy 10," ibid., HUAC 8907.370.10.56.

62. George Santayana, "History," in *The Life of the Reason, or the Phases of Human Progress*, vol. 5 of *Reason in Science*, 5 vols. (New York: Charles Scribner's sons, 1906), 40.

63. Santayana, "History," 39, 47, 19, 42, 46, 54, 49, 57, 53, 46, 64, 67, 61.

64. Ibid., 47, 62.

65. Morison, "The Early Travels of Peter the Great, 1697–1698," May 1907, written for History 27: Modern European History, taught by Haskins, HUA HU 92.7.580, 2, 10, 17, 19, 34, 38.

66. Morison, "Pope Alexander VI and the Temporal Power, 1492–1503," Thesis for History 7, HUC 8907.338.7.56, 1, 3, 7, 4, 8, 11–12, 15.

67. Morison, *Three Centuries of Harvard*, 388.

68. Morison, "The Ottoman Empire under Suleiman the Magnificent, 1520–1566," Thesis for Semitic 14, HUC 8907.380.14.56.

69. Ibid., i–ii, 1, 18, 8–11, 7, 3, 6, 28, 32, 33–36.

70. Toy's comments were made on the front page of Morison's paper at an unspecified date. Morison's "degree with distinction" was voted at a meeting of the Division of History and Political Science in the spring of 1907; see "Minutes of the Meeting of the Division of History and Political Science," 27 May 1907, Records of the History Department, HUA UAV 454.1.

71. Morison, "Albert Bushnell Hart, 1889–1939," Proceedings of the Massachusetts Historical Society 66 (1936–1941): 435–36.

72. Ibid.

73. Morison, "A Memoir and Estimate of Albert Bushnell Hart," 41.

74. Morison, "Albert Bushnell Hart, 1889–1939," 436.

75. Morison, "A Memoir and Estimate of Albert Bushnell Hart," 41.

76. Morison, "Albert Bushnell Hart, 1889–1939," 436.

77. Albert Bushnell Hart, *Manual of American History, Diplomacy, and Government for Class Use* (Cambridge, Mass.: Harvard University Press, 1908), 5–7, 12–16, 300–4.

78. Albert Bushnell Hart, "History 13 and History 17," *Topical Outline of the Courses in Constitutional and Political History of the United States Given at Harvard College* (Cambridge, Mass.: W. H. Wheeler, Publisher, 1886).

79. Bert J. Loewenberg, *American History in American Thought: Christopher Columbus to Henry Adams* (New York: Simon and Schuster, 1972), 455–56; Albert Bushnell Hart, "Methods of Teaching American History," in G. Stanley Hall, *Methods of Teaching History* (Boston: D. C. Heath, 1895), 1–3; and "Course Methods Taught By Hart," Papers of Albert Bushnell Hart, Harvard University Archives, Pusey Library, Cambridge, Massachusetts (hereafter cited as ABH), ABH HUG 4448.22 box 11.

80. Morison, "A Memoir and Estimate of Albert Bushnell Hart," 39.

81. Henry Lea cited in Ibid., 38–39. See also "From Who's Who in America by Kind Permission," in *Harvard Bulletin* 13 (7 February 1912), a roast article presented at a Testimonial Dinner for Albert Bushnell Hart, 29 December 1909, collected in "Personal and Personal Business Papers, 1876–1926," ABH HUG 4448.5.

82. For more on Hart's professional commitment to the issue of slavery, see Albert Bushnell Hart, *Slavery and Abolition, 1831–1841* (New York: Harper & Brothers, 1906). See also Morison, "A Memoir and Estimate of Albert Bushnell Hart," 39.

83. Morison, "Albert Bushnell Hart 1889–1939," 436.

84. Ibid.

85. Ibid.

CHAPTER 3: THE GREAT TRIUMVIRATE

1. John H. Morison to SEM, [1909], "Samuel Eliot Morison's Correspondence with his Father," Personal and Family Correspondence, SEMC HUG(FP)—33.6 box 3.

2. Morison, "A Memoir and Estimate of Albert Bushnell Hart," Proceedings of the Massachusetts Historical Society 77 (March 1965): 32, 46.

3. William R. Keylor, *Academy and Community: The Foundation of the French Historical Profession* (Cambridge, Mass.: Harvard University Press, 1975), 12, 257 n. 37.

4. Morison, *Vistas of History* (New York: Alfred A. Knopf, 1964), 20. These French historians wrote primarily political and institutional history, including Charles Seignobas's *La Méthode historique appliquée aux sciences sociales* (Paris: F. Alcan, 1901), Anatole Leroy-Beaulieu's *Christianisme et démocratic, christianisme et socialisme* (Bloud, 1911), and Maurice Caudel's *Nos libertés politiques* (Paris: A. Colin, 1910). Caudel was also editor of the *Revue des sciences politiques*.

5. Morison, "Autobiographical Sketch," SEMC HUG(FP)—33.1 box 1.

6. Keylor, *Academy and Community*, 211–12.

7. Morison, *Fullness of Life: A Memoir of Elizabeth Shaw Morison, 1886–1945* (Privately printed, 1945), 2–4.

8. Ibid., 5.

9. Morison, "Autobiographical Sketch," SEMC HUG(FP)—33.1 box 1.

10. Morison, *Fullness of Life*, 6.

11. Morison, "Star Chamber Club," SEMC HUG(FP)—33.55 box 7. See also, Morison, "Autobiographical Sketch," SEMC HUG(FP)—33.1 box 1.

12. "The Degree of Ph.D. in History," Records of the History Department, HUA UAV 453.5.

13. Morison, "Autobiographical Sketch," SEMC HUG(FP)—33.1 box 1.

14. Morison, *Fullness of Life*, 7. Bishop McVicar of Rhode Island officiated. "Is your principal sober?" he asked Morison's best man just prior to the ceremony. "Reasonably so," was the reply, since Morison "was still suffering from the ushers' dinner." "No matter," said the Bishop, "drunk or sober, we'll see him through!"

15. Morison, "A Memoir and Estimate of Albert Bushnell Hart," 37–39, 40. "My cup was full of happiness," Morison wrote later of his History 13 appointment.

16. Morison, "The Life and Correspondence of Harrison Gray Otis, 1765–1815," Ph.D. diss. in History, Harvard University, 1912, HUA, HU 90.918.

17. Albert Bushnell Hart, "Specimen Questions," *Manual of History, Diplomacy, and Government* (Cambridge, Mass.: Harvard University Press, 1908), 396; Hart's response appears in Albert Bushnell Hart, *Epochs of American History Formation of the Union, 1750–1829* (New York: Longmans, Green, and Co., 1892), 175.

18. Morison, "The Life and Correspondence of Harrison Gray Otis," 374, 126.

19. Hart, *Epochs of American History*, 168–70.

20. Morison, "The Life and Correspondence of Harrison Gray Otis," 190.

21. Albert Bushnell Hart to SEM, 5 March 1914, letter 2, SEMC HUG(FP)—33.15 box 6. Hart wrote two letters to Morison on 5 March. I have designated them letter 1 and letter 2.

22. Morison, "Edward Channing: A Memoir," in *By Land and by Sea: Essays and Addresses by Samuel Eliot Morison* (New York: Alfred A. Knopf, 1953), 320, introductory remarks, 316.

23. Ibid., 299–300, 303, 315, 319, 320.

24. Morison, "A Memoir and Estimate of Albert Bushnell Hart," 35.

25. Morison, "Edward Channing: A Memoir," 29, 22, 7, 11, 306. Morison cites Thomas Wentworth Higginson on Channing's loneliness as a boy: "His one chosen companion is the imaginary Mr. Dowdy, whose individuality is hopelessly intertwined with his own, he is Dowdy, but Dowdy is not he;—in fact, as he confidently whispered to me, 'There's a great many of them'; he peoples the world with Dowdies."

26. Morison, "A Memoir and Estimate of Albert Bushnell Hart," 35.

27. Morison, "Edward Channing: A Memoir," 307–8. Channing said of Adams: "I cannot express, no words of mine could, the debt I owe to Henry Adams. He was the greatest teacher that I ever encountered. He could draw out from a man the very best that was in him."

28. Channing's paper for the American Historical Association meeting, "Town and Country Government," is abstracted in Papers of the American Historical Association 1 (1886): 23.

29. Edward Channing, "Town and County Government in English Colonies," Johns Hopkins University Studies in Historical and Political Science 1 (1884).

30. Ralph Ray Fahrney, "Edward Channing," in The Marcus W. Jernegan Essays in American Historiography, ed. William T. Hutchinson (Chicago: University of Chicago Press, 1937), 297. See also, Carl Russell Fish, "Edward Channing, American Historian," Current History 32 (March 1931): 863.

31. Edward Channing, A History of the United States, 6 vols. (New York: Macmillan Company, 1905–25).

32. James Ford Rhodes, History of the United States from the Compromise of 1850 to the End of Roosevelt's Administration, 9 vols. (New York: Macmillan Company, 1928).

33. Channing, A History of the United States, vol. i, v, vi, vii.

34. Morison, "Edward Channing: A Memoir," 30.

35. Edward Channing, "The Present State of Historical Writing in America," Reprinted from the Proceedings of the American Antiquarian Society for October 1910 (Worcester, Mass.: Davis Press, 1910), 10.

36. Ibid.

37. Morison, "Edward Channing: A Memoir," 319–20.

38. Ibid., 301, 324.

39. Ibid., 319.

40. Morison, Fullness of Life, 15.

41. Edward Channing to SEM, 3 November 1915, SEMC HUG(FP)—33.15 box 3; Channing, The History of the United States, vol. 4, 563. Channing called Morison's biography of Otis "the best account, by far" of the Hartford Convention and listed it among several works in which "abundant citations for further research" could be found by students.

42. Morison, "Edward Channing: A Memoir," 319.

43. Edward Channing to SEM, 3 November 1915, SEMC HUG(FP)—33.15 box 3. "I am delighted with Harrison Gray Otis," Channing wrote. "It is historical and readable—a difficult combination."

44. Ray Allen Billington, Frederick Jackson Turner: Historian, Scholar, Teacher (New York: Oxford University Press, 1973), 12–15, 25.

45. For more on Allen, see David B. Frankenberger, "William Francis Allen," in William Francis Allen: Memorial Volume (Boston: G. H. Ellis, 1890); and Owen G. Stearns, "William Francis Allen: Wisconsin's First Historian," Master's thesis, University of Wisconsin, 1955.

46. For more on Adams, see Herbert Baxter Adams, Tributes of His Friends (Baltimore: Johns Hopkins University Press, 1902), 9–49; and Bert J. Loewenberg, American History in American Thought (New York: Simon & Schuster, 1972), 363–79.

47. Billington, Frederick Jackson Turner, 65–66. For a discussion of Turner and his classmates at Hopkins, see Loewenberg, "History at Hopkins: J. Franklin Jameson, John Spencer Bassett, William Trent, Woodrow Wilson," in Loewenberg, American History in American Thought, 400–24.

48. Frederick Jackson Turner, "The Significance of the Frontier in American History," in The Frontier in American History (New York: Holt, Rinehart, and Winston, 1920), 267.

For a discussion of the background of the Turner thesis, see Ray A. Billington, *The Genesis of the Frontier Thesis: A Study in Historical Creativity* (San Marino, Calif.: Huntington Library, 1971).

49. SEM to Professor G. W. Pierson, 15 November 1941, SEMC HUG(FP)—33.15 box 8.

50. Warren Susman, *Culture as History: The Transformation of American Society in the Twentieth Century* (New York: Pantheon Books, 1984), 17.

51. Billington, *Frederick Jackson Turner*, 297–98.

52. Ibid., 298.

53. Morison, introductory remarks to "Edward Channing: A Memoir," 299.

54. Billington, *Frederick Jackson Turner*, 311–12, 327. The student comments were recorded in Edward E. Dale, "Turner—the Man and Teacher," *University of Kansas City Review* 18 (Autumn 1951): 25–26.

55. Ibid., 330.

56. Ibid., 310.

57. Edward Channing, *A Student's History of the United States* (New York: Macmillan Company, 1898).

58. Frederick Jackson Turner, "A Student's History of the United States," *Educational Review* 18 (October 1899): 301–4. Other reviewers of Channing's works noted the same tendency. See "The Story of the Great Lakes, by Edward Channing," *American Historical Review* 15 (October 1909): 190; Fahrney, "Edward Channing," 297. For an excellent discussion of the Turner-Channing rift, see Billington, *Frederick Jackson Turner*, 177–78.

59. Morison, "Edward Channing: A Memoir," 32. See also C. H. Van Tyne's review in *American Historical Review* 18 (April 1913): 604, in which Van Tyne complains of Channing's "textual indifference" to Turner.

60. Turner, "The Significance of the Frontier in American History," 1.

61. For more on "Turner's Dilemma," see David Noble, *Historians against History: The Frontier Thesis and the National Covenant in American Historical Writing Since 1830* (Minneapolis: University of Minnesota Press, 1965), 38.

62. Frederick Jackson Turner, *The Rise of the New West, 1819–1829*, vol. 14 of The American Nation Series, 26 vols., ed. Albert B. Hart (New York: Harpers and Brothers 1906). Morison notes: "Hart was a tough, rigorous editor, blue-penciling texts liberally and enforcing deadlines. He was the only person who ever managed to get a complete book out of Turner, which he is said to have accomplished by sending that distinguished Western historian collect telegrams demanding copy, until Turner concluded it would be cheaper to finish the book."

63. Channing as cited in Billington, *Frederick Jackson Turner*, 311.

64. Turner to Frederick Merk, 26 March 1931 as cited in ibid., 310.

65. See, for instance, Turner's description of Henry Adams as the "Porcupinus Angelicus" in *The Historical World of Frederick Jackson Turner*, narrated by Wilbur R. Jacobs (New Haven, Conn.: Yale University Press, 1968), 53.

66. Billington, *Frederick Jackson Turner*, 311.

67. Morison, "Edward Channing: A Memoir," 22.

68. Morison, "The Life and Correspondence of Harrison Gray Otis," chapter 11, "Oratory, Law, and Personality," 400–44, especially 402, 404, 405.

69. Worthington C. Ford to Charles Haskins, 6 April 1912, SEMC HUG(FP)—33.15 box 5.

70. Frederick Jackson Turner to Charles Haskins, 21 April 1912, ibid.

71. Morison, *The Life and Letters of Harrison Gray Otis: Federalist, 1765–1848*, 2 vols. (Boston: Houghton Mifflin, 1913), vol 1, ix.

72. Review of *Harrison Gray Otis*, *New York Times*, 4 January 1914.

73. Review of *Harrison Gray Otis, Springfield Republican* 14 May 1914, 5.

74. Morison, Introduction to *Harrison Gray Otis, 1765–1848: The Urbane Federalist* (Boston: Houghton Mifflin, 1969), ix. For other reviews, see *Nation* 93 (19 February 1914): 184; *American Historical Review* 19 (April 1914): 655; *American Political Science Review* 8 (May 1914): 291; *Boston Transcript*, 5 November 1913, 24; *English Historical Review* 29 (October 1914): 799.

75. Morison talk, "Theodore Roosevelt and Theodore Roosevelt, Jr.," 27 October 1956, SEMC HUG(FP)—33.55 box 7.

76. Morison, *Vistas of History*, 22, 25.

77. Frederick Jackson Turner to SEM, 14 September 1912, SEMC HUG(FP)—33.15 box 8.

78. SEM to Samuel Flagg Bemis, 22 April 1953, ibid., box 2.

79. Frederick Jackson Turner to SEM, 14 September 1912, ibid., box 8.

80. Morison, introductory remarks, "Edward Channing: A Memoir," 299.

81. For more on this Balkans trip, see SEM and Elizabeth S. Morison ("Bessie") to Emily M. Morison, "Letters from the Balkans, 1913," SEMC HUG(FP)—33.6 box 6.

82. Morison, "A Memoir and Estimate of Albert Bushnell Hart," 41. Morison later said of Stephens, "Great teachers do far more good to the cause of history than mediocre writers. Such men, for instance, as the late H. Morse Stephens, who stopped writing (which he never liked) as soon as he obtained a chair in this country . . . inspired thousands of young men and initiated scores of valuable books" (Morison, "History as a Literary Art," in *By Land and by Sea*, 290).

83. C. H. Rieber [on behalf of H. Morse Stephens] to SEM, 9 February 1914, SEMC HUG(FP)—33.15 box 12.

84. H. Morse Stephens to SEM, 4 March 1914, ibid.

85. Albert Bushnell Hart to SEM, 5 March 1914, letter 1, ibid., box 6.

86. SEM to Stephens, 13 March 1914, SEMC HUG(FP)—33.15, ibid., box 12.

87. Hart to SEM, 5 March 1914, letter 1, ibid., box 6.

88. Morison, *Three Centuries of Harvard*, (Cambridge, Mass.: Harvard University Press, 1936), 398–99, 439–46.

89. Morison, "A Memoir of Albert Bushnell Hart," 43–44; see also Albert Bushnell Hart, "Government," in Morison ed., *The Development of Harvard University 1869–1929* (Cambridge, Mass.: Harvard University Press, 1930), 181–85.

90. Ibid.

91. Morison, *Three Centuries of Harvard*, 447–48.

92. Hart to SEM, 3 November 1914, SEMC HUG(FP)—33.15 box 12. For more on the offer to Morison, see A. Lawrence Lowell, 27 October 1914, ibid., box 8.

93. SEM to Hart, [1914], ibid., box 6.

94. Frederick Jackson Turner to SEM, 21 December 1916, ibid., box 8.

95. Edward Channing to SEM, 30 September 1914, SEMC HUG(FP)—33.15 box 3.

96. Channing to Barrett Wendell, 24 October 1914, ibid.

97. Barrett Wendell to "Emily" (Morison's mother), 26 October 1914, ibid.

98. Channing to Barrett Wendell, 24 October 1914, ibid.

99. Channing to Morison, 4 November 1914, ibid.

100. Morison to Wendell, 31 October 1914, The Wendell Papers, bMS Am 1907 I(913), Houghton Library, Harvard University; hereafter cited as WP.

101. Channing to SEM, 4 November 1914, SEMC HUG(FP)—33.15 box 3. See also Michael Scott, *Tom Cringle's Log* (New York: Macmillan, 1895).

102. Wilcomb Washburn, "Samuel Eliot Morison, Historian," *William and Mary Quarterly*, 3d ser., 36 (July 1979): 333.

103. William Bentinck-Smith, "Samuel Eliot Morison," Proceedings of the Massachusetts Historical Society 88 (1976): 123.

104. Morison, introductory remarks, "Edward Channing: A Memoir," 299.

CHAPTER 4: THE "USABLE PAST"

1. William McDonald, review of *The Life and Letters of Harrison Gray Otis*, by Samuel Eliot Morison, *American Historical Review* 19 (April 1914): 655–57.

2. SEM to Frank Maloy Anderson, 5 January 1942, SEMC HUG (FP)—33.15 box 8.

3. Albert Bushnell Hart, *Commonwealth History of Massachusetts* (New York: States History Company, 1927–30).

4. For an account of the bright young historians associated with Hart's *Commonwealth History*, see Morison, "A Memoir and Estimate of Albert Bushnell Hart," Proceedings of the Massachusetts Historical Society 77 (March 1965): 49.

5. SEM to Barrett Wendell, 26 Septemer 1914, WP bMS Am 1907, 1 (913).

6. SEM to A. Lawrence Lowell, 1914, SEMC HUG(FP)—33.15 box 7.

7. SEM to Barrett Wendell, 26 September 1914, WP bMs Am 1907, 1 (913).

8. SEM to H. Morse Stephens, 10 May 1914, SEMC HUG(FP)—33.15 box 12.

9. Arthur Schlesinger, Sr., *In Retrospect: The History of a Historian* (New York: Harcourt, Brace, & World, 1963), 87.

10. Morison, Introduction to *Sailor Historian: The Best of Samuel Eliot Morison*, ed. Emily Morison Beck (Boston: Houghton Mifflin, 1977), 1.

11. Channing to SEM, 4 November 1914, SEMC HUG(FP)—33.15 box 3.

12. Kenneth W. Porter to SEM, 5 December 1964, SEMC HUG(FP)—33.15 box 10; Porter is best known for his biography *John Jacob Astor* (New York: Russell & Russell, 1931).

13. W. S. Ferguson to SEM, 6 February 1915, ibid., box 5.

14. Frederick Jackson Turner to SEM, 21 December 1916, ibid., box 8.

15. SEM to Curtis Brown, "Account of Writings," 17 November 1952, SEMC HUG(FP)—33.1 box 1.

16. Ferris Greenslet to SEM, 31 January 1914, The Manuscripts of Samuel Eliot Morison, Houghton Library, Harvard University (hereafter referred to as MSEM), bMS Am 1925 (1271). "The first sale, of more than three hundred copies, is not entirely a bad one for a book of this type and price," wrote Greenslet. "It is furthermore, the type of book that does not always have the largest sales at first. We shall hope to see it show some continued life."

17. SEM to Curtis Brown, "Account of Writings," 17 November 1952, SEMC HUG(FP)—33.1 box 1.

18. SEM to Frank Anderson, 5 January 1942, ibid., 33.15 box 8. "James assured me, in 1916, that he was going to write the book himself, which the old stuffed shirt never did," wrote Morison.

19. James Harvey Ropes to SEM, 9 September 1915, ibid., box 11.

20. SEM to James Harvey Ropes, 10 September 1915, ibid.

21. SEM to Ferris Greenslet, 8 April 1917, 3 March 1920, 31 July 1920, MSEM bMS Am 1925 (1271).

22. Henry H. Edes to Whom It May Concern, 26 August 1918, SEMC HUG(FP)—33.20 box 1.

23. SEM to Ernest C. Oberholtzer, 22 February 1914, ibid., 33.15 box 9.

24. Carl Becker, "Detachment and the Writing of History," *Atlantic Monthly* 106 (October 1910): 525–36.

25. Billington, *Frederick Jackson Turner: Historian, Scholar, Teacher* (New York: Oxford University Press, 1973), 329.

26. Frederick Jackson Turner, "Social Forces in American History," in Turner, *The Frontier in American History* (New York: Holt, Rinehart, and Winston, 1920), 328.

27. Morison, "Final Report of Editor of Leaflets," June 1921, SEMC HUG(FP)—33.15 box 9.

28. Albert J. Beveridge to George Harvey, 25 September 1921, The Papers of Albert J. Beveridge, General Correspondence, 1890–1927, file M, Library of Congress; hereafter referred to as PAJB.

29. Trade Union College to SEM, 13 October 1919, SEMC HUG(FP)—33.15 box 11.

30. Frederick Merk to SEM, 9 November 1921, SEMC HUG(FP)—33.15 box 9.

31. Morison, "Autobiographical Sketch," ibid, 33.1 box 1.

32. Wilcomb Washburn, "Samuel Eliot Morison, Historian," *William and Mary Quarterly*, 3d ser., 36 (July 1979): 326.

33. Morison, *Vistas of History* (New York: Alfred A. Knopf, 1964), 56.

34. D. W. Brogan, "The Admiral as Historian," SEMC HUG(FP)—33.1 box 1.

35. Morison, "Autobiographical Sketch," ibid.; also see SEM to Remes Renfrew, 6 September 1947, ibid., 33.15 box 10.

36. Morison, *Fullness of Life: A Memoir of Elizabeth Shaw Morison, 1886–1945* (Privately printed, 1945), 20.

37. Claude Bowers, *Beveridge and the Progressive Era* (New York: Literary Guild, 1932), 2–44, 79–93, 178–79, 333–51, 352–80, 384, 438–57. This biography, written by a personal friend shortly after Beveridge's death, remains the best source on Beveridge's career; see also, John Braeman, *Albert J. Beveridge, American Nationalist* (Chicago: University of Chicago Press, 1971), and Tracy E. Strevey, "Albert J. Beveridge," in *The Marcus W. Jernegan Essays in American Historiography*, ed. William T. Hutchinson (Chicago: University of Chicago Press, 1937), 374–93.

38. Strevey, "Albert J. Beveridge," 376. For more on Ridpath, see William W. Carson, "John Clark Ridpath," in *Dictionary of American Biography*, 20 vols., ed. Dumas Malone (New York: Charles Scribner's Sons, 1935–1938), vol. 15, 599. Carson writes of Ridpath: "His books sold in such numbers that he may certainly be regarded as one of the most popular writers of historical works of his time. The enormous quantity and scope of his work, however, precluded that scrupulous regard for fact and reliance on authority that characterizes the more scholarly historian" (599).

39. Bowers, *Beveridge and the Progressive Era*, 547.

40. Albert J. Beveridge to Clarence Alvord, 6 August 1915, PAJB AC 9316.

41. Bowers, *Beveridge and the Progressive Era*, 545.

42. SEM to Beveridge, 2 August 1918, PAJB.

43. Beveridge to Edwin M. Lee, 17 April 1916, as cited in Bowers, *Beveridge and the Progressive Era*, 545.

44. Albert J. Beveridge, "The Making of a Book," *Saturday Evening Post*, 23 October 1926, 187.

45. Bowers, *Beveridge and the Progressive Era*, 554.

46. Morison, "The Faith of an Historian," in *By Land and by Sea: Essays and Addresses by Samuel Eliot Morison* (New York: Alfred A. Knopf, 1953), 356–57.

47. Bowers, *Beveridge and the Progressive Era*, 555–58.

48. Albert J. Beveridge, *The Life of John Marshall*, 4 vols. (Boston: Houghton Mifflin, 1919), vol. 3, 274–545.

49. SEM to Beveridge, 2 August 1918, PAJB.

50. Beveridge to SEM, 18 May 1918, ibid.

51. Beveridge to William E. Dodd, 4 February 1915, ibid.

52. Charles Beard to Beveridge, 24 February [1918], ibid.

53. See "Jefferson or Burr?" in Morison, *The Life and Letters of Harrison Gray Otis: Federalist, 1765–1848*, 2 vols. (Boston: Houghton Mifflin, 1913), vol. 1, 199–216.

54. Morison, "The Education of John Marshall," *Atlantic Monthly* 126 (July 1920): 54.

55. Beveridge to Clarence Alvord, 27 December 1918, PAJB.

56. Morison, "Comedy in 2 Acts: The Education of John Marshall; act 1, according to Senator Beveridge," SEMC HUG(FP)—33.55 box 8.

57. Morison, "Comedy in 2 Acts: The Education of John Marshall; act 2, as it really happened," ibid.

58. Beveridge to SEM, 3 May 1920, PAJB.

59. Charles Beard, *The Supreme Court and the Constitution* (New York: Macmillan, 1912). For more on the historical implications of the debate, see Charles A. Miller, *The Supreme Court and the Uses of History* (Cambridge, Mass.: Harvard University Press, 1969).

60. Isaac Hunt to Beveridge, 9 December 1919, PAJB.

61. A. C. McLaughlin, Review of *The Life of John Marshall*, *American Bar Association Journal* 7 (March 1927): 231.

62. L. C. Bell, "John Marshall: Albert J. Beveridge as a Biographer," *Virginia Law Register* 12 (March 1927): 641–42.

63. Thomas Woodrow Wilson, *Congressional Government: A Study in American Politics* (Boston: Houghton, Mifflin, 1885).

64. Quoted in Loewenberg, *American History in American Thought: Christopher Columbus to Henry Adams* (New York: Simon & Schuster, 1972), 411–12.

65. Morison, "Woodrow Wilson Was Right," Address delivered before the Phi Beta Kappa Society of Washington and Lee University, Lexington, Virginia, 27 March 1941, SEMC HUG(FP)—33.55 box 8.

66. Oliver Marble Gale, ed., *Americanism: Woodrow Wilson's Speeches on the War— Why He Made Them and What They Have Done* (Chicago: Baldwin Syndicate Publishers, 1918).

67. Morison, "Woodrow Wilson Was Right," SEMC HUG(FP)—33.55 box 7.

68. Morison, *The Oxford History of the United States*, 2 vols. (London: Oxford University Press, 1927), vol. 2, 463.

69. Beveridge to Edward S. Corwin, 25 February 1918, PAJB.

70. Beveridge to William E. Dodd, 14 April 1919, ibid.

71. Beveridge to Corwin, 25 February 118, ibid.

72. Beveridge to Dodd, 4 February 1916, ibid. Beveridge wrote a book about his experiences in Germany during the early war, entitled *What Is Back of the War* (Indianapolis: Bobbs-Merrill, 1915). See also, *North American Review* 201 (May 1915): 655–56.

73. H. J. Eckenrode to Beveridge, 3 March 1917, 6 May 1917, PAJB.

74. Beveridge to Dodd, 9 August 1915, ibid.

75. Albert J. Beveridge, *The Meaning of the Times and Other Speeches* (Indianapolis: Bobbs-Merrill, 1908), 37, as quoted in Strevey, "Albert J. Beveridge," 379.

76. Bowers, *Beveridge and the Progressive Era*, 550–51.

77. Beveridge to SEM, 5 April 1920, PAJB.

78. SEM to Beveridge, 2 August 1918, ibid.

79. Morison, "Woodrow Wilson Was Right," SEMC HUG(FP)—33.55 box 7. See also, "Lecture Notes for History 10," HUC 8953.238.160; "Lecture Notes in History 10," HUC 8953.238.160; "Lecture Notes in History 10, taken by J. C. Borden," HUA HUC 8930.338.10.

80. Morison, "Woodrow Wilson Was Right," ibid.

81. Morison, "Diary, 1917" as cited in "Woodrow Wilson Was Right," ibid.

82. SEM to Professor Kuno Meyer, 10 January 1915, SEMC HUG(FP)—33.15 box 9.

83. Billington, *Frederick Jackson Turner*, 348.

84. Turner to John Franklin Jameson, 20 May 1917, as quoted in Elizabeth Donnan and Leo F. Stock, eds., *An Historian's World* (Philadelphia: American Philosophical Society, 1956), 207 n. 126.

85. For more on Channing's attitude toward New History, see Harvey Wish, *The American Historian: A Social-Intellectual History of the Writing of the American Past* (New York: Oxford University Press, 1960), 128–30. See also Ralph Ray Fahrney, "Edward Channing," in *The Marcus W. Jernegan Essays in American Historiography*.

86. Turner to Jameson, 20 May 1917, in Donnan and Stock, *An Historian's World*, 207.

87. Billington, *Frederick Jackson Turner*, 217–23.

88. Turner to Jameson, 20 May 1917, in Donnan and Stock, *An Historian's World*, 207.

89. Morison, "My Diary of the Peace Conference," 1, 2, 3 January 1919, The Peace Conference Papers, SEMC HUG(FP)—33.20. See also Morison, "Autobiographical Sketch," ibid., 33.1 box 1; and Bentinck-Smith, "Samuel Eliot Morison," Proceedings of the Massachusetts Historical Society 88 (1976): 123.

90. SEM to Hon. Henry White, 29 November 1918, SEMC HUG(FP)—33.20.

91. Morison, "My Diary of the Peace Conference," 12 January 1919, ibid.

92. SEM to A. Lawrence Lowell, 31 August 1918, ibid., 33.1 box 2.

93. A. Lawrence Lowell to SEM, 3 July 1918, "Department of Justice Row," SEMC HUG(FP)—33.1 box 2.

94. SEM to Emily M. Morison, 31 August 1918, ibid.

95. SEM to A. Lawrence Lowell, 31 August 1918, ibid. Morison noted that in the first few months of the war he had stayed neutral but that "within a short time of our Declaration I became convinced that the only way to a just and lasting peace was through a complete victory over Germany."

96. David H. Thurn, indexer, "Guide to the Samuel Eliot Morison Collection in the Harvard University Archives," ibid., 33.1 box 2.

97. The Army Historical Section was headed by historian Robert Johnston, who initiated a series of studies in the military history of war, including "First Reflection on the Campaign of 1918" (1920) (Dexter Perkins, "Robert Johnston," in *Dictionary of American Biography*, vol. 10, 149–50). Morison wrote to a former student of Johnston's: "I was interested in your article on R. M. Johnston in *Military Affairs*. I, too, was a pupil of his and found him a most inspiring teacher. He did me the compliment of trying to get me a commission on his historical staff; but I finished World War I as a private" (SEM to Alexander Baltzley, 30 September 1957, SEMC HUG[FP]—33.15 box 2).

98. SEM to White, 29 November 1918, SEMC HUG(FP)—33.20.

99. Morison, "My Diary of the Peace Conference," 14 January 1919, ibid.

100. Ibid.

101. SEM to Upton Sinclair, 5 February 1940, ibid. Sinclair wrote a novel, *Presidential Agent*, in which his young American hero served as a translator and secretary for one of the American experts at the Paris peace conference. In preparation for the work, Sinclair asked Morison for information on the most important figures at the conference, and Morison pointed to many of his Harvard colleagues. Some of the Harvard people went on to write their own reminiscences. See, for instance, Robert H. Lord and Charles H. Haskins, *Some Problems of the Peace Conference* (Cambridge, Mass.: Harvard University Press, 1920); and Robert H. Lord, *Archibald Cary Coolidge: Life and Letters* (Boston: Houghton Mifflin, 1932).

102. James Truslow Adams, "How Our Peace Agents Lived," *New York Times*, 27 July

1919. For more on the work of historians at home, see George T. Blakey, *Historians on the Home Front: American Propagandists for the Great War* (Lexington: University of Kentucky Press, 1970).

103. SEM to Sinclair, 5 February 1940, SEMC HUG)FP)—33.20; Morison, "Statement on Policy," ibid.

104. Morison, "Statement on Policy," ibid.

105. Ibid.

106. Ibid.

107. Ibid.

108. SEM to the *New York Times*, "Recognition of the Baltic Republics," 30 November 1919, ibid., 33.20. See also Morison's articles "The Eastern Baltic: (1) The Peace Conference and the Baltic; (2) Latvia; (3) Latvia, Continued; (4) Esthonia; (5) Finland," which appeared in *New Europe* in 1919. See also SEM to the *Boston Globe*, 14 November 1941, ibid., 33.15 box 2.

109. Morison, "My Diary of the Peace Conference," 7 May 1919 through 12 June 1919, SEMC HUG(FP)—33.15 box 2. See also SEM to Sinclair, 5 February 1940, SEMC HUG(FP)—33.20.

110. SEM to Sinclair, 5 February 1940, SEMC HUG(FP)—33.20.

111. Morison, "Statement of Policy," ibid.

112. SEM to Sinclair, 5 February 1940, ibid.

113. Morison wrote later, "The real reason for the United States recognizing the Republic of Finland was that Mr. Hoover wanted it done so that he could use the contributions of Finnish Americans deposited in National City Bank, to buy food for Finland. I recommended that Finland be recognized because a stable government had been established, but Hoover's was the *real* reason." SEM to Michigan State University, 22 June 1966, ibid, 33.15 box 9.

114. SEM letter to the *New York Times*, "Recognition of the Baltic Republics," 30 November 1919, ibid, 33.20.

115. SEM to Sinclair, 5 February 1940, ibid.

116. Morison, "My Diary of the Peace Conference," 12 June 1919, ibid. R. S. Baker and Lincoln Steffens were journalists and political activists covering the peace conference. Baker, a friend and admirer of Wilson, became head of the U.S. delegation's press bureau; whereas Steffens was on assignment for *McClure's* magazine.

117. SEM to Joseph C. Grew, 15 June 1919, ibid.

118. "Mock Letter," ibid.

119. SEM to Sinclair, 5 February 1940, ibid.

120. Morison, "Statement on Policy," ibid.

121. SEM to Sinclair, 5 February 1940, ibid.

122. Morison, "Woodrow Wilson Was Right," ibid., 33.55 box 8.

123. Morison, "The Eastern Baltic: (1) The Peace Conference and the Baltic," *New Europe* 12, 7 August 1919, 82.

124. Ibid., "The Eastern Baltic: (5) Finland, *New Europe* 12, 2 October 1919, 275. "On our side, the time has come to extend *de jure* recognition to the new *regime*, and to admit the Finnish Republic to the League of Nations," Morison wrote.

125. Morison, "My Diary of the Peace Conference," SEMC HUG(FP)—33.20.

126. Beveridge to Alvord, 28 March 1919, 4 December 1918, PAJB. See also, Beveridge to Clarence Alvord, 27 December 1918, PAJB; and Albert J. Beverdige, "Pitfalls of a League of Nations," *North American Review* 209 (March 1919): 305–14.

127. Bowers, *Beveridge and the Progressive Era*, 517–20.

128. Beveridge to Henry Cabot Lodge, 4 April 1919, PAJB.

129. Beveridge to Alvord, 27 December 1918, PAJB.

130. Morison, "Woodrow Wilson Was Right," SEMC HUG(FP)—33.55 box 8.

131. Ibid.

132. Bowers, *Beveridge and the Progressive Era*, 506.

133. Alvord to Beveridge, 20 March 1919, PAJB.

134. Beveridge to D. R. Anderson, 6 December 1915, ibid.

135. Beveridge to Clarence Alvord, 27 December 1918, ibid.

136. Beveridge to Corwin, 24 October 1918, ibid.

137. Beveridge to Alvord, 3 January 1919, ibid.

138. Beveridge to Corwin, 8 August 1918, ibid.

139. Beveridge to SEM, 5 April 1920, ibid.

140. Beveridge to SEM, 27 February 1920, ibid.

141. Bowers, *Beveridge and the Progressive Era*, 510.

142. SEM to Beveridge, 3 March 1920, PAJB. See also Beveridge to SEM, 5 February 1927, ibid.

143. Morison, "Autobiographical Sketch," SEMC HUG(FP)—33.1 box 1.

144. SEM to Beveridge, 3 March 1920, PAJB.

145. Morison, *Fullness of Life*, 20.

146. Morison, "Memoranda 1919, written early 1920 as a summary of year," ibid., 33.55 box 8.

147. Ibid.

CHAPTER 5: HISTORICAL RELATIVISM

1. Peter Novick, *That Noble Dream: The "Objectivity Question" and the American Historical Profession* (Cambridge, England: Cambridge University Press, 1988), 130.

2. John Higham, *History: Professional Scholarship in America* (Baltimore: Johns Hopkins University Press, 1965), 55.

3. Clarence Alvord, "Musings of an Inebriated Historian," *American Mercury* 5 (1925): 434, 436, 441, as cited in Novick, *That Noble Dream*, 132.

4. Morison, *Fullness of Life: A Memoir of Elizabeth Shaw Morison, 1886–1945* (Privately printed, 1945), 34.

5. Morison, "Autobiographical Sketch," SEMC HUG(FP)—33.1 box 1.

6. Morison, *Fullness of Life*, 20.

7. Morison, "Autobiographical Sketch," SEMC HUG(FP)—33.1 box 1.

8. Ibid.

9. Morison, *Fullness of Life*, 45.

10. Ibid., 10. Dexter was a leader in the Church League for Industrial Democracy and the Fellowship of Youth. Morison noted that Dexter had "that sense of balance without which his ardor to regenerate the world would have burned him up."

11. Morison, "Smith Owen Dexter: An Address on the First Anniversary of Dexter's Death," 2 May 1937, SEMC HUG(FP)—33.55 box 2.

12. Morison, *Vistas of History* (New York: Alfred A. Knopf, 1964), 56.

13. Ibid.

14. Morison, *Fullness of Life*, 45.

15. Morison, "Autobiographical Sketch," SEMC HUG(FP)—33.1 box 1.

16. SEM to Sinclair, 5 February 1940, ibid., 33.20.

17. Channing to Morison, 30 September 1914, SEMC HUG(FP)—33.15 box 3.

18. Channing to Morison, 14 December 1922, ibid.

19. On Abbott, see Morison, "History," in Morison, ed., *The Development of Harvard University, 1869–1929* (Cambridge, Mass.: Harvard University Press, 1930), 173.

20. Morison, *Three Centuries of Harvard* (Cambridge, Mass.: Harvard University Press, 1936), 465–66.

21. Morison, "History," 169.

22. Arthur Schlesinger, Sr., later wrote of the Harvard history department in the 1920s: "In this onetime Yankee stronghold Morison, for instance, was the only full-time American historian with a Harvard A.B., Merk as well as I being state-university graduates from that far-off clime which Channing called Transappalachia." Arthur M. Schlesinger, Sr., *In Retrospect: The History of a Historian* (New York: Harcourt, Brace & World, 1963), 99.

23. SEM to G. W. Pierson, 15 November 1941, SEMC HUG(FP)—33.15 box 8.

24. The student cited here was Morris Hadley, author of *Arthur Twining Hadley* (New Haven, Conn.: Yale University Press, 1948).

25. SEM to G. W. Pierson, 15 November 1941, SEMC HUG(FP)—33.15 box 8.

26. Morison, "A Memoir and Estimate of Albert Bushnell Hart," Proceedings of the Massachusetts Historical Society 77 (March 1965): 47–48. See also remarks made by Roosevelt at Hart's testimonial dinner in 1909, "From Who's Who in America by Kind Permission," in *Harvard Bulletin* 13 (7 February 1912) in "Personal and Personal Business Papers, 1876–1926," ABH HUG 4448.5.

27. Morison, "My Diary of the Peace Conference," 6 January 1919, SEMC HUG(FP)—33.20. The officers were still in uniform because they had not yet been officially released from duty.

28. Bentinck-Smith, "Samuel Eliot Morison," Proceedings of the Massachusetts Historical Society 88 (1976): 127.

29. Bernard Bailyn et al. "Samuel Eliot Morison," *Harvard University Gazette* 72, 10 June 1977.

30. Bentinck-Smith, "Samuel Eliot Morison," 127.

31. Wilcomb E. Washburn, "Samuel Eliot Morison, Historian," *William and Mary Quarterly*, 3d ser., 36 (July 1979): 334, 336.

32. Arthur Schlesinger, Sr., *In Retrospect: The History of a Historian*, 77–78. See also Richard W. Leopold, " 'Not Merely High Scholarship but High Character and Personality': The Harvard History Department of Half-Century Ago," Proceedings of the Massachusetts Historical Society 95 (1983): 119.

33. Morison, *Three Centuries of Harvard*, 463.

34. Upton Sinclair, *The Goose Step: A Study of American Education* (Pasadena, Calif.: Published by the author, 1922), ix–x.

35. Morison, *Three Centuries of Harvard*, 464.

36. Richard Hofstadter, *The Progressive Historians: Turner, Beard, Parrington* (New York: Alfred A. Knopf, 1968), 285–88.

37. Morison, *The Oxford History of the American People* (New York: Oxford University Press, 1965), 909.

38. Van Wyck Brooks, "On Creating a Usable Past," *Dial* 64, 11 April 1918, 337–41.

39. Van Wyck Brooks, "Harvard and American Life," *Contemporary Review* 94 (December 1908): 613, 617. Brooks's complaints were the product of a lifelong struggle for survival as a free-lance writer amidst the growing commercialism and specialization of American life. For more, see Raymond Nelson, *Van Wyck Brooks: A Writer's Life* (New York: E. P. Dutton, 1981), 26–50; and James Hoopes, *In Search of American Culture* (Amherst: University of Massachusetts Press, 1977), 39.

40. James Truslow Adams, "A Business Man's Civilization," *Harper's* 159 (July 1929): 140, 142.

41. Allan Nevins, *James Truslow Adams: Historian of the American Dream* (Urbana: University of Illinois Press, 1968), 33, 179–80.

42. James Truslow Adams to Mark Howe, 18 March 1929, as cited in John Higham, *History: Professional Scholarship in America*, 75–76.

43. SEM to Beveridge, 3 March 1920, PAJB.

44. SEM to Frank Anderson, 5 January 1942, SEMC HUG(FP)—33.15 box 1.

45. Carl Becker to William Dodd, 17 June 1920, as cited in Novick, *That Noble Dream*, 130.

46. James Harvey Robinson, "After Twenty Years," *Survey* 53 (1924): 18–19, as cited in ibid., 131.

47. For a discussion of historical relativism and Becker's attitudes toward it, see Carl Becker, "Everyman His Own Historian," Presidential Address delivered before the American Historical Association, 29 December 1931, in Becker, *Everyman His Own Historian: Essays on History and Politics* (New York: F. S. Crofts, 1935).

48. Brooks, "On Creating a Usable Past," 339, 340–41.

49. Albert J. Beveridge, "The Making of a Book," *Saturday Evening Post*, 23 October 1926, 182.

50. John Hohenberg, *The Pulitzer Prizes* (New York: Columbia University Press, 1974), 65, 67.

51. Benjamin Woods Labaree, Foreword to Morison, *The Maritime History of Massachusetts, 1783–1860*, anniversary edition, (Boston: Northeastern University Press, 1979), x. See also Morison, "The Writing of History," SEMC HUG(FP)—33.55 box 8.

52. Ferris Greenslet to SEM, 29 July 1920, MSEM HL bMS Am 1925 (1271). "I have begun to fiddle with our spring list," Greenslet wrote. "What about the 'History of Massachusetts'?"

53. Morison, *Vistas of History*, 27.

54. SEM to Greenslet, 31 July 1920, MSEM HL bMS Am 1925 (1271).

55. SEM to Beveridge, 3 October 1921, PAJB.

56. Morison, *Vistas of History*, 50. Uncle Dudley, "History of an Historian," *Boston Sunday Globe*, 15 April 1951, SEMC HUG(FP)—33.1 box 1.

57. Washburn, "Samuel Eliot Morison, Historian," 334.

58. Peter Gay, *Freud for Historians* (New York: Oxford University Press, 1985).

59. Morison, *Vistas of History*, 46.

60. Morison, *The Maritime History of Massachusetts, 1783–1860*, (Boston: Houghton Mifflin, 1921), 7, 6, 41, 46, 319.

61. Morison, *The Maritime History of Massachusetts*, 42, 227, 22, vii, 22, 349, 318, 335, 171, 324, 259, 143.

62. Labaree, Foreword to *The Maritime History of Massachusetts*, x.

63. Morison, *The Maritime History of Massachusetts*, 192, 197, 198.

64. Ibid., 4, 371, 2, 1, 3, 14, 2, 5, 6, 4, 3, 2, 372, 106, 6, 7.

65. Ibid., 1, 369, 365, 370.

66. Ibid., 370, 371, 372.

67. Uncle Dudley, "History of an Historian," SEMC HUG(FP)—33.1 box 1. Uncle Dudley was Morison's friend Lucien Price, writer for the *Boston Globe*.

68. Ibid.

69. SEM to Curtis Brown, "Account of Writings, Books by Samuel Eliot Morison," 17 November 1952, ibid., box 2.

70. "Best Possible Choice," 6 July 1942, *Herald*, ibid., box 1.

71. SEM to Beveridge, 3 October 1921, PAJB.

72. Beveridge to SEM, 18 May 1918 and 6 July 1920, PAJB.

73. T. W. Van Metre, Review of *The Maritime History of Massachusetts 1783–1860*, by Samuel Eliot Morison, *American Historical Review* 27, no. 3 (April 1922): 600–1.

74. SEM to Lincoln Colcord, 18 September 1927, SEMC HUG(FP)—33.15 box 3.

75. Harold E. Stearns, ed., *Civilization in the United States* (Rahway, N.J.: Quinn & Boden Company, 1922), vii; Hendrik Willem Van Loon, "History," ibid., 303, 305; Morison, *The Oxford History of the American People*, 910.

76. Morison, "A Prologue to American History," *By Land and by Sea*, 3.

77. Morison, "Teaching American History to Young Englishmen," *Boston Sunday Globe*, 4 October 1925.

78. Frank Aydelotte, *The Oxford Stamp and Other Essays: Articles from the Educational Creed of an American Oxonion* (New York: Oxford University Press, 1917), 16.

79. Morison, "An American Professor's Reflections on Oxford," 7, 14 November 1925, SEMC HUG(FP)—33.15 box 5. See also, Morison, "Teaching American History to Young Englishmen."

80. Morison, Introductory remarks to "A Prologue to American History," *By Land and by Sea: Essays and Addresses by Samuel Eliot Morison* (New York: Alfred A. Knopf, 1953), 3.

81. SEM to Beveridge, 17 September 1921, PAJB.

82. Beveridge to George Harvey, 25 September 1921, SEMC HUG(FP)—33.15 box 2.

83. Beveridge to SEM, 17 September 1921, PAJB.

84. Beveridge to SEM, 1 November 1921, ibid.

85. SEM to Beveridge, 20 September 1921, ibid.

86. SEM to Beveridge, 3 October 1921, ibid. Beveridge predicted to Harvey that Morison would be at the "head of American historians in fifteen years."

87. SEM to Beveridge, 29 October 1921, ibid.

88. Channing to SEM, 18 October 1923, SEMC HUG(FP)—33.15, box 3.

89. Channing to Morison, 9 July 1922, ibid.

90. Morison, "An American Professor's Reflections on Oxford," 14 November 1925, ibid., 33.15 box 5.

CHAPTER 6: THE RETREAT FROM RELATIVISM

1. Morison, "An American Professor's Reflections on Oxford," *Spectator*, 11 November 1925, 866.

2. Morison, "Autobiographical Sketch," SEMC HUG(FP)—33.1 box 1.

3. SEM to Emily M. Morison, 10 November 1922, "The Oxford Correspondence," ibid., 33.15 box 5.

4. Morison, *Fullness of Life: A Memoir of Elizabeth Shaw Morison, 1886–1945* (Privately printed, 1945), 35.

5. Morison, introductory remarks, "A Prologue to American History," in *By Land and by Sea: Essays and Addresses by Samuel Eliot Morison* (New York: Alfred A. Knopf, 1953), 3, 6.

6. Ibid., 8, 7, 8.

7. SEM to Robert M. McElroy, 4 June 1925, SEMC HUG(FP)—33.21. See also, SEM to Emily M. Morison, 10 November 1922, "The Oxford Correspondence," ibid., 33.21.

8. Morison, "Teaching American History to Young Englishmen," *Boston Sunday Globe*, 4 October 1925.

9. Ibid.

10. Ibid.

11. Ibid.

12. James M. Perry, "An Admiral Talks About History," *National Observer*, 3 May 1965.

13. Morison, Preface to *The Oxford History of the United States*, 2 vols. (London: Oxford University Press, 1927), vol. 1, v.

14. SEM to Beveridge, 17 September 1921, PAJB; Morison, "Autobiographical Sketch," SEMC HUG(FP)—33.1 box 1.

15. SEM to President A. Lawrence Lowell, 18 October 1923, ibid., 33.21.

16. A Lawrence Lowell to SEM, 6 November 1923, ibid.

17. Channing to SEM, 18 October 1923, SEMC HUG(FP)—33.15 box 3.

18. Channing to SEM, 12 December 1923, ibid.

19. Morison, ed., *The Development of Harvard University, 1869–1929*, (Cambridge, Mass.: Harvard University Press, 1930), 170. See also, Arthur M. Schlesinger, Sr., *New Viewpoints in American History* (New York: Macmillan, 1922).

20. Channing to Morison, 12 December 1923, SEMC HUG(FP)—33.15 box 3.

21. Lucien Price to SEM, 23 December 1923, ibid., 33.21.

22. SEM to Lord Harmsworth, [1924], [1925], ibid.

23. Morison, "Teaching American History to Young Englishmen."

24. Comments of H. W. C. Davis, "Discussion of Proposal to Establish a Paper on Imperial and American History," 29 May 1925, "Oxford," SEMC HUG(FP)—33.55 box 6.

25. SEM to Robert M. McElroy, 4 June 1925, ibid., 33.21.

26. Morison, "Teaching American History to Young Englishmen."

27. Ibid.

28. Comments of Mr. Weaver, "Discussion of Proposal to Establish a Paper on Imperial and American History," 29 May 1925, SEMC HUG(FP)—33.55 box 6.

29. Comments of Wickham Legg, ibid.

30. Morison, "Teaching American History to Young Englishmen." See also SEM to Robert M. McElroy, 4 June 1925, SEMC HUG(FP)—33.21.

31. The vote was seven members of the board for the proposal, eight against.

32. Morison, "Teaching American History to Young Englishmen."

33. "Study of History: American Life Distorted on the Films," 7 July 1925, unattributed newspaper clipping in Morison's Oxford Correspondence, SEMC HUG(FP)—33.21.

34. Morison, "Teaching American History to Young Englishmen."

35. Morison, *The Oxford History of the American People* (New York: Oxford University Press, 1965), 910.

36. Ibid.

37. For further discussion of this "relativist dilemma," see Peter Novick, *That Noble Dream, The "Objectivity Question" and the American Historical Profession* (Cambridge, England: Cambridge University Press, 1988), 163–67.

38. Morison, "Teaching American History to Young Englishmen."

39. Morison, "An American Professor's Reflections on Oxford," 7 November 1925, SEMC HUG(FP)—33.21.

40. Lincoln Colcord to SEM, 23 May 1923, ibid., box 3.

41. SEM to Colcord, 4 June 1923, ibid.

42. Morison, *Fullness of Life*, 38.

43. Emily M. Morison to Elizabeth Shaw Morison, "The Oxford Correspondence," SEMC HUG(FP)—33.21.

44. SEM to Martha Mitchell, 28 October 1944, SEMC HUG(FP)—33.1 box 1.

45. Morison, *The Oxford History of the United States*, vi.

46. Morison, *The Oxford History of the United States*, v. See also, Novick, *That Noble Dream*, 180.

47. Morison, "Autobiographical Sketch," SEMC HUG(FP)—33.1 box 1.

48. Morison, "An American Professor's Reflections on Oxford," 14 November 1925, ibid., 33.21.

49. SEM to Albert J. Beveridge, 30 July 1926, PAJB.

50. Beveridge to SEM, 27 February 1922, PAJB.

51. Charles W. Duke, "The 'Man of the Ages' as Beveridge Sees Him," *Philadelphia Public Ledger*, 11 February 1923.

52. Ida M. Tarbell, *The Life of Abraham Lincoln*, 2 vols. (New York: S. S. McClure Co., 1895).

53. H. J. Eckenrode to Beveridge, 4 January 1926, PAJB.

54. Beveridge to Charles Beard, 26 September 1926, ibid.

55. Morison to Beveridge, 25 November 1924, ibid.

56. Ibid. Here Morison refers to John Nicolay and John Hay, *Abraham Lincoln: A History* (New York: Century Co., 1890).

57. Morison to Beveridge, 15 October 1924, PAJB.

58. Beveridge to SEM, 28 June 1925, ibid.

59. Beveridge to H. J. Eckenrode, 28 April 1925, ibid.; these comments were originally expressed by Eckenrode in a letter of 22 April 1925, to which Beveridge remarked, "I shall have to agree with you all down the line."

60. Morison, "A Prologue to American History," in *By Land and by Sea*, 21.

61. SEM to Beveridge, 25 November 1924, PAJB.

62. Morison, *The Oxford History of the United States*, vol. 2, 83, 91.

63. SEM to Beveridge, 19 February 1926, General Correspondence, 1890–1927, File M, PAJB.

64. Beveridge to SEM, 5 May 1925, ibid.

65. Beveridge to SEM, 19 February 1926, ibid.

66. SEM to Beveridge, 15 February 1926, ibid.

67. SEM to Beveridge, 23 February 1926, ibid.

68. Charles Beard to Beveridge, 23 April 1925, PAJB.

69. Charles Beard, *The Rise of American Civilization*, 2 vols. (New York: Macmillan, 1927), vol. 2, 98.

70. Beveridge to Beard, 16 March 1926, PAJB.

71. Frederick Jackson Turner, "The Children of Pioneers," *Yale Review* 15, no. 4 (July 1926): 663.

72. Ray Allen Billington, "From Association to Organization: The OAH in the Bad Old Days," *Journal of American History* 65 (1978): 76, as cited in Novick, *That Noble Dream*, 182.

73. John Higham, *History: Professional Scholarship in America* (Baltimore: Johns Hopkins University Press, 1965), 176.

74. Morison, "History as Literary Art," in *By Land and by Sea*, 290–91.

75. Beveridge to SEM, 13 July 1926, PAJB.

76. SEM to G. W. Pierson, 15 November 1941, SEMC HUG(FP)—33.15 box 7.

77. Morison, *The Oxford History of the United States*, vol. 1, 4, 3, 5.

78. Ibid., 5.

79. SEM to G. W. Pierson, 15 November 1941, SEMC HUG(FP)—33.15 box 7.

80. For a discussion of the historical uses of the frontier, see David Noble, *Historians Against History: The Frontier Thesis and the National Covenant in American Historical Writing Since 1830* (Minneapolis: University of Minnesota Press, 1965), 37–55.

81. Morison, *The Oxford History of the United States*, vol. 1, 5, 7, 10, 8.

82. Ibid., 5–9, 69.

83. Ibid., 30, 37, 41, 12, 16.

84. SEM to Channing, 8 November 1923, SEMC HUG(FP)—33.15 box 3.

85. Ralph Ray Fahrney, "Edward Channing," in *The Marcus W. Jernegan Essays in American Historiography*, ed. William T. Hutchinson (Chicago: University of Chicago Press, 1937), 296.

86. Channing, *A History of the United States*, vol. 3, chapter 13.

87. Morison, *The Oxford History of the United States*, vol. 1, 24–25, 4, 2, 19.

88. Ibid., 65–66, 67, 68–69, 66.

89. Ibid., vol. 1, 413, 419, 426, 425; vol. 2, 360.

90. Ibid., vol. 2, 83, 91.

91. Review of *The Oxford History of the United States*, by Samuel Eliot Morison, in *English Historical Review* 43 (July 1928): 464.

92. Review of *The Oxford History of the United States*, by Samuel Eliot Morison, in *Times [London] Literary Supplement*, 8 December 1927, 919.

93. Frederick Jackson Turner to SEM, 12 August 1925, as cited in Wilbur R. Jacobs, narrator, *The Historical World of Frederick Jackson Turner* (New Haven, Conn.: Yale University Press, 1968), 232–33.

94. For more on the unfinished biography, see W. E. Barton, "A Noble Fragment: Beveridge's Life of Lincoln," *Mississippi Valley Historical Review* 15 (March 1929): 497.

95. For more on Beard and the critical reception of *The Rise of American Civilization*, see Ellen Nore, *Charles A. Beard: An Intellectual Biography* (Carbondale: University of Southern Illinois Press, 1983).

CHAPTER 7: IN DEFENSE OF THE IVORY TOWER

1. Charles and Mary Beard, *The Rise of American Civilization*, 2 vols. (New York: Macmillan, 1927), vol. 2, 794–95, 792, 793. See also Charles Beard, "The Social Studies Curriculum," *The Social Frontier* 2 (1935): 78–79 as cited in Peter Novick, *That Noble Dream: The "Objectivity Question" and the American Historical Profession* (Cambridge, England: Cambridge University Press, 1988), 186.

2. Novick, *That Noble Dream*, 188.

3. For more on the social studies movement, see "The Social Studies—For What?" *School and Society* 36 (1932): 362; and "National Education Association Report," *The Social Studies in Secondary Education* (Washington, D.C.: National Education Association of the United States, 1916). See also, Charles A. Beard, *A Charter for the Social Sciences in the Schools* (New York: Charles Scribner's Sons, 1932).

4. John Dewey, *Democracy in Education* (1916; reprint, New York: Macmillan, 1961), 51, as cited in David W. Marcell, *Progress and Pragmatism: James, Dewey, Beard, and the American Idea of Progress* (Westport, Conn.: Greenwood Press, 1974), 238.

5. Novick, *That Noble Dream*, 189–92.

6. Morison, "Lucien Price: Memoir for the Saturday Club," SEMC HUG(FP)—33.55 box 6. See also, Alexander Meiklejohn, *The Experimental College* (New York: Harper & Brothers, 1932).

7. Lucien Price, *Prophets Unawares—The Romance of an Idea* (New York: Century Co., 1924).

8. Morison, *The Oxford History of the American People* (New York: Oxford University Press, 1965), 910.

9. Morison, *Vistas of History* (New York: Alfred A. Knopf, 1964), 42.

10. Morison, "Faith of an Historian," in *By Land and by Sea: Essays and Addresses by Samuel Eliot Morison* (New York: Alfred A. Knopf, 1953), 348.

11. Morison, "Address on Harvard and the University of Chicago, 1936," *Harvard Alumni Bulletin* 38, no. 5, 3 July 1936, 1209.

12. SEM to Howard Mumford Jones, [n.d.], SEMC HUG(FP)—33.15 box 7.

13. Charles M. Andrews, "These Forty Years," *American Historical Review* 30 (January 1925): 226, 227.

14. Ibid., 228, 229, 228, 229, 242, 237, 227, 238, 241, 242, 229, 242, 243, 246.

15. Carl Russell Fish to Congressman Brooks Fletcher, 9 March 1927, as cited in Novick, *That Noble Dream*, 194.

16. Eisenstadt, *Charles McLean Andrews: A Study in American Historical Writing* (New York: Columbia University Press, 1956), 193–95.

17. Morison wrote Lincoln Colcord: "Of course it is a relief to be free from 'figuring,' at least to keep no accounts, buy a sail-boat and a car and build a float, and still find money in the bank; but it is going to be quite a struggle to prevent being ridden by possessions" (18 September 1927, SEMC HUG(FP)—33.15 box 3).

18. Ibid.

19. Morison, "Impressions of Harvard After Oxford: I and II," *Harvard Alumni Bulletin*, vol. 28, nos. 30 and 31, 6 and 13 May 1926, 891–93 and 917–20; I: 891.

20. SEM to Lincoln Colcord, 18 September 1927, SEMC HUG(FP)—33.15 box 3.

21. Morison, "Impressions of Harvard After Oxford: I," 891.

22. Morison, *Fullness of Life: A Memoir of Elizabeth Shaw Morison, 1886–1945* (Privately printed, 1945), 46.

23. SEM to Frederick Merk, 9 November 1921, SEMC HUG(FP)—33.15 box 9.

24. "Report of the Harvard Student Council Committee on Education," *Harvard Alumni Bulletin*, 15 April 1926, 1–24.

25. "President Lowell's Inaugural Address," *Harvard Alumni Bulletin*, 13 October 1909; and "From President Lowell's Annual Report," *Harvard Alumni Bulletin*, 25 March 1914.

26. Morison, *Three Centuries of Harvard* (Cambridge, Mass.: Harvard University Press, 1936), 443, 477.

27. "Harvard Under President Lowell," *Harvard Alumni Bulletin*, 21 May 1925; "Building Going on at the University," ibid., 28 June 1926; "Correspondents Send Letters on Various Topics of Interest," ibid., 29 April 1926; Odin Roberts, "What Harvard Can Learn in England," ibid., 15 April 1926.

28. Morison, "Impressions of Harvard After Oxford: I," 891–93; II, vol. 28, no. 31, 13 May 1926, 917–20.

29. Ibid., 1: 891–93.

30. Roberts, "What Harvard Can Learn in England," 829.

31. Morison, "Impressions of Harvard After Oxford," 2:918.

32. Morison, "Talk to History Students in Graduate School," 6 October 1927, SEMC HUG(FP)—33.50 box 3.

33. Ibid.

34. Morison, "Impressions of Harvard After Oxford: I," 892.

35. Ibid., 2: 920.

36. Morison, *Three Centuries of Harvard*, 476–77.

37. Morison, "Address on Harvard and the University of Chicago," 1209.

38. Morison, "Lucien Price, Memoir for the Saturday Club," SEMC HUG(FP)—33.55 box 6.

39. Morison, "Harvard and Academic Oaths," *Harvard Alumni Bulletin* 37 (1934–35), 683–84.

40. Morison, "Oath: Some Reasons Why the Teacher's Oath Law Ought to Be Repealed," 1 February 1939, SEMC HUG(FP)—33.55 box 7.

41. Richard Hofstadter, *The Progressive Historians: Turner, Beard, Parrington* (New York: Alfred A. Knopf, 1963), 291.

42. Morison, "Citizenship and Freedom in Teaching," An address before the State of Education Women's Club, 20 January [1936], 8, SEMC HUG(FP)—33.55 box 7.

43. Morison, "Three Oathless Centuries," Remarks by Samuel E. Morison at Hearing on the Bill to Repeal the Teacher's Oath Act, at the State House, Boston, Massachusetts, 19 March 1936 (Boston: Massachusetts Society for Freedom in Teaching, 1936), 10.

44. Senator Charles G. Miles to SEM, 28 March 1936 and 4 April 1936, SEMC HUG(FP)—33.55 box 7.

45. SEM to Charles Miles, 30 March 1936, ibid.

46. SEM to Lucien Price, 10 April 1936, SEMC HUG(FP)—33.55 box 6.

47. Lucien Price, "The Ivory Tower," *Boston Globe*, 10 April 1936, ibid. See also Eric Goldman, "Historians and the Ivory Tower," *Social Frontier* 2 (1936): 280.

48. SEM to Lucien Price, 10 April 1936, ibid.

49. Ibid.

50. W. C. Saegen to SEM, [1926], SEMC HUG(FP)—33.15 box 6.

51. Morison, introductory remarks to "Harvard's Past," in *By Land and by Sea*, 250.

52. Morison, *Vistas of History*, 37.

53. Morison, *Harvard in the Seventeenth Century*, 2 vols. (Cambridge, Mass.: Harvard University Press, 1936), vol. 1, 25. See also, Morison, *The Founding of Harvard College* (Cambridge, Mass.: Harvard University Press, 1935), 247–48, 8.

54. Morison, *Three Centuries of Harvard*, 24, 12; Morison, *The Founding of Harvard College* (Cambridge, Mass.: Harvard University Press, 1935), 9, 339–41, 9.

55. Morison, *Three Centuries of Harvard*, 321, 335, 342, 389.

56. Morison, *The Puritan Pronaos* (New York: New York University Press, 1936), 16; Morison repeated the phrase in *The Scholar in America: Past, Present, and Future* (New York, 1961), 15.

57. Charles M. Andrews, *These Forty Years*, 237.

58. Morison, *The Development of Harvard University, 1869–1929* (Cambridge, Mass.: Harvard University Press, 1930), 177.

59. Harold Larabee, Review of *Three Centuries of Harvard*, by Samuel Eliot Morison, *New England Quarterly* 10 (September 1937): 594–96.

60. Review of *Three Centuries of Harvard*, by Samuel Eliot Morison, *Christian Science Monitor*, 11 July 1936, 14.

61. Morison, *Vistas of History* (New York: Alfred A. Knopf, 1964), 39.

62. Albert Bushnell Hart to SEM, 19 June 1936, SEMC HUG(FP)—33.15 box 6.

63. George Santayana to SEM, 4 September 1936, ibid., box 11.

64. "Honorary Degrees" in "The Modern University and the 'University Professor,' " *Harvard Alumni Bulletin*, 3 July 1936, 1193.

65. Morison, *Three Centuries of Harvard*, 461.

66. Morison, "Remarks," *Harvard Alumni Bulletin*, 3 July 1936, 1206–9.

67. Morison, "Autobiographical Sketch," SEMC HUG(FP)—33.1 box 1. For a discussion of the tercentenary activities and Morison's involvement in them see *The Tercentenary of Harvard College: A Chronicle of the Tercentenary Year, 1935–36* (Cambridge, Mass.: Harvard University Press, 1937), 5, 40, 47, 75, 85, 196.

68. Morison, *Vistas of History*, 55.

69. Richard W. Leopold, " 'Not merely High Scholarship but High Character and Personality': The Harvard History Department a Half-Century Ago," *Proceedings of the Massachusetts Historical Society* 95 (1983): 119. Leopold was a graduate student at Harvard in the 1930s, 119.

CHAPTER 8: THE RAGGED EDGE OF TRUTH

1. Eugen Rosenstock-Huessy, "The Predicament of History," as cited in Henry E. Bourne, "The Fiftieth Anniversary Meeting," *American Historical Review* 40, no. 3 (April 1935): 427.

2. Morison, "Faith of an Historian," in *By Land and by Sea: Essays and Addresses by Samuel Eliot Morison* (New York: Alfred A. Knopf, 1953), 354.

3. Theodore Clark Smith, "The Writing of American History in America, from 1884 to 1934," *American Historical Review* 40, no. 3 (April 1935): 439–49.

4. Charles Beard, "That Noble Dream," *American Historical Review* 41, no. 1 (October 1935): 75, 76, 79, 87.

5. John Higham, *History: Professional Scholarship in America* (Baltimore: Johns Hopkins University Press, 1965), 128.

6. Charles Beard, "Written History as an Act of Faith," in *The Historian and the Climate of Opinion*, Robert Allen Skotheim (Reading, Mass: Addison-Wesley Publishing Company, 1969), 18.

7. Quoted in Morison, *The Oxford History of the American People* (New York: Oxford University Press, 1965), 911–12. See the following rebuttals to Beard: Charles H. McIlwain, "The Historian's Part in a Changing World," *American Historical Review* 42 (1937): 209–15; Arthur O. Lovejoy, "Present Standpoints and Past History," *Journal of Philosophy* 36 (1939): 477–89; and Robert L. Schuyler, "The Usefulness of Useless History," *Political Science Quarterly* 56 (1941): 23–37.

8. Morison, *Fullness of Life: A Memoir of Elizabeth Shaw Morison, 1886–1945* (Privately printed, 1945), 22.

9. Morison, "Faith of an Historian," 354.

10. Morison, "History Through a Beard," in *By Land and by Sea*, 335.

11. Morison, "Citizenship and Freedom in Teaching," An address before the State of Education Women's Club, 20 January [1936], 2, SEMC HUG(FP)—33.55 box 7.

12. Morison, "Faith of an Historian," 352, 347.

13. Ibid., 347–48, 348, 347.

14. Morison, "History Through a Beard," 332.

15. Morison, "Talk to History Students in Graduate School," 6 October 1927, SEMC HUG(FP)—33.50, box 3.

16. Morison, "Faith of an Historian," 351. Beard influenced historians such as William Dodd, Edward Channing, Max Farrand, and Walter Lippmann. For more see Harvey Wish, *The American Historian* (New York: Oxford University Press, 1960), 274.

17. Morison, Review of *The Colonial Period in American History, I: The Settlements*, by Charles M. Andrews, *New England Quarterly* 7 (December 1934): 729–32.

18. Charles M. Andrews to SEM, 12 January 1935, SEMC HUG(FP)—33.15 box 1.

19. Morison, "Faith of an Historian," 354–55.

20. Morison, *Vistas of History* (New York: Alfred A. Knopf, 1964), 24.

21. R. H. Tawney, *Religion and the Rise of Capitalism* (London: J. Murray, 1926).

22. Beard, *The Rise of American Civilization*, 2 vols. (New York: Macmillan Company, 1927), vol. 1, 54, 56.

23. H. L. Mencken, "Puritanism as a Literary Force," in *Mencken* (Carbondale: Southern Illinois University Press, 1969). Also see, Randolph Bourne, "The Puritan Will to Power," in *Randolph Bourne: The Radical Will—Selected Writings, 1911–1918*, ed., Olaf Hansen (New York: Urizen Books, 1977), 301; James Truslow Adams, *The Founding of New England* (Boston: Atlantic Monthly Press, 1921), 2–7, 121, 122, 193, 264, 279–309; Warren Susman, "Uses of the Puritan Past," in *Culture as History: The Transformation of American Society in the Twentieth Century* (New York: Pantheon Books, 1984), 42.

24. Morison, Review of *The Founding of New England*, by James Truslow Adams, *American Historical Review* 27 (October 1921): 129–31.

25. Morison, *Vistas of History*, 38.

26. Morison, *Builders of the Bay Colony* (Boston: Houghton Mifflin, 1930), x.

27. Morison, *Builders of the Bay Colony*, vi.

28. Morison, "Those Misunderstood Puritans," *Forum* 85 (March 1931): 142. See also Morison, *Builders of the Bay Colony*, 58.

29. Morison, *Builders of the Bay Colony*, vi. Morison devoted an entire appendix in *Builders of the Bay Colony* to an attack on Adams. Perry Miller cited this appendix as one of three inspirations for the writing of *The New England Mind in the Seventeenth Century* (New York: Macmillan, 1939), x.

30. Morison, "Faith of an Historian," 354.

31. Morison, *Puritan Pronaos* (New York: New York University Press, 1936), 29.

32. Morison, *Builders of the Bay Colony*, 131, 104, 53, 79.

33. Ibid., 104, 16.

34. Ibid., 119, 121, 125.

35. Ibid., 117, 125.

36. Morison, "Those Misunderstood Puritans," 147. For more on the conservatism of Morison's work, see Robert Allen Skotheim, *American Intellectual Histories and Historians* (Princeton, N.J.: Princeton University Press, 1966), 173–212.

37. Morison, "Faith of an Historian," 356.

38. Morison, *Builders of the Bay Colony*, 119, 380, x, 100.

39. Ibid., 379–80.

40. SEM to James Truslow Adams, 25 November 1929, SEMC HUG(FP)—33.15 box 1.

41. Morison, *Builders of the Bay Colony*, vi; James Truslow Adams to SEM, 11 December 1929, SEMC HUG(FP)—33.15 box 1; see also, James Truslow Adams, "My Methods as a Historian," *Saturday Review of Literature* 50, 30 June 1934, 277–78. For more on Adams's methods, see James Truslow Adams, "Why Historians Get Headaches," *Rotarian* (January 1940).

42. Morison, "Faith of an Historian," 347–48, 356; see also Morison, "History Through a Beard," 345.

43. Morison, Preface to the Second Edition, *The Intellectual Life of Colonial New England* (New York: New York University Press, 1956).

44. Morison, "Faith of an Historian," 356. For more on Murdock, see Emil Oberholzer, "Puritanism Revisited," in *Perspectives on Early American History*, ed. Alden T. Vaughan and George Athan Billias (New York: Harper & Row, 1973), 37–45.

45. Perry Miller, *Orthodoxy in Massachusetts: A Genetic Study* (Cambridge, Mass.: Harvard University Press, 1930), viii. For more on Miller, see Edmund S. Morgan, "Perry Miller and the Historians," *Proceedings of the American Antiquarian Society* 74, part 1 (1964): 11–18.

46. Allyn B. Forbes, Review of *Provincial Society, 1690–1763*, by James Truslow Adams, *New England Quarterly* 1 (July 1928): 415.

47. B[ernard]. De V[oto], Review of *Henry Adams*, by James Truslow Adams, *New England Quarterly* 7 (March 1934): 195–96. See also Clifford Shipton, "Secondary Education in the Puritan Colonies," *New England Quarterly* 7 (December 1934): 649; James J. Walsh, "Scholasticism in the Colonial Colleges," *New England Quarterly* 5 (July 1932): 483; H. B. Parkes, "Sexual Mores and the Great Awakening," *New England Quarterly* 3 (January 1930): 135.

48. Perry Gilbert Miller, "Thomas Hooker and the Democracy of Early Connecticut," *New England Quarterly* 4 (October 1931): 663.

49. SEM to James Truslow Adams, 25 November 1929, SEMC HUG(FP)—33.15 box 1.

50. Worthington C. Ford, "Correspondence," *New England Quarterly* 7 (June 1934): 398.

51. Ford to James Truslow Adams, 17 May 1934, as quoted in Nevins, *James Truslow Adams: Historian of the American Dream* (Urbana: University of Illinois Press, 1968), 244.

52. Morison, "Faith of an Historian," 347–48.

53. Adams to SEM, 15 November 1929, SEMC HUG(FP)—33.15 box 1.

54. James Truslow Adams, Review of *Builders of the Bay Colony*, by Samuel Eliot Morison, *New England Quarterly* 3 (October 1930): 741–46.

55. Van Wyck Brooks, *The Wine of the Puritans: A Study of Present Day America* (New York: M. Kennerley, 1909), 14, 29, 134. For a contemporary review of the work by a perceptive Harvard student, see T. S. Eliot, "The Wine of the Puritans," 7 May 1909, *Harvard Advocate*, 80.

56. Morison, *The Puritan Pronaos*, 5.

57. Ibid., 17, 16, 5, 58, 27, 71.

58. Morison, "Address: Amherst College," SEMC HUG(FP)—33.55 box 1. See also Morison, "New England in Higher Education," [1932], SEMC HUG(FP)—33.55 box 5; "Puritan Education and the Founding of Harvard College," Providence College, December 1936, ibid., 33.41 box 1.

59. Morison, *The Puritan Pronaos*, 13.

60. Van Wyck Brooks, *The Flowering of New England, 1815–1865* (1936; New and revised edition, E. P. Dutton, 1940), 1, 210, 211, 214, 215; see also Morison, Preface to the Second Edition, *The Puritan Pronaos*, xi.

61. George Santayana to SEM, 4 September 1936, SEMC HUG(FP)—33.15 box 11.

62. Laura Richards to SEM, 13 April 1937, ibid., box 2.

63. SEM to Santayana, 28 September 1936, ibid., box 11.

64. Santayana to SEM, 11 October 1936, ibid.

65. Morison, Review of *The Flowering of New England, 1815–1865*, by Van Wyck Brooks, *American Historical Review* 42 (1937): 564.

66. Ibid., 562–63, 563–64.

67. Ibid. For more on this point, see Brooks to SEM, 24 February 1940, SEMC HUG(FP)—33.15 box 2.

68. SEM to Brooks, 25 January 1937, ibid.

69. Brooks to SEM, 8 October 1936, 27 April 1937, 8 October 1936, ibid.

70. Robert E. Spiller, ed., *The Van Wyck Brooks–Lewis Mumford Letters: The Record of a Literary Friendship, 1921–63* (New York: E. P. Dutton, 1970), 248–49.

71. Brooks to SEM, 27 April 1937, SEMC HUG(FP)—33.15 box 2.

72. Brooks to SEM, 2 February 1937, 19 December 1936, ibid.

73. Brooks, "On Creating a Usable Past," 338; SEM to Brooks, 5 February 1937, SEMC HUG(FP)—33.15 box 2.

74. Charles M. Andrews to SEM, 13 May 1935, ibid., box 1.

75. Raymond Nelson, *Van Wyck Brooks: A Writer's Life* (New York: E. P. Dutton, n.d.), 227–79.

76. SEM to Andrews, 30 November 1934, 7 November 1938, SEMC HUG(FP)—33.15 box 2.

77. SEM to Van Wyck Brooks, 14 May 1948, ibid., box 1.

78. Brooks's italics. Van Wyck Brooks to SEM, 31 May 1948, ibid.

79. Skotheim, *American Intellectual Histories and Historians*, 178–79.

80. Morison, "Faith of an Historian," 355.

CHAPTER 9: THE VOYAGE OF DISCOVERY

1. Morison, "History as a Literary Art," in *By Land and by Sea: Essays and Addresses by Samuel Eliot Morison* (New York: Alfred A. Knopf, Inc., 1953), 289.

2. Ibid., 289–91.

3. Ibid., 297.

4. Rosemary Jann, *The Art and Science of Victorian History* (Columbus: Ohio State University Press, 1985), xii.

5. Morison, *Vistas of History* (New York: Alfred A. Knopf, 1964), 26–27.

6. Emily Morison Beck, ed., *Sailor Historian: The Best of Samuel Eliot Morison* (Boston: Houghton Mifflin, 1977), 1.

7. Morison, *Admiral of the Ocean Sea: A Life of Christopher Columbus*, 2 vols., (Boston: Little, Brown, 1942), vol. 1, 143.

8. Justin Winsor, ed., *Narrative and Critical History of the United States*, 8 vols. (Boston: Houghton Mifflin, 1884–89).

9. R. Comissione Columbiana, *Raccolta di documenti e studi pubblicati dalla R. Comissione Columbiana* (Roma: Ministero della pubblica istruzione, 1892–96).

10. Beck, *Sailor Historian*, 1.

11. For a discussion of Columbus historiography, see Morison, *Admiral of the Ocean Sea*, 1: 76–79, 101–6.

12. Morison, *Vistas of History*, 28–29.

13. Morison, *Admiral of the Ocean Sea*, vol. 1, xvi.

14. Robert van Gelder, "An Interview with Samuel Eliot Morison: The Author of 'Admiral of the Ocean Sea' Discusses His Life and Work," *New York Times Book Review*, 13 March 1943.

15. SEM to Lincoln Colcord, 29 January 1937, SEMC HUG(FP)—33.15 box 3.

16. For details of this arrangement, see SEM to Andrews, 4 November 1937, Charles M. Andrews Papers, Yale University; hereafter cited as CMAP.

17. For more on William Goodwin, see Barry Fell, *America B.C.: Ancient Settlers in the New World* (New York: Quadrangle/New York Times Book Co., 1976), vii, 18, 291.

18. Andrews to SEM, 29 April 1939, SEMC (HUG(FP)—33.15 box 1.

19. William B. Goodwin, "The Oldest Community Site in America," An address given before the annual meeting of the Florida Historical Society, 24 January 1939, in *Florida Historical Quarterly* 17 (April 1939): 330. Goodwin eventually published his findings in *The Ruins of Great Ireland in New England* (Boston: Meador, 1946).

20. Andrews to SEM, 2 February 1939, 29 April 1939, SEMC HUG(FP)—33.15 box 1.

21. Goodwin, "Report on Three Expeditions to the Island of Haiti; Undertaken in the Years 1935, 1936, and 1938," The William B. Goodwin Papers, The Connecticut State Archives, Capitol Building, Hartford, Connecticut; hereafter cited as WBGP.

22. Goodwin to Wesley Winans Stout, 19 July 1939, ibid.

23. SEM to Andrews, 12 April 1939, SEMC (HUG(FP)—33.15 box 1.

24. Ibid.

25. Andrews to SEM, 29 April 1939, ibid.

26. SEM to Andrews, 12 April 1939, ibid.

27. Andrews to SEM, 29 April 1939, ibid.

28. Goodwin to Louis Mercier, 29 August 1939, WBGP.

29. Goodwin to Coplin Yates, 8 May 1940, ibid.; Goodwin to Wesley Winans Stout, 19 July 1939, ibid.

30. SEM to Andrews, 18 July 1939, 3 May 1939, CMAP.

31. SEM to Andrews, 26 January 1939, ibid. See also SEM to Andrews, 29 April 1939, SEMC HUG(FP)—33.15 box 1.

32. SEM to Andrews, 3 May 1939, CMAP.

33. Andrews to SEM, 29 April 1939, SEMC HUG(FP)—33.15 box 1.

34. Grace A. Fendler to Carnegie Corporation of New York, 3 November 1939, ibid., 33.55 box 3.

35. SEM to Andrews, 24 July 1939, CMAP.

36. SEM to Andrews, 18 July 1939, SEMC HUG(FP)—33.15 box 1.

37. SEM to James B. Conant, 27 April 1939, SEMC HUG(FP)—33.15 box 3.

38. Conant to SEM, 15 May 1939, ibid.

39. SEM to Andrews, 12 April 1939, ibid., box 1.

40. Walter H. Marx, ed., "The Story of the Columbus Expedition (told via letters printed in the *Harvard Alumni Bulletin*, 29 September 1939–1 March 1940)," ibid., 33.75.

41. Cox and Stern to SEM, 2 June 1939, ibid., 33.15 box 3.

42. Commandante Luis Toro Buiza, "Harvard Columbus Expedition," *Falange*, 9 January 1940.

43. Morison, *Admiral of the Ocean Sea*, vol. 1, xix–xx.

44. SEM to F. R. Bolster, 15 July 1940, SEMC HUG(FP)—33.55 box 3.

45. "News Release," 11 August 1939, Harvard University News Office, ibid.

46. SEM to W. J. Peters, 27 July 1939, 3 August 1939, ibid. See also SEM to Sr. Don Janeval Valeria, n.d., ibid.

47. President and Fellows of Harvard College to SEM, 12 April 1940, ibid.

48. SEM to Mr. du Bois, 13 April 1940, ibid.

49. M. A. Lettand [White House Private Secretary] to SEM, 10 July 1939, ibid; Division of Foreign Service to SEM, 17 June 1939, ibid. One reviewer called the expedition "an adventure in international cooperation," see Marx, ed., "The Story of the Harvard Columbus Expedition," ibid., 33.75.

50. SEM to Colonel Devers, 30 January 1940, SEMC HUG(FP)—33.55 box 3.

51. SEM to Charles Andrews, 18 July 1939, CMAP.

52. "News Release," 11 August 1939, SEMC HUG(FP)—33.55 box 3.

53. "Food List," 7 August 1939, ibid., 33.72, box 1

54. "News Release," 11 August 1939, ibid., 33.55 box 3.

55. Ibid.

56. Morison, "Family Bulletin No. 1—Capitana," 11 September 1939, SEMC HUG(FP)—33.55 box 3. During the Harvard Columbus Expedition, Morison sent letters to the *Harvard Alumni Bulletin* explaining his activities. These have been republished in Morison, *By Land and by Sea*, 99–123. He also sent some private letters to his immediate family and a few friends. I have designated these as "Family Bulletin."

57. Morison, "Journal of the Harvard Columbus Expedition—Brooklyn to Tenerife," 29 August 1939, ibid.

58. Morison, "Letter No. 1," *Harvard Alumni Bulletin*, 29 September 1939, in *By Land and by Sea*, 100.

59. Morison, "Journal of the Harvard Columbus Expedition," 3 September 1939, SEMC HUG(FP)—33.55 box 3.

60. "Family Bulletin No. 1," 16 September 1939, ibid.

61. Susan Hammond, "Lecture on the Harvard Columbus Expedition," c. 1941, SEMC HUG(FP)—33.71 series 2. Susan Hammond, wife of Captain Paul Hammond, gave several lectures on the expedition to the Colony Club and the English-Speaking Union. The typescript of one of these lectures is preserved in the Harvard University Archives. The Hammonds and Morison also kept an elaborate photographic record of the voyage. See "Harvard Columbus Expedition, Glass Slides—series 1 and 2," ibid.

62. "Family Bulletin No. 1," 11 September 1939, ibid., 33.55 box 3.

63. Hammond, "Lecture on the Harvard Columbus Expedition," ibid., 33.71 series 2.

64. "Letter No. 7, 15 February 1940," *By Land and by Sea*, 118.

65. "Transcriptions from the Journal of Samuel Eliot Morison," 6 October 1939, SEMC HUG(FP)—33.73 box 3.

66. "Family Bulletin No. 10," 5 December 1939, ibid.

67. Hammond, "Lecture on the Harvard Columbus Expedition," ibid., 33.71 series 2.

68. "Family Bulletin No. 11," 23 December 1939, ibid., 33.55 box 3.

69. "Family Bulletin No. 2," 23 September 1939, SEMC HUG(FP)—33.55 box 3.

70. "Family Bulletin No. 3," 30 September 1939, ibid.

71. Morison, "Journal of the Harvard Columbus Expedition, Brooklyn to Tenerife," 16 November 1939, ibid., 33.73.

72. "Family Bulletin No. 4," 10 October 1939, SEMC HUG(FP)—33.55 box 3.

73. "Family Bulletin No. 5," 14–18 October 1939, ibid.

74. "Family Bulletin No. 6," 23 October 1939, ibid.

75. Hammond, "Lecture on the Harvard Columbus Expedition," ibid., 33.71 series 2.

76. Kenneth R. Spear to SEM, n.d., SEMC HUG(FP)—33.55 box 3.

77. Morison, "Journal of the Harvard Columbus Expedition," 20 November 1939, ibid., 33.73.

78. Morison, "Journal of the Harvard Columbus Expedition," 20 September 1939, ibid.

79. "Ship's Log, kept by Jarillo Walters (sailing master)," 10, 11, 12 October 1939, ibid., 33.55 box 3.

80. "Family Bulletin No. 11," 23 December 1939," ibid.

81. Morison, *Admiral of the Ocean Sea*, vol. 2, 262.

82. "Family Bulletin No. 11," 23 December 1939, SEMC HUG(FP)—33.55 box 3.

83. "Family Bulletin No. 12," 6 January 1940, ibid.

84. "Letter No. 7, 15 February 1940," *By Land and by Sea*, 120.

85. Ibid., 121.

86. Morison returned to the Caribbean to complete some of the unfinished work of the Harvard Columbus Expedition in the summer of 1940. See "Harvard Columbus Expedition—Cuban Cruise," Family Letters 1–6: 12 June 1940, 17 June 1940, 23 June 1940, 30 June 1940, 3 July 1940, 8 July 1940, SEMC HUG(FP)—33.55 box 4.

87. "Family Bulletin No. 6," 23 October 1939, SEMC HUG(FP)—33.55 box 3; "Family Bulletin No. 7," 6 November 1939, ibid.

88. "Letter No. 7," 15 February 1940, *By Land and by Sea*, 122.

89. "Columbus Upheld!" *New York Times*, 2 February 1940.

90. "Life Resails Columbus's Routes," *Life* 8, 25 March 1940, 102–6.

91. Uncle Dudley, "Sailor Historian," *Boston Globe*, 16 February 1939.

92. Morison, *Admiral of the Ocean Sea*, vol. 1, xxi, xxi–xlv.

93. Ibid., vol. 1, 3, 4, 5, 3, 4, 6.

94. Ibid., vol. 1, xxxix; vol. 2, 74.

95. Ibid., vol. 1, 77, 8, xv, xix–xx, 26–27, 17, 182–83.

96. Ibid., vol. 1, 295, 298.

97. Morison, "History as Literary Art," 297.

98. Ibid., vol. 1, 135; vol. 2, 228; vol. 1, 275–76, 285, 64.

99. Ibid., vol. 1, 262, 210, 26–27, 29, 282.

100. Ibid., vol. 1, 115, 438; vol. 2, 10; vol. 1, 437; vol. 2, 53, 54.

101. Ibid., vol. 1, 48, 117, 91, 273, 91, 137.

102. Ibid., vol. 1, 285, 79, 111, 31; vol. 2, 164.

103. Morison, *Admiral of the Ocean Sea*, single volume edition, (Boston: Little, Brown, 1942), 670, 671, 667, 669.

104. Morison, "History as Literary Art," 293.

CHAPTER 10: PARTICIPATORY HISTORY

1. See, for instance, Alexander Marchant, Review of *Admiral of the Ocean Sea*, by Samuel Eliot Morison, *American Historical Review* 49 (January 1944): 269–70; Garrett Mattingly, "Professor with a Roll," *New Republic* 106, 9 March 1942, 337; J. B. Brebner, "The Great Navigator," *Yale Review* 31 (Spring 1942): 606–8; William McFee, "The Discoverer," *Nation* 154, 14 March 1942, 314; Lincoln Colcord, Review of *Admiral of the Ocean Sea*, by Samuel Eliot Morison, *Books* 3, 1 March 1942, 14; Leonard Olschki, Review

of *Admiral of the Ocean Sea*, by Samuel Eliot Morison, *Saturday Review of Literature*, 25, 28 February 1942, 5; Review of *Admiral of the Ocean Sea*, by Samuel Eliot Morison, in *Time* 39, 2 March 1942, 16; E. C. Kiessling, "Historian Who Lives History," *Milwaukee Journal* (1 November 1964).

2. SEM to Curtis Brown, 17 November 1952, SEMC HUG(FP)—33.1 box 1. The figure $30,000 was based on the accumulated royalties as of 1952.

3. Clifton Fadiman, "Admiral of the Ocean Sea," *New Yorker* 18 (28 February 1942): 57.

4. Robert van Gelder, An Interview with Samuel Eliot Morison, *New York Times*, 13 March 1943.

5. SEM to Franklin D. Roosevelt, 1 June 1940, SEMC HUG(FP)—33.15 box 11.

6. SEM to the *Harvard Crimson*, 9 December 1940, ibid., box 4.

7. SEM to Franklin D. Roosevelt, 20 December 1940, Franklin Delano Roosevelt File—5720 OF3900 boxes 1–4, Hyde Park, New York; hereafter cited as FDR HP.

8. SEM to Commodore D. W. Knox, 14 October 1946, Office Files of Rear Admiral Samuel E. Morison, 1911–1969, series 2, box 9; The Naval Operational Archives, housed in the Washington Naval Yard, Washington, D.C.: hereafter cited as NOA.

9. SEM to Capt. John A. Gade, 9 December 1941, SEMC HUG(FP)—33.15 box 5.

10. SEM to Franklin D. Roosevelt, 23 March 1942, ibid., 33.41 box 1.

11. Morison, *Vistas of History* (New York: Alfred A. Knopf, 1964), 28–29.

12. Ibid., 32.

13. SEM to Franklin D. Roosevelt, 23 March 1942, SEMC HUG(FP)—33.41 box 1.

14. John L. McCrea, Letters to the Editor, *Boston Sunday Globe*, 6 June 1976.

15. Franklin D. Roosevelt to Captain McCrea, 7 April 1942, SEMC HUG(FP)—33.41 box 1.

16. Frank Knox to SEM, 11 April 1942, ibid.

17. James Forrestal, Preface to *Operations in North African Waters*, vol. 2 of *The History of United States Naval Operations in World War II*, by Samuel Eliot Morison (Boston: Little, Brown, 1947).

18. John L. McCrea, Letters to the Editor, *Boston Sunday Globe*, 6 June 1976.

19. "Lt. Comdr S. E. Morison's Talk with President Roosevelt," 12 June 1942, NOA, box 14, series 3, vol. F, folder 90.

20. Morison, *Fullness of Life: A Memoir of Elizabeth Shaw Morison, 1886–1945* (Privately printed, 1945), 52. "When we entered the war, Bessie thoroughly approved of my ambition to write the History of United States Naval Operations, and my method of doing it, which took me far from her for months at a time. Her typically cheerful reaction was, 'Go to sea, Sam, if you must, I shall enjoy being *sur la branche.*'"

21. Morison, *Vistas of History*, 32.

22. Henry Saloman, Jr., "Historian at War: Chronicling American Naval Operations in World War II," *Harvard Alumni Bulletin*, 22 February 1947, 425.

23. John Heffernan to [Secretary of the Navy], 1 January 1946, NOA, series 2, box 7.

24. Morison, "Impressions of the Moroccan Expedition and the Battle of Casablanca, 18 November 1942; written at sea on the return voyage, November 20–24, from my rough notes and memory," SEMC HUG(FP)—33.55 box 5, 1.

25. "War Room Conversations: Patton," ibid., 2–4.

26. Ibid., 6.

27. Ibid. Morison also noted the historical significance of the crossing: "As this was the 450th anniversary of the discovery of America by Columbus, there was a sentimental significance in the fact that on 31 October, and again on 3 November, Task Force 34 crossed the track made by the *Santa Maria, Pinta,* and *Nina* on their westward voyage in 1492. It seemed that America was at last repaying her debt to the first Admiral of the

Ocean Sea, and in a sense fulfilling his ambition to deliver Jerusalem; for these seventy thousand young men from the New World of his discovery were returning to rescue the Old World of his affections from the most iniquitous bondage to which she had been subjected in a thousand years" (Morison, *Operations in North African Waters*, 49).

28. Morison, "Sail Easy Mike," Ballads: SEMC HUG(FP)—33.55 box 1. This file also includes Morison's humorous notes on the "Rules and Regulations from Mess Attendants in the United States Navy," the "Battle of the Privies," and "Discreetly Secret—Report on Operation Tortoga—2 Sea turtles mating."

29. Franklin D. Roosevelt, "Memorandum for Mr. Shipman," 18 December 1942, FDR Presidential Library File, box 3, FDR HP.

30. Morison, "Impressions of the Moroccan Expedition," 6.

31. SEM to Edgar E. Weis[s], 5 February 1943, NOA, series 2, box 5.

32. Morison, "Impressions of the Moroccan Expedition," 31.

33. Salomon, "Historian at War," 426.

34. Ibid. See also, SEM to Secretary of the Navy, 7 January 1943, NOA, series 2, box 9.

35. Roger Pineau to Greg Pfitzer, 3 January 1989; letter in possession of the author and cited with permission.

36. Morison, "Morison's Talk with Pres. Roosevelt," 16 December 1942, NOA, series 3, box 14, vol F, folder 90.

37. Morison, "Autobiographical Sketch," SEMC HUG(FP)—33.15 box 1.

38. Morison, *Vistas of History*, 32.

39. SEM to Captain Ralph C. Parker, [n.d.], NOA, sereis 2, box 5.

40. Morison, "MacArthur, D.A., Gen.: Admiral Morison's notes on his interview with General MacArthur," 12 January 1943, NOA, series 1, box 13, folder 66.

41. Morison, "Autobiographical Sketch," SEMC HUG(FP)—33.1 box 1.

42. Morison, "My Night," 9 July 1943, ibid. 33.55 box 1.

43. A. T. Primm, III, "Review of Samuel Eliot Morison's *Operations in North African Waters*," *St. Louis Dispatch*, [1947].

44. Salomon, "Historian at War," 426.

45. Morison, "Personal Impressions of Gilbert Island and Marshall Operations: November–December 1945, written aboard U.S.S. *Baltimore*," 6 December 1943, NOA, series 3, box 35, folder 13.

46. Ibid.

47. Ibid. See also Salomon, "Historian at War," 427.

48. Ibid.

49. Morison, "Autobiographical Sketch," SEMC HUG(FP)—33.1 box 1.

50. Morison, "Morison Has Lunch with Pres. Roosevelt," 12 February 1944, NOA box 14, series 3, vol. F, folder 90.

51. March Hatch, "Busy Writing a 14-Volume History of the United States Navy in World War II," *Boston Sunday Post*, 20 October 1946.

52. Ibid.

53. Morison, "Memoir of FDR; written near Okinawa, 13 April 1945," SEMC HUG(FP)—33.55 box 6.

54. Morison, *Fullness of Life*, 52–56.

55. Morison, "Autobiographical Sketch," SEMC HUG(FP)—33.1 box 1.

56. Salomon, "Historian at War," 429.

57. Roger Pineau to Greg Pfitzer, 3 January 1989.

58. Ibid. In pursuing these duties, Pineau became acquainted with Japanese Foreign Minister Mamoru Shigemitsu, Commanders in Chief Combined Fleet Jisaburo Ozawa and Soemu Toyoda, Admiral Sadotoshi Tomioka, Captains Mitsuo Fuchida, Toshikazu Ohmae, and Yasuji Watanabe, all of whom provided Morison with valuable information about Japanese naval operations.

59. Ibid. In addition to his responsibilities as Japanese translator and researcher, Pineau also worked in French and British naval archives.

60. "Pearl Harbor Questionaire," 17 October 1945, NOA, series 3, box 20, folder 39a.

61. Roger Pineau to Greg Pfitzer, 3 January 1989.

62. SEM to Chief of Naval Operations, 12 December 1953, SEMC HUG(FP)—33.47, Naval History box 1.

63. Dudley Wright Knox, Introduction to *The Battle of the Atlantic, September 1939–May 1943*, vol. 1 of *The History of United States Naval Operations in World War II*, by Sameul Eliot Morison (Boston: Little, Brown, 1947), xxxiv.

64. SEM to Commodore D. W. Knox, 14 October 1946, NOA, series 2, box 9.

65. Morison, *The Battle of the Atlantic*, 133, 135.

66. Ibid., 28.

67. Sam Adkins, "Lady Luck Was Our Strongest Ally in the U-Boat Campaign," *Courier Journal*, Louisville, Kentucky, 30 November 1947, 4.

68. Morison, *The Battle of the Atlantic*, xiii–xiv.

69. Ibid., 133.

70. Harry C. Butcher, "Grand Strategy and Action," *Saturday Review of Literature* 31, 3 January 1948, 13.

71. Morison, *Operations in North African Waters*, 83, 55–64.

72. Harry C. Butcher, "Navy Inexplicables Explained," *Saturday Review of Literature* 30, 29 March 1947, 12.

73. Hanson W. Baldwin, "The Navy's Role in World War II," *New York Times Book Review*, 23 February 1947, 12.

74. William Reitzel, Review of *Operations in North African Waters*, by Samuel Eliot Morison, *American Historical Review* 53 (October 1947): 81.

75. John M. McCullough, "Grand Strategy of North African Invasion: Historian Analyzes America's Strengths and Weaknesses in 1942–43," *Philadelphia Inquirer*, 2 March 1947.

76. Butcher, "Navy Inexplicables," 17.

77. Morison, *Operations in North African Waters*, 44. See also Thomas C. Mendenall, "History-Writing and the War," *Yale Review* 37 (Autumn 1947): 157.

78. W. Barton Leach, "Review of S. E. Morison's *Operations in North African Waters*," NOA, series 3, box 18, folder 29.

79. Charles Beard, *President Roosevelt and the Coming of the War, 1941* (New Haven, Conn.: Yale University Press, 1948), 3, 443–45.

80. Ibid., 493–500, 512.

81. Morison, *The Rising Sun in the Pacific*, vol. 3 of *The History of United States Naval Operations in World War II* (Boston: Little, Brown, 1948), ix.

82. Morison, "History Through a Beard," in *By Land and by Sea: Essays and Addresses by Samuel Eliot Morison* (New York: Alfred A. Knopf, 1953), 337.

83. Morison, *The Rising Sun in the Pacific*, 53–55, 68, 73.

84. Morison, "History Through a Beard," 333, 335.

85. For more on Beard's pacifism, see Charles Beard, *The Devil Theory of War* (New York: The Vanguard Press, 1936).

86. Morison, "History Through a Beard," 334.

87. Ibid., 333.

88. Philip A. Crowl, "Ships and Sailors vs Nippon," *Saturday Review of Literature* 31, 27 November 1948, 131.

89. Ed Rankin to SEM, 29 October 1961, SEMC HUG(FP)—33.55 box 6.

90. "What Makes Sammy Run," 15 November 1961, *Chicago Sunday Tribune*.

91. Morison, *The Rising Sun in the Pacific*, 80–141.

92. "A Hired Liar," *Chicago Sunday Tribune,* 10 October 1948. See also, Morison, "Comments on *Chicago Sunday Tribune* Editorial, 'A Hired Liar,' " NOA, series 3, box 10, folder 17.

93. "A Court Historian Comes in Out of the Rain," *Chicago Daily Tribune,* 25 September 1948.

94. "Doing Good by Stealth," *Chicago Daily Tribune,* 2 August 1948.

95. "A Hired Liar," *Chicago Sunday Tribune,* 10 October 1948; also ibid.

CHAPTER 11: SAFEGUARDING HISTORY

1. FDR to Professor W. Y. Eliot, 16 March 1938, FDR HP.

2. FDR to SEM, 28 February 1938, 3 December 1938, 14 December 1938, ibid. See also, Morison, "My Visit to the White House," 19 November 1938, SEMC HUG(FP)—33.55 box 6.

3. Morison, "The Very Essence of History," *New York Times Magazine,* 88, Sect. 8, 19 March 1939, 4–5, 22.

4. "Historian Laments Losses," 10 December 1938, as cited in "Hearing Before the Committee on the Library, House of Representatives on H. J. Res. 268, 7 May 1939," FDR HP.

5. Walter Trohan, "Mr. Roosevelt's Memorial," *Chicago Tribune,* 29 September 1939, FDR HP.

6. Boothby's italics. Clarence S. Boothby to FDR, 13 December 1938, ibid.

7. D. W. Alspaugh, to FDR, 28 December 1938, ibid.

8. Eleanor Roosevelt to Justice Frankfurter, 8 June 1945, NOA, series 2, box. 2.

9. SEM to FDR, 11 March 1938, ibid. See also, "Memorandum on the Archives of the Franklin Delano Roosevelt Library," 17 November 1938, SEMC HUG(FP)—33.55 box 6.

10. FDR to W. Y. Elliott, 16 March 1938, FDR HP. See also, Charles A Beard to FDR, 6 December 1938, ibid.

11. Charles Beard to Kent E. Keller, [n.d.], and Julian P. Boyd to FDR, 12 December 1938, FDR HP.

12. Charles Beard, "Who's to Write the History of the War," *Saturday Evening Post,* 220, 4 October 1947, 172.

13. Howard K. Beale, "The Professional Historian: His Theory and His Practice," *Pacific Historical Review* 22 (August 1953): 239.

14. Herman Kahn, "World War II and Its Background: Research Materials at the Franklin D. Roosevelt Library and Policies Concerning Their Use," FDR HP. See also, "Exercises at the Dedication of the FDR Library," 13 June 1941, SEMC HUG(FP)—33.55 box 6.

15. William Neumann to SEM, 21 November 1953, SEMC HUG(FP)—33.55 box 1.

16. SEM to William Neumann, 30 November 1952, ibid.

17. For more on the political uses of history in the postwar period, see Roy F. Nichols, "Postwar Reorientation of Historical Thinking," *American Historical Review* 54 (1948): 78–89.

18. SEM to Leverett Saltonstall, 7 June 1948, SEMC HUG(FP)—33.41, box 1.

19. Richard Lloyd Jones, "Harvard's Fuzzy-Minded Teachers," *Tulsa Tribune,* 27 November 1948.

20. Jones's italics. Richard Lloyd Jones to SEM, 8 September 1948, SEMC HUG(FP)—33.55 box 1.

21. Jones's italics. Richard Lloyd Jones to SEM, 26 September 1948, ibid.

22. Morison, Introductory remarks to "History Through a Beard," *Atlantic Monthly* 182 (August 1948): 91–97; I have consulted the version that appears in *By Land and by*

Sea: Essays and Addresses by Samuel Eliot Morison (New York: Alfred A. Knopf, 1953), 328.

23. Ibid., 339.

24. Ibid., 331, 332.

25. SEM to Van Wyck Brooks, 19 May 1948, SEMC HUG(FP)—33.55 box 1.

26. Morison, Introductory remarks to "History Through a Beard," 345.

27. Justice Felix Frankfurter to SEM, 5 May 1948, SEMC HUG(FP)—33.55 box 1.

28. Bernard De Voto to SEM, 20 July 1948, ibid.

29. William Langer to SEM, 22 July 1948, ibid; Storer Lunt to SEM, 27 July 1948, ibid.

30. Beale, "The Professional Historian: His Theory and His Practice," 247–49.

31. M. L. Deyo to SEM, 17 May 1945, NOA, series 2, box 4.

32. Charles Beard to SEM, 19 July 1948, SEMC HUG(FP)—33.55, box 1; and Charles Beard to SEM, [n.d.], ibid., 33.15 box 2.

33. "A Hired Liar," *Chicago Sunday Tribune*, 10 October 1948.

34. Morison, Introductory remarks to "History Through a Beard," 328. Alfred Knopf, who republished the article in *By Land and by Sea*, never approved of the piece. Knopf wrote: "I agreed with many mutual friends that 'History Through a Beard,' a poor title to begin with, did not represent Samuel Eliot Morison at his best and did not deserve the kind of immortality that a hard-bound book inevitably involves." See Alfred A. Knopf, "Historian and Publisher," *American Heritage*, 28, no. 3 (April 1977): 103.

35. Dixon Wechter to SEM, 27 July 1948, SEMC HUG(FP)—33.55 box 1; and SEM to Wechter, 18 September 1948, ibid.

36. Morison, Introductory remarks to "Faith of an Historian," in *By Land and by Sea*, 346.

37. SEM to Cyril Falls, 3 October 1952, NOA, series 2, box 4.

38. Charles A. Beard, "Written History as an Act of Faith," as cited in Robert Allen Skotheim, ed., *The Historian and the Climate of Opinion* (Reading, Mass.: Addison-Wesley, 1969), 9–20.

39. Morison, "Faith of an Historian," 351.

40. Howard K. Beale to SEM, 28 January 1953, SEMC HUG(FP)—33.55 box 1.

41. Beale's italics. Beale, "The Professional Historian," 251–52.

42. Howard K. Beale to SEM, 28 January 1953, SEMC HUG(FP)—33.55 box 1.

43. SEM to Richard Lovell, 3 February 1953, ibid.

44. Brooks Beck to SEM, 9 February 1953, ibid.

45. Curtis Nettels to SEM, 5 February 1953, ibid.

46. Ibid. See also, Curtis Nettels to SEM, 13 February 1953, ibid.

47. Beale, "The Professional Historian," 244.

48. "Remarks by President Truman," Annual Report of the American Historical Association, 1950, Proceedings, 1 (Washington, D.C.: United States Government Printing Office, 1950), 4.

49. Beale, "The Professional Historian," 245.

50. "When History Serves the State," *Chicago Sunday Tribune*, 30 September 1951, 26–27.

51. Grace Davidson, "Morison for More A-Bombs; Naval Historian Says Reds Respect Strength," *Boston Post*, 23 November 1950.

52. Ibid. See also, "Historian's View of War," *Worcester Independent Gazette*, 5 October 1951.

53. Morison, *Coral Sea, Midway, and Submarine Actions, May 1942–August 1942*, vol. 4 of *The History of United States Naval Operations in World War II* (Boston: Little, Brown, 1949), 63, 106.

54. Ibid., 38.

55. Ibid., 102.

56. Morison, *Breaking the Bismarcks Barrier, 22 July 1924–1 May 1944*, vol. 6 of *The History of United States Naval Operations in World War II* (Boston: Little, Brown, 1950), 20.

57. Morison, *The Struggle for Guadalcanal*, vol. 5 of *The History of United States Naval Operations in World War II* (Boston: Little, Brown, 1949), 40, 17, 3.

58. Morison, *Breaking the Bismarcks Barrier*, 50.

59. Morison, *Aleutians, Gilberts and Marshalls, June 1942–April 1944*, vol. 7 of *The History of United States Naval Operations in World War II* (Boston: Little, Brown, 1951), 46–47.

60. Ibid., 157–59.

61. Morison, *Aleutians, Gilberts, and Marshalls*, 132.

62. Morison, *Breaking the Bismarcks Barrier*, 46.

63. Morison, "MacArthur, D. A., Gen.: Admiral Morison's notes on his interview with General MacArthur," 12 January 1943, NOA, series 1, box 13, folder 66.

64. Morison, *New Guinea and the Mariannas*, vol. 8 of *The History of United States Naval Operations in World War II* (Boston: Little, Brown, 1953), 4, 6–7.

65. Morison, *The Oxford History of the American People* (New York: Oxford University Press, 1965), 1072.

66. Ibid., 1068; see also, "Korea: A Costly Renewal of U. S. Lesson in Japan War," *Christian Science Monitor*, 13 November 1950; and J. Malcolm, "U. S. Sea Power Saved Day in Korea, Says Morison," *Boston Globe*, 13 November 1950.

67. Morison, *The Oxford History of the American People*, 1071–72.

68. Ibid., 1071.

69. "MacArthur, D. A., Gen: Admiral Morison's notes on his interview with General MacArthur," 12 January 1943, NOA, series 1, box 13, folder 66.

70. Morison, *The Oxford History of the American People*, 1072–73.

71. C. Vann Woodward, "Between Defeats in the Pacific," *Saturday Review of Literature*, 32, 29 October 1949, 20.

72. Ira Wolfert, "The Guadalcanal Story: Blood, Blunders, Tears, and Victory," *New York Times Book Review*, 27 November 1949, 3. See also, the reply of Morison's staff: James Shaw, "Letter to the Editor," *New York Times Book Review*, 25 December 1949, 9.

73. Morison, "Faith of an Historian," 350.

CHAPTER 12: CONSENSUS HISTORY

1. John Higham, "The Cult of the 'American Consensus': Homogenizing Our History," *Commentary* (February 1959): 95. See also, John Higham, "Beyond Consensus: The Historian as Moral Critic," *American Historical Review* (April 1962): 609–25.

2. Richard Hofstadter, *The American Political Tradition* (New York: Alfred A. Knopf, 1948), xxxvi–xxxvii, as cited in Peter Novick, *That Noble Dream: The "Objectivity Question" and the American Historical Profession* (New York: Cambridge University Press, 1988), 333.

3. Higham, "The Cult of 'American Consensus,'" 96.

4. Arthur Schlesinger, Jr., *The Vital Center: the Politics of Freedom* (Boston: Houghton Mifflin, 1949).

5. Daniel Bell, *The End of Ideology*, (Glencoe, Ill.: Free Press, 1960).

6. Higham, "The Cult of 'American Consensus,'" 94.

7. Morison, "Faith of an Historian," in *By Land and by Sea: Essays and Addresses by Samuel Eliot Morison*, (Alfred A. Knopf, 1953), 357.

8. Morison, "Statement by Samuel Eliot Morison of Boston, in favor of General Eisenhower," *Boston Post,* 27 October 1952.

9. Ibid.

10. SEM to Dwight D. Eisenhower, 18 November 1952, SEMC HUG(FP)—33.15 box 3.

11. Morison, *Freedom in Contemporary Society* (Boston: Little, Brown, 1956), 104.

12. SEM to Dwight D. Eisenhower, 18 November 1952, SEMC HUG(FP)—33.15 box 3.

13. Morison, *The Oxford History of the American People* (New York: Oxford University Press, 1965), 1079.

14. Ibid.

15. Morison, *The Invasion of France and Germany,* vol. 11 of *The History of United States Naval Operations in World War II* (Boston: Little, Brown, 1957), 22, 37.

16. Morison, *Sicily-Salerno-Anzio,* vol. 9 of *The History of the United States Naval Operations in World War II* (Boston: Little, Brown, 1954), 7, 10–11.

17. Ibid., 138, 140.

18. Morison, *The Atlantic Battle Won, May 1943–May 1945,* vol. 10 of *The History of the United States Naval Operations in World War II* (Boston: Little, Brown, 1956), 363–64, 95.

19. M. L. Deyo, "Comments on Admiral Morison's First Draft," February 1956, NOA, series 3, box 81, folder 33.

20. Morison, *The Invasion of France and Germany,* 53, 83.

21. Ibid., 86–87.

22. Ibid., 330.

23. Morison, *The Oxford History of the American People,* 1079.

24. Ibid., 1081.

25. Ibid., 1091–94.

26. Ibid., 1106.

27. Morison, "Report on Lunch with President Eisenhower at the White House," 28 October 1953, NOA, box 53, folder 69.

28. Morison, *The Oxford History of the American People,* 1106.

29. SEM to Brooks Beck, 19 October 1950, SEMC HUG(FP)—33.15 box 2.

30. "*The Hinge of Fate,* by Winston Churchill," *New York Times,* 17 October 1950.

31. SEM to Brooks Beck, 19 October [1950], SEMC HUG(FP)—33.15 box 2.

32. Ibid.

33. Winston Churchill, *The Hinge of Fate,* vol. 4 of *The Second World War,* (Boston: Houghton, Mifflin, 1950), vii.

34. Morison, "Sir Winston Churchill: Nobel Prize Winner," *Saturday Review Gallery* (New York: Simon & Schuster, 1959), 415–16.

35. Ibid., 418.

36. Novick, *That Noble Dream,* 281–361.

37. Morison, "Faith of an Historian," 353.

CHAPTER 13: ADMINISTERING HISTORY

1. For more on the conspiracy theory of history, see Richard Hofstadter, *The Paranoid Style in American Politics* (New York: Alfred A. Knopf, 1952); and Morison, *The Oxford History of the American People* (New York: Oxford University Press, 1965), 1074–75.

2. Peter Novick, *That Noble Dream: The "Objectivity Question" and the American Historical Profession* (New York: Cambridge University Press, 1988), 326–29.

3. Morison, "History Through a Beard," in *By Land and by Sea: Essays and Addresses of Samuel Eliot Morison* (New York: Alfred A. Knopf, 1953), 333–34; see also, "Faith of an Historian," ibid., 353–55.

4. SEM to Sir Arnold Lunn, 17 November 1952 and 5 January 1954, SEM HUG(FP)—33.15 box 5.

5. Morison, *Freedom in Contemporary Society* (Boston: Little, Brown, 1956), 32–35.

6. Ibid., 34, 136.

7. Howard K. Beale, "The Professional Historian: His Theory and His Practice," *Pacific Historical Review* 22 (August 1953): 254.

8. Morison, *Freedom in Contemporary Society*, 6.

9. Ibid., 35–42, 133.

10. Morison, *The Oxford History of the American People*, 1083.

11. Morison, *Freedom in Contemporary Society*, 110, 43–44.

12. Ibid., 40–44.

13. R.A.P. in comments scribbled across the top of the *Chicago Tribune* article "What Makes Sammy Run," 5 November 1961.

14. Morison, *Freedom in Contemporary Society*, 36.

15. Morison wrote Henry Steele Commager in 1937: "I have been trying to keep my foot off that escalator for years" Commager Papers, Amherst, Mass.; cited with permission.

16. Morison also turned down an offer to accept a position at the Institute for Advanced Studies at Princton University for the same reasons.

17. For an account of Morison's last lecture at Harvard, see "Class Gives Ovation as Morison Retires," *Harvard Crimson*, 3 May 1955; see also, Morison, *Vita Nuova: A Memoir of Priscilla Barton Morison* (Printed privately, 1975), 92.

18. SEM to Admiral Arthur Radford, 29 January 1954, SEMC HUG(FP)—33.15 box 10.

19. SEM to H. R. Askins, 31 March 1952, NOA, series 3, box 41.

20. "History '68', 1947," NOA, series 1, box 14.

21. Philip Lundeberg to Greg Pfitzer, 1 November 1989; in possession of the author and cited with permission.

22. SEM to Bern Anderson, 26 January 1956, NOA, series 1, box 2.

23. Jim Shaw to SEM, 21 April 1951, NOA, series 1, box 4.

24. Morison, *The Two-Ocean War: A Short History of the United States Navy in the Second World War* (Little, Brown, 1963).

25. Roger Pineau to Greg Pfitzer, 3 January 1989; in possession of the author and cited with permission.

26. SEM to Secretary of the Navy, 23 March 1954, NOA, series 2, box 5.

27. SEM to Roger Pineau, "Duty Orders and Related Correspondence," 1952–57, NOA, series 1, box 3.

28. For more on "Victory at Sea," see Howard B. Hitchens, ed., *America on Film and Tape* (Westport, Conn.: Greenwood Press, 1985), 143.

29. SEM to Richard H. Lovell, 2 October 1951, SEMC HUG(FP)—33.41 box 1.

30. SEM to Henry Salomon, 25 October 1952, ibid.

31. Richard Lovell to Ted Kupferman, 25 October 1952, ibid.

32. SEM to Richard Lovell, 10 November 1952, ibid; SEM to Harold B. Gross, 24 January 1953, ibid.

33. Richard Lovell to Ted Kupferman, 25 October 1952, ibid.

34. Kent Roberts Greenfield to SEM, 30 October 1946, SEMC HUG(FP)—33.15 box 3; see also, Morison's reply: 1 November 1946, ibid.

35. Roger Pineau to Greg Pfitzer, 3 January 1989.

36. "The Nevins Committee to Study the Navy's Historical Organization and Programs," submitted to the Secretary of the Navy, 7 April 1955, NOA, series 1, box 1.

37. SEM to John Gingrich, 29 January 1954, SEMC HUG(FP)—33.15, box 5.

38. SEM to Capt. Mundorff, 11 May 1951, NOA, series 2, box 4.

39. Roger Pineau to Goro Nakano, 5 January 1955, ibid.

40. H. Salomon to SEM, 30 August 1944, series 2, box 9, folder 15.

41. A. C. Brown to SEM, 20 July 1945, ibid., box 7.

42. SEM to A. C. Brown, 23 July 1945, ibid.

43. SEM to Vice Admiral Paul F. Foster, 17 May 1952, (letter 1), ibid, box 4. Morison wrote two letters to Foster on 17 May 1952; I have designated them letter 1 and letter 2.

44. Ibid., letter 2.

45. Richard W. Bates, *Battle Evaluation Plan* (1946–57), Ms. Collection 28, box 13, Naval War College, Newport, Rhode Island; hereafter cited as NWC.

46. Morison, *Leyte, June 1944*, vol. 12 of *The History of United States Naval Operations in World War II* (Little, Brown, 1958), 199–200.

47. Morison, "Faith of an Historian," 349.

48. Thomas Synnott to Greg Pfitzer, "Miscellaneous Notes, [1982]"; in possession of the author and cited with permission.

49. Morison, "Faith of an Historian," 350.

50. SEM to Admiral E. M. Eller, 30 October 1957, NOA, series 2, box 7, file 10.

51. Robert B. Carney, "Review of Admiral Morison's Volume XII," series 3, box 93, folder 6.

52. "Admiral Morison's Observations on Admiral Carey's Review," ibid.

53. Thomas Synnott to Greg Pfitzer, 25 November 1988 and "miscellaneous notes"; in possession of the author and quoted with permission.

54. Morison, *Freedom in Contemporary Society*, 108.

55. Morison, *Leyte, June 1944*, 336, 247.

56. Morison, "Admirals I Have Known—and a General or Two," Address given at the Maine Maritime Academy, 29 April 1967, 8.

57. SEM to Admiral Joseph J. Clark, 10 June 1968; SEM HUG(FP)—33.15 box 2.

58. Morison, *The Liberation of the Philippines, Luzon, Mindano, the Visayas, 1944–45*, vol. 13 of *The History of United States Naval Operations in World War II* (Little, Brown, 1960), 68, 69, 59.

59. Morison, *Victory in the Pacific, 1945*, vol. 14 of *The History of the United States Naval Operations in World War II* (Little, Brown, 1960), 308.

60. William F. Halsey to Robert B. Carney, 10 November 1958, as cited in Michael Vlahos, *The Blue Sword: The Naval War College and the American Mission, 1919–1941* (Newport, R.I.: Naval War College Press, 1980), 157.

61. E. B. Potter to SEM, 8 January 1963, SEMC HUG(FP)—33.15 box 10.

62. Carney, "Review of Admiral Morison's Volume XII," NOA, series 3, box 93, folder 6.

63. William F. Halsey to SEM, 26 January 1951, SEMC HUG(FP)—33.15 box 4.

64. SEM to William F. Halsey, 29 January 1951, ibid.

65. Ibid.; see also, Halsey to Carney, 10 November 1958, as cited in Vlahos, *The Blue Sword*, 157.

66. Morison, *Supplement and General Index*, vol. 15 of *The History of United States Naval Operations in World War II* (Boston: Little, Brown, 1962), 17.

67. Morison, *Strategy and Compromise: A Reappraisal of the Crucial Decisions Confronting the Allies in the Hazardous Years, 1940–1945* (Boston: Little, Brown, 1958), 114–16.

68. Morison, *Leyte, June 1944*, 223.

69. Ibid.

CHAPTER 14: THE BREAKDOWN OF CONSENSUS

1. Morison, "Autobiographical Sketch," SEMC HUG(FP)—33.1 box 1.

2. Morison, *Vita Nuova: A Memoir of Priscilla Morison* (Privately printed, 1975), 104.

3. SEM to Bergdorf Goodman, 9 April 1951, SEMC HUG(FP)—33.15 box 2.

4. Henry Steele Commager to SEM, 6 October 1954, ibid., box 3.

5. SEM to Curtis Brown, "Account of Writings," 17 November 1952, ibid.,—33.1 box 2.

6. Morison, *Vita Nuova*, 104.

7. Ibid., 134.

8. Ibid.

9. SEM to Priscilla Morison, 24 January 1957, as cited in ibid.

10. Morison, *Vita Nuova*, 139.

11. Charles Francis Adams to SEM, 25 April 1949, SEMC HUG(FP)—33.15 box 1; SEM to Curtis Brown, "Account of Writings," 17 November 1952, SEMC HUG(FP)—33.1 box 2.

12. Morison, *Vita Nuova*, 139.

13. Don Agger, "The Art of a Historian," *Central Program Services Division Talks*, SEMC HUG(FP)—33.1 box 2. Morison, *John Paul Jones: A Sailor's Biography* (Boston: Little, Brown, 1959), 405–6.

14. Ibid., *John Paul Jones*, 8, 91, 425.

15. Ibid., 396.

16. John Hohenberg, *The Pulitzer Prizes* (New York: Columbia University Press, 1974), 277. See also, Morison, "Fiat Pulitzia, Ruat Coelum: A Brief Account of Pulitzer Prize Day on 44 Brimmer Street," SEMC HUG(FP)—33.1 box 2.

17. Ted Weeks to SEM, 8 October 1959, SEMC HUG(FP)—33.15 box 13.

18. Walter Teller, "On Deck with the Little Captain," *Saturday Review of Literature*, 42, 19 September 1959, 35.

19. Morison, *Vita Nuova*, 145.

20. Allan Collins to SEM, 22 May 1962, SEMC HUG(FP)—33.15 box 1.

21. Drake de Kay to SEM, 2 August 1956, ibid.

22. SEM to Drake de Kay, 7 August 1956, ibid.

23. Alfred A. Knopf, "Historian and Publisher," *American Heritage* 28, no. 3 (April 1977), 102.

24. SEM to Curtis Brown, "Account of Writings," 17 November 1952, SEMC HUG(FP)—33.1 box 2.

25. Knopf, "Historian and Publisher," 103.

26. SEM to Alfred A. Knopf, 17 November 1952, SEMC HUG(FP)—33.15 box 8.

27. Knopf, "Historian and Publisher," 103.

28. SEM to Curtis Brown, "Account of Writings," 17 November 1952, SEMC HUG(FP)—33.1 box 2.

29. Ibid.

30. Ibid. Morison and Henry Steele Commager, *Growth of the American Republic*, 2 vols. (New York: Oxford University Press, 1930, 1937, 1942, 1950, 1962).

31. SEM to Commager, 11 August 1948, SEMC HUG(FP)—33.15 box 3.

32. Allan Nevins, "To Take the Poison Out of Textbooks," *New York Times Magazine*, 13 February 1947.

33. *Time* 57, 26 February 1951, 48–49, as cited in Peter Novick, *That Noble Dream: The "Objectivity Question" and the American Historical Profession* (New York: Cambridge University Press, 1988), 350n.

34. SEM to Henry Steele Commager, 11 August 1948, SEMC HUG(FP)—33.15 box 3.

35. Henry Steele Commager to SEM, 27 January 1956 and 25 November 1956, ibid.

36. SEM to Henry Steele Commager, 3 August 1961, ibid.

37. Henry Steele Commager to SEM, 9 August [1961], ibid.; see also, Commager to Mr. Hollinshead, 31 May 1968, ibid.

38. SEM to Curtis Brown, "Account of Writings," ibid., SEMC HUG(FP)—33.1 box 2.

39. Henry Steele Commager to Mr. Hollinshead, 31 May 1968, ibid, 33.15 box 3; Commager to SEM, 26 July 1966, ibid.; SEM to Henry Steele Commager, 26 February 1937, Commager Papers, Amherst Mass., cited with permission.

40. SEM to Curtis Brown, "Account of Writings," SEMC HUG(FP)—33.1 box 2.

41. Morison, Henry Steele Commager, and William E. Leuchtenberg, *Growth of the American Republic* (New York: Oxford University Press, 1969). See also, Henry Steele Commager to SEM, 26 July [1966], SEMC HUG(FP)—33.15 box 3.

42. SEM to Henry Steele Commager, 22 January 1962, ibid.

43. Henry Steele Commager to SEM, August 9 [1961], ibid.

44. SEM to Curtis Brown, "Account of Writings," 17 November 1952, ibid., 33.1 box 2.

45. Ibid.

46. Knopf, "Historian and Publisher," 106.

47. Henry Steele Commager to SEM, 3 February 1962, SEMC HUG(FP)—33.15 box 3.

48. William Bentinck-Smith, "Samuel Eliot Morison," Proceedings of the Massachusetts Historical Society, 88 (1977, offprint), 129.

49. Ibid. For a nearly complete bibliography of Morison's prolific works, see K. Jack Bauer, "Bibliography of Writings by Samuel Eliot Morison," *North American Society of Oceanic History* Newsletter 4 (1978).

50. Ibid.

51. Morison, *One Boy's Boston, 1887–1901* (Houghton Mifflin, 1962), frontispiece.

52. Morison, *Vita Nuova*, 196.

53. Morison, *One Boy's Boston*, 21, 75, 19, 30–31, 29.

54. Morison and Commager, *The Growth of the American Republic*, 1950, 180.

55. Morison, *One Boy's Boston*, 14, 17–18, 20, 73, 45, 77.

56. Morison, *Vita Nuova*, 189.

57. Edmund Morgan to Howard Mumford Jones, 20 March 1961, SEMC HUG(FP)—33.55 box 7.

58. Morison, *Vistas of History* (New York: Alfred A. Knopf, 1964), vii.

59. Morison, *Vita Nuova*, 203. See also, Morison, *Vistas of History*, 18.

60. Albert Strobl, "Salty Historian," *Milwaukee Reader*, 29 July 1963.

61. Morison, "The Experiences and Principles of an Historian," *Vistas of History*, x, 24.

62. Ibid., 56–57.

63. Ibid., 63.

64. Morison, "Excerpt from Diary," December 1958, in *Vita Nuova*, 151.

65. Ibid., February 1959.

66. Morison, "The Oxford History of the American People, 1965: Morison's Address on Its Critical Reception," SEMC HUG(FP)—33.47 box 1.

67. Ibid.

68. Morison, *The Oxford History of the American People* (New York: Oxford University Press, 1965), vii.

69. James M. Perry, "An Admiral Talks About History," 3 May 1965, *National Observer*; George Troy, "The National Book Award Winners," *Providence Sunday Journal*, 14 March 1965.

70. Alexander Theroux, "Good Old with Everything," *Esquire*, 83, April 1975, 158.

71. "Books," *Newsweek*, 26 April 1965, 102.

72. Morison, "The Oxford History of the American People, 1965: Morison's Address on Its Critical Reception," SEMC HUG(FP)—33.47 box 1.

73. Ibid.

74. David H. Donald, Review of Morison's *Oxford History of the American People*, by Samuel Eliot Morison, *Washington Post* [1965] as found in ibid.

75. John E. Wiltz, Review of *The Oxford History of the American People*, by Samuel Eliot Morison, *Chicago Tribune*, as found in ibid.

76. "OHAP—Excerpts from Reviews," April 1965, SEMC HUG(FP)—33.47, box 1.

77. W. H. Masterson, "America Seen From the NE Corner," *Houston Post*, 4 April 1965.

78. Richard D. Heffner, "The Fact and Spirit of Our Past," *Saturday Review*, 1 May 1965, 37.

79. Prof. Edgar Yokley, [n.d.], SEMC HUG(FP)—33.47 box 1.

80. Daniel Boorstin, "Damn the libidos, full speed, ahead," *Book Week*, 25 April 1965, 5, 10–12.

81. Ibid., 12.

82. Heffner, "The Fact and Spirit of Our Past," 37.

83. Max Lerner, "A Bold History," *New York Post*, 23 April 1965.

84. Morison, *The Oxford History of the American People*, vii.

85. Morison, "The Oxford History of the American People, 1965: Morison's Address on Its Critical Reception," SEMC HUG(FP)—33.47 box 1.

86. Ibid. Morison noted: "It was fun to write, too, and if I can communicate to my readers some of the laughter there is in American history, without being sarcastic like Mencken, I am satisfied."

CHAPTER 15: THE "REUSABLE PAST"

1. Paul Katzeff, "Admiral Morison: A New Book at 87," *Sunday Herald Advertiser*, 29 September 1974, summary of an interview.

2. "30 Men and Women Winners of 1964 Medal of Freedom," *Providence Journal*, 4 July 1964.

3. Henry Steele Commager to SEM, 13 February [n.d.], SEMC HUG(FP)—33.15 box 3.

4. Ibid., 19 March 1968.

5. Ibid., 13 February [n.d.]

6. SEM to President Lyndon B. Johnson, 14 March 1965 and 23 October 1965, SEMC HUG(FP)—33.15 box 7.

7. Ibid., 5 August 1967. See also, Walt W. Rostow to SEM, 10 October 1967, ibid.

8. Robert J. Donovan, "Vietnam, a Case of Overstretch," *Los Angeles Times*, 10 July 1972, ibid., 33.55 box 8.

9. SEM to President Lyndon B. Johnson, 5 August 1967, ibid., 33.15 box 7.

10. Morison, *Old Bruin: Commodore Matthew C. Perry, 1748–1858* (Little, Brown, 1967), 29.

11. Morison, *Vita Nuova: A Memoir of Priscilla Morison* (Privately printed, 1975), 235, 246–52.

12. Priscilla Morison, as quoted in ibid.

13. *Old Bruin*, 161, 216, 319.

14. Ibid., 412, 429.

15. Ibid., 338; see also Morison's discussion of twentieth-century imperialism in the Pacific.

16. Ibid., 425.

17. SEM to Denis Brogan, 3 November 1965, SEMC HUG(FP)—33.15 box 2.

18. Robert L. Beisner, "New Biography of Matthew Perry," *Evening Star*, Washington, D.C., 19 November 1967.

19. Gerald W. Johnson, "Where Liberty Means Death," *Book World*, 19 November 1967.

20. J. D. Hutchinson, "50-Year Naval Career Vividly Recounted," *Sunday Denver Post,* 19 November 1967.

21. Alexander C. Brown, "The 'Open Door' Expedition to Japan—A Sailor's Account of M. C. Perry," *Daily Press,* Newport News, Virginia, 3 December 1967.

22. Morison, *Vita Nuova,* 230.

23. SEM to Denis Brogan, 13 June 1969, SEMC HUG(FP)—33.15 box 2.

24. John Higham, *History: Professional Scholarship in America* (Baltimore: Johns Hopkins University Press, 1965), 234.

25. Morison, *Old Bruin,* 442.

26. Don Alfonso to SEM, 5 May 1969, SEM HUG(FP)—33.15 box 1.

27. SEM to D. Alfonso, 26 May 1969, ibid.

28. SEM to R. B. M. Barton, 19 June 1969, ibid., box 2.

29. Page Smith, "The Historian as Skinny-Dipper," *Baltimore Sun,* 3 June 1976.

30. Louise J. Salome, "A Conversation with Samuel Eliot Morison," *Evening Gazette,* Worcester, Mass., 21 February 1968.

31. SEM to D. Alfonso, 18 September 1973, SEMC HUG(FGP)—33.15 box 1.

32. Novick, *That Noble Dream: The "Objectivity Question" and the American Historical Profession* (Cambridge, England: Cambridge University Press, 1988), 416.

33. Ibid., 537.

34. Ibid., 520–623.

35. Joan Hoff-Wilson, "Is the Historical Professional an 'Endangered Species'?" *Public Historian* 2 (Winter 1980): 6, 7–8, 16 as cited in Novick, *That Noble Dream,* 520.

36. Lawrence Stone, "The Revival of Narrative: Reflections on a New Old History," *Past and Present* 85 (November 1979) as cited in Novick, *That Noble Dream,* 622.

37. C. Vann Woodward, "Short History," as cited in Novick, *That Noble Dream,* 622.

38. Jack Hexter, "The Rhetoric of History," *International Encyclopedia of the Social Sciences* (New York: Macmillan and the Free Press, 1968) as cited in Novick, *That Noble Dream,* 623.

39. Novick, *That Noble Dream,* 623.

40. Morison, "Prescott: The American Thucydides," *Atlantic Monthly* 200 (November 1957): 165–168.

41. Ibid.

42. Morison, *The Parkman Reader* (Boston: Little, Brown, 1955), 3.

43. Violetta Hill, "Samuel Eliot Morison: The Amphibious Historian," 5 January 1971, SEMC HUG(FP)—33.1 box 2.

44. Morison, *The Parkman Reader,* ix.

45. Salome, "A Conversation with Samuel Eliot Morison," 7.

46. Hayden White, *Metahistory: The Historical Imagination in Nineteenth-Century Europe* (Baltimore: Johns Hopkins University Press, 1973) as mentioned in Novick, *That Noble Dream,* 599.

47. John Fiske, *The Discovery of America,* 2 vols. (Boston: Houghton Mifflin Company, 1892).

48. SEM to Bernadotte Schmitt, 7 February 1961, SEMC HUG(FP)—33.15 box 11.

49. Morison, *The European Discovery of America: The Northern Voyages* (New York: Oxford University Press, 1971), vii.

50. SEM to Ted Weeks, 21 December 1960, SEMC HUG(FP)—33.15 box 13.

51. Katzeff, "Admiral Morison: A New Book at 87."

52. R. A. Skelton, Thomas E. Marston, and George D. Painter, eds., *The Vinland Map and the Tartar Relation* (New Haven, Conn.: Yale University Press, 1965).

53. SEM to David Quinn, 24 April 1968, SEMC HUG(FP)—33.41 box 1, folder 2.

54. Morison, "It All Boils Down to What We Know Before," *Italian-American Review* (November 1965): 12, 16.

55. Edmund Morgan to SEM, 11 November 1965, SEMC HUG(FP)—33.41 box 3, folder 9.

56. George C. Caner, Jr., "Review of Morison's Comments on the Vinland Map," ibid.

57. "Morison Adds Insult to Columbus Injury," SEMC HUG(FP)—33.1 box 2.

58. SEM to Miss Helen Wallis, 4 February 1974, ibid., 33.41 box 1, folder 7.

59. Ted Weeks to Perry Knowlton, 17 April 1969, ibid., 33.15 box 13. Weeks's figures may not include other royalties that would bring the total sum to $212,000.

60. P[ublisher's] W[eekly] Interviews, "Samuel Eliot Morison," Publisher's Weekly, 4 November 1974, 6.

61. Perry Knowlton to Bryon Hollinshead, Jr., 21 March 1969, SEMC HUG(FP)—33.41 box 1.

62. SEM to Perry Knowlton, 4 July 1969, ibid.

63. Morison, Vita Nuova, 325.

64. SEM to Antha Card, "Instructions to Antha Card," 22 March 1973, SEMC HUG(FP)—33.41 box 2, folder 10.

65. John Barkham, "Historian Follows Magellan by Air," [1972] Daily Press, Newport News, Virginia.

66. Priscilla Morison as cited in Morison, Vita Nuova, 331.

67. Morison, ibid.

68. Morison, The European Discovery of America: The Southern Voyages (New York: Oxford University Press, 1974), x.

69. SEM to A. L. Rowse, 23 January 1969, SEMC HUG(FP)—33.41 box 1, folder 4.

70. Morison, The Southern Voyages, x–xi.

71. Ibid., ix.

72. Katzeff, "Admiral Morison: A New Book at 87."

73. Morison, The Northern Voyages, 587; Southern Voyages, 238, x.

74. Morison, Northern Voyages, 49, 309, 147.

75. Morison, Southern Voyages, 297, 372; Northern Voyages, 679.

76. Morison, Northern Voyages, 3, 488; Southern Voyages, 165.

77. Morison, Southern Voyages, 403, 404; Northern Voyages, 417.

78. Morison, Northern Voyages, xii, 496–97.

79. Ibid., xii, 583.

80. Morison, "History as Literary Art," in By Land and by Sea: Essays and Addresses of Samuel Eliot Morison (New York: Alfred A. Knopf, 1953), 293.

81. David Hackett Fischer, Historians' Fallacies: Toward a Logic of Historical Thought (New York: Harper & Row, 1970), 4.

82. "Professor of the Ocean Sea," News Leader, 9 December 1974.

83. "Samuel Eliot Morison, Renowned Historian, Dies," Ellsworth American, 20 May 1976.

84. Alexander Theroux, "Good Old Everything," Esquire 83, April 1975, 158.

85. "P. W. Interviews," 6.

86. Beck, Sailor Historian: The Best of Samuel Eliot Morison (Boston: Houghton Mifflin, 1977), xxvi–xxvii.

87. "P. W. Interviews," Interviews, 6.

88. Theroux, "Good Old Everything," 152.

89. August Heckscher, "For SEM," 9 July 1975, SEMC HUG(FP)—33.1 box 2.

90. Theroux, "Good Old Everything," 158.

91. Morison, The Southern Voyages, xii.

92. Morison, Vita Nuova, 359.

93. M. J. Wilson, "Morison, 84, Top American Historian," St. Louis Globe Democrat, 14 August 1971.

94. Ibid. See also, Theroux, "Good Old Everything," 79.

95. "Denatured History," *Boston Globe,* 12 March 1965.

96. Mrs. August Belmont to SEM, 28 March 1963, SEMC HUG(FP)—33.15 box 2.

97. John A. Garraty to SEM, 1 April 1970, ibid., box. 1

98. Ibid., 19 August 1970.

99. Morison, *The Parkman Reader,* 23.

100. Mrs. August Belmont to SEM, 3 April 1975, SEMC HUG(FP)—33.15 box 2.

101. Theroux, "Good Old Everything," 79.

102. Wilcomb Washburn, "Samuel Eliot Morison," *William and Mary Quarterly* 3d series, 36 (July 1979): 351.

103. Jim Brunell, "Sad Transition of 1972," [n.d.], SEMC HUG(FP)—33.1 box 2.

104. Walter Muir Whitehill, Foreword to *Sailor Historian,* xxix.

105. Theroux, "Good Old Everything," 79.

106. Whitehill, Foreword to *Sailor Historian,* xxvii–xxviii.

107. Novick, *That Noble Dream,* 628.

108. Ibid., 622. Novick cites Joan C. Scott, Erik Monkkonen, and Allan Bogue as major proponents of this position.

109. Beck, *Sailor Historian,* viii.

EPILOGUE

1. "The Presentation of the Samuel Eliot Morison Award," *American Heritage* 28 (October 1977): 96–97.

2. Bruce Catton, "The Way I See It," *American Heritage* 27 (October 1976): 54.

3. "Making History for Others to Record," Material Relating to the Frigate U.S.S. *Samuel Eliot Morison,* SEMC HUG(FP)—33.55 box 8. See also, "Launching of the Guided Missile Frigate *Samuel E. Morison,*" Program, ibid.

4. "Coat of Arms: U.S.S. *Samuel Eliot Morison* (FFG-13)," in "Booklet: Facts and Data," FFG Program Manager's Office, February 1980, ibid.

5. Morison, "Prescott: The American Thucydides," *Atlantic Monthly* 200 (November 1957): 167, 172.

SELECT BIBLIOGRAPHY

MANUSCRIPT SOURCES

The most valuable source of information about Morison's career as a historian is The Samuel Eliot Morison Collection, Harvard University Archives, Pusey Library, Cambridge, Massachusetts. A guide has been prepared by David Thurn of the Harvard Archives, who directs researchers to the introductory notes that precede each major division of the collection. These notes provide explanations of the ordering principles of each section and explain possible exceptions or special instructions for locating particular materials. The major divisions include:

Biographical Papers   HUG (FP)—33.1
The first of two boxes contains general biographical information on Morison, including autobiographical statements, memoirs, news clippings, and a bibliography. The second box contains papers of a more personal nature relating, for example, to 44 Brimmer Street or family manuscripts.

Memoirs of Elizabeth S. Morison and   HUG (FP)—33.3
Priscilla B. Morison

Diaries and Notebooks Kept by Morison   HUG (FP)—33.5
Personal Diaries from 1907 to 1976 (sealed until the year 2000)

Family and Personal Correspondence   HUG (FP)—33.6
The letters in this series range in date from 1807 to 1975, embracing several generations of Morison's family correspondence. These boxes do not constitute a single unbroken chronological sequence, nor do they hold similar contents. The family correspondence begins with Eliot family letters and ends with Morison's correspondence with his children (and their families), although there is some overlapping among the early letters. Here the researcher will find Morison's first letter (written at age five), notes from the family servant, Lizzie Turner, letters from his grandfather, historian Samuel Eliot, his college correspondence with his mother, addressed as "Chitty."

General Correspondence   HUG (FP)—33.15
Twenty-four boxes of correspondence relating to all aspects of Morison's public and private life. These boxes include letters to and from other historians as well as business dealings, financial transactions, and travel plans. These letters are arranged alphabetically. Letters include those from Charles Francis Adams on the possibility of writing a biography of John Adams, from Don Alfonso D'Orleans Y Bourbon on his escape into exile with King Alfonso of Spain in 1931, from Lincoln Colcord on the founding of the Penebscot Marine Museum, from Malcolm Cowley on slave trade, from Grossadmiral A. D. Donitz on German U-boat campaigns in World War II, from Dwight D. Eisenhower on politics and academics, to Alfred A. Knopf on historical writing, to Lyndon B. Johnson on the need for a "peace offensive" in Vietnam, and so on.

The Peace Conference Papers   HUG (FP)—33.20
Morison was called to the peace conference in Paris in January of 1919 and remained there until June of the same year; he wrote a letter of resignation on June 14, which was

accepted soon thereafter. Morison was attached to the Russian division of the American Commission to Negotiate Peace under R. H. Lord, and his job was "to handle all the material coming in from consulates, embassies, M.I.D., and missions in the field, on Finland, Esthonia, Latvia and Lithuania, and make reports and recommendations thereupon; also to keep in touch with the delegations of those countries." This box contains Morison's diary, correspondence, and a statement on U.S.-Russian policy.

Oxford Correspondence, 1922–1925   HUG (FP)—33.21

Morison was elected the Harold Vyvyan Harmsworth Professor of American History at Oxford in the fall of 1921. He held the post from 1922 to 1925. This box contains Morison's correspondence during those years, arranged alphabetically.

Correspondence: Antha Card and Samuel Eliot HUG (FP)—33.22
Morison

These two boxes contain Morison's correspondence with his secretary, Antha E. Card, from 1963 to 1975. Occasionally there is an exchange of letters between Antha E. Card and Priscilla Barton Morison.

Books: Research Material   HUG (FP)—33.41

These boxes contain research material of diverse nature, from notes, card files, and articles, scholarly correspondence with publishers, to illustrations collected for certain of Morison's books. Some of the material was never published, as for example, "The History of Massachusetts," and "Harvard History: 18th–20th Centuries." Owing to the likelihood of future acquisitions, the boxes in this portion of the collection do not benefit from an overall numerical ordering sequence.

Manuscripts   HUG (FP)—33.45

These boxes contain the manuscripts and/or typescripts of several of Morison's books. Included in the first box is a list of manuscripts Morison gave the Harvard Archives in 1974.

Book Reviews   HUG (FP)—33.47

These two boxes contain photocopies of book reviews written by Morison and arranged chronologically by dates of publication. Box 2 also contains some advertisements and reviews saved by Morison.

Articles   HUG (FP)—33.50

Morison's articles have been divided into the following categories: box 1: American History; box 2: Harvard History; box 3: On History and Writing; box 4: Columbus/Maritime/Discovery; box 5: World War II/Navy; box 6: Memoirs; box 7: Miscellaneous.

Subject File   HUG (FP)—33.55

The subject file is an alphabetical arrangement of folders containing various materials (correspondence, lectures and addresses, research notes, and so on) ranging over Morison's entire career. Morison did not, apparently, anticipate the researcher when he assigned headings in the file, because the headings are not always helpful in identifying the contents of a particular folder.

Miscellaneous Research Notes and Files HUG (FP)—33.60

Harvard Columbus Expedition   HUG (FP)—33.71–74
Materials relating to Morison's transatlantic voyage in late 1939 and early 1940 to retrace
the discoveries of Columbus: Glass Slides: 33.71; Food List: 33.72; Ships' Logs: 33.73;
Maps: 33.74.

Visual Material   HUG (FP)—33.80
The photographs of Morison are arranged chronologically whenever possible. Folder
headings have been underscored, followed by descriptive entries regarding individual
photographs. Several of the later folders have been given "subject" headings.

Audio Matieral   HUG (FP)—33.85

General Index
This index does not attempt to be an exhaustive guide to the collection, but merely a
finding aid for material that might otherwise remain obscure. The entries under each
heading are not in any particular order.

The Guide to the Samuel Eliot Morison Collection includes two additional aids for the
researcher: "The Appendix to the General Correspondence" (following the General Correspondence) and the "General Index" (at the back).

There is also a much smaller holding of Morison papers at Harvard's Houghton Library,
The Letters of Samuel Eliot Morison, correspondence that is related to the publishing of
Morison's earliest works. Here I have quoted mainly from Morison's correspondence with
his editor at Houghton Mifflin Company, Ferris Greenslet, with permission of Houghton
Library.

In addition I have cited several manuscript collections with papers of importance to
Morison's career. These include:

The Papers of Henry Steel Commager. [Unprocessed]. Amherst College, Amherst, Mass.
The Papers of Samuel Eliot. The Boston Athenaeum, Boston, Mass.
The Papers of Barrett Wendell. Houghton Library, Harvard University, Cambridge, Mass.
The Papers of Albert Bushnell Hart. Pusey Library, Harvard University, Cambridge, Mass.
Records of the History Department; Records of the Department of History and Govern-
     ment, 1890–1910. Pusey Library, Harvard University, Cambridge, Mass.
The Papers of Arthur M. Schlesinger, Sr. Pusey Library, Harvard University, Cambridge,
     Mass.
The Papers of Emily M. Morison. Schlesinger Library, Harvard University, Cambridge,
     Mass.
The William B. Goodwin Papers. Connecticut State Library, Hartford, Conn.
Charles M. Andrews Papers. Yale University Library, New Haven, Conn.
James Truslow Adams Papers. Rare Book and Manuscript Library, Columbia University,
     New York, NY.
The Papers of Admiral Richard Bates. Naval War College, Newport, R.I.
The Albert J. Beveridge Papers. The Library of Congress, Washington, D.C.
The Papers of Samuel Eliot Morison Relating to the *History of United States Naval
     Operations in World War II.* The Naval Operational Archives, Washington Navy Yard,
     Washington, D.C.

WRITINGS BY MORISON, 1912–1942

*Below is a chronological listing of articles and books by Morison cited in this study. The
most thorough bibliography of Morison's works is K. Jack Bauer's "Bibliography of*

Writings by Samuel Eliot Morison," *North American Society of Oceanic History* Newsletter 4 (1978).

"The Life and Correspondence of Harrison Gray Otis, 1765–1815." Ph.D. diss., Harvard University, 1912.

The Life and Letters of Harrison Gray Otis. 2 vols. Boston: Houghton Mifflin, 1913.

A History of the Constitution of Massachusetts. Boston: Wright & Potter, 1917.

"The Eastern Baltic: (1) The Peace Conference and the Baltic; (2) Latvia; (3) Latvia, Continued; (4) Esthonia; (5) Finland." *New Europe* 12 (7 August 1919–2 October 1919): 77–82, 127–32, 155–59, 200–5, 270–75.

"The Education of John Marshall." *Atlantic Monthly* 126 (July 1920): 45–54.

"The New Baltic Republics: (1) Esthonia and Latvia; (2) Lithuania and Finland." *Youths' Companion,* 7 October 1920, 28 October 1920.

The Maritime History of Massachusetts, 1783–1860. Boston: Houghton Mifflin, 1921, 1941. London: Heinemann, 1923. Paperback edition, Houghton Mifflin, 1961.

Review of *The Founding of New England,* by James Truslow Adams. *American Historical Review* 27 (October 1921): 129–31.

"Memoir of Alden Bradford," Proceedings of the Massachusetts Historical Society 55 (1921–22): 153–64.

"A Prologue to American History, An Inaugural Lecture." Oxford: Clarendon Press, 1922.

"An American Professor's Reflections on Oxford." *London Spectator,* 7, 14 November 1925; *The Living Age,* 8th ser., 41, 2 January 1926, 44–48.

"Impressions of Harvard After Oxford I and II," *Harvard Alumni Bulletin* vol. 28, nos. 30 and 31 (6 May 1926, 13 May 1926), 891–93, 917–20.

The Class Lives of Samuel Eliot and Nathaniel Holmes Morison, Harvard 1839. Boston: Privately printed, 1926.

Oxford History of the United States. 2 vols. Oxford: Oxford University Press, 1927.

Builders of the Bay Colony. Boston: Houghton Mifflin, 1930, 1958; London: Heinemann, 1931; paperback edition, Houghton Mifflin, 1964.

With Henry Steele Commager. *Growth of the American Republic.* New York: Oxford University Press, 1930, 1937, 1942, 1950, 1962, 1969. 2 vols. in 1937 and later editions. William Leuchtenberg coauthor for 1969 edition.

With Ephraim Emerton. "History, 1838–1929." In *The Development of Harvard College Since the Inauguration of President Eliot,* edited by Samuel Eliot Morison. Cambridge, Mass.: Harvard University Press, 1930.

"Edward Channing: A Memoir." Proceedings of the Massachusetts Historical Society 64 (1930–32): 250–84.

"Those Misunderstood Puritans." *Forum,* 85 (March 1931): 142–47.

Review of *The Colonial Period in American History,* vol. 1, by Charles M. Andrews. *New England Quarterly* 7 (December 1934): 729–32.

"Harvard and Academic Oaths." *Harvard Alumni Bulletin* 37 (1934–35): 682–86.

The Founding of Harvard College. Cambridge, Mass.: Harvard University Press, 1935.

"Harvard's Past." *Harvard Alumni Bulletin* 38 (1935–36): 265–74.

"Address at the Tercentenary Celebration." *Harvard Alumni Bulletin* 39 (1936–37): 13–15.

Harvard College in the Seventeenth Century. 2 vols. Cambridge, Mass.: Harvard University Press, 1936.

The Puritan Pronaos. New York: New York University Press, 1936; reissued 1956 as *The Intellectual Life of Colonial New England;* paperback edition, Cornell University Press, 1960.

Three Centuries of Harvard, 1636–1936. Cambridge, Mass.: Harvard University Press, 1936, 1963.

"Three Oathless Centuries in Massachusetts." *Massachusetts Law Quarterly* (April 1936).

"Tribute to Albert Bushnell Hart." Proceedings of the Massachusetts Historical Society 66 (1936–41): 434–38.

Review of *The Flowering of New England*, by Van Wyck Brooks. *American Historical Review* 42 (1937): 564.

"A Reading Period in Haiti." *Harvard Alumni Bulletin* 41 (1938–39): 802–7.

"Discovering the Great Discoverer." *New York Times Magazine*, 9 October 1938, 6–7, 25–26.

"*Life* Resails Columbus's Routes." *Life* 6, 25 March 1939, 102–6.

"Reports on the Harvard Columbus Expedition." *Harvard Alumni Bulletin* 42 (29 September 1939–1 March 1940), 42–43.

Second Voyage of Christopher Columbus. New York: Oxford University Press, 1939.

Portuguese Voyages to America in the Fifteenth Century. Cambridge, Mass.: Harvard University Press, 1940; paperback edition, Octagon Books, 1965.

"Route of Columbus Along the North Coast of Haiti, and the Site of Navidad." *Transactions of the American Philosophical Society* new series, 31 (1940): 239–85.

Admiral of the Ocean Sea. 2 vols. Boston: Little Brown, 1942. Also 1 vol. edition Little Brown, 1942; Time, Inc., 1962.

"The Landing at Fedhala, Morocco, November 8, 1942," *American Neptune* 3 (1943): 99–105.

"Historical Notes on the Gilbert and Marshall Islands," *American Neptune* 4 (1944): 87–118.

Memoir of Elizabeth Shaw Morison, 1886–1945. Boston: Merrymount Press, 1945.

History as a Literary Art. Boston: Old South Association, 1946.

History of the United States Naval Operations in World War II. 15 vols. Boston: Little, Brown, 1947–62. vol. 1, *The Battle of the Atlantic.* 1947, 1964; vol. 2, *Operations in North African Waters.* 1947, 1962; vol. 3, *The Rising Sun in the Pacific.* 1948, 1963; vol. 4, *Coral Sea, Midway, and Submarine Actions.* 1950, 1962; vol. 5, *The Struggle for Guadalcanal.* 1950, 1962; vol. 6, *Breaking the Bismarcks Barrier.* 1950, 1962; vol. 7, *Aleutians, Gilberts and Marshalls.* 1951, 1962; vol. 8, *New Guinea and the Marianas.* 1953, 1962; vol. 9, *Sicily, Salerno, Anzio.* 1954, 1964; vol. 10, *The Atlantic Battle Won.* 1956, 1964; vol. 11, *The Invasion of France and Germany.* 1957, 1964; vol. 12, *Leyte.* 1958, 1963; vol. 13, *The Liberation of the Philippines.* 1959, 1963; vol. 14, *Victory in the Pacific.* 1960; vol. 15, *Supplement and General Index.* 1962.

"History Through a Beard." *Atlantic Monthly* 182 (August 1948): 91–97.

"Notes on Writing Naval (not Navy) English." *American Neptune* 9 (1949): 5–10.

Ropemakers of Plymouth. Boston: Houghton, Mifflin, 1950.

"Faith of a Historian." *American Historical Review* 56 (1951): 261–75.

"Two Minutes That Changed the Pacific War," *New York Times Magazine*, 1 June 1952, 10, 44–47.

ed. William Bradford. *Of Plymouth Plantation.* New York: Alfred A. Knopf, 1952.

By Land and by Sea: The Essays and Addresses of Samuel Eliot Morison. New York: Alfred A. Knopf, 1953.

With Arthur Meier Schlesinger, Sr., Frederick Merk, Arthur Meier Schlesinger, Jr., and Paul Herman Buck. *Harvard Guide to American History.* Cambridge, Mass.: Harvard University Press, 1953.

"Sir Winston Churchill, Nobel Prize Winner," *Saturday Review* 36, 31 October 1953, 22–23.

"A Letter and a Few Reminiscences of Henry Adams." *New England Quarterly* 27 (1954): 95–97.

Christopher Columbus, Mariner. Boston: Little, Brown, 1955.

ed. *The Parkman Reader*. Boston: Little, Brown, 1955.

"The Sea in Literature." *Atlantic Monthly* 196 (September 1955): 67–71.

Freedom in Contemporary Society. Boston: Little, Brown, 1956; Freeport, Books for Libraries, 1969.

Nathaniel Homes Morison. Baltimore: Peabody Institute, 1957.

ed. William H. Prescott, *History of the Conquest of Peru*. New York: Limited Editions Club, 1957; Heritage Press, 1957.

"Prescott: The American Thucydides." *Atlantic Monthly* 200 (November 1957): 165–72.

William Hickling Prescott. Boston: Massachusetts Historical Society, 1958.

Strategy and Compromise. Boston: Little, Brown, 1958.

"The Centenary of Prescott's Death." *New England Quarterly* 32 (1959): 243–48.

"The Greatest Voyage Ever Made." *Saturday Evening Post* 231, 3 October 1959, 42–43, 148–53.

John Paul Jones: A Sailor's Biography. Boston: Little, Brown, 1959: paperback edition, Time, Inc., 1964.

"The Real John Paul Jones." *Saturday Evening Post*, 231, 1 August 1959, 26–27, 55–57.

"Reminiscences of Charles Eliot Norton," *New England Quarterly* 38 (1960): 364–68.

"The Lessons of Pearl Harbor." *Saturday Evening Post* 234, 28 October 1961, 19–27.

The Scholar in America, Past, Present, and Future. New York: Oxford University Press, 1961.

One Boy's Boston, 1887–1901. Boston: Houghton Mifflin, 1962.

ed. *Journals and Other Documents on the Life and Voyages of Christopher Columbus*. New York: Limited Edition Club, 1963; Heritage Press, 1963.

Two-Ocean War. Boston: Little, Brown, 1963.

With Maurice Obregón, *The Caribbean as Columbus Saw It*. Boston: Little, Brown, 1964.

"A Memoir and Estimate of Albert Bushnell Hart." Proceedings of the Massachusetts Historical Society 77 (1965): 28–52.

The Oxford History of the American People. New York: Oxford University Press, 1965; paperback edition, New American Library, 3 vols. (1972).

"Arthur Meier Schlesinger," Proceedings of the American Antiquarian Society 76 (1967): 227–30.

"Old Bruin": Commodore Matthew Calbraith Perry, 1796–1858. Boston: Little, Brown. 1967.

Harrison Gray Otis, 1765–1848: The Urbane Federalist. Boston: Houghton Mifflin, 1969.

The European Discovery of America. 2 vols. New York: Oxford University Press, 1971–74. vol. 1, *The Northern Voyages*, 1971; vol. 2, *The Southern Voyages*, 1974.

Francis Parkman. Boston: Massachusetts Historical Society, 1973.

Vita Nuova. A Memoir of Prescilla Barton Morison. Northeast Harbor: Privately printed, 1975.

With Henry Steele Commager and William E. Leuchtenberg. *A Concise History of the American Republic*. New York: Oxford University Press, 1977.

Emily Morison Beck, ed. *Sailor Historian: The Best of Samuel Eliot Morison*. Boston: Houghton Mifflin, 1977.

SECONDARY WORKS CONSULTED

Little has been written about Morison or his career. The best biographical sources are the memorials written by representatives of various scholarly and professional organizations, including Bernard Bailyn, "Samuel Eliot Morison: Memorial Minute Adopted by the Faculty of Arts and Sciences, Harvard University." Harvard University Gazette 72 (10 June 1977); *William Bentinck-Smith, "Samuel Eliot Morison." Proceedings of the Massa-*

chusetts Historical Society 88 (1976): 123; Wilcomb Washburn, "Samuel Eliot Morison, Historian." *William and Mary Quarterly*, 3d series, 36 (July 1979): 326. The most thorough biographical essay written while Morison was still alive is Walter Muir Whitehill, "Portrait of the Admiral As a Renaissance Man." *Boston Magazine* (September 1965): 24. See also E. C. Kiessling, "Historian Who Lives History." *Milwaukee Journal*, 1 November 1964; James M. Perry, "An Admiral Talks About History." *National Observer*, 3 May 1965; Uncle Dudley, "Sailor Historian." *Boston Globe*, 16 February 1939.

Several general works in historiography have sections on Morison. These include: Bert J. Loewenberg, *American History in American Thought: Christopher Columbus to Henry Adams*. New York: Simon and Schuster, 1972; Richard Middlekauf, *Pastmasters: Some Essays on American Historians*. Edited by Marcus Cunliffe and Robin W. Winks. New York: Harper & Row, 1969; Robert Allen Skotheim, *American Intellectual Histories and Historians*. Princeton. N.J.: Princeton University Press, 1966.

Small selections of Morison's correspondence with other historians have been published. These include: Parker Albee, Jr., ed. "Portrait of a Friendship: Selected Correspondence of Samuel Eliot Morison and Lincoln Colcord, 1921–1947." *New England Quarterly* part 1: 66 (June 1983): 163–99; part 2: 66 (September 1983): 398–424; Elizabeth Donnan, and Leo F. Stock, eds. *John Franklin Jameson: An Historian's World*. Philadelphia, 1956; Robert Spiller, ed. *The Van Wyck Brooks-Lewis Mumford Letters: The Record of a Literary Friendship, 1921–63*. New York: E. P. Dutton, 1970.

Information concerning the historians mentioned in this study can be found in the following sources.

For more on Samuel Eliot, see George Harvey Genzmer, "Samuel Eliot." *The Dictionary of American Biography* 5 (1936): 81; Barrett Wendell, "Samuel Eliot." Proceedings of the American Academy of Arts and Sciences 34 (1899): 651. See also the following works by Eliot: Samuel Eliot, *History of Liberty*. 4 vols. Boston: Little, Brown and Company, 1853; *The Liberty of Rome: A History with Historical Account of the Liberty of Ancient Nations*. 2 vols. New York: George P. Putnam, 1849; *William Samuel Eliot, 1854–1874*. Cambridge, Mass.: Riverside Press, 1875.

On Albert Bushnell Hart, see the following works: *American History Told by Contemporaries*. 5 vols. New York: Macmillan Company, 1885–1929; gen. ed. *The American Nation: A History*. 27 vols. New York: Harper & Brothers, 1907. Vol 27: *National Ideas Historically Traced, 1607–1907*; *Commonwealth History of Massachusetts*. New York: The States History Company, 1927–30; *Epochs of American History: Formation of the Union, 1750–1829*. New York: Longmans, Green, and Co., 1892; "History 13 and History 17." *Topical Outline of the Courses in Constitutional and Political History of the United States Given at Harvard College*. Cambridge, Mass.: Harvard University Press, 1886. *How to Study History, Literature, the Fine Arts*. Meadville, Pa.: The Chautauqua-Century Press, 1895; *Manual of History, Diplomacy, and Government*. Cambridge, Mass.: Harvard University Press, 1908; "Methods of Teaching American History." In *Methods of Teaching History*, by G. Stanley Hall. Boston, 1885, 1–3; *Slavery and Abolition, 1831–1841*. New York: Harper & Brothers, 1906.

On Charles Homer Haskins, see the following works: "The Historical Curriculum in Colleges." *Minutes of the Association of History Teachers of the Middle States and Maryland for 1904*, 2–8; With Lord, Robert. *Some Problems of the Peace Conference*. Cambridge, Mass.: Harvard University Press, 1920.

For more on Albert J. Beveridge, see Lawrence F. Abbott, "Senator Beveridge." *Outlook* 146, 11 May 1927, 43–44; W. E. Barton, "A Noble Fragment: Beveridge's Life of Lincoln." *Mississippi Valley Historical Review* 15 (March 1929): 497; John Spenser Bassett, Review of *The Life of John Marshall*, by Albert J. Beveridge. *American Historical Review* 12 (April 1920): 515–17; L. C. Bell, "John Marshall: Albert J. Beveridge as a Biographer." *Virginia Law Register* 12 (March 1927): 61–42; Claude Bowers, *Beveridge and the Progressive Era.* New York: The Literary Guild, 1932; Edwin Corwin, Review of *The Life of John Marshall*, by Albert J. Beveridge. *Mississippi Valley Historical Review* 4 (March 1920); Charles W. Duke, "The 'Man of the Ages' as Beveridge Sees Him." *Philadelphia Public Ledger*, 11 February 1923; A. C. McLaughlin, Review of *The Life of John Marshall. American Bar Association Journal* 7 (March 1927): 231; Tracy E. Strevey, "Albert J. Beveridge." In *The Marcus W. Jernegan Essays in American Historiography*, edited by William T. Hutchinson. Chicago: University of Chicago Press, 1937, 374–93. See also the following works by Beveridge: *Abraham Lincoln, 1809–1858.* 4 vols. Boston: Houghton Mifflin, 1928; "Historical Research as a Public Interest." *Annual Report of the American Historical Association for the Year 1925.* Washington, D.C.: U.S. Government Printing Office, 1929; *The Life of John Marshall.* 4 vols. Boston: Houghton Mifflin, 1919; "The Making of a Book." *Saturday Evening Post*, 23 October 1926, 187; *The Meaning of the Times and Other Speeches.* Indianapolis, 1908; "Pitfalls of a League of Nations." *North American Review* 209 (March 1919): 305–14; *What Is Back of the War.* Indianapolis: The Bobbs-Merrill Company, 1915.

On Edward Channing, see Lester J. Cappon, "Channing and Hart: Partners in Bibliography." *New England Quarterly* 29 (September 1956): 318–40; Ralph Ray Fahrney, "Edward Channing." In *The Marcus W. Jernegan Essays in American Historiography*, edited by William T. Hutchinson. Chicago: The University of Chicago Press, 1937; Carl Russell Fish. "Edward Channing, American Historian." *Current History* 32 (March 1931): 863; Review of *A Student's History of the United States*, by Edward Channing. *Educational Review* 18 (October 1899), 301–4; C. H. Van Tyne, Review of *History of the United States*, by Edward Channing. *American Historical Review* 18 (April 1913): 604. See also the following works by Channing: "The Companions of Columbus." In *Narrative and Critical History of America.* 8 vols., edited by Justin Winsor. Boston: Houghton Mifflin, 1884–89; *A History of the United States.* 6 vols. New York: Macmillan Company, 1905–25; "The Present State of Historical Writing in America." Reprinted from the Proceedings of the American Antiquarian Society for October 1910. Worcester, Mass.: Davis Press, 1–11.

On Frederick Jackson Turner, see Charles A. Beard, "The Frontier in American History." *New Republic* 25, 16 February 1921, 349–50; Ray Allen Billington, *Frederick Jackson Turner: Historian, Scholar, Teacher.* New York: Oxford University Press, 1973; Ray Allen Billington, *The Genesis of the Frontier Thesis: A Study in Historical Creativity.* San Marino, California, 1971; Wilbur R. Jacobs, narrator, *The Historical World of Frederick Jackson Turner.* New Haven, Conn.: Yale University Press, 1968. See also the following work by Turner: *The Frontier in American History.* New York: Holt, Rinehart, and Winston, 1920.

For more on James Truslow Adams, see De Voto, B[ernard]. Review of *Henry Adams*, by James Truslow Adams. *New England Quarterly* 7 (March 1934): 195–96; Allyn B. Forbes, Review of *Provincial Society, 1690–1763*, by James Truslow Adams. *New England Quarterly* 1 (July 1928): 415; Worthington C. Ford, "Correspondence." *New England Quarterly* 7 (June 1934): 398; Allan Nevins. *James Truslow Adams: Historian of the American Dream.* Urbana: University of Illinois Press, 1968. Also see the following books and articles written by Adams: "A Business Man's Civilization." *Harper's Magazine* 159 (July 1929): 140–42; *The Founding of New England*. Boston: Atlantic Monthly Press, 1921; "How Our Peace Agents Lived." *New York Times*, 27 July 1919; "My Methods as a Historian." *Saturday Review of Literature* 50, 30 June 1934, 277–78; *Provincial Society, 1690–1763*. New York: Macmillan, 1927; Review of *Builders of the Bay Colony*, by Samuel Eliot Morison. *New England Quarterly* 3 (October 1930): 741–46; "Why Historians Get Headaches," *Rotarian*, January 1940.

For more on Van Wyck Brooks, see James Hoopes, *Van Wyck Brooks: In Search of American Culture*. Amherst: University of Massachusetts Press, 1977; Raymond Nelson, *Van Wyck Brooks: A Writer's Life*. New York: E. P. Dutton, 1981. T. S. Eliot, Review of *The Wine of the Puritans*, by Van Wyck Brooks. *Harvard Advocate*, 7 May 1909, 80. Also see the following works by Brooks: *An Autobiography: Scenes and Portraits, Days of the Phoenix* and *From the Shadow of the Mountain*. New York: E. P. Dutton, 1965; *The Flowering of New England, 1815–1865*. New revised edition. E. P. Dutton, 1940; "Harvard and American Life." *Contemporary Review* 94 (December 1908): 613–17; "On Creating a Usable Past." *Dial* 64, 11 April 1918, 337–41; *The Wine of the Puritans: A Study of Present Day America*. New York: M. Kennerley, 1909.

On Charles M. Andrews, see Carl Bridenbaugh, Review of *The Colonial Period in American History*, by Charles M. Andrews. *Pennsylvania Magazine of History and Biography* 61 (1937): 332; A[braham] S. Eisenstadt, *Charles McLean Andrews: A Study in American Historical Writing*. New York: Columbia University Press, 1956; Benjamin Woods Labaree, "Charles McLean Andrews: Historian, 1863–1943." *William and Mary Quarterly*, 3d series, 1 (January 1944): 3–14; Jernegan, Marcus W. Review of *The Colonial Period in American History*, by Charles M. Andrews. *Yale Review* 28 (Spring 1938): 646; Nettels, Curtis. Review of *The Colonial Period in American History* by Charles M. Andrews. *New England Quarterly* 10 (December, 1937): 795. See also the following works by Andrews: *The Colonial Period in American History*. 4 vols. New Haven, Conn.: Yale University Press, 1934–38; *Our Earliest Colonial Settlements, Their Diversities of Origin and Later Characteristics*. New York: New York University Press, 1933; "These Forty Years." *American Historical Review* 30 (January 1925): 225–49.

For more on amateur historian William B. Goodwin, see Barry Fell, *America B.C.: Ancient Settlers in the New World*. New York: Quadrangle/New York Times Book Co., 1976. Also see the following works by him: "The Oldest Community Site in America," *Florida Historical Quarterly* 17 (April 1939): 330; *The Ruins of Great Ireland in New England*. Boston: Meador Publishing Co., 1946; *Spanish and English Ruins in Jamaica*. Boston: Meador Publishing Co., 1946.

Charles Beard's writings were so voluminous that it is not possible here to give a thorough accounting of them. The best place to begin is with two bibliographic studies: Jack Frooman, and Edmund D. Cronon. In *Charles A. Beard: An Appraisal*, edited by Howard K. Beale. Lexington: University of Kentucky Press, 1945; and Bernard C. Borning, *The Political and Social Thought of Charles A. Beard* (Seattle: University of Washington Press, 1962). For biographical accounts of Beard, see Cushing Stout, *The Pragmatic Revolt in American History*, 1958; Matthew Josephson, "Charles A. Beard: A Memoir," *Virginia Quarterly Review*, 25 (1949): 585–901.

For more on historians mentioned briefly in this study, see: David B. Frankenburger, "William Francis Allen." *William Allen Francis: Memorial Volume*. Boston: G. H. Ellis,

1890; Owen G. Stearns, "William Francis Allen: Wisconsin's First Historian." M. A. Thesis, University of Wisconsin, 1955; Charles Beard, *The Supreme Court and the Constitution.* New York: Macmillan Company, 1912; William W. Carson, "John Clark Ridpath." In *Dictionary of American Biography.* vol 15., edited by Dumas Malone. New York: Charles Scribner's Sons, 1935; George Santayana, *The Life of the Reason, or The Phases of Human Progress,* 5 vols. New York: Charles Scribner's Sons, 1906. Oliver Marble Gale, ed. *Americanism: Woodrow Wilson's Speeches on the War—Why He Made Them and What They Have Done.* Chicago: The Baldwin Syndicate Publishers, 1918; Woodrow Wilson, *Congressional Government: A Study in American Politics.* Boston: Houghton Mifflin, 1885; Justin Winsor, ed. *Narrative and Critical History of America.* 8 vols. Boston: Houghton Mifflin, 1884–89.

INDEX

Numerals in italics refer to an illustration or photograph of the entry.